D1526499

# Couple Relationships in the Middle and Later Years

# Couple Relationships in the Middle and Later Years

Their Nature, Complexity,
and Role in Health and Illness

Edited by Jamila Bookwala

AMERICAN PSYCHOLOGICAL ASSOCIATION

WASHINGTON, DC

Published by
American Psychological Association
750 First Street, NE
Washington, DC 20002
www.apa.org

To order
APA Order Department
P.O. Box 92984
Washington, DC 20090-2984
Tel: (800) 374-2721; Direct: (202) 336-5510
Fax: (202) 336-5502; TDD/TTY: (202) 336-6123
Online: www.apa.org/pubs/books
E-mail: order@apa.org

In the U.K., Europe, Africa, and the Middle East, copies may be ordered from
American Psychological Association
3 Henrietta Street
Covent Garden, London
WC2E 8LU England

Typeset in Goudy by Circle Graphics, Inc., Columbia, MD

Printer: Bang Printing, Brainerd, MN
Cover Designer: Berg Design, Albany, NY

The opinions and statements published are the responsibility of the authors, and such opinions and statements do not necessarily represent the policies of the American Psychological Association.

Library of Congress Cataloging-in-Publication Data

Names: Bookwala, Jamila, author.
Title: Couple relationships in the middle and later years : their nature, complexity, and role in health and illness / Jamila Bookwala.
Description: Washington, DC : American Psychological Association, [2016] | Includes bibliographical references and index.
Identifiers: LCCN 2015038125 | ISBN 9781433822094 | ISBN 1433822091
Subjects: LCSH: Older couples—Psychology. | Older people—Psychology. | Aging—Psychological aspects. | Interpersonal relations—Psychological aspects. | Interpersonal relations—Health aspects.
Classification: LCC BF724.8 .B63 2016 | DDC 155.67/192—dc23
LC record available at http://lccn.loc.gov/2015038125

British Library Cataloguing-in-Publication Data
A CIP record is available from the British Library.

Printed in the United States of America
First Edition

http://dx.doi.org/10.1037/14897-000

# CONTENTS

Contributors ....................................................................................... *ix*

Introduction: Current Perspectives on Couple Relationships
in the Middle and Later Years ................................................................ 3
*Jamila Bookwala*

**I. Nature and Quality of Older Couple Relationships** ........................ **15**

Chapter 1.     Happily Ever After? Marital Satisfaction During
               the Middle Adulthood Years ......................................... 17
               *Barbara A. Mitchell*

Chapter 2.     Marital Discord in the Later Years ................................. 37
               *Timothy W. Smith and Carolynne E. Baron*

Chapter 3.     Older Couple Relationships and Loneliness .................. 57
               *Jenny de Jong Gierveld and Marjolein Broese van Groenou*

Chapter 4.      Intimacy and Obligations in LAT Relationships
                in Late Life ....................................................... 77
                *Sofie Ghazanfareeon Karlsson and Majen Espvall*

Chapter 5.      Same-Sex Relationships in Middle
                and Late Adulthood ...................................... 95
                *Bozena Zdaniuk and Christine Smith*

Chapter 6.      Sexual Intimacy in Mid- and Late-Life Couples .......... 115
                *Amy C. Lodge and Debra Umberson*

Chapter 7.      Spousal Role Allocation and Equity
                in Older Couples ........................................ 135
                *Liat Kulik*

Chapter 8.      These Happy Golden Years? The Role
                of Retirement in Marital Quality .............................. 157
                *Amy Rauer and Jakob F. Jensen*

Chapter 9.      Health Contributions to Marital Quality:
                Expected and Unexpected Links ................................ 177
                *Jeremy B. Yorgason and Heejeong Choi*

**II. Marriage, Health, and Adaptation to Illness
    in Middle and Late Life** ................................................. **197**

Chapter 10.     Marital Biography and Health in Middle
                and Late Life ................................................. 199
                *Zhenmei Zhang, Hui Liu, and Yan-Liang Yu*

Chapter 11.     Collaborative Cognition in Middle and Late Life:
                Couple Negotiation of Everyday Tasks ....................... 219
                *Jennifer A. Margrett and Celinda Reese-Melancon*

Chapter 12.     Spousal Interrelationships in Health Across
                Adulthood: Health Behaviors and Everyday
                Stress as Potential Underlying Mechanisms ................ 239
                *Christiane A. Hoppmann, Victoria Michalowski,
                and Denis Gerstorf*

Chapter 13.    A Developmental Perspective to Dyadic
               Coping Across Adulthood ............................................ 259
               *Cynthia A. Berg, Kelsey K. Sewell,*
               *Amy E. Hughes Lansing, Stephanie J. Wilson,*
               *and Carrie Brewer*

Chapter 14.    Emotion Regulation in the Context of Spousal
               Caregiving: Intrapersonal and Interpersonal
               Strategies ...................................................................... 281
               *Joan K. Monin*

Chapter 15.    Chronic Disease Management in Older Couples:
               Spousal Support Versus Control Strategies .................. 303
               *Melissa M. Franks, Elizabeth Wehrspann,*
               *Kristin J. August, Karen S. Rook,*
               *and Mary Ann Parris Stephens*

Chapter 16.    Harnessing the Power of the Marital Relationship
               to Improve Illness Management: Considerations
               for Couple-Based Interventions ................................... 325
               *Lynn M. Martire, Rachel C. Hemphill,*
               *and Courtney A. Polenick*

Index  .................................................................................................... 345

About the Editor ................................................................................... 357

# CONTRIBUTORS

**Kristin J. August, PhD,** Department of Psychology, Rutgers University, Camden, NJ

**Carolynne E. Baron, MS,** Department of Psychology, University of Utah, Salt Lake City

**Cynthia A. Berg, PhD,** Department of Psychology, University of Utah, Salt Lake City

**Jamila Bookwala, PhD,** Department of Psychology, Lafayette College, Easton, PA

**Carrie Brewer, BA,** Graduate School of Education and Psychology, Pepperdine University, Malibu, CA

**Marjolein Broese van Groenou, PhD,** Department of Sociology, Vrije Universiteit, Amsterdam, The Netherlands

**Heejeong Choi, PhD,** Consumer and Family Sciences, Sungkyunkwan University, Seoul, Republic of Korea

**Jenny de Jong Gierveld, PhD,** Department of Sociology, Vrije Universiteit, Amsterdam, and Netherlands Interdisciplinary Demographic Institute, The Hague, The Netherlands

**Majen Espvall, PhD,** Department of Social Work, Mid-Sweden University, Östersund

**Melissa M. Franks, PhD,** Department of Human Development and Family Studies, Purdue University, West Lafayette, IN

**Denis Gerstorf, PhD,** Department of Psychology, Humboldt University, Berlin, Germany

**Sofie Ghazanfareeon Karlsson, PhD,** Department of Social Work, Mid-Sweden University, Östersund

**Rachel C. Hemphill, PhD,** Center for Healthy Aging, Pennsylvania State University, University Park

**Christiane A. Hoppmann, PhD,** Department of Psychology, University of British Columbia, Vancouver, Canada

**Amy E. Hughes Lansing, PhD,** Department of Psychiatry, Dartmouth University, Lebanon, NH

**Jakob F. Jensen, PhD,** Department of Child Development and Family Relations, East Carolina University, Greenville, NC

**Liat Kulik, PhD,** School of Social Work, Bar-Ilan University, Ramat Gan, Israel

**Hui Liu, PhD,** Department of Sociology, Michigan State University, East Lansing

**Amy C. Lodge, PhD,** Center for Social Work Research, The University of Texas at Austin

**Jennifer A. Margrett, PhD,** Department of Human Development and Family Studies, Iowa State University, Ames

**Lynn M. Martire, PhD,** Department of Human Development and Family Studies and Center for Healthy Aging, Pennsylvania State University, University Park

**Victoria Michalowski, MA,** Department of Psychology, University of British Columbia, Vancouver, Canada

**Barbara A. Mitchell, PhD,** Department of Sociology/Anthropology and Department of Gerontology, Simon Fraser University, Burnaby, BC, Canada

**Joan K. Monin, PhD,** Chronic Disease Epidemiology, Social and Behavioral Sciences, Yale School of Public Health, New Haven, CT

**Mary Ann Parris Stephens, PhD,** Department of Psychological Sciences, Kent State University, Kent, OH

**Courtney A. Polenick, MS,** Department of Human Development and Family Studies, Pennsylvania State University, University Park

**Amy Rauer, PhD,** Department of Human Development and Family Studies, Auburn University, Auburn, AL

**Celinda Reese-Melancon, PhD,** Department of Psychology, Oklahoma State University, Stillwater

**Karen S. Rook, PhD,** Department of Psychology and Social Behavior, University of California, Irvine

**Kelsey K. Sewell, MS,** Department of Psychology, University of Utah, Salt Lake City

**Christine Smith, PhD,** Department of Human Development and Psychology, University of Wisconsin, Green Bay

**Timothy W. Smith, PhD,** Department of Psychology, University of Utah, Salt Lake City

**Debra Umberson, PhD,** Department of Sociology and Population Research Center, The University of Texas at Austin

**Elizabeth Wehrspann, MS,** Department of Human Development and Family Studies, Purdue University, West Lafayette, IN

**Stephanie J. Wilson, MS,** Department of Human Development and Family Studies, Pennsylvania State University, University Park

**Jeremy B. Yorgason, PhD,** School of Family Life, Brigham Young University, Provo, UT

**Yan-Liang Yu, MA,** Department of Sociology, Michigan State University, East Lansing

**Bozena Zdaniuk, PhD,** Interdisciplinary Studies Graduate Program, University of British Columbia, Vancouver, Canada

**Zhenmei Zhang, PhD,** Department of Sociology, Michigan State University, East Lansing

# Couple Relationships in the Middle and Later Years

# INTRODUCTION: CURRENT PERSPECTIVES ON COUPLE RELATIONSHIPS IN THE MIDDLE AND LATER YEARS

JAMILA BOOKWALA

Older couple relationships are recognized to be complex, multidimensional, and vital to health and well-being (Bookwala, 2012, 2014b). With life expectancy at its highest levels and the baby-boom generation's entry first into the midlife years and now into late adulthood, scholars, clinicians, and society at large have shown an ever-increasing interest in understanding couple relationships as people age. The present volume focuses exclusively on these couple relationships, providing a rich resource for those who study and work with middle-aged and older adults and couples. As described in this introduction, the chapters in this book cover a broad range of topics central to older couple relationships: the quality of these relationships and their evolving nature and definition in contemporary society; older couples' loneliness, sexual intimacy, relationship history, and role equity and how these factors are linked to relationship quality and well-being; the role of major life transitions such as retirement and illness in shaping older couple

http://dx.doi.org/10.1037/14897-001
*Couple Relationships in the Middle and Later Years: Their Nature, Complexity, and Role in Health and Illness,*
J. Bookwala (Editor)

relationships; and dyadic influences on health, cognitive function, and coping with and managing illness.

The volume is organized into two broad sections. Part I characterizes the nature, characteristics, and quality of couple relationships among middle-aged and older adults in today's society. Both positive (marital satisfaction) and negative (marital discord) dimensions of relationship quality in older couples are considered, as well as factors that can play a role in improving or diminishing relationship quality (e.g., the allocation of roles, sexual satisfaction, the retirement of one and/or both partners, and the occurrence of a long-term illness). Although the loss of a spouse or partner is clearly linked to a high risk of loneliness, this section offers insights into how older individuals can experience loneliness in an ongoing relationship. Part I also includes chapters on less traditional but equally significant older couple relationships that are gaining in prevalence (living-apart-together [LAT] relationships) and visibility (same-sex relationships).

An area that has witnessed perhaps the most prolific theoretical and empirical advances in the field of older couple relationships is their integral role in health and well-being (Bookwala, 2012, 2014b). The chapters in Part II address a variety of topics at the intersection of marriage and health as individuals age. The beneficial role of married status in late-life health is widely established; in this section we learn more about the emerging importance of individuals' cumulative marital history for their health during the midlife years and beyond. Other topics include the significant role of couples' negotiations in improving cognitive performance on daily tasks and the potential mechanisms that can explain convergence that is seen on health indicators within couples. Part II also focuses on the challenge for the dyad as a unit when a spouse becomes chronically ill, a normative life transition and stressor as people age. Related chapters discuss useful emotion regulation strategies in the context of spousal caregiving when one spouse requires care due to illness, review the essential role of dyadic coping in the face of a stressor such as chronic illness, consider the developmental bases of dyadic coping from a lifespan perspective, and describe ways that spouses can hinder, promote, and be trained to enhance adaptation to and management of chronic illness.

Overall, the 16 chapters offer critical analyses of relevant theory and empirical findings in specific areas of research on mid- and late-life couple relationships. They identify existing limitations in and future directions for research on older couple relationships, offering recommendations that can enhance current understanding about their nature and complexity and how they can shape and be shaped by intra- and interpersonal contexts. Recognizing the importance of high-quality couple relationships in aging well, the chapters in this volume also consider clinical and policy issues relevant to maintaining and enhancing older couple relationships. It should be noted that although the chapters in this volume mostly focus on marital relationships in midlife and late life, reflecting the vast majority of existing research on older couple relationships, the volume also addresses nontraditional adult couple relationships as feasible based on the extant literature. In the following paragraphs, I provide a brief summary of each chapter in the volume, highlighting overarching themes in and major points addressed by each.

## PART I: NATURE AND QUALITY OF OLDER COUPLE RELATIONSHIPS

Part I includes nine chapters that focus on key aspects related to the quality of couple relationships during the middle and late adulthood years. Research on marital quality across the adult life span has seen considerable growth in recent decades (Bookwala, 2012). The construct is widely regarded as a multidimensional one that encompasses both positive dimensions (e.g., satisfaction, closeness, happiness, adjustment in the marriage) and negative dimensions (e.g., marital disagreement, discord, or conflict; Fincham & Linfield, 1997). In Chapter 1, Barbara A. Mitchell summarizes early and contemporary developments related to marital satisfaction in middle adulthood, providing a historical analysis of definitions of the construct and methodologies for measuring it. Mitchell reviews changing trends in research emphases over several decades; theoretical perspectives that explain midlife marital (dis)satisfaction including adult attachment theory and life-cycle forces; and empirical findings on correlates of marital satisfaction at the level of the individual, relationship, context, and environment.

Of course, older couple relationships are not characterized exclusively by positive dimensions. Indeed, intimate relationships are typically marked by ambivalence, such that criticism and other hurtful emotional behaviors co-occur with positive feelings and behaviors (Akiyama, Antonucci, Takahashi, & Langfahl, 2003; Fingerman, Hay, & Birditt, 2004). Studies have found that mid- and late-life marriages are not free from disagreement and conflict (Bookwala & Jacobs, 2004; Bookwala, Sobin, & Zdaniuk, 2005; Henry, Miller, & Giarrusso, 2005). In Chapter 2, Timothy W. Smith and Carolynne E. Baron review theoretical, methodological, and empirical advances in the area of marital discord and aging. They use a variety of theoretical frameworks to explain marital discord in older couples including models that incorporate both positive and negative dimensions to measure marital quality; interpersonal theory that incorporates both affiliative and controlling aspects of behavior and motivation; and the application of life-span models to the understanding of interpersonal relationships. Smith and Baron also identify links from marital discord to physical health, emotional adjustment, and well-being with a particular emphasis on coronary disease.

Chapter 3 focuses on loneliness in older couples. We know from longitudinal research that experiencing the loss of a spouse or partner has adverse effects on health and well-being (e.g., Bookwala, Marshall, & Manning, 2014; Das, 2013). In their chapter, Jenny de Jong Gierveld and Marjolein Broese van Groenou stress that these adverse effects occur because the loss of this significant intimate relationship seriously increases the risk for both emotional and social loneliness. However, loneliness also has been found to occur in poor-quality relationships among aging individuals (De Jong Gierveld, Broese van Groenou, Hoogendoorn, & Smit, 2009). In their chapter, De Jong Gierveld and Broese van Groenou review conceptual and methodological advances on loneliness and identify distal and proximal factors associated with loneliness in midlife and late life. Most notably, they discuss the role of the couple relationship as a potentially decisive factor in alleviating both emotional and social loneliness as individuals age.

An ongoing need in research on older couple relationships remains the study of the nature and quality of couple relationships that are less traditional than marriage between opposite-sex members. Changing social attitudes and cultural norms have resulted in increasing numbers of adults opting for other types of intimate relationships. For example, among middle-aged and older persons, there is an increase in LAT relationships, which are noncohabiting intimate relationships in which a couple does not share the same household but self-identifies and is recognized by their social network as a couple (Levin, 2004). Older LAT relationships bring new challenges especially in terms of role definitions and caregiving dynamics. Same-sex marriages and unions in midlife and late life also represent an important area of research, especially given the growing legal recognition of same-sex marriage in many parts of the Western hemisphere and most recently in the United States. Given the emerging importance of LAT and same-sex relationships, Chapters 4 and 5 in this section focus on these relationships.

Specifically, in Chapter 4, Sofie Ghazanfareeon Karlsson and Majen Espvall describe such LAT relationships and consider the implications for caregiving and care receiving within these relationships in the event of poor health and how these demands vary by gender. They also analyze care-related expectations and obligations in LAT relationships against the backdrop of cultural and social influences using Sweden as a case study, where the state—rather than the spouse or family—bears the primary responsibility for caring for elders' needs.

In Chapter 5, Bozena Zdaniuk and Christine Smith review the literature on the formation, maintenance, and quality of same-sex couples' relationships during the mid- and late-life years. The empirical literature in this area is still developing and does not have the methodological sophistication seen in other relationship research. Zdaniuk and Smith highlight the need for theoretically guided and methodologically rigorous studies on older same-sex relationships. The growing visibility of same-sex unions and marriages presents gerontology scholars who focus on relationship research with a unique and timely opportunity to make substantial strides in our understanding of these relationships.

Contrary to pervasive stereotypes and conventional wisdom, sexual intimacy and sexual satisfaction are important to older adults (Cain et al., 2003; Gott & Hinchliff, 2003). In Chapter 6, Amy C. Lodge and Debra Umberson review the literature on sexuality in older couples, an understudied and sometimes controversial topic. Increasingly, studies show that sexual intimacy and satisfaction remain important as people age, and more frequent sexual activity is associated with more positive evaluations of relationship quality and greater relationship satisfaction (Bookwala, 2012). Lodge and Umberson consider the importance of sexual behavior to relationship quality and the reciprocal relationship between sexual behavior and overall well-being. They draw our attention to the need for theoretically guided research on sexual behavior and intimacy in the mid- and late-life years and for this research to be more inclusive of nonheterosexual sexualities.

Another aspect of couple relationships that can play a significant role in marital satisfaction and well-being is the level of (in)equity in marital role allocation or division of household labor (Bookwala, 2012). Inequities in the division of labor are quite common in midlife (Bookwala, 2009; Feeney, Peterson, & Noller, 1994), although they tend to decline in the late adulthood years (Hagedoorn et al., 2006; Kulik, 2002). In Chapter 7, Liat Kulik describes the importance of equity in role allocation within couples during and after the midlife years and highlights the significance of role equity for relationship quality. Kulik reviews theoretical explanations for inequities in marital role allocation and changes in role allocations over the adult life span and analyzes the extent to which different life transitions—adult children leaving the home, retirement from work, and taking on the caregiving role—are accompanied by changes in household division of labor.

A normative life transition that has strong implications for the quality of the couple relationship is retirement from one's primary employment (Trudel, Turgeon, & Piche, 2000). Recent retirement trends show that individuals presently around the age of retirement are electing to delay their retirement, opt for partial employment, or transition in and out of the workforce depending on personal circumstances and available opportunities (National Institute on Aging, 2007). Regardless of the growing complexity in the definition of retirement, the retirement of one or both spouses can have significant implications for the quality of the couple relationship. In Chapter 8, Amy Rauer and Jakob F. Jensen review the lack of consistent empirical findings on the role of retirement in marital quality, with studies showing positive, negative, or no links between these variables. They provide explanations for these inconsistencies and delineate potential factors that can significantly facilitate or impede the individual's and couple's adjustment to retirement.

Part I ends with an examination of how health-related changes in a spouse can influence the quality of the couple's relationship. Changes in the health of one spouse have been found to have significant implications for the health of the other spouse as evidenced in the caregiving context (e.g., Burton et al., 2003; Schulz & Beach, 1999) and in the marital context more broadly (e.g., Bookwala, 2014c; Zivin & Christakis, 2007). Equally as important, a growing body of research has documented that the effects of spousal illness also occur at the relationship level. In Chapter 9, Jeremy B. Yorgason and Heejeong Choi review the evidence for the sometimes adverse and sometimes beneficial consequences of spousal illness on the quality of the relationship. They develop an integrated theoretical framework that incorporates well-established gerontology models related to stress and adaptation and to interpersonal and dyadic relationships, and they use this framework to explain how and why spousal illness can have expected and unexpected ramifications for relationship quality. Yorgason and Choi's chapter serves as a fitting segue to Part II, which focuses on couple relationships and their links to health and coping with illness.

## PART II: MARRIAGE, HEALTH, AND ADAPTATION TO ILLNESS IN MIDDLE AND LATE LIFE

Research has flourished in recent years on the health benefits of being married, especially as people age. Relative to other marital status categories (being divorced or separated, widowed, never married) and even cohabiting relationships, being married is consistently linked to superior health (e.g., Pienta, Hayward, & Jenkins, 2000; Zhang & Hayward, 2006). The health benefits associated with marriage are broad in scope (ranging from functional levels to fatal and nonfatal health conditions to mortality) and application (although the protective effects of marriage are stronger for men than women; Bookwala, 2012). Studies also have found that being in a better quality marriage is a strong predictor of better health in middle-aged and older adults (e.g., Bookwala, 2005; Umberson, Williams, Powers, Liu, & Needham, 2006) and can act as a buffer in the face of midlife and late-life stressors (Bookwala, 2011; Bookwala & Franks, 2005; Mancini & Bonanno, 2006). The chapters contained in this section further advance our understanding about the complex links between marriage and health.

In Chapter 10, Zhenmei Zhang, Hui Liu, and Yan-Liang Yu review the literature linking marital history and health in the mid- and late-life years.

Zhang and colleagues demonstrate that understanding the health benefits of being married requires a far more nuanced and careful analysis that takes into account the various elements of individuals' lifetime marital histories such as the type, number, timing, and sequencing of marital transitions. They also emphasize that the health impact of marital transitions must be evaluated in terms of the contexts in which marital transitions are embedded as defined by individuals' gender, race, and marital quality.

Cognition is a vital domain of health and well-being as individuals age, and research on maintaining and improving late-life cognition continues to be an important need. Spouses and similar intimate partners can play an influential role as supportive collaborators in the cognitive realm by helping to enhance each other's cognitive performance (Strough & Margrett, 2002). In Chapter 11, Jennifer A. Margrett and Celinda Reese-Melancon review theoretical and empirical advances in the field of collaborative cognition in adulthood, highlighting the significant role spouses can and do play in enhancing performance when individuals age, especially on familiar (everyday) cognitive tasks. Margrett and Reese-Melancon's review of the literature shows that the effectiveness of collaborative cognition between spouses is a function of a number of factors related to the task, the dyad, and the environmental context.

Not only do older couples share cognitive resources, they also share health trajectories. Partners in an intimate relationship such as marriage are especially likely to show convergence on emotional experiences and health and well-being (Bookwala & Schulz, 1996; Hoppmann, Gerstorf, & Hibbert, 2011; Strawbridge, Wallhagen, & Shema, 2011; Tower & Kasl, 1996), sometimes viewed as a form of contagion (Bookwala, 2014a; Hatfield, Cacioppo, & Rapson, 1993). In Chapter 12, Christiane A. Hoppmann, Victoria Michalowski, and Denis Gerstorf use the intricate tango dance as a metaphor to represent the complex interplay of individual and relationship factors that are relevant to similarities between spouses' health trajectories with age. Hoppmann and colleagues identify spouses' influence on each other's engagement in health behaviors and their ability to transmit emotions to each other on a day-to-day basis as potential mechanisms that explain the synchrony in spousal health trajectories.

With increasing age, individuals are at greater risk for developing a serious or chronic illness. The last four chapters in this volume address the broad topic of aging couples coping with illness. To date, scholars have focused considerable attention on how older couples cope with losses (e.g., cognitive decline) and life stressors (e.g., illness of one or both spouses). Ill health experienced by a spouse makes coping demands on the ill person, the other spouse, and the dyad as a unit, and thus has consequences for individual and dyadic adjustment (Berg & Upchurch, 2007). Furthermore, dyadic coping varies over the life span and the trajectory of the illness and as a function of the relationship and illness context (Berg & Upchurch, 2007). In Chapter 13, Cynthia A. Berg, Kelsey K. Sewell, Amy E. Hughes Lansing, Stephanie J. Wilson, and Carrie Brewer review the literature on dyadic coping in healthy couples and those coping with illness. They explain why dyadic coping, which is associated with health benefits throughout adulthood, may be especially beneficial as couples age and how dyadic coping efforts develop and change over the course and stages of a chronic illness. They further propose that interactions with parents and romantic partners earlier in life shape dyadic coping strategies used later in life in spousal and similar relationships.

The development of a chronic or serious health condition in one member of a couple typically brings with it the demands of caregiving. Caring for an ill spouse is a well-known stressor known to be associated with adverse psychological and physical health effects (e.g., Burton, Zdaniuk, Schulz, Jackson, & Hirsch, 2003; Schulz & Beach, 1999). A factor that can contribute to the negative toll on spouse caregivers is the ongoing exposure to their loved one's suffering (Monin & Schulz, 2009), which can trigger a range of negative emotions including distress, sadness, and frustration. Managing these emotions is an important task for both spouse caregivers and their ill partners. In Chapter 14, Joan K. Monin reviews intrapersonal and interpersonal emotional regulation processes relevant to the spouse caregiving context and their associated health benefits for both the spouse caregiver and the care recipient. Monin makes a case for emotion regulation as a powerful strategy within the spousal caregiving context for mitigating negative consequences and enhancing positive ones in both spouses.

A considerable body of research has relied on social control theory, which refers to tactics used by an individual to instrument change in another person's behavior, to understand the mechanisms and strategies through which spouses can play an influential role in managing their partner's health-related behaviors when she or he is diagnosed with an illness (e.g., Lewis & Rook, 1999). Notwithstanding the potential benefits of dyadic coping in the face of a spouse's illness, mixed results have been found in situations where one spouse attempts to influence the other's disease management. In Chapter 15, Melissa M. Franks, Elizabeth Wehrspann, Kristin J. August, Karen S. Rook, and Mary Ann Parris Stephens discuss how spouses can be effective or ineffective in helping a chronically ill spouse manage his or her disease. The authors identify contextual factors that influence the choice of strategies and their eventual efficacy. Their review also informs us about the costs and benefits of different types of spousal involvement strategies in disease management for the ill partner, the spouse, and the dyadic relationship.

Given that individuals have the potential to yield beneficial effects for an ill spouse's management of and adaptation to a chronic health condition, training spouses to use effective strategies can be a valuable approach for better disease management. Recent years have witnessed a growing interest in couple-based intervention programs for promoting adjustment to chronic illness (Martire, Schulz, Helgeson, Small, & Saghafi, 2010). In the final chapter of this volume, Lynn M. Martire, Rachel C. Hemphill, and Courtney A. Polenick argue that couple-based interventions designed to promote adjustment to chronic illness can be especially efficacious if they target specifically how spouses influence the ill partner's disease management. They use findings from observational studies on spousal influence in illness management and from couple-based interventions with populations at risk for serious health conditions as supporting evidence for their position and offer recommendations for designing and implementing couple-based interventions that directly target beneficial spousal behaviors to enhance the ill partner's management of the disease. Such interventions have the potential to improve self-care, influence the trajectory of the chronic illness, and enhance both spouses' well-being.

Significant gaps still exist in the literature. Notably, there is a relative paucity of research on older same-sex marriages and nonmarital heterosexual and same-sex relationships; research that uses the dyad as the unit of analysis; and research that examines the cultural, ethnic, and demographic influences on the nature and quality of couple relationships. There is also an ongoing need for the use of sophisticated methodologies (e.g., observational research, longitudinal studies, time sampling techniques) in studying older couple relationships, methodologies that can provide a more granular level of analysis. Nonetheless, as this brief introduction shows, tremendous strides have been made in the field of research on older couple relationships. Collectively, the chapters in this volume offer a multilayered and comprehensive view on the nuances and complexities that characterize couple relationships as people age and on the integral role of older couple relationships in health and well-being. This volume provides a rich, topical, and comprehensive resource for those who study and work with adults and couples in the mid- and late-life years.

## REFERENCES

Akiyama, H., Antonucci, T., Takahashi, K., & Langfahl, E. S. (2003). Negative interactions in close relationships across the life span. *The Journals of Gerontology: Series B. Psychological Sciences and Social Sciences, 58*, 70–79. http://dx.doi.org/10.1093/geronb/58.2.P70

Berg, C. A., & Upchurch, R. (2007). A developmental-contextual model of couples coping with chronic illness across the adult life span. *Psychological Bulletin, 133*, 920–954. http://dx.doi.org/10.1037/0033-2909.133.6.920

Bookwala, J. (2005). The role of marital quality in physical health during the mature years. *Journal of Aging and Health, 17*, 85–104. http://dx.doi.org/10.1177/0898264304272794

Bookwala, J. (2009). The impact of parent care on marital quality and well-being in adult daughters and sons. *The Journals of Gerontology: Series B. Psychological Sciences and Social Sciences, 64*, 339–347. http://dx.doi.org/10.1093/geronb/gbp018

Bookwala, J. (2011). Marital quality as a moderator of the effects of poor vision on quality of life among older adults. *The Journals of Gerontology: Series B. Psychological Sciences and Social Sciences, 66*, 605–616. http://dx.doi.org/10.1093/geronb/gbr091

Bookwala, J. (2012). Marriage and other partnered relationships in middle and late adulthood. In R. Blieszner & V. Bedford (Eds.), *Handbook of families and aging* (2nd ed., pp. 91–123). Westport, CT: Greenwood/ABC-CLIO.

Bookwala, J. (2014a). Affective contagion. In A. C. Mihalos (Ed.), *Encyclopedia of quality of life and well-being research* (pp. 88–91). Dordrecht, the Netherlands: Springer. http://dx.doi.org/10.1007/978-94-007-0753-5_44

Bookwala, J. (2014b). Marital quality and well-being in mid and late life. In A. C. Mihalos (Ed.), *Encyclopedia of quality of life and well-being research* (pp. 3804–3808). Dordrecht, the Netherlands: Springer. http://dx.doi.org/10.1007/978-94-007-0753-5_3891

Bookwala, J. (2014c). Spouse health status, depressed affect, and resilience in mid and late life: A longitudinal study. *Developmental Psychology, 50*, 1241–1249. http://dx.doi.org/10.1037/a0035124

Bookwala, J., & Franks, M. M. (2005). Moderating role of marital quality in older adults' depressed affect: Beyond the main-effects model. *The Journals of Gerontology: Series B. Psychological Sciences and Social Sciences, 60*, 338–341. http://dx.doi.org/10.1093/geronb/60.6.P338

Bookwala, J., & Jacobs, J. (2004). Age, marital processes, and depressed affect. *The Gerontologist, 44*, 328–338. http://dx.doi.org/10.1093/geront/44.3.328

Bookwala, J., Marshall, K. I., & Manning, S. W. (2014). Who needs a friend? Marital status transitions and physical health outcomes in later life. *Health Psychology, 33*, 505–515. http://dx.doi.org/10.1037/hea0000049

Bookwala, J., & Schulz, R. (1996). Spousal similarity in subjective well-being: The Cardiovascular Health Study. *Psychology and Aging, 11*, 582–590. http://dx.doi.org/10.1037/0882-7974.11.4.582

Bookwala, J., Sobin, J., & Zdaniuk, B. (2005). Gender and aggression in marital relationships: A life span perspective. *Sex Roles, 52*, 797–806. http://dx.doi.org/10.1007/s11199-005-4200-1

Burton, L. C., Zdaniuk, B., Schulz, R., Jackson, S., & Hirsch, C. (2003). Transitions in spousal caregiving. *The Gerontologist, 43*, 230–241. http://dx.doi.org/10.1093/geront/43.2.230

Cain, V. S., Johannes, C. B., Avis, N. E., Mohr, B., Schocken, M., Skurnick, J., & Ory, M. (2003). Sexual functioning and practices in a multi-ethnic study of midlife women: Baseline results from SWAN. *Journal of Sex Research, 40,* 266–276. http://dx.doi.org/10.1080/00224490309552191

Das, A. (2013). Spousal loss and health in late life: Moving beyond emotional trauma. *Journal of Aging and Health, 25,* 221–242. http://dx.doi.org/10.1177/0898264312464498

De Jong Gierveld, J. J., Broese van Groenou, M., Hoogendoorn, A. W., & Smit, J. H. (2009). Quality of marriages in later life and emotional and social loneliness. *The Journals of Gerontology: Series B. Psychological Sciences and Social Sciences, 64,* 497–506. http://dx.doi.org/10.1093/geronb/gbn043

Feeney, J., Peterson, C., & Noller, P. (1994). Equity and marital satisfaction over the family life cycle. *Personal Relationships, 1,* 83–99. http://dx.doi.org/10.1111/j.1475-6811.1994.tb00056.x

Fincham, F. D., & Linfield, K. J. (1997). A new look at marital quality: Can spouses feel positive and negative about their marriage? *Journal of Family Psychology, 11,* 489–502. http://dx.doi.org/10.1037/0893-3200.11.4.489-502

Fingerman, K. L., Hay, E. L., & Birditt, K. S. (2004). The best of ties, the worst of ties: Close, problematic, and ambivalent social relationships. *Journal of Marriage and Family, 66,* 792–808. http://dx.doi.org/10.1111/j.0022-2445.2004.00053.x

Gott, M., & Hinchliff, S. (2003). How important is sex in later life? The views of older people. *Social Science & Medicine, 56,* 1617–1628. http://dx.doi.org/10.1016/S0277-9536(02)00180-6

Hagedoorn, M., Van Yperen, N. W., Coyne, J. C., van Jaarsveld, C. H. M., Ranchor, A. V., van Sonderen, E., & Sanderman, R. (2006). Does marriage protect older people from distress? The role of equity and recency of bereavement. *Psychology and Aging, 21,* 611–620. http://dx.doi.org/10.1037/0882-7974.21.3.611

Hatfield, E., Cacioppo, J. T., & Rapson, R. L. (1993). Emotional contagion. *Current Directions in Psychological Science, 2,* 96–99. http://dx.doi.org/10.1111/1467-8721.ep10770953

Henry, R. G., Miller, R. B., & Giarrusso, R. (2005). Difficulties, disagreements, and disappointments in late-life marriages. *International Journal of Aging & Human Development, 61,* 243–264. http://dx.doi.org/10.2190/EF1G-PNXF-J1VQ-6M72

Hoppmann, C. A., Gerstorf, D., & Hibbert, A. (2011). Spousal associations between functional limitation and depressive symptom trajectories: Longitudinal findings from the study of Asset and Health Dynamics Among the Oldest Old (AHEAD). *Health Psychology, 30,* 153–162. http://dx.doi.org/10.1037/a0022094

Kulik, L. (2002). His and her marriage: Differences in spousal perceptions of marital life in late adulthood. In S. P. Shohov (Ed.), *Advances in psychology research* (pp. 21–32). Huntington, NY: Nova Science.

Levin, I. (2004). Living apart together: A new family form. *Current Sociology, 52,* 223–240. http://dx.doi.org/10.1177/0011392104041809

Lewis, M. A., & Rook, K. S. (1999). Social control in personal relationships: Impact on health behaviors and psychological distress. *Health Psychology, 18,* 63–71. http://dx.doi.org/10.1037/0278-6133.18.1.63

Mancini, A. D., & Bonanno, G. A. (2006). Marital closeness, functional disability, and adjustment in late life. *Psychology and Aging, 21,* 600–610. http://dx.doi.org/10.1037/0882-7974.21.3.600

Martire, L. M., Schulz, R., Helgeson, V. S., Small, B. J., & Saghafi, E. M. (2010). Review and meta-analysis of couple-oriented interventions for chronic illness. *Annals of Behavioral Medicine, 40,* 325–342. http://dx.doi.org/10.1007/s12160-010-9216-2

Monin, J. K., & Schulz, R. (2009). Interpersonal effects of suffering in older adult caregiving relationships. *Psychology and Aging, 24,* 681–695. http://dx.doi.org/10.1037/a0016355

National Institute on Aging. (2007). *Growing older in America: The Health and Retirement Study* (NIH Publication No. 07-5757). Bethesda, MD: National Institutes of Health.

Pienta, A. M., Hayward, M. D., & Jenkins, K. R. (2000). Health consequences of marriage for the retirement years. *Journal of Family Issues, 21,* 559–586. http://dx.doi.org/10.1177/019251300021005003

Schulz, R., & Beach, S. R. (1999). Caregiving as a risk factor for mortality: The Caregiver Health Effects Study. *JAMA, 282,* 2215–2219. http://dx.doi.org/10.1001/jama.282.23.2215

Strawbridge, W. J., Wallhagen, M. I., & Shema, S. J. (2011). Spousal interrelations in self-reports of cognition in the context of marital problems. *Gerontology, 57,* 148–152. http://dx.doi.org/10.1159/000318637

Strough, J., & Margrett, J. (2002). Overview of the special section on collaborative cognition in later adulthood. *International Journal of Behavioral Development, 26,* 2–5. http://dx.doi.org/10.1080/01650250143000300

Tower, R. B., & Kasl, S. V. (1996). Depressive symptoms across older spouses: Longitudinal influences. *Psychology and Aging, 11,* 683–697. http://dx.doi.org/10.1037/0882-7974.11.4.683

Trudel, G., Turgeon, L., & Piche, L. (2000). Marital and sexual aspects of old age. *Sexual and Relationship Therapy, 15,* 381–406. http://dx.doi.org/10.1080/713697433

Umberson, D., Williams, K., Powers, D. A., Liu, H., & Needham, B. (2006). You make me sick: Marital quality and health over the life course. *Journal of Health and Social Behavior, 47,* 1–16. http://dx.doi.org/10.1177/002214650604700101

Zhang, Z., & Hayward, M. D. (2006). Gender, the marital life course, and cardiovascular disease in late midlife. *Journal of Marriage and Family, 68,* 639–657. http://dx.doi.org/10.1111/j.1741-3737.2006.00280.x

Zivin, K., & Christakis, N. A. (2007). The emotional toll of spousal morbidity and mortality. *The American Journal of Geriatric Psychiatry, 15,* 772–779. http://dx.doi.org/10.1097/JGP.0b013e318050c9ae

# I

# NATURE AND QUALITY OF OLDER COUPLE RELATIONSHIPS

# 1

# HAPPILY EVER AFTER? MARITAL SATISFACTION DURING THE MIDDLE ADULTHOOD YEARS

BARBARA A. MITCHELL

Despite significant transformations in the meanings and behaviors associated with the institution of marriage, marriage continues to be regarded as one of the most intimate and enduring of all close family ties. Beginning with the publication of a landmark scientific study of the sex lives and problems of married people (Hamilton, 1929), the topic of marital satisfaction, in particular, has emerged as a highly popular thematic area central to marital research. Not surprisingly, the rationale for studying this field stems from numerous issues and concerns, ranging from its centrality to individual, family, and societal well-being (e.g., Stack & Eshleman, 1998) to the need to develop empirically defensible interventions that can prevent or alleviate marital distress and divorce (Jose & Alfons, 2007). With the aging of the large baby boomer generation (ca. 1946–1965), we have witnessed a historically unprecedented number of couples in middle adulthood. Indeed, this subject matter is particularly timely against the backdrop of population shifts,

http://dx.doi.org/10.1037/14897-002
*Couple Relationships in the Middle and Later Years: Their Nature, Complexity, and Role in Health and Illness,*
J. Bookwala (Editor)

economic challenge, changing family structures, and related alterations in family roles and responsibilities.

The primary goal of this chapter is to review and critique conceptual, theoretical, and empirical work on marital satisfaction, with special attention paid to the correlates of marital satisfaction during the middle adulthood years. In addition, a number of salient clinical and policy implications and recommendations for future work are identified.

## CONCEPTUALIZING AND THEORIZING MIDLIFE MARITAL SATISFACTION

*Midlife marital satisfaction* has been broadly defined and conceptualized as a powerful multidimensional aspect of marital quality during the "middle years." Although conceptualizations of the middle years are gradually being revised to reflect changes in family and life-span-related processes (e.g., increased longevity, delayed family transitions), typical conceptualizations tend to focus on either chronological markers (i.e., one's relative age, commonly considered as being between ages 45 and 64) or life course developmental transitions (i.e., unique phases of family life, such as child launching).

Moreover, it is recognized that although some midlife couples have been married only for a few years because of late marriage or remarriage, the majority have been married for at least 10 years, with some being married as long as 30 years (Hollist & Miller, 2005). Therefore, most studies on midlife marriages assume that couples have already experienced the adjustments and early transitions that characterize younger couples, such as parenthood. It is also often assumed that midlife couples have already survived the early years of marriage (which have the highest risk of divorce), shared a relationship history, and established patterns of relating to each other.

### Defining Midlife Marital Satisfaction

Despite varied terminology, marital satisfaction and other indicators of marital quality—such as marital conflict, marital commitment, social support, marital interaction, and marital discord—are often combined as a single indicator of marital quality at specific times of the marriage (Stanley, 2007; see also Chapter 2, this volume). Kamp Dush, Taylor, and Kroeger (2008) observed that marital quality is typically used to indicate global evaluations of marriage that could include behavioral indicators (e.g., conflict in the marriage) or indicators of social comparison (e.g., I would marry my spouse again if I had to live my life over). And although the concept of marital satisfaction—that is, an overall appraisal of the degree of happiness with various dimensions of one's marriage—is often used as a single indicator of marital quality, it is also used interchangeably with terms such as *marital happiness*.

## Shifting Focal Interests

As reviewed by McCabe (2006), research foci reflect changes in popular theories and methodologies that shape empirical studies. They also mirror transformations in the wider societal understandings of marriage and of what constitutes a satisfying marriage. For example, in the 1930s and 1940s, emphasis was almost exclusively on psychological factors (including perceptions of the spouse's personality) and personality profiles. In the 1950s, the spotlight shone more on the interactional and cognitive style of couples, as well as a movement from questionnaire data to observations of couple interactions.

However, many scholars criticized research conducted from the 1950s to the 1970s for its failure to fully address deeper issues of power structure imbalances and gender inequities. These issues were viewed as especially salient amid the emergence of more "alternative" relationship patterns (e.g., stepfamilies) and the changing roles of men and women. Thus, during the 1970s and 1980s, the study of factors leading to unhappy marriages (and especially divorce, given a dramatic surge in divorce rates) became a strong focal point. There was also a growing recognition that there may be a health-buffering effect of marriage, particularly for men (e.g., Bernard, 1982). A burgeoning interest in how marital satisfaction changes from the early years of marriage until old age also emerged; however, many of these studies were cross-sectional and plagued by methodological issues (McCabe, 2006). In the 1990s, researchers continued with these streams of inquiry but also showed renewed interest in husband–wife interactions (Bradbury, Fincham, & Beach, 2000).

Generally, over the past 2 decades, studies have continued to address issues of health, well-being, and aging, as well as stronger recognition of diversity within relationships. This variability is due to aspects such as differing partnership histories and trajectories, and changing racial/immigration patterns. There has also been growing attention to the topic of lesbian, gay, bisexual, and transgender (LGBT) partnerships, although research remains limited (see Chapter 5, this volume).

With the increased economic independence, educational attainment, and labor force participation of women, gendered and work-related issues (both paid and unpaid) have become more salient. Furthermore, in tandem with the aging of the baby boomer population, we have also witnessed increasing interest in aging and sexuality and its role in marital satisfaction (see Chapter 6, this volume, for a discussion of sexual intimacy in older couples), a focus that coincides with changing ideas about growing old and the rising strength of mass marketing and the pharmaceutical and medical industries. Moreover, the sociopolitical environment has also played an influential role in the direction and type of research that has been generated. Notably, there have been greater funding opportunities and policy mandates for research that will strengthen marriages across a wide variety of family situations (Fincham & Beach, 2010).

## Conceptual and Theoretical Perspectives on Midlife Marital Satisfaction

Researchers have tended to use conceptual models that explain why (or why not) the couple is happy in the marriage. Although there has been a broadening of disciplinary approaches as applied to this topic, psychological theorizing remains highly influential. For instance, Hazan and Shaver (1987) applied attachment theory to marital satisfaction, generating the hypothesis that securely attached couples have higher marital satisfaction and are more likely to describe feeling comfortable with emotional intimacy and in finding joy in their relationships.

Another body of literature focuses more on psychosocial and/or family-related lifespan developmental or life-cycle changes (e.g., Duvall, 1977). Li and Fung (2011) proposed a dynamic goal theory of marital satisfaction drawing on a lifespan developmental perspective. Their theory argues that people have multiple goals to achieve in their marriage (e.g., personal growth, companionship, instrumental) that change in priority as one ages and determine the level of marital satisfaction. Middle-aged couples tend to prioritize instrumental goals, whereas young couples emphasize personal growth and older couples focus on companionship.

Generally, marital scholars tend to view marital happiness as a dynamic state that is highly fluid over the family life course. Although early studies suggested that marital satisfaction declines steadily during the first 10 years of marriage (e.g., Blood & Wolfe, 1960; Pineo, 1969), more recent research purports that marital satisfaction over the family life cycle is curvilinear, or follows a "U-shaped curve" (Aldous, 1978; Duvall, 1977; Rodgers, 1964; Vaillant & Vaillant, 1993) that is characterized by high marital happiness in the early (or preparental) years of marriage, a decline during the middle (or parental) years, and a rise in marital happiness in the later (or postparental) years. It is assumed that children create demands on parents' time and income and that this can negatively affect parents' feelings of stress, burden, and the availability of time to devote to personal or leisure activities (VanLaningham, Johnson, & Amato, 2001).

This model is not without its criticisms because there is a heavy reliance on cross-sectional data, and selection processes may explain the U-shaped trend as marriages that have problems (i.e., the "worst" marriages) often end in divorce and therefore do not survive until midlife or later life (Peek, 2009). Moreover, Anderson, Van Ryzin, and Doherty (2010) argued that this model of "continuous decline" until the midlife years is inadequate for theorizing, because there may be different subgroup trajectories of marital happiness. Some (unhappy) midlife couples may stay together "for the sake of the children" and, even if the children are grown and have left home, because they belong to certain religious or cultural groups that are less likely than others to approve of separation/divorce (Mitchell, 2012).

Developmental and lifespan psychologists also highlight how midlife is a stage of life characterized as having specific normative developmental challenges that need to be resolved (Erikson, 1963; Lachman & James, 1997). Prior studies have often assumed that there is a crisis of identity that can create further crises or turning points and hence new strains on marriages. One of the most popular images is that of a middle-aged married man experiencing a "midlife crisis" who becomes disenchanted with his wife, family, and career and subsequently buys a red sports car while daydreaming of younger women. However, this theory (and related research) has received little support as a universal developmental phenomenon and for being an exclusively male phenomenon.

More recent theoretical developments focusing on psychosocial aspects of human development are increasingly incorporating concepts of resilience, resources, and coping styles to demanding midlife circumstances. For example, Huber, Navarro, Womble, and Mumme (2010) used a family adaptation model, along with Duvall's (1977) family life cycle's "middle-aged family" stage task conceptualization. Stage tasks such as rebuilding the marriage are simultaneously incorporated with vulnerability in family processes (e.g., a problem or crisis situation) and various buffering or protective factors (e.g., social network support). Other researchers have formulated more positive conceptualizations of crises, such as the benefits of ego development, self-esteem, and wisdom, all of which are seen to positively impact midlife marital experiences (e.g., see Pudrovska, 2009, for a review).

The life course perspective has also been applied to the study of midlife marriages (e.g., Lodge & Umberson, 2012; Mitchell, 2010b; Umberson, Williams, Powers, Chen, & Campbell, 2005). Elder and O'Rand (2005) described this perspective as "temporal and contextual in locating people in history through birth years and in the life course through the social meanings of age-graded events and activities" (p. 454). Midlife is noted to be a period of life during which couples are navigating a number of overlapping, highly fluctuating, and stressful transitions, such as menopause, the transition to the "empty nest" and retirement, caregiving, health declines, and the death of parents.

# RESEARCH STUDIES ON MARITAL SATISFACTION

Quantitative researchers have typically tried to capture multiple dimensions of marital satisfaction by using self-report measures that reflect feelings toward various aspects of the marital relationship (e.g., see Haynes et al., 1992; Steinberg & Silverberg, 1987; VanLaningham et al., 2001). Although used to study marital satisfaction irrespective of marital stage, two well-established measures that appeared in seminal research (e.g., Gottman & Levenson, 1988) include the 22-item Locke-Williamson Scale (Burgess, Locke, & Thomes, 1971) and the 15-item Locke-Wallace Marital Adjustment Test (Locke & Wallace, 1959). More recently, researchers (e.g., see Anderson et al., 2010) have continued to use variants of these early measures. Other researchers (e.g., Heiman et al., 2011; Lee, Zarit, Rovine, Birditt, & Fingerman, 2012; Mitchell & Gee, 1996) have used self-reported single indicators of overall marital satisfaction or happiness to produce one interval or binary measure (e.g., *very satisfied* vs. *less than very satisfied*). Finally, a few researchers have tried to assess marital satisfaction by observing interactions between couples in therapy sessions or laboratory settings (e.g., see Henry, Berg, Smith, & Florsheim, 2007).

Happiness is typically a self-perceived indicator of a positive personal feeling (Stack & Eshleman, 1998). This section reviews the factors associated with midlife marital happiness or satisfaction organized in terms of (a) individual, psychological, and inter/intrapersonal; (b) microcontextual; and (c) macroenvironmental factors.

## Individual, Psychological and Inter/intrapersonal Factors

Research in this domain has commonly identified demographic (e.g., age, gender, length of marriage), health, physical intimacy, sexual behavior, sexual function, and sexual history variables as predictive of relationship happiness (Heiman et al., 2011). In a comprehensive meta-analysis, Karney and Bradbury (1995) found that sexual satisfaction was among the strongest predictors of both marital satisfaction and stability. This is consistent with the general observation that despite pervasive negative stereotypes regarding the sexuality of aging individuals, sexual intimacy and satisfaction are salient (Bookwala, 2012). More frequent sexual activity is associated with more positive marital relationships and relationship quality in the later years (DeLamater & Moorman, 2007; Galinsky & Waite, 2014; Yeh, Lorenz, Wickrama, Conger, & Elder, 2006). Heiman et al. (2011) also found that although sexual functioning was a common predictor of relationship satisfaction for both genders, physical intimacy was a stronger and more consistent predictor for men compared with women. In a sample of midlife to later life long-term married couples (ages 50–69), Lodge and Umberson (2012) also found that, overall, sexual experiences are gendered and characterized by change over time, with some couples distressed by changes in their sex lives due to age-related physical changes. A key physiological factor related to sexual issues among women is menopause. Although this is not necessarily a difficult transition for the majority of aging women, it has been linked to mood states such as anger, anxiety, and depression. In addition, men may also experience a decline in sexual arousal and functioning, which can increase the risk of sexual problems (Matthews, 1992).

Overall, declining health has been found to be associated with a decline in marital satisfaction, particularly for the healthy spouse (e.g., Booth & Johnson, 1994). This effect has been found to be particularly magnified when the spouse assumes the role of the caregiver for a partner whose illness is chronic or progressive. Detrimental emotional patterns initiated by the ill spouse (especially when it is the husband), for instance, have been found to be problematic. This is particularly evident when there are excessive demands for care and attention (Kosberg & Garcia, 1987). Researchers have also established a strong link between mental health and marital satisfaction, although the causal direction of the relationship is not clear, and there may be gender differences. Also, some research has suggested that when marital problems arise, women may be more likely than men to assume the role of repairing the discordant relationship. Conversely, men are more likely to withdraw emotionally (e.g., see Gagnon, Hersen, Kabacoff, & Van Hasselt, 1999).

Other studies have focused more on attachment, interaction, communication styles, personality, and cognitive/affective dimensions. Although studies on the role of personality on midlife marriages have been rare and inconclusive (e.g., see Schmitt, Kliegel, & Shapiro, 2007; Shiota & Levenson, 2007), research has generally supported the idea that securely attached individuals (versus insecurely attached individuals) have better marital relationships. Secure attachment is also found to be predictive of successful conflict resolution, relationship independence, commitment, trust, and positive emotions in marriage (Hollist & Miller, 2005).

Indeed, many studies have found that one of the most important determinants of marital satisfaction is the ability of couples to resolve conflict by solving problems through cooperative, positive, interactive behaviors (Gottman & Levenson, 1988; Leggett, Byczek, & Morese, 2012). Although these associations are observed across all age groups, increased length of marriage is linked to the development of better conflict resolution skills. Older-aged couples tend to use expressions of affection along with expressions of discontent and disagreement during arguing, whereas younger couples use more negative expression (Carstensen, Gottman, & Levenson, 1995). Length of marriage is also related to the tendency for couples to cite "friendship" as an important characteristic of marriage, along with commitment, liking their spouse, and having their best friend for a spouse (Charles & Carstensen, 2002). Orbuch, House, Mero, and Webster (1996), however, argued that satisfaction tends to rise after the period when most marriages end in divorce, with satisfaction tending to rise after about 20 years of marriage (Kreider, 2005).

## Microcontextual Factors

Because midlife is a time when couples are facing the aging of their own parents and making the substantial transition of launching their children and living alone as a couple, the role of children and competing responsibilities on marriages has also been a popular topic of interest. The idea that coresident young adult children, in particular, have a negative impact on midlife marriages is rapidly being accepted as a social fact by the media, the general public, and some social scientists. This "failure to launch" discourse has instigated study into the presumed (negative) effects of refilled nests on parental marriages. Notably, the extended dependency of adult children on parental households and/or resources is assumed to impede the transition to the empty nest, a transition that many midlife parents look forward to as they make plans to retire, "downsize" their homes, pursue hobbies, and spend more time together as a couple (Mitchell, 2006).

Yet, findings on parental responsibilities and marital quality have been mixed. Some studies have shown that the transition to parenthood leads to lower marital quality, with a rise in marital happiness after the nest empties (e.g., White & Edwards, 1990). Yet, Ward and Spitze (2005) found no effects of coresidence with adult children (including returns home) on the marital satisfaction of parents. Mitchell and Gee (1996) found that although most parents were satisfied with adult child coresident living arrangements and their marriages, they generally did not want it to be a permanent living arrangement. Also, parents who were in first marriages (vs. remarried) and those that were in better health tended to have greater marital satisfaction. Moreover, Mitchell and Gee found that when children "boomeranged" home multiple times (three or more), it could negatively impact their marriage, but if the child only returned once or twice, it did not seem to cause the same set of problems. Parents also reported that they felt that they were "doing their job as parents" by helping their young adult children successfully transition into adulthood, and this positively affected their parental roles and marriages. Indeed, when parents and children had strong, supportive relations, there were positive benefits of coresidence for midlife marriages, including the pooling of resources, emotional support and companionship, and help with the household tasks. These perceived benefits offset any negative effects on parental marital satisfaction related to lack of privacy and/or independence or the additional financial pressures.

Generally, researchers have consistently demonstrated the importance of support (both emotional and instrumental) for improved family and marital relations, regardless of age. In particular, with increasing levels of stress in relationships, supports both within and outside the marriage are found to be an important variable in affecting marital satisfaction (McCabe, 2006). Furthermore, research specifically centered on the "sandwiched generation" has been mixed, with much of this literature guided by a stress-burden model. This model assumes that increased support to parents negatively impacts marital interactions and satisfaction. Although some studies have failed to find this (e.g., Ward & Spitze, 2005), other studies have found a significant association between higher caregiving burden and greater marital stress (Bookwala, 2009; Ron, 2006).

Yet other research has considered support also received by parents as an important contextual aspect of intergenerational relationships. For example, Lee et al. (2012) found that regardless of whether it was the husband or wife, whichever spouse gave more support to parents and received more support from parents than the other spouse reported lower marital satisfaction. In particular, if there was perceived unfairness in family work, marital satisfaction tended to be lower. This finding mirrors a general consensus that perceived equity, fairness, and reciprocity in relationships (e.g., the division of labor in households) plays an important role in marital satisfaction.

Other research has suggested that work and income-related issues and stressors can impact midlife marriages. Some studies have suggested that socioeconomic status (i.e., income) plays a negligible role in marital satisfaction (Schmitt et al., 2007). However, chronic economic adversity and long-term economic difficulties are consistently found to influence marital functioning in the later years (e.g., Wickrama, Surjadi, Lorenz, Conger, & O'Neal, 2012). Notably, persistent economic hardship is found to lead to an accumulation of disagreements and conflicts that may have long-term marital consequences. Conversely, economic prosperity in the midadult years can contribute to decreased marital conflicts and increased positive marital interaction.

The retirement transition is also shown to be stressful and may have consequences for marriage (see Chapter 8, this volume). Retirement is often associated with relocation and changes in health insurance, income, and one's daily schedule. The loss of the worker role is accompanied by the loss of coworkers as a source of social support in addition to the loss of identity and worker tasks (Rohwedder & Willis, 2010). All of these changes suggest potentially deleterious effects of retirement on marriages. However, outcomes vary based on spousal similarity in retirement status, the stress level of the job, how wives and husbands influence each other's adjustment to retirement, whether health problems are affecting activities and leisure, and caregiving responsibilities (Wickrama, O'Neal, & Lorenz, 2013).

Finally, the cultural background of the couple appears to influence midlife marital happiness. Not only are race and ethnicity associated with individual and other social support level factors (e.g., economic marginalization; availability of social networks), they also are relevant for understanding couple experiences including mate selection, values, practices, norms, obligations, and expectations of partnership roles. Although some limited research has examined cross-cultural variations in marital satisfaction (e.g., see Rehman & Holtzworth-Munroe, 2007), virtually no research has focused explicitly on midlife marital relations. One exception is a recent study (Mitchell, 2010b) that examined the association between midlife marital happiness and ethnic culture among four diverse cultural groups (British, Chinese, South Asian, and Southern European Canadians). Although ethnic identification per se was not associated with marital satisfaction, certain cultural factors played a role in subjective evaluations of how internal/external stressors affected marriage and what constituted a happy, fulfilling marriage. Those from more familistic/ collectivist cultural orientations (e.g., Asian, Southern European) tended to perceive competing midlife caregiving responsibilities as less detrimental to their marriages compared with those from more individualistic backgrounds (e.g., British). This latter group was more likely to value independence and autonomy and the pursuit of personal goals such that competing demands were evaluated more negatively and were viewed as interfering with marital experiences.

**Macroenvironmental Factors**

Mounting attention has been paid to the broader macrolevel context to improve our understanding of spouse behavior and marital processes. These wider contexts range from the economic climate of the neighborhood/region to overall societal/cultural and the sociopolitical contexts that have shaped these processes. Downward economic cycles and reduced labor market opportunities in certain neighborhoods and geographical areas, for instance, are associated with marital instability and dissolution. However, Eckstein and Ginsburg (2010) argued that in times of economic uncertainty, some couples may delay the decision to divorce and stay together in unpleasant, emotionally detached relationships for financial convenience. Neighborhood economic disadvantage has also been found to be positively related to crime, high levels of stress, and spousal abuse/violence (Fox, Benson, DeMaris, & Van Wyk, 2002).

Cultural discourses surrounding the acceptability of different sexual practices at different ages also can affect how midlife couples experience sexuality and intimacy (Lodge & Umberson, 2012). These processes may be gendered, given that practices and attitudes are mediated by social meanings.

Moreover, with the rise of prescription drugs (e.g., Viagra) and cultural imperatives to remain sexually active into later life, some midlife adults may feel social pressure to conform to a normative heterosexuality that defines sexual intimacy in a narrowly confined manner (Loe, 2004).

Similarly, dominant discourses related to cultural and religious ideas can create norms and expectations regarding marital experiences. Beliefs about marriage vary across historical and cultural locations; for example, the idea that marriages should be based on romantic love is a relatively new social invention in Western cultures (Mitchell, 2012). Generally, there has been a growth in individualistic values in North American culture (e.g., Glenn, 1996), which have been shown to affect family experiences. Individualistic spouses may invest relatively little effort in resolving disagreements because the larger social environment has become less hospitable to marriage (VanLaningham et al., 2001). The general secularization of society is also known to influence how couples perceive the quality of their marriages, including generating a greater premium on individual choice and a liberalization of sexual beliefs and behaviors.

Finally, public policies (including laws and legislation, such as retirement policies and Social Security) and access to social services and good quality health care can shape work and family trajectories and careers. Income-related supports for disadvantaged families, for instance, reduce chronic financial strain and buffer marital stresses. Overall, these kinds of macrolevel environmental structures can influence family resources, decisions, and behaviors and influence the quality of marital relationships during midlife.

## CLINICAL APPLICATIONS AND POLICY/PRACTICAL IMPLICATIONS

Midlife couples face many of the same relationship issues that younger and older couples face. Regardless of age, research consistently finds that factors such as good conflict resolution skills, positive marital interactions, and supportive environments are critical to marital satisfaction and overall marital quality. Yet, midlife couples typically confront a complicated set of challenges, stressors, and opportunities by virtue of their unique developmental phase. From a clinical perspective, therefore, there is a need for tailored therapeutic counseling and other family-related interventions.

As noted earlier, middle-aged couples typically experience multiple overlapping life course transitions. Therefore, professionals (e.g., therapists) working with midlife couples require specialized training in these areas. This kind of knowledge will be useful to prevent potential problems that can escalate into more serious ones, as well as to intervene with existing problems so that the marriage can be strengthened or salvaged. However, it is important for health professionals, family life educators, social workers, therapists, and counselors to acknowledge gendered and ethnic/racial differences in the experiences of middle-aged couples. Women, in particular, are more likely to feel the pressure and strain of competing work roles and caregiving responsibilities and are more likely to make sacrifices to their careers to take care of other family members (Mitchell, 2014). They are also more likely to be prescribed medications for stress and depression than men when confronting midlife challenges such as child launching (e.g., see Mitchell & Lovegreen, 2009), highlighting the need for professionals to understand the root sources of problem behaviors (e.g., substance abuse). Culturally sensitive therapeutic approaches are also needed to disentangle issues that may overlap with structural conditions (e.g., limited access to opportunities for support) and ethnic culture (e.g., norms, preferences, meanings and expressions of marital problems and experiences).

In the larger policy arena and at the local community level, it would be helpful to offer supports, services, and programs that prevent marital problems from occurring and/or to intervene in problems to alleviate marital distress. Opportunities for participation in community, professional, and religious organizations, for instance, have the potential to generate shared spousal activities, which is positively related to marital happiness (Voydanoff, 2004). Programs that provide information and resources for "sandwiched" caregivers (e.g., respite care) or for those confronted with specific health problems (e.g., chronic illness) are also found to be helpful in alleviating midlife stressors (Mitchell, 2014).

Finally, public policies that facilitate work–family balance and that acknowledge the changing context of income security and retirement are critical. For example, loss of work roles due to economic downsizing has increased during the recent recession, potentially magnifying certain kinds of marital conflict. Recognition of the potential challenges faced by midlife couples to maintain economic security (and good health/well-being) in preparation for retirement is fundamental to clinical, programmatic, and policy initiatives.

## FUTURE DIRECTIONS FOR THEORY AND RESEARCH

Although much has been learned about the constellation of factors that contribute to midlife marital satisfaction, there remain a number of areas that provide promising directions for the future. With regard to definitions (and operationalizations) of the concept of marital happiness, there has been a tendency to consider marital happiness as a multidimensional concept and/or as a global subjective evaluation of marital quality. Yet, it is often considered (and measured) on a continuum as a dichotomous/binary state (e.g., relatively "satisfied" or relatively "dissatisfied," characterized by "positive" or "negative" marital interactions). Windsor and Butterworth (2010) argued that we need to refine this concept and integrate the concept of ambivalence as an expression of both positive and negative (or indifferent) sentiments about the same social partner.

We also need to advance our conceptual models to emphasize the dynamic and fluid nature of midlife marital satisfaction indicators. In this regard, ecological system models (e.g., Bronfenbrenner, 1989) combined with lifespan/life course perspectives offer potential as a useful overarching framework for examining relationships among nested individual, interpersonal, family, work, and community systems. This kind of flexible, transdisciplinary approach is particularly timely given the increased complexity of family and work arrangements in midlife. However, little research has examined the extent to which inter/intrapersonal marital processes embedded in microcontexts interact with the macrocontexts at the community or societal level. This perspective could also be integrated with recent theorizing on the role of family vulnerabilities and stressors (e.g., cumulative disadvantage, resilience, and adaptive coping mechanisms), genetic and environmental influences, and family processes/resources.

Thus, there is a need to use more sophisticated research designs to incorporate multiple levels of data, because many previous studies have relied on cross-sectional samples and have often included the perspective of only one spouse/family member. As Townsend (2012) noted, multiple-member research designs provide many opportunities to assess potential bias in theories, results, and conclusions as well as the variability that can occur in perceptions within the same family unit. Longitudinal designs are also needed to tap into issues of fluidity in family life to incorporate changing transitions, circumstances, and contexts. The rising use of growth-curve longitudinal analyses shows promise for understanding complex and diverse marital trajectories (Anderson et al., 2010). We also need to incorporate more mixed methods in single studies to better contextualize larger scale survey data. These kinds of data can link broader findings, such as population patterns, to the lived experiences of midlife couples (e.g., see Mitchell, 2010a, 2014).

Research gaps continue to exist in relation to many emerging family problems that result from long military deployment, including issues of substance abuse, mental illness, and family violence. This is especially critical given the high rate of posttraumatic stress disorder of the returning service member (e.g., see Monson, Taft, & Fredman, 2009).

Limited research has also focused on ethnicity, despite the fact that marital traditions, meanings, and practices can vary widely across families and cultures. There is also a need to study the understudied midlife subgroups, such as economically disadvantaged ethnic minorities (Fincham & Beach, 2010). This focus becomes even more salient as families continue to diversify because of immigration patterns and trends in globalization (e.g., transnational families). Moreover, marital happiness in interracial unions and among couples from different religious or spiritual backgrounds has received scant attention. Furthermore, greater attention needs to be paid to changing trends that are due to population aging, economic uncertainty, and divorce/remarriage. Many midlife parents are postponing retirement and are providing substantial economic and housing support to younger and older generations at a time when they are beginning to experience some of their own health declines (Mitchell, 2014).

We also know little about those who marry later in life as well as the "marrying kind" (i.e., those that have remarried more than once or twice), because virtually all studies focus on long-term marriages. Divorce rates among all age groups have increased over time, and especially among older aged adults (Brown & Lin, 2012). However, a research gap remains with respect to midlife couples who have been married for a relatively short period of time and/or those who have divorced and remarried. Studies addressing the intersectionality between rapidly changing gendered ideologies and identities and how this can affect midlife marital satisfaction are also warranted. Indeed, women are increasingly becoming the primary breadwinners in many families, and there is a stronger convergence of gender roles (Parker & Wang, 2013).

Additional research is also required to further our understanding of the impact of medical technologies and innovations on midlife relationships. New reproductive advances allow women to conceive at later ages, and we are witnessing a general delay in the age at (first) parenthood. However, little is known about how midlife parenthood (or involuntary childlessness, on the other hand), as well as how other nonnormative parental or living arrangement patterns can impact midlife marriages. In this regard, the topics of middle-aged stepparenting and same-sex or LAT relationships (those who live apart but are together as a couple) are rarely discussed in the midlife marital satisfaction literature (for the latter, see Chapters 4 and 5, this volume). New information technologies and social media have also transformed communication patterns, although research on such topics as sex in cyberspace is still in its infancy (Hertlein & Webster, 2008). This area can complement research on issues related to love, trust, sexuality, and intimacy.

Finally, it is important that research translates knowledge into practice. This will not only allow us to better understand midlife marriages on a scholarly level but also provide evidence-based research that is capable of generating timely practical and policy-relevant recommendations. Indeed, emergent trends occurring over recent decades—such as population aging, more egalitarian gender roles, and greater economic insecurity and fragility—underscore the complex and dynamic landscape against which marital relationships develop and change. Researchers, clinicians, practitioners, and policymakers are left with this challenge as the field moves forward.

# REFERENCES

Aldous, J. (1978). *Family careers: Developmental changes in families*. New York, NY: Wiley.

Anderson, J. R., Van Ryzin, M. J., & Doherty, W. J. (2010). Developmental trajectories of marital happiness in continuously married individuals: A group-based modeling approach. *Journal of Family Psychology, 24*, 587–596. http://dx.doi.org/10.1037/a0020928

Bernard, J. (1982). *The future of marriage*. New Haven, CT: Yale University Press.

Blood, R. O., & Wolfe, D. M. (1960). *Husbands and wives: The dynamics of married living*. Glencoe, IL: Free Press.

Bookwala, J. (2009). The impact of parent care on marital quality and well-being in adult daughters and sons. *Journal of Gerontology, 64*, 339–347. http://dx.doi.org/10.1093/geronb/gbp018

Bookwala, J. (2012). Marriage and other partnered relationships in middle and late adulthood. In R. Blieszner & V. Hilkevitch Bedford (Eds.), *Handbook of families and aging* (2nd ed., pp. 91–123). Santa Barbara, CA: Praeger.

Booth, A., & Johnson, D. R. (1994). Declining health and marital quality. *Journal of Marriage and Family, 56*, 218–223. http://dx.doi.org/10.2307/352716

Bradbury, T. N., Fincham, F. D., & Beach, S. R. (2000). Research on the nature and determinants of marital satisfaction: A decade in review. *Journal of Marriage and Family, 62*, 964–980. http://dx.doi.org/10.1111/j.1741-3737.2000.00964.x

Bronfenbrenner, U. (1989). Ecological systems theory. *Annals of Child Development, 6*, 187–249.

Brown, S. L., & Lin, I. F. (2012). The gray divorce revolution: Rising divorce among middle-aged and older adults, 1990–2010. *The Journals of Gerontology: Series B: Psychological Sciences and Social Sciences, 67*, 731–741. http://dx.doi.org/10.1093/geronb/gbs089

Burgess, E. W., Locke, H. J., & Thomes, M. M. (1971). *The family*. New York, NY: Van Nostrand Reinhold.

Carstensen, L. L., Gottman, J. M., & Levenson, R. W. (1995). Emotional behavior in long-term marriage. *Psychology and Aging, 10*, 140–149. http://dx.doi.org/10.1037/0882-7974.10.1.140

Charles, S. T., & Carstensen, L. L. (2002). Marriage in old age. In M. Yalom & L. L. Carstensen (Eds.), *Inside the American couple: New thinking/new challenges* (pp. 236–254). Berkeley: University of California Press.

DeLamater, J., & Moorman, S. M. (2007). Sexual behavior in later life. *Journal of Aging and Health, 19*, 921–945. http://dx.doi.org/10.1177/0898264307308342

Duvall, E. M. (1977). *Marriage and family development* (5th ed.). Philadelphia, PA: Lippincott.

Eckstein, D., & Ginsburg, P. (2010). The "staying together in needy times" (STINT) couple's questionnaire. *The Family Journal: Therapy for Couples and Families, 18,* 310–315. http://dx.doi.org/10.1177/1066480710372128

Elder, G. H., & O'Rand, A. (2005). Adult lives in a changing society. In K. S. Cook, G. A. Fine, & J. S. House (Eds.), *Sociological perspectives on social psychology* (pp. 452–475). Needham Heights, MA: Allyn and Bacon.

Erikson, E. (1963). *Childhood and society* (2nd ed.). New York, NY: Norton.

Fincham, F. D., & Beach, S. R. (2010). Marriage in the new millennium: A decade in review. *Journal of Marriage and Family, 72,* 630–649. http://dx.doi.org/10.1111/j.1741-3737.2010.00722.x

Fox, G. L., Benson, M. L., DeMaris, A. A., & Van Wyk, J. (2002). Economic distress and intimate violence. *Journal of Marriage and Family, 64,* 793–807. http://dx.doi.org/10.1111/j.1741-3737.2002.00793.x

Gagnon, M. D., Hersen, M., Kabacoff, R. I., & Van Hasselt, V. B. (1999). Interpersonal and psychological correlates of marital dissatisfaction in late life: A review. *Clinical Psychology Review, 19,* 359–378. http://dx.doi.org/10.1016/S0272-7358(97)00048-2

Galinsky, A. M., & Waite, L. J. (2014). Sexual activity and psychological health as mediators of the relationship between physical health and marital quality. *The Journals of Gerontology: Series B. Psychological Sciences and Social Sciences, 69,* 482–492. http://dx.doi.org/10.1093/geronb/gbt165

Glenn, N. D. (1996). Values, attitudes, and the state of American marriage. In D. Popenoe, J. Elshtain, & D. Blankenhorn (Eds.), *Promises to keep: Decline and renewal of marriage in American* (pp. 15–34). New York, NY: Rowman and Littlefield.

Gottman, J. M., & Levenson, R. W. (1988). The social psychophysiology of marriage. In P. Noller & M. A. Fitzpatrick (Eds.), *Perspectives on marital interactions* (pp. 182–200). Clevedon, England: Multilingual Matters.

Hamilton, G. V. (1929). *A research in marriage.* New York, NY: Albert & Charles Boni.

Haynes, S. N., Floyd, F. J., Lemsky, C., Rogers, E., Winemiller, D., Heilman, N., . . . Cardone, L. (1992). The marital satisfaction questionnaire for older persons. *Psychological Assessment, 4,* 473–482. http://dx.doi.org/10.1037/1040-3590.4.4.473

Hazan, C., & Shaver, P. (1987). Romantic love conceptualized as an attachment process. *Journal of Personality and Social Psychology, 52,* 511–524. http://dx.doi.org/10.1037/0022-3514.52.3.511

Heiman, J. R., Long, J. S., Smith, S. N., Fisher, W. A., Sand, M. S., & Rosen, R. C. (2011). Sexual satisfaction and relationship happiness in midlife and older couples in five countries. *Archives of Sexual Behavior, 40,* 741–753. http://dx.doi.org/10.1007/s10508-010-9703-3

Henry, N. J. M., Berg, C. A., Smith, T. W., & Florsheim, P. (2007). Positive and negative characteristics of marital interaction and their association with marital satisfaction in middle-aged and older couples. *Psychology and Aging, 22*, 428–441. http://dx.doi.org/10.1037/0882-7974.22.3.428

Hertlein, K. M., & Webster, M. (2008). Technology, relationships, and problems: A research synthesis. *Journal of Marital and Family Therapy, 34*, 445–460. http://dx.doi.org/10.1111/j.1752-0606.2008.00087.x

Hollist, C. S., & Miller, R. B. (2005). Perceptions of attachment style and marital quality in midlife marriages. *Family Relations, 54*, 46–57. http://dx.doi.org/10.1111/j.0197-6664.2005.00005.x

Huber, C. H., Navarro, R. L., Womble, M. W., & Mumme, F. L. (2010). Family resilience and midlife marital satisfaction. *The Family Journal, 18*, 136–145. http://dx.doi.org/10.1177/1066480710364477

Jose, O., & Alfons, V. (2007). Do demographics affect marital satisfaction? *Journal of Sex & Marital Therapy, 33*, 73–85. http://dx.doi.org/10.1080/00926230600998573

Kamp Dush, C. M., Taylor, M. G., & Kroeger, R. A. (2008). Marital happiness and psychological well-being across the life course. *Family Relations, 57*, 211–226. http://dx.doi.org/10.1111/j.1741-3729.2008.00495.x

Karney, B. R., & Bradbury, T. N. (1995). The longitudinal course of marital quality and stability: A review of theory, method, and research. *Psychological Bulletin, 118*, 3–34. http://dx.doi.org/10.1037/0033-2909.118.1.3

Kosberg, J. I., & Garcia, J. L. (1987). The problems of older clients seen in a family service agency: Treatment and program implications. *Journal of Gerontological Social Work, 11*, 141–153. http://dx.doi.org/10.1300/J083V11N03_11

Kreider, R. M. (2005). Number, timing, and duration of marriages and divorces: 2001. *Current Population Reports*. Washington, DC: U.S. Census Bureau.

Lachman, M. E., & James, J. B. (1997). Charting the course of midlife development: An overview. In M. E. Lachman & J. B. James (Eds.), *Multiple paths of midlife development* (pp. 1–20). Chicago, IL: University of Chicago Press.

Lee, J. E., Zarit, S. H., Rovine, M. J., Birditt, K. S., & Fingerman, K. L. (2012). Middle-aged couples' exchanges of support with aging parents: Patterns and association with marital satisfaction. *Gerontology, 58*, 88–96. http://dx.doi.org/10.1159/000324512

Leggett, D. G., Byczek, S., & Morese, D. T. (2012). Cooperation, conflict, and marital satisfaction: Bridging theory, research, and practice. *The Journal of Individual Psychology, 68*, 182–199.

Li, T., & Fung, H. H. (2011). The dynamic goal theory of marital satisfaction. *Review of General Psychology, 15*, 246–254. http://dx.doi.org/10.1037/a0024694

Locke, H. J., & Wallace, K. M. (1959). Short marital-adjustment and prediction tests: Their reliability and validity. *Marriage and Family Living, 21*, 251–255. http://dx.doi.org/10.2307/348022

Lodge, A. C., & Umberson, D. (2012). All shook up: Sexuality of mid- to later life married couples. *Journal of Marriage and Family, 74*, 428–443. http://dx.doi.org/10.1111/j.1741-3737.2012.00969.x

Loe, M. (2004). *The rise of Viagra: How the little blue pill changed sex in America.* New York, NY: New York University Press.

Matthews, K. A. (1992). Myths and realities of the menopause. *Psychosomatic Medicine, 54*, 1–9. http://dx.doi.org/10.1097/00006842-199201000-00001

McCabe, M. P. (2006). Satisfaction in marriage and committed heterosexual relationships: Past, present and future. *Annual Review of Sex Research, 17*, 39–58.

Mitchell, B. A. (2006). *The boomerang age: Transitions to adulthood in families.* New Brunswick, NJ: Aldine-Transaction.

Mitchell, B. A. (2010a). Happiness in midlife parental roles: A mixed methods analysis. *Family Relations, 59*, 326–339. http://dx.doi.org/10.1111/j.1741-3729.2010.00605.x

Mitchell, B. A. (2010b). Midlife marital happiness and ethnic culture: A life course perspective. *Journal of Comparative Family Studies, 41*, 167–183.

Mitchell, B. A. (2012). *Family matters: An introduction to family sociology in Canada* (2nd ed.). Toronto, Ontario, Canada: Canadian Scholar's Press.

Mitchell, B. A. (2014). Generational juggling acts in midlife families: Gendered and ethnocultural intersections. *Journal of Women & Aging, 26*, 332–350. http://dx.doi.org/10.1080/08952841.2014.907666

Mitchell, B. A., & Gee, E. M. (1996). Boomerang kids and midlife parental marital satisfaction. *Family Relations, 45*, 442–448. http://dx.doi.org/10.2307/585174

Mitchell, B. A., & Lovegreen, L. (2009). The empty nest syndrome in midlife families: A multi-method exploration of parental gender differences and cultural dynamics. *Journal of Family Issues, 30*, 1654–1670.

Monson, C. M., Taft, C. T., & Fredman, S. J. (2009). Military-related PTSD and intimate relationships: From description to theory-driven research and intervention development. *Clinical Psychology Review, 29*, 707–714. http://dx.doi.org/10.1016/j.cpr.2009.09.002

Orbuch, T. L., House, J. S., Mero, R. P., & Webster, P. S. (1996). Marital quality over the life course. *Social Psychology Quarterly, 59*, 162–171. http://dx.doi.org/10.2307/2787050

Parker, K., & Wang, W. (2013, March 14). *Modern parenthood: Roles of moms and dads converge as they balance work and family.* Washington, DC: Pew Research Center Social and Demographic Trends.

Peek, M. K. (2009). Marriage in later life. In D. Carr (Ed.), *Encyclopedia of the life course and human development: Vol. 3. Later life* (pp. 241–245). Detroit, MI: Macmillan Reference Books.

Pineo, P. C. (1969). Development patterns in marriage. *The Family Coordinator, 18*, 135–140. http://dx.doi.org/10.2307/582229

Pudrovska, T. (2009). Parenthood, stress, and mental health in late midlife and early old age. *The International Journal of Aging & Human Development*, 68, 127–147. http://dx.doi.org/10.2190/AG.68.2.b

Rehman, U. S., & Holtzworth-Munroe, A. (2007). A cross-cultural examination of the relation of marital communication behavior to marital satisfaction. *Journal of Family Psychology*, 21, 759–763. http://dx.doi.org/10.1037/0893-3200.21.4.759

Rodgers, R. H. (1964). Toward a theory of family development. *Journal of Marriage and Family*, 26, 262–270. http://dx.doi.org/10.2307/349456

Rohwedder, S., & Willis, R. J. (2010). Mental retirement. *The Journal of Economic Perspectives*, 24, 119–138. http://dx.doi.org/10.1257/jep.24.1.119

Ron, P. (2006). Caregiving offspring to aging parents: How it affects their marital relations, parenthood, and mental health. *Illness, Crisis & Loss*, 14, 1–21.

Schmitt, M., Kliegel, M., & Shapiro, A. (2007). Marital interaction in middle and old age: A predictor of marital satisfaction? *The International Journal of Aging & Human Development*, 65, 283–300. http://dx.doi.org/10.2190/AG.65.4.a

Shiota, M. N., & Levenson, R. W. (2007). Birds of a feather don't always fly farthest: Similarity in Big Five personality predicts more negative marital satisfaction trajectories in long-term marriages. *Psychology and Aging*, 22, 666–675. http://dx.doi.org/10.1037/0882-7974.22.4.666

Stack, S., & Eshleman, J. R. (1998). Marital status and happiness: A 17-nation study. *Journal of Marriage and Family*, 60, 527–536. http://dx.doi.org/10.2307/353867

Stanley, S. M. (2007). Assessing couple and marital relationships: Beyond form and toward a deeper knowledge of function. In L. M. Casper & S. L. Hoffereth (Eds.), *Handbook of measurement issues in family research* (pp. 85–100). Mahwah, NJ: Erlbaum.

Steinberg, L., & Silverberg, S. B. (1987). Influences on marital satisfaction during the middle stages of the family life cycle. *Journal of Marriage and Family*, 49, 751–760. http://dx.doi.org/10.2307/351969

Townsend, A. L. (2012). Innovative research methods in family gerontology. In R. Blieszner & V. Hilkevitch Bedford (Eds.), *Handbook of families and aging* (2nd ed., pp. 61–88). Santa Barbara, CA: Praeger.

Umberson, D., Williams, K., Powers, D. A., Chen, M. D., & Campbell, A. M. (2005). As good as it gets? A life course perspective on marital quality. *Social Forces*, 84, 493–511. http://dx.doi.org/10.1353/sof.2005.0131

Vaillant, C. O., & Vaillant, G. E. (1993). Is the U-curve of marital satisfaction an illusion? A 40-year study of marriage. *Journal of Marriage and the Family*, 55, 230–239. http://dx.doi.org/10.2307/352971

VanLaningham, J., Johnson, D. R., & Amato, P. (2001). Marital happiness, marital duration, and the U-shaped curve: Evidence from a five-wave panel study. *Social Forces*, 79, 1313–1341. http://dx.doi.org/10.1353/sof.2001.0055

Voydanoff, P. (2004). Implications of work and community resources and demands for marital quality. *Community, Work & Family, 7,* 311–325. http://dx.doi.org/10.1080/1366880042000295736

Ward, R. A., & Spitze, G. D. (2005). Marital implications of parent–adult child coresidence: A longitudinal view. *The Journals of Gerontology: Series B. Psychological Sciences and Social Sciences, 59,* S2–S8.

White, L., & Edwards, J. (1990). Emptying the nest and parental well-being: Evidence from national panel data. *American Sociological Review, 55,* 235–242. http://dx.doi.org/10.2307/2095629

Wickrama, K. A. S., O'Neal, C. W., & Lorenz, F. O. (2013). Marital functioning from middle to later years: A life course–stress process framework. *Journal of Family Theory & Review, 5,* 15–34. http://dx.doi.org/10.1111/jftr.12000

Wickrama, K. A. S., Surjadi, F. F., Lorenz, F. O., Conger, R. D., & O'Neal, C. W. (2012). Family economic hardship and progression of poor mental health in middle-aged husbands and wives. *Family Relations, 61,* 297–312. http://dx.doi.org/10.1111/j.1741-3729.2011.00697.x

Windsor, T. D., & Butterworth, P. (2010). Supportive, aversive, ambivalent, and indifferent partner evaluations in midlife and young-old adulthood. *The Journals of Gerontology: Series B. Psychological Sciences and Social Sciences, 65,* 287–295. http://dx.doi.org/10.1093/geronb/gbq016

Yeh, H. C., Lorenz, F. O., Wickrama, K. A., Conger, R. D., & Elder, G. H., Jr. (2006). Relationships among sexual satisfaction, marital quality, and marital instability at midlife. *Journal of Family Psychology, 20,* 339–343. http://dx.doi.org/10.1037/0893-3200.20.2.339

# 2

# MARITAL DISCORD IN THE LATER YEARS

TIMOTHY W. SMITH AND CAROLYNNE E. BARON

Marriage and similar intimate relationships are central in the lives of most adults, and the number of older adults in such relationships continues to grow (Brown & Lin, 2012). Simply being a partner in these relationships confers protection from health problems and emotional difficulties associated with aging (Holt-Lunstad, Smith, & Layton, 2010; Shiovitz-Ezra & Leitsch, 2010). The quality of such relationships, however, matters as well. Conflict, strain, and disruption in intimate relationships are common, and these indications of marital discord confer risk of age-related diseases, such as coronary heart disease (CHD; Robles, Slatcher, Trombello, & McGinn, 2014). Further, the development of age-related chronic illness is often a significant stressor affecting marital quality, as the couple attempts to cope with the many related concerns, demands, and limitations in functioning. Hence, health and marital discord may be reciprocally related over time (Smith, Baron, & Grove, 2014). Marital discord also increases the risk of depression and loneliness (Ayalon, Shiovitz-Ezra, &

http://dx.doi.org/10.1037/14897-003
*Couple Relationships in the Middle and Later Years: Their Nature, Complexity, and Role in Health and Illness,*
J. Bookwala (Editor)

Palgi, 2013; Whisman & Uebelacker, 2009) and is a strong predictor of life satisfaction (Whisman, Uebelacker, Tolejko, Chatav, & McKelvie, 2006).

Difficulties in marriage and similar intimate relationships may become an even more important influence on the health and well-being of older adults, given that the incidence of divorce among U.S. adults ages 50 and above doubled from 1990 to 2010. This age group now accounts for approximately 25% of divorces in the United States (Brown & Lin, 2012). Hence, marital discord in the later years is an important topic for behavioral and biobehavioral research. The findings of such efforts could guide efforts to maximize the health, functioning, and well-being of the growing population of older adults.

The present chapter reviews issues in research on marital discord in the later years, including age-related differences in levels and sources of marital discord. We also review research on associations of marital discord with physical health, emotional adjustment, and well-being in the later years. In examining the health implications of marital discord, we emphasize CHD because it is the most common cause of death and becomes increasingly common with age.

## CONCEPTUAL AND METHODOLOGICAL ISSUES

Given the changing nature of marriage and similar intimate relationships, we review relationship discord in both the context of legal marriage and "marriage-like" relationships (e.g., cohabitation). For convenience, we refer to *marital* discord (and related terms, such as marital disruption and marital adjustment), even though for a growing number of individuals these relationships do not involve formal marriage.

### Models of Marital Discord

Research on marital discord and related processes in later adulthood is guided by conceptual models of the structure of these constructs. Careful examination of the most commonly used models may identify opportunities to develop a more complete understanding of the nature and correlates of discord in intimate relationships in this growing group.

*Single Versus Two-Dimensional Models of Marital Quality and Adjustment*

Research on marital quality generally and marital discord in particular is often hampered by issues involving conceptual definitions and their translation into measurement procedures. Marital *quality* and *adjustment* are perhaps the most commonly used terms, describing intimate relationships as varying in warmth, affection, support, and closeness versus hostility, conflict, distance, and disaffection. The closely related and often used term marital satisfaction refers to the subjective evaluation of relationship quality by members of the couple. Such evaluations are based on the elements of marital quality and adjustment, so measures of marital quality, adjustment, and satisfaction are highly correlated. Traditionally, the terms marital *discord, distress*, and *conflict* refer to the negative end of this continuum, and widely used measures are conceptualized, worded, and scored consistent with this single-dimension model. For example, items reflecting hostility, conflict, and disaffection are reversed and added to items reflecting affection, support, agreement, and closeness to form a dimension score for marital quality.

However, recent developments have suggested that this single-dimension model is limited (Fincham & Rogge, 2010). Positive and negative aspects of intimate relationships are distinct dimensions, even though they are inversely correlated as suggested in the single-dimension model. Further, these positive and negative aspects of marital functioning are independently related to overall marital quality or satisfaction (e.g., Herrington et al., 2008). This two-factor structure and the independent associations of positive and negative aspects of marital functioning with measures of general marital quality has been demonstrated in middle-aged and older couples (N. J. M. Henry, Berg, Smith, & Florsheim, 2007). However, in many studies of older adults, it is unclear if findings reflect discord specifically, low levels of positive aspects of the relationship, or both.

Separate measurements of positive and negative relationship characteristics could refine our understanding of marital discord among older adults. These two aspects of relationship quality may change differently with age or relate differently to health and well-being, or their respective roles may differ for men and women. Combinations of these two dimensions could have differing effects. Low levels of both positivity and negativity describe *indifference*, whereas high levels of both describe *ambivalence* (Fincham & Rogge, 2010; Uchino, Holt-Lunstad, Uno, & Flinders, 2001). These two patterns could also differ across middle and later adulthood. Further, recent evidence has suggested that ambivalence in marriage predicts coronary artery disease in older couples independent of the effects of high negativity or discord (Uchino, Smith, & Berg, 2014).

### Interpersonal Perspective on Marital Discord

Interpersonal theory (Pincus & Ansell, 2013) suggests that traditional models of marital adjustment are incomplete because they do not consider *control*, an additional, major dimension of interpersonal behavior and motivation. In this perspective, two broad dimensions describe social behavior. Affiliation resembles closely the single dimension model of marital quality, ranging from warmth, affection, and friendliness to hostility, coldness, and quarrelsomeness. *Control* describes behavior as ranging from dominant and directive to submissive, yielding, and deferential.

Compared with a clear emphasis on the affiliation dimension in marital research, the control dimension has been relatively neglected. Yet, the perception of excessive or unfair control by the spouse and related behaviors (e.g., criticism, blame) are related to low marital quality (Ehrensaft, Langhinrichsen-Rohling, Heyman, O'Leary, & Lawrence, 1999; Sanford, 2010; Smith, Traupman, Uchino, & Berg, 2010). Measures of marital conflict are associated with high levels of both hostility and control (Cundiff, Smith, Butner, & Critchfield, 2015; Smith et al., 2010). Also, women and men may differ in the importance of affiliation and control in intimate relationships or in their sensitivity to variations in behavior along these dimensions. Women may be more responsive to difficulties along the affiliation dimension, whereas men may be more responsive to issues related to control (Smith, Gallo, Goble, Ngu, & Stark, 1998). Marital processes related to control might also differ with age, and its correlates and consequences could as well, especially given age-related concerns about autonomy and independence. Hence, assessment of both dimensions could provide a better understanding of marital discord in older adults.

In couple interactions, one partner's displays of affiliation and control are reciprocally related to the other's, in an ongoing process of mutual influence. In interpersonal theory, this pattern is described in the *complementarity principle*, where an actor's behavior tends to "pull, elicit, invite, or evoke 'restricted classes' of responses" from partners (Pincus & Ansell, 2013, p. 149). In the specific definition of complementarity in interpersonal theory, the "invited" or evoked behavior is similar to the initial actor's behavior in terms of affiliation and opposite in control. That is, warmth invites warmth in return, whereas cold or hostile actions invite hostility. Expressions of dominance or control invite submissiveness or deference; submissive actions invite controlling or dominant responses from interaction partners. Research has indicated that complementarity as defined in the interpersonal perspective is more apparent for affiliation than control (Cundiff et al., 2015; Sadler, Ethier, & Woody, 2011) because unfriendly dominance (i.e., the combination of low affiliation and high control) tends to evoke dominance in return (rather than submissiveness), often reflecting effortful struggles for control or the assertion of independence. Complementarity in control is more common for warm interactions (i.e., high affiliation). In understanding marital discord in older adults, complementarity could be important. The tendency to reciprocate hostile behavior is a hallmark of distressed marriages (Snyder, Heyman, & Haynes, 2005). Older couples' ability to avoid or interrupt cycles of negative complementarity involving hostile or controlling behavior may be an important influence on their health and well-being.

## Aging and Lifespan Perspectives on Marital Discord

In research on marital discord in later adulthood, a life-span developmental approach highlights the unique nature and correlates of intimate relationships in this group. Older adults face distinct life challenges and stressors, may approach these situations with different goals, and often do so with declining cognitive and self-regulatory abilities.

### Life-Stage Perspectives

As adults enter into later stages of life, stressors, roles, identity, and goals shift. Physical stressors common to older adults include limitations in vision, hearing, and functional activity, as well as chronic disease and physical disability (Federal Interagency Forum on Aging-Related Statistics, 2012). Older adults are also more likely to be caregivers (National Alliance for Caregiving and AARP, 2009) and are more susceptible to a variety of illnesses, leaving them more vulnerable to the stress of marital discord (Robles et al., 2014).

With retirement, the transition from middle to late adulthood also often involves spouses spending more time together and engaged in leisure activities (Federal Interagency Forum on Aging-Related Statistics, 2012). This transition also often results in changes in personal identity and changes in roles and power within the couple (Kulik, 2002; Wang, Henkens, & van Solinge, 2011). Identities connected to one's vocation are challenged, and roles such as being the financial provider are discontinued. Common outcomes are a more balanced division of household tasks and equality of roles (Kulik, 2002). The transition from work and parenthood into retirement typically reduces the retiree's social network but also allows time for the couple to spend more time together and focus primarily on the spousal relationship (Wang et al., 2011).

Each of these age-related processes involves potentially far-reaching changes in the couple's context, an important influence on their ongoing marital transactions as just described. Preexisting strengths and vulnerabilities of the relationship may be magnified, and new sources of potential conflict and discord may emerge as others fade in importance. Thus, the overall level of marital discord may change in the later years, and the sources and consequences of such difficulties are likely to change as well.

### Socioemotional Selectivity Theory

Socioemotional selectivity theory has informed much of the research on aging, relationship quality, and well-being. In this perspective, individuals in the later stages of life perceive limitations of time, inspiring shifts in priorities and interpersonal goals and motivating changes in behavior (Carstensen,

Isaacowitz, & Charles, 1999). Specifically, as people grow into old age they prioritize their emotional well-being and high-quality, meaningful close relationships, focusing less on attaining knowledge and information through diverse and numerous interactions. Because of perceived time limitations and a focus on well-being and high-quality relationships, older individuals tend to accept intimate relationships as they are (Carstensen et al., 1999). Older couples minimize negative affect and enhance positive affect by selectively attending to positive information and regulating emotions in negative interactions. From this perspective, older couples will experience less marital discord and react to it more constructively when it occurs.

### Aging and Executive Functioning

Other perspectives suggest that declining self-regulatory abilities in older adults can contribute to negative relationship interactions. Decreases in cognitive executive functioning are associated with lack of restraint and lower empathy in older adults (Bailey & Henry, 2008; J. D. Henry, von Hippel, & Baynes, 2009; Moran, 2013), resulting in decreased inhibitory ability that in turn contributes to less appropriate social behavior (von Hippel, 2007). In marital transactions, reduced restraint and empathy could promote more frequent and severe cycles of negative reciprocity or hostile complementarity. Executive functioning has not been related specifically to marital functioning in elderly couples. However, in elderly adults, these declining cognitive functions are associated with general social difficulties that parallel the reduced positivity and increased negativity in marital difficulties (Andrew, Fisk, & Rockwood, 2011; J. D. Henry et al., 2009).

## Methods in Studying Marital Discord

The most common approach in studies of marital quality among older adults involves self-reports of relationship characteristics. As described previously, this typically involves a single dimension model of relationship quality, with items reflecting only positive relationship qualities or combining positive and negative aspects to form a single score. A much greater variety of methodological approaches is available, however (Snyder et al., 2005). For key constructs in this domain, multiple measurement methods are available, including structured interviews, self-reports, partner reports, and behavioral observation procedures. These methods can be used to measure relationship *behaviors* (e.g., levels and reciprocity of positive and negative responses during conflict; frequency and severity of conflict), *cognitions* (e.g., attributions for marital events and partner behavior; relationship beliefs, expectancies, and standards regarding spouse behavior), and *affect* (e.g., frequency, degree, duration, and reciprocity of positive and negative affect during couple interaction; general sentiments about the spouse and relationship; emotion regulation in couple interactions). For studies of potentially stressful marital discord, in particular, psychophysiological assessments are valuable (Smith et al., 2011; Smith, Uchino, et al., 2009).

Compared with multifaceted and multimethod current approaches to relationship functioning, most research on marital discord in older adults has been limited in methodological scope. Self-reports that capture only the single dimension of relationship sentiment or overall quality may not capture adequately the variety of aspects of marital functioning that are important in the health and well-being of older adults. As described previously, measures based on single dimension models combine the separate positivity and negativity dimensions that could differ in their associations with age or have distinct and varying associations with health and well-being among older adults. Measures that capture only affiliation fail to assess the potentially important effects of control in couple interactions. Moreover, the commonly used self-report approaches are susceptible to social desirability artifacts. Hence, age-group differences in levels and correlates of marital discord could reflect cohort or age differences in self-report artifacts.

Behavioral observations are less susceptible to limitations of self-reports, and observations during laboratory tasks predict important outcomes (Smith et al., 2011; Snyder et al., 2005). However, analogue enactments of relationship conflict or other couple interactions may be less negative and briefer than in natural environments. Daily experience sampling is a valuable complementary approach in this regard, with well-developed methodological and quantitative methods for examining couples (Laurenceau & Bolger, 2005). Overall, more complete and sophisticated assessment of couple functioning will be essential in future research on older adults.

## EMPIRICAL FINDINGS

A growing body of research has focused on levels of marital discord in later adulthood and their health-related consequences. Evidence from these studies illustrates the importance of the conceptual and methodological issues that are discussed above. Age differences in relationship quality vary as a function of the assessment methods used, and the association with emotional and physical health tends to differ based on the specific aspects of marital functioning and relationship discord that are assessed.

### Levels of Discord

A number of studies have examined age differences in marital quality generally, and marital discord in particular. Results are mixed, but when age differences are found, they typically suggest that older couples report higher marital quality and less discord. For example, in one study rates of negative interactions across multiple relationships were generally lower for older groups, but rates of negative interactions with spouses were consistent across age groups (Akiyama, Antonucci, Takahashi, & Langfahl, 2003). Similar findings of limited age differences have been reported in cross-sectional (Hatch & Bulcroft, 2004) and prospective studies (Krause & Rook, 2003). Other studies have demonstrated lower behavioral and affective indicators of negativity and conflict in interactions of older couples compared with middle-aged couples (Carstensen, Gottman, & Levenson, 1995; Levenson, Carstensen, & Gottman, 1994) and increasing avoidant behavior during conflict over time (Holley, Haase, & Levenson, 2013).

In the Utah Health and Aging Study (Smith, Berg, et al., 2009; Smith, Uchino, et al., 2009), 300 middle-aged and older couples completed a variety of self-report measures of marital quality, as well as a conflict discussion and a collaborative problem-solving task, in counterbalanced order. Task behavior was rated for variations in both affiliation and control. On general measures of marital quality, older couples reported higher marital adjustment than middle-aged couples, though this age difference was stronger for husbands than wives. On measures examining self-reported warm and hostile marital processes separately, the age difference was stronger for positive marital behaviors than for hostility or marital discord (N. J. M. Henry et al., 2007). Older couples reported less negative affect (e.g., anger) in response to the conflict task and rated their spouses' behavior as less hostile, even though observer ratings indicated either no age differences or differences in which older participants displayed less warmth than their middle-aged counterparts. Some age differences varied for husbands and wives. For example, compared with middle-aged men, older men displayed more warm dominance, a combination of high affiliation and high control that was evident, for example, when they gently and constructively made suggestions or led the couples' collaborative efforts. They also displayed less hostile dominance than middle-aged men, a blend of low affiliation and high control that is evident in criticism and blame. In contrast, older women displayed less warmth overall than middle-aged women (Smith, Berg, et al., 2009).

This difference between self-report and behavioral measures underscores the importance of multiple assessment methods and could suggest that older couples display a stronger tendency to minimize negative experiences in their self-reports. However, older couples' greater discrepancy between self-reports of negative affect and appraisals of spouse behavior on the one hand and independent behavior ratings on the other could reflect greater positive sentiment override (Story et al., 2007), in which older couples are more likely to base their appraisals and affective responses on overarching sentiments, as opposed to momentary behaviors by the spouse. The latter interpretation is consistent with the fact that control of general marital satisfaction eliminated many of the age effects in affect and appraisal (Smith, Berg, et al., 2009), as well as the discrepancy between self-reports and behavioral measures of marital interaction quality (Story et al., 2007).

The focus of marital discord and efforts to deal with it differ between middle-aged and older couples. Levenson, Carstensen, and Gottman (1993) found that middle-aged couples disagreed more about money, religion, and children, whereas older individuals ranked communication and recreation as greater sources of conflict. In other studies, older couples reported fewer difficulties with intimacy and personality differences, but greater difficulties regarding intergenerational relations, household duties, and leisure activities (R. G. Henry, Miller, & Giarrusso, 2005). Gender role changes resulting from retirement are often associated with decreased marital quality (Myers & Booth, 1996). Older couples are also more bothered by unwanted advice from the spouse (Sorkin & Rook, 2006). Older couples also reported similar levels of tension and conflict, but less arguing and more avoidance of difficult topics (Birditt, Fingerman, & Almeida, 2005; Bookwala, Sobin, & Zdaniuk, 2005; Holley et al., 2013). A systematic review found that issues that influence marital relations and satisfaction in late-life couples include equality of roles, communication, and transitions to living apart (Walker & Luszcz, 2009).

Physiological responses during marital interactions provide mixed evidence regarding differences between middle-aged and older couples. Generally, discordant marital interactions evoke greater physiological stress responses than neutral or positive interactions, and the magnitude of those reactions is greater in couples reporting higher levels of marital distress (Robles et al., 2014). Levenson et al. (1994) found that older couples responded to marital interaction with smaller cardiovascular stress responses than middle-aged couples. However, it is difficult to determine if this was true during a negative disagreement interaction task or in the positive and neutral tasks they used. In the Utah Health and Aging Study, middle-aged and older couples displayed similar elevations in blood pressure during the conflict discussion task (see Figure 2.1), which were significantly larger than those during the collaboration task (i.e., planning a day of errands; Smith, Berg, et al., 2009). In the only significant age difference, older men displayed larger increases in blood pressure during collaboration than did middle-aged men.

Overall, these results provide some support for predictions based on socioemotional selectivity theory that older adults are more positive in appraisal, affect, and behavior in marriage, as well as more skilled at managing negative emotions and interactions compared with younger individuals (Charles & Carstensen, 2010). However, there is also considerable evidence inconsistent with this model, suggesting that middle-aged and older couples differ more in subjective responses and reports than in independently rated behavioral or

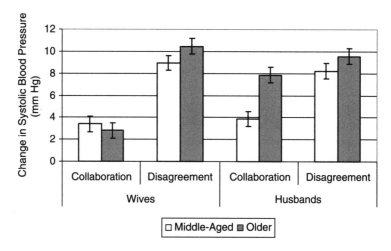

*Figure 2.1.* Systolic blood pressure reactivity during marital disagreement and collaborative problem solving in middle-aged and older couples. From "Conflict and Collaboration in Middle-Aged and Older Couples: II. Cardiovascular Reactivity During Marital Interaction," by T. W. Smith, B. N. Uchino, C. A. Berg, P. Florsheim, G. Pearce, M. Hawkins, . . . C. Olsen-Cerny, 2009, *Psychology and Aging, 24*, p. 280. Copyright 2009 by the American Psychological Association.

physiological responses to marital conflict. It is important to note that the sources of marital difficulties differ across age groups, suggesting the importance of a contexualized approach to marital discord later in life.

Consistent with predictions based on age-related declines in cognitive executive function, older individuals show more inappropriate social behavior compared with younger individuals and decreases in restraint and inhibition (e.g., J. D. Henry et al., 2009; von Hippel & Gonsalkorale, 2005). Further, older adults demonstrate declines in the ability to take the perspective of another, and this reduced empathy is also associated with impairments in executive cognitive functioning and disinhibition of a self-focused perspective (Bailey & Henry, 2008). Hence, declines in cognitive functioning in older adults can lead to social deficits that have deleterious effects on the quality of close interpersonal relationships (Andrew et al., 2011; Aron, Aron, Tudor, & Nelson, 1991).

Such age-related difficulties in inhibitory control could result in greater sequences of negative couple interaction (i.e., greater complementarity of low affiliation). That is, poor inhibition could make it more difficult to resist the "invitation" to respond to a spouse's hostile remarks with additional hostility. High levels of such negative reciprocity are typical in couples experiencing significant discord (Snyder et al., 2005).

To examine this issue in the Utah Health and Aging Study, we conducted further analyses of previously reported data (Smith, Berg, et al., 2009).

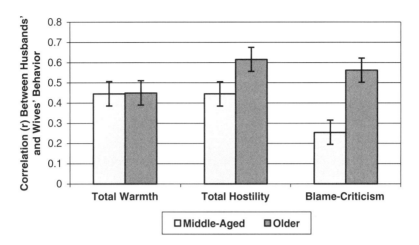

*Figure 2.2.* Complementarity in warm and hostile behavior during marital disagreement, as represented by the correlation (and SE of the correlation) between husbands' and wives' behavior in middle-aged and older couples.

Specifically, we calculated the correlation of husbands' and wives' levels of warm and hostile behavior during the conflict discussion and tested the age-group differences in these associations. As seen in Figure 2.2, middle-aged and older couples displayed similar levels of the expected positive complementarity in which higher levels of warmth by one partner are significantly associated with higher levels displayed by the other. Also as expected, negative complementarity was significant in both age groups. However, this association between partners' levels of hostile behavior was significantly stronger in older couples than in middle-aged couples. Also as depicted in Figure 2.2, this significant age group difference was particularly evident in the behavior category that blends high hostility and high control. Compared with middle-aged couples, older couples showed a much stronger correlation between husbands' and wives' levels of criticism and blame during the conflict. This pattern is consistent with reduced ability to exert restraint and resist the invitation to trade criticism and blame in a classic defensive and discordant manner.

However, older couples did not display overall higher levels of hostile control during the conflict discussion (Smith, Berg, et al., 2009). It is possible that older couples are characterized by both greater difficulties in exercising restraint, but also more interest in doing so, and a greater tendency to avoid such discussions when they can, responses consistent with socioemotional selectivity theory (Carstensen et al., 1999). The greater vulnerability to negative reciprocity and the greater interest in avoiding it may be offsetting in typical daily lives of couples. That is, the relationship costs of disinhibition in older adults may be offset by gains facilitated by the tendency in older adults to be more positive compared with younger adults (von Hippel, Henry,

& Matovic, 2008). Negative marital interactions such as hostile reciprocity predict lower overall marital satisfaction in both middle-aged and older couples (Bookwala & Jacobs, 2004; Cundiff et al., 2015; Schmitt, Kliegel, & Shapiro, 2007).

## Correlates of Marital Discord

Correlates of marital discord among older adults are of interest in efforts to identify contributing factors and potential consequences. Prospective studies have suggested that depression is both a contributing factor and a consequence of marital discord (Whisman & Uebelacker, 2009). It is important to note that the association between depression and marital discord may or may not be stronger for older couples compared with middle-aged and younger couples (Bookwala & Jacobs, 2004; Whisman, 2007). Discord in older couples is also associated with poor physical health and related effects of poor health, such as levels of functional activity versus disability and depression (Bookwala, 2005, 2011; Bookwala & Franks, 2005; Umberson, Williams, Powers, Liu, & Needham, 2006). Some evidence has suggested gender differences in these associations; in one study, husbands' poor health was associated with greater marital distress reported by their wives, whereas the opposite association was not found (Iveniuk, Waite, Lauman, McClintock, & Tiedt, 2014).

The effects of marital discord on physical health have been examined in detail in the case of CHD. Reports of greater conflict in marriage and similar intimate relationships are associated with increased risk of incident CHD (e.g., fatal and nonfatal myocardial infarction; De Vogli, Chandola, & Marmot, 2007). In CHD patients, low marital quality predicts greater risk of recurrent coronary events and reduced survival (Idler, Boulifard, & Contrada, 2012; King & Reis, 2012; Orth-Gomér et al., 2000; Rohrbaugh, Shoham, & Coyne, 2006). The negative general health effects of marital disruption (i.e., separation, divorce) are well established (Sbarra, Law, & Portley, 2011) and are also seen in the specific instance of CHD. For example, divorce is associated with increased levels of asymptomatic coronary atherosclerosis in otherwise healthy older adults (Smith et al., 2011) and increased risk of clinically apparent CHD (Matthews & Gump, 2002). Given the prevalence and seriousness of CHD among older adults, this association has important implications for their health and well-being.

As noted previously, behavioral measures of marital discord have potential advantages over self-report assessments, and examination of multiple aspects of discord may lead to a more refined understanding of this general association. To examine these possibilities in the Utah Health and Aging Study, Smith et al. (2011) tested associations of ratings of affiliation and control evident in husbands' and wives' behavior during the discussion of a marital problem with the severity of coronary artery calcification (CAC), a noninvasive index of coronary atherosclerosis. The 150 older couples in these analyses were outwardly healthy, with no prior evidence of cardiovascular disease (CVD).

The first analysis tested associations of wives' affiliation, husbands' affiliation, and the interaction between these first-order effects with CAC severity. These behavioral ratings of affiliation predicted wives' coronary atherosclerosis, controlling demographic, biomedical, and behavioral risk factors. Women who displayed low levels of affiliation during conflict discussions had significantly more severe atherosclerosis, and a significant interaction indicated that this was especially the case if their husbands also displayed low affiliation. Levels of affiliation displayed by wives and husbands did not predict husbands' atherosclerosis, suggesting a gender or marital role difference.

The coding system permitted separate examination of hostile and warm components of the overall affiliation dimension. Surprisingly, wives' and husbands' levels of hostility were unrelated to wives' atherosclerosis. Rather, low levels of warmth during conflict discussions predicted greater atherosclerosis among wives, underscoring the importance of separate measurements of positive and negative aspects of affiliation.

In the next analysis, ratings of control predicted husbands' atherosclerosis, controlling traditional risk factors. Husbands who displayed high levels of control and husbands whose wives displayed high levels of control during the conflict discussion had significantly more severe atherosclerosis. These first-order effects were qualified by an interaction, such that husbands in couples where both partners displayed little control had the least atherosclerosis. Examining dominance and submissiveness separately, neither partner's submissive behavior was related to husbands' disease, but wives' and husbands' dominance predicted husbands' atherosclerosis. Suggesting another gender difference, neither spouse's controlling behavior during the conflict task predicted wives' disease.

These results suggest that more refined dimensional models of relationship quality may improve our understanding of the role of marital discord in coronary artery disease in older adults. The common practice of measuring only affiliation could lead to an underestimate of the association of marital processes with CVD in men, but the interpersonal perspective calls attention to the possible effects of control. Further, measurement of both ends of these two dimensions can provide further explication of the specific aspects of marital interaction that predict health in older adults. Conflict discussions that involve warmth might insulate older women from the otherwise deleterious effects of marital discord, for example. For men, the couple's expressions of dominance predicted disease, but submissive or deferential behavior afforded no protection from the apparent atherogenic effects of marital discord. It is important to note that none of the self-report measures of general marital adjustment or marital discord were significantly related to atherosclerosis. Hence, commonly used self-reports could underestimate the role of marital discord in cardiovascular disease among older adults.

## CONCLUSION

Marital discord is important in the health, emotional adjustment, and well-being of older adults, but there are inconsistencies and limitations in this literature. Conceptual models and some research suggest that older couples experience less discord, but most of the support for this conclusion is based on self-reports. Behavioral observations and physiological assessments suggest that middle-aged and older couples experience similar levels of marital discord. Further, marital discord is often measured as the negative pole of a dimension that also includes positive aspects of marital quality. As a result, it is often difficult to determine if findings involve discord (e.g., hostility, conflict, criticism), low levels of positive aspects of marital quality (e.g., warmth, affection, support), or both.

Further, prior research has emphasized the affiliation dimension and ignored control, even though the latter is involved in marital discord and its effects on health. Current concepts and methods in marital research (Snyder et al., 2005) are useful in addressing these issues, as are concepts and methods in the interpersonal perspective (Pincus & Ansell, 2013; Smith et al., 2014). Finally, much of the research on marital discord among older adults is cross-sectional. Given continuing cultural and demographic changes in marriage and similar intimate relationships, distinguishing cohort and aging effects, and cohort by aging interactions, requires prospective designs.

Despite these limitations, consistent associations of marital discord with health, emotional adjustment, and well-being suggest the need for evidence-based assessment and intervention approaches. However, marital assessment and intervention research has often neglected possible moderating effects of age (Lambert-Shute & Fruhauf, 2011). Given the growing number of older adult intimate relationships with varying levels of discord, a full set of intervention options could be useful, from low-cost, Internet-based, and self-directed approaches available on a broad scale to traditional marital therapies tailored to address the needs of older adults. Typically, psychological services for older adults emphasize traditional mental health issues and cognitive aging. Increasing the availability of evidence-based services focused on intimate relationship issues for older couples and integrating those services in interdisciplinary care is an important challenge in the development and delivery of comprehensive health care for our aging population.

# REFERENCES

Akiyama, H., Antonucci, T., Takahashi, K., & Langfahl, E. S. (2003). Negative interactions in close relationships across the life span. *The Journals of Gerontology: Series B. Psychological Sciences and Social Sciences, 58,* P70–P79. http://dx.doi.org/10.1093/geronb/58.2.P70

Andrew, M. K., Fisk, J. D., & Rockwood, K. (2011). Social vulnerability and prefrontal cortical function in elderly people: A report from the Canadian Study of Health and Aging. *International Psychogeriatrics, 23,* 450–458. http://dx.doi.org/10.1017/S1041610210001195

Aron, A., Aron, E. N., Tudor, M., & Nelson, G. (1991). Close relationships as including other in the self. *Journal of Personality and Social Psychology, 60,* 241–253. http://dx.doi.org/10.1037/0022-3514.60.2.241

Ayalon, L., Shiovitz-Ezra, S., & Palgi, Y. (2013). Associations of loneliness in older married men and women. *Aging & Mental Health, 17,* 33–39. http://dx.doi.org/10.1080/13607863.2012.702725

Bailey, P. E., & Henry, J. D. (2008). Growing less empathic with age: Disinhibition of the self-perspective. *The Journals of Gerontology: Series B. Psychological Sciences and Social Sciences, 63,* P219–P226. http://dx.doi.org/10.1093/geronb/63.4.P219

Birditt, K. S., Fingerman, K. L., & Almeida, D. M. (2005). Age differences in exposure and reactions to interpersonal tensions: A daily diary study. *Psychology and Aging, 20,* 330–340. http://dx.doi.org/10.1037/0882-7974.20.2.330

Bookwala, J. (2005). The role of marital quality in physical health during the mature years. *Journal of Aging and Health, 17,* 85–104. http://dx.doi.org/10.1177/0898264304272794

Bookwala, J. (2011). Marital quality as a moderator of the effects of poor vision on quality of life among older adults. *The Journals of Gerontology: Series B. Psychological Sciences and Social Sciences, 66,* 605–616. http://dx.doi.org/10.1093/geronb/gbr091

Bookwala, J., & Franks, M. M. (2005). Moderating role of marital quality in older adults' depressed affect: Beyond the main-effects model. *The Journals of Gerontology: Series B. Psychological Sciences and Social Sciences, 60,* P338–P341. http://dx.doi.org/10.1093/geronb/60.6.P338

Bookwala, J., & Jacobs, J. (2004). Age, marital processes, and depressed affect. *The Gerontologist, 44,* 328–338. http://dx.doi.org/10.1093/geront/44.3.328

Bookwala, J., Sobin, J., & Zdaniuk, B. (2005). Gender and aggression in marital relationships: A life-span perspective. *Sex Roles, 52,* 797–806. http://dx.doi.org/10.1007/s11199-005-4200-1

Brown, S. L., & Lin, I. F. (2012). The gray divorce revolution: Rising divorce among middle-aged and older adults, 1990–2010. *The Journals of Gerontology: Series B. Psychological Sciences and Social Sciences, 67,* 731–741. http://dx.doi.org/10.1093/geronb/gbs089

Carstensen, L. L., Gottman, J. M., & Levenson, R. W. (1995). Emotional behavior in long-term marriage. *Psychology and Aging, 10,* 140–149. http://dx.doi.org/10.1037/0882-7974.10.1.140

Carstensen, L. L., Isaacowitz, D. M., & Charles, S. T. (1999). Taking time seriously: A theory of socioemotional selectivity. *American Psychologist, 54,* 165–181. http://dx.doi.org/10.1037/0003-066X.54.3.165

Charles, S. T., & Carstensen, L. L. (2010). Social and emotional aging. *Annual Review of Psychology, 61,* 383–409. http://dx.doi.org/10.1146/annurev.psych.093008.100448

Cundiff, J. M., Smith, T. W., Butner, J., & Critchfield, K. (2015). Affiliation and control in marital interaction: Interpersonal complementarity is present but does not predict affect or relationship quality. *Personality and Social Psychology Bulletin, 41,* 35–51. http://dx.doi.org/10.1177/0146167214557002

De Vogli, R., Chandola, T., & Marmot, M. G. (2007). Negative aspects of close relationships and heart disease. *Archives of Internal Medicine, 167,* 1951–1957. http://dx.doi.org/10.1001/archinte.167.18.1951

Ehrensaft, M. K., Langhinrichsen-Rohling, J., Heyman, R. E., O'Leary, K. D., & Lawrence, E. (1999). Feeling controlled in marriage: A phenomenon specific to physically aggressive couples? *Journal of Family Psychology, 13,* 20–32. http://dx.doi.org/10.1037/0893-3200.13.1.20

Federal Interagency Forum on Aging-Related Statistics. (2012). *Older Americans 2012: Key indicators of well-being.* Washington, DC: U.S. Government Printing Office.

Fincham, F. D., & Rogge, R. (2010). Understanding relationship quality: Theoretical challenges and new tools for assessment. *Journal of Family Theory & Review, 2,* 227–242. http://dx.doi.org/10.1111/j.1756-2589.2010.00059.x

Hatch, L. R., & Bulcroft, K. (2004). Does long-term marriage bring less frequent disagreements? Five explanatory frameworks. *Journal of Family Issues, 25,* 465–495. http://dx.doi.org/10.1177/0192513X03257766

Henry, J. D., von Hippel, W., & Baynes, K. (2009). Social inappropriateness, executive control, and aging. *Psychology and Aging, 24,* 239–244. http://dx.doi.org/10.1037/a0013423

Henry, N. J. M., Berg, C. A., Smith, T. W., & Florsheim, P. (2007). Positive and negative characteristics of marital interaction and their association with marital satisfaction in middle-aged and older couples. *Psychology and Aging, 22,* 428–441. http://dx.doi.org/10.1037/0882-7974.22.3.428

Henry, R. G., Miller, R. B., & Giarrusso, R. (2005). Difficulties, disagreements, and disappointments in late-life marriages. *International Journal of Aging & Human Development, 61,* 243–264. http://dx.doi.org/10.2190/EF1G-PNXF-J1VQ-6M72

Herrington, R. L., Mitchell, A. E., Castellani, A. M., Joseph, J. I., Snyder, D. K., & Gleaves, D. H. (2008). Assessing disharmony and disaffection in intimate relationships: Revision of the Marital Satisfaction Inventory factor scales. *Psychological Assessment, 20,* 341–350. http://dx.doi.org/10.1037/a0013759

Holley, S. R., Haase, C. M., & Levenson, R. W. (2013). Age-related changes in demand-withdraw communication behaviors. *Journal of Marriage and Family*, *75*, 822–836. http://dx.doi.org/10.1111/jomf.12051

Holt-Lunstad, J., Smith, T. B., & Layton, J. B. (2010). Social relationships and mortality risk: A meta-analytic review. *PLoS Medicine*, *7*, e1000316. http://dx.doi.org/10.1371/journal.pmed.1000316

Idler, E. L., Boulifard, D. A., & Contrada, R. J. (2012). Mending broken hearts: Marriage and survival following cardiac surgery. *Journal of Health and Social Behavior*, *53*, 33–49. http://dx.doi.org/10.1177/0022146511432342

Iveniuk, J., Waite, L. J., Lauman, E., McClintock, M. K., & Tiedt, A. (2014). Marital conflict in older couples: Positivity, personality, and health. *Journal of Marriage and Family*, *76*, 130–144. http://dx.doi.org/10.1111/jomf.12085

King, K. B., & Reis, H. T. (2012). Marriage and long-term survival after coronary artery bypass grafting. *Health Psychology*, *31*, 55–62. http://dx.doi.org/10.1037/a0025061

Krause, N., & Rook, K. S. (2003). Negative interaction in late life: Issues in the stability and generalizability of conflict across relationships. *The Journals of Gerontology: Series B. Psychological Sciences and Social Sciences*, *58*, P88–P99. http://dx.doi.org/10.1093/geronb/58.2.P88

Kulik, L. (2002). Marital equality and the quality of long-term marriage in later life. *Ageing and Society*, *22*, 459–481. http://dx.doi.org/10.1017/S0144686X02008772

Lambert-Shute, J., & Fruhauf, C. A. (2011). Aging issues: Unanswered questions in marital and family therapy literature. *Journal of Marital and Family Therapy*, *37*, 27–36. http://dx.doi.org/10.1111/j.1752-0606.2009.00152.x

Laurenceau, J.-P., & Bolger, N. (2005). Using diary methods to study marital and family processes. *Journal of Family Psychology*, *19*, 86–97. http://dx.doi.org/10.1037/0893-3200.19.1.86

Levenson, R. W., Carstensen, L. L., & Gottman, J. M. (1993). Long-term marriage: Age, gender, and satisfaction. *Psychology and Aging*, *8*, 301–313. http://dx.doi.org/10.1037/0882-7974.8.2.301

Levenson, R. W., Carstensen, L. L., & Gottman, J. M. (1994). The influence of age and gender on affect, physiology, and their interrelations: A study of long-term marriages. *Journal of Personality and Social Psychology*, *67*, 56–68. http://dx.doi.org/10.1037/0022-3514.67.1.56

Matthews, K. A., & Gump, B. B. (2002). Chronic work stress and marital dissolution increase risk of posttrial mortality in men from the Multiple Risk Factor Intervention Trial. *Archives of Internal Medicine*, *162*, 309–315. http://dx.doi.org/10.1001/archinte.162.3.309

Moran, J. M. (2013). Lifespan development: The effects of typical aging on theory of mind. *Behavioural Brain Research*, *237*, 32–40. http://dx.doi.org/10.1016/j.bbr.2012.09.020

Myers, S. M., & Booth, A. (1996). Men's retirement and marital quality. *Journal of Family Issues*, *17*, 336–357. http://dx.doi.org/10.1177/019251396017003003

National Alliance for Caregiving and AARP. (2009). *Caregiving in the U.S.* Washington, DC: Authors.

Orth-Gomér, K., Wamala, S. P., Horsten, M., Schenck-Gustafsson, K., Schneiderman, N., & Mittleman, M. A. (2000). Marital stress worsens prognosis in women with coronary heart disease: The Stockholm Female Coronary Risk Study. *JAMA, 284,* 3008–3014. http://dx.doi.org/10.1001/jama.284.23.3008

Pincus, A. L., & Ansell, E. B. (2013). Interpersonal theory of personality. In T. Millon & M. J. Lerner (Eds.), *Handbook of psychology: Vol. 5. Personality and social psychology* (2nd ed., pp. 141–159). New York, NY: Wiley.

Robles, T. F., Slatcher, R. B., Trombello, J. M., & McGinn, M. M. (2014). Marital quality and health: A meta-analytic review. *Psychological Bulletin, 140,* 140–187. http://dx.doi.org/10.1037/a0031859

Rohrbaugh, M. J., Shoham, V., & Coyne, J. C. (2006). Effect of marital quality on eight-year survival of patients with heart failure. *The American Journal of Cardiology, 98,* 1069–1072. http://dx.doi.org/10.1016/j.amjcard.2006.05.034

Sadler, P., Ethier, N., & Woody, E. (2011). Interpersonal complementarity. In L. M. Horowitz & S. Strack (Eds.), *Handbook of interpersonal psychology: Theory, research, assessment, and therapeutic interventions* (pp. 123–142). Hoboken, NJ: Wiley.

Sanford, K. (2010). Perceived threat and perceived neglect: Couples' underlying concerns during conflict. *Psychological Assessment, 22,* 288–297. http://dx.doi.org/10.1037/a0018706

Sbarra, D. A., Law, R. W., & Portley, R. M. (2011). Divorce and death: A meta-analysis and research agenda for clinical, social, and health psychology. *Perspectives on Psychological Science, 6,* 454–474. http://dx.doi.org/10.1177/1745691611414724

Schmitt, M., Kliegel, M., & Shapiro, A. (2007). Marital interaction in middle and old age: A predictor of marital satisfaction? *The International Journal of Aging & Human Development, 65,* 283–300. http://dx.doi.org/10.2190/AG.65.4.a

Shiovitz-Ezra, S., & Leitsch, S. A. (2010). The role of social relationships in predicting loneliness: The National Social Life, Health, and Aging Project. *Social Work Research, 34,* 157–167. http://dx.doi.org/10.1093/swr/34.3.157

Smith, T. W., Baron, C. E., & Grove, J. L. (2014). Personality, emotional adjustment, and cardiovascular risk: Marriage as a mechanism. *Journal of Personality, 82,* 502–514.

Smith, T. W., Berg, C. A., Florsheim, P., Uchino, B. N., Pearce, G., Hawkins, M., . . . Olsen-Cerny, C. (2009). Conflict and collaboration in middle-aged and older couples: I. Age differences in agency and communion during marital interaction. *Psychology and Aging, 24,* 259–273. http://dx.doi.org/10.1037/a0015609

Smith, T. W., Gallo, L. C., Goble, L., Ngu, L. Q., & Stark, K. A. (1998). Agency, communion, and cardiovascular reactivity during marital interaction. *Health Psychology, 17,* 537–545. http://dx.doi.org/10.1037/0278-6133.17.6.537

Smith, T. W., Traupman, E. K., Uchino, B. N., & Berg, C. A. (2010). Interpersonal circumplex descriptions of psychosocial risk factors for physical illness: Application to hostility, neuroticism, and marital adjustment. *Journal of Personality, 78*, 1011–1036. http://dx.doi.org/10.1111/j.1467-6494.2010.00641.x

Smith, T. W., Uchino, B. N., Berg, C. A., Florsheim, P., Pearce, G., Hawkins, M., . . . Olsen-Cerny, C. (2009). Conflict and collaboration in middle-aged and older couples: II. Cardiovascular reactivity during marital interaction. *Psychology and Aging, 24*, 274–286. http://dx.doi.org/10.1037/a0016067

Smith, T. W., Uchino, B. N., Florsheim, P., Berg, C. A., Butner, J., Hawkins, M., . . . Yoon, H.-C. (2011). Affiliation and control during marital disagreement, history of divorce, and asymptomatic coronary artery calcification in older couples. *Psychosomatic Medicine, 73*, 350–357. http://dx.doi.org/10.1097/PSY.0b013e31821188ca

Snyder, D. K., Heyman, R. E., & Haynes, S. N. (2005). Evidence-based approaches to assessing couple distress. *Psychological Assessment, 17*, 288–307. http://dx.doi.org/10.1037/1040-3590.17.3.288

Sorkin, D. H., & Rook, K. S. (2006). Dealing with negative social exchanges in later life: Coping responses, goals, and effectiveness. *Psychology and Aging, 21*, 715–725. http://dx.doi.org/10.1037/0882-7974.21.4.715

Story, T. N., Berg, C. A., Smith, T. W., Beveridge, R., Henry, N. J. M., & Pearce, G. (2007). Age, marital satisfaction, and optimism as predictors of positive sentiment override in middle-aged and older married couples. *Psychology and Aging, 22*, 719–727. http://dx.doi.org/10.1037/0882-7974.22.4.719

Uchino, B. N., Holt-Lunstad, J., Uno, D., & Flinders, J. B. (2001). Heterogeneity in the social networks of young and older adults: Prediction of mental health and cardiovascular reactivity during acute stress. *Journal of Behavioral Medicine, 24*, 361–382. http://dx.doi.org/10.1023/A:1010634902498

Uchino, B. N., Smith, T. W., & Berg, C. A. (2014). Spousal relationship quality and cardiovascular risk: Dyadic perceptions of relationship ambivalence are associated with coronary-artery calcification. *Psychological Science, 25*, 1037–1042. http://dx.doi.org/10.1177/0956797613520015

Umberson, D., Williams, K., Powers, D. A., Liu, H., & Needham, B. (2006). You make me sick: Marital quality and health over the life course. *Journal of Health and Social Behavior, 47*, 1–16. http://dx.doi.org/10.1177/002214650604700101

von Hippel, W. (2007). Aging, executive functioning, and social control. *Current Directions in Psychological Science, 16*, 240–244. http://dx.doi.org/10.1111/j.1467-8721.2007.00512.x

von Hippel, W., & Gonsalkorale, K. (2005). "That is bloody revolting!" Inhibitory control of thoughts better left unsaid. *Psychological Science, 16*, 497–500. http://dx.doi.org/10.1111/j.0956-7976.2005.01563.x

von Hippel, W., Henry, J. D., & Matovic, D. (2008). Aging and social satisfaction: Offsetting positive and negative effects. *Psychology and Aging, 23*, 435–439. http://dx.doi.org/10.1037/0882-7974.23.2.435

Walker, R. B., & Luszcz, M. A. (2009). The health and relationship dynamics of late-life couples: A systematic review of the literature. *Ageing and Society, 29,* 455–480. http://dx.doi.org/10.1017/S0144686X08007903

Wang, M., Henkens, K., & van Solinge, H. (2011). Retirement adjustment: A review of theoretical and empirical advancements. *American Psychologist, 66,* 204–213. http://dx.doi.org/10.1037/a0022414

Whisman, M. A. (2007). Marital distress and DSM–IV psychiatric disorders in a population-based national survey. *Journal of Abnormal Psychology, 116,* 638–643.

Whisman, M. A., & Uebelacker, L. A. (2009). Prospective associations between marital discord and depressive symptoms in middle-aged and older adults. *Psychology and Aging, 24,* 184–189. http://dx.doi.org/10.1037/a0014759

Whisman, M. A., Uebelacker, L. A., Tolejko, N., Chatav, Y., & McKelvie, M. (2006). Marital discord and well-being in older adults: Is the association confounded by personality? *Psychology and Aging, 21,* 626–631. http://dx.doi.org/10.1037/0882-7974.21.3.626

# 3

# OLDER COUPLE RELATIONSHIPS AND LONELINESS

JENNY de JONG GIERVELD AND MARJOLEIN BROESE van GROENOU

*Find Loneliness scale*

The couple relationship is a major factor in alleviating loneliness. Midlife and older adults without a couple relationship, especially after widowhood or divorce, are at serious risk of loneliness. Outcomes of empirical research, both dating back to the former century (Lopata, 1980, 1996), as well as based on recent research (Aartsen & Jylhä, 2011, Ben-Zur, 2012; Guiaux, Van Tilburg, & Broese van Groenou, 2007), have shown that widowed and divorced older adults are frequently characterized by high levels of loneliness. Yet, some older adults within a couple relationship also report loneliness. About one in six older married men and women experiences moderate or strong levels of emotional loneliness (De Jong Gierveld, Broese van Groenou, Hoogendoorn, & Smit, 2009). This calls for more attention to the determinants of loneliness, especially those that may operate differently for adults in couple relationships and those without couple relationships in midlife and later life.

http://dx.doi.org/10.1037/14897-004
*Couple Relationships in the Middle and Later Years: Their Nature, Complexity, and Role in Health and Illness,*
J. Bookwala (Editor)

This chapter assesses the concept and measurement of loneliness, a theoretical model to investigate the interplay of the main determinants of loneliness, several types of couple relationships, and the association between couple relationships and loneliness; the chapter rounds off with suggestions for interventions to alleviate loneliness.

## THE CONCEPT OF LONELINESS, MEASURING INSTRUMENTS, AND THE THEORETICAL MODEL OF LONELINESS

Loneliness concerns the manner in which individuals subjectively experience and evaluate a lack of communication with other people. A widely used definition of loneliness is the subjective, unpleasant experience of a perceived discrepancy between the quantity and quality of existing relationships (e.g., with spouse, children, friends) and the relationships one wishes (De Jong Gierveld, Van Tilburg, & Dykstra, 2006; Perlman & Peplau, 1981). So, it is the discrepancy subjectively experienced between the desired personal relationships and actually realized relationships—feelings of missing certain personal relationships—that is of crucial importance for the onset and continuation of loneliness. The absence of loneliness includes feelings of social embedment.

Loneliness is distinct from social isolation, which concerns the objective characteristics of a situation and refers to a small or reduced network of kin and nonkin relationships. Common characteristics of socially isolated individuals are the near absence of relationships with others. We identify a continuum from social isolation on the one hand to social participation on the other. Persons with a very small number of ties with others are, by definition, socially isolated.

Loneliness is but one of the possible outcomes of the subjective evaluation of a situation characterized by a small number of relationships. Socially isolated persons are not necessarily lonely, and lonely persons are not necessarily socially isolated in the objective sense. A varied social network with regular contacts and exchanges of support with members of one's social network are crucial elements for affecting social embedment and alleviating loneliness, and consequently quality of life and life expectancy (Hawkley et al., 2008; Holt-Lunstad, Smith, & Layton, 2010; Pinquart & Sörensen, 2001). Having at least three or four intimate social ties provides the greatest protection against loneliness; the protection provided by additional relationships has only a small additional impact (Van Tilburg & De Jong Gierveld, 2007).

Although the size of the social network is important, many other aspects are worth mentioning in this context, too, such as the composition and functioning of the social network.

## Components of Loneliness

Most people wish to have at least one social contact in whom they can confide their personal worries and feelings. A romantic partner, an adult child, or a best friend is most frequently identified as such an intimate figure. If such a confidant is missing, the risk of loneliness increases. This type of loneliness was designated by Weiss (1973) as *emotional* loneliness. Feelings of missing related to a broader group of contacts or an engaging social network (e.g., peripheral kin, casual friends, colleagues, neighbors) is designated as the *social* type of loneliness. In this case, one misses small talk and conversation about daily hassles and feels there is no one to turn to for social companionship or support in times of need. Some people are especially prone to emotional loneliness, others to social loneliness; however, it is the combination of emotional and social loneliness that leads to the most intense feelings of loneliness.

## Measurement of Loneliness

Loneliness has a negative connotation. Lonely people report that loneliness carries a social stigma, and for that reason many of them are reluctant to talk about feelings of loneliness. Consequently, people with deficiencies in their relationships do not always admit to being lonely. The use of direct questions including the words *lonely* or *loneliness* to investigate loneliness is likely to result in underreporting, partly associated with a "diagnosis threat." For that reason, we prefer to use a set of questions that do not explicitly use the word *loneliness* and opt for loneliness scales. In empirical investigations into loneliness, two well-known and validated scales are available and frequently used.

One scale is the De Jong Gierveld Loneliness Scale, which consists of 11 items; six of the items are grouped together as the emotional loneliness subscale (range 0–6), and five items constitute the social loneliness subscale (range 0–5; De Jong Gierveld & Kamphuis, 1985; De Jong Gierveld & Van Tilburg, 1999). Dependent on the research question, one can choose to use either the overarching 11-item loneliness scale or the subscales. The scales have proven to be reliable and valid (Dykstra & Fokkema, 2007; Pinquart & Sörensen, 2001; Van Tilburg & De Leeuw, 1991). A shortened scale of six items, encompassing a three-item emotional and three-item social loneliness subscale, also has reliability and validity (De Jong Gierveld & Van Tilburg, 2006, 2010; Leung, De Jong Gierveld, & Lam, 2008). The second scale, the UCLA Loneliness Scale, was developed by Russell, Peplau, and Ferguson (1978) and consists of 20 items; the revised version (Version 3) of the scale is published by Russell (1996) and also has 20 items (10 items worded in the loneliness direction and 10 items worded in the nonloneliness direction). The UCLA scale is constructed as a unidimensional scale that does not differentiate between emotional and social loneliness. The scale has proven to be reliable and valid (Pinquart & Sörensen, 2001). Recently, both scales were evaluated and tested for use in middle-aged and older adults (Penning, Liu, & Chou, 2014); the authors recommended the De Jong Gierveld Loneliness Scale as the most appropriate measure of loneliness among this group, to be used either as a unidimensional or bidimensional measure of emotional and social loneliness.

## Theoretical Model of Loneliness

The main approaches to loneliness focus exclusively on individual-level characteristics that predispose people to become lonely. For that reason we start with these characteristics. According to Weiss (1973), emotional loneliness can only be resolved by starting a (new) couple relationship, and to alleviate social loneliness one needs more friends and others. This theoretical line of thinking is called the *deficit* approach, which posits that the absence of specific types of relationships is associated with specific forms of loneliness. Social loneliness is largely attributable to support network deficits related to friends, neighbors, and colleagues; emotional loneliness is associated with the absence of a partner or another close confidant. In the deficit approach, alleviating loneliness is directly associated with starting one or more new relationships.

Others posit that loneliness is not the direct result of the absence of specific personal relationships but results primarily from the differences between desired and actually achieved relationships. So the kernel of the cognitive discrepancy theory is the perceived discrepancy between one's desired size, composition, and functioning of social relationships and the corresponding size, composition, and functioning of existing relationships (Dykstra & De Jong Gierveld, 1994; Dykstra & Fokkema, 2007; Perlman & Peplau, 1981). The cognitive discrepancy theory recognizes both the size, composition, and functioning of the network of personal relationships (*proximal* factors related to loneliness), as well as the individual-level desires and expectations regarding these aspects of the network as the key factors in the onset and continuation of loneliness. Other factors are important as well, such as gender, education, income, health, and marital status, so-called *distal* characteristics, which operate partly through the proximal factors to influence loneliness (De Jong Gierveld & Tesch-Römer, 2012; Hawkley et al., 2008).

## DISTAL ANTECEDENTS

In the following sections, we first discuss several of the distal antecedents of loneliness: gender, deprived living conditions, and health.

## Gender

Mean differences in loneliness reveal that older women tend to be more emotionally lonely than older men, and older men are socially lonelier than their age-matched female peers (Dykstra & De Jong Gierveld, 2004). However, these gender differences in emotional and social loneliness mask within-group differences among men and women, as related to marital status and marital history. The unequal distribution of widowhood among men and women is the most important factor in explaining differences in mean emotional loneliness between men and women; women's higher risk of widowhood is associated with higher mean levels of emotional loneliness (Aartsen & Jylhä, 2011). Also, men are more likely to remarry after divorce or widowhood, which also contributes to the relatively high proportion of single women in later life. In addition, compared with men's socialization, women's socialization is oriented toward more complex affective needs and a varied and satisfying social network (Chodorow, 1978) and motivates women in later life (and earlier in life as well) to realize a broader and more varied network of kin and nonkin, consequently decreasing the risks of social loneliness.

## Deprived Living Conditions

The risk of being affected by multiple forms of deprived living conditions (e.g., a low educational level, low income, dependency on Social Security, and difficulties in making ends meet) is known to be especially high for those ages 70 years and over (Phillipson, 2004; Victor, Scambler, Marston, Bond, & Bowling, 2006). Such conditions negatively influence older persons' ability to optimize and diversify social contacts during the life course and contribute to loneliness in late adulthood (Ajrouch, Blandon, & Antonucci, 2005; Fokkema, De Jong Gierveld, & Dykstra, 2012). Recent research among Canadian older adults showed that especially changes toward worse financial situations and unmet needs were associated with loneliness (De Jong Gierveld, Keating, & Fast, 2015). Both couples and individuals living in economic-deprived conditions in certain neighborhoods of large cities (Scharf & De Jong Gierveld, 2008) and in socially excluded rural areas (Russell, Cutrona, de la Mora, & Wallace, 1997; Theeke & Mallow, 2013; Wenger & Burholt, 2004) are known to experience low levels of well-being and high levels of loneliness. Because of partner homogeneity in socioeconomic status, this may be even more so for couples in lower status groups. Those in the lowest income brackets tend to meet and marry partners in about the same income brackets; climbing the social ladder continues to be difficult for these individuals, and social exclusion problems faced during young adulthood are prominent also in later age (Ferraro & Shippee, 2009).

## Health

Empirical evidence consistently supports a negative association between general health indicators and loneliness (Dykstra, Van Tilburg, & De Jong Gierveld, 2005; Hawkley et al., 2008). Part of the effect is indirect, as health is an important resource for maintaining a large and diverse social network in later life (Aartsen, Van Tilburg, Smits, & Knipscheer, 2004). Whereas good physical health facilitates mobility and fosters social interaction outside the home, good cognitive health is required to communicate with others and preserve a balanced exchange of support with all relationships in the personal network (Broese van Groenou, Hoogendijk, & Van Tilburg, 2013). For married older adults, experiencing spousal health problems leads to significant changes in marital and social roles and may affect the level of well-being of both partners (Bookwala & Schulz, 1996; Siegel, Bradley, Gallo, & Kasl, 2004). However, Warner and Kelley-Moore (2012) found that positive marital quality moderated the association between functional limitations and loneliness, offering protection from the deleterious socioemotional consequences of disablement. Generally, the adaptation pattern may be one of growing closer together in a smaller social world, in which the importance and meaning of the marital bond is positively reevaluated (van Nes, Jonsson, Abma, & Deeg, 2013). Yet, disabling health problems may also hamper the quality of the marital relationship because of a lack of emotional closeness and intimacy, decreased shared activities, and problematic behavior of the disabled spouse (Lyons, Sullivan, Ritvo, & Coyne 1995; Walker & Luszcz, 2009). Other research using dyadic data on older couples has shown how both own and spousal health impact loneliness, but that these associations are highly gendered (Korporaal, Broese van Groenou, & Van Tilburg, 2008, 2013). After controlling for indicators of the support exchanged with network members and the spouse, own and spousal health problems for men were related to higher levels of social loneliness, but not to emotional loneliness. For women, poor spousal health impacted emotional loneliness, and only their own health problems increased the level of social loneliness (Korporaal et al., 2008). These gender differences corroborate that men socially benefit from being married but are less emotionally dependent on the quality of the marital bond. For them, spousal health problems affect, in particular, their levels of social interaction, whereas for women spousal health hampers the quality of the marriage, evoking feelings of emotional loneliness.

## PROXIMAL ANTECEDENTS: COUPLE RELATIONSHIPS

Of the different proximal factors—size and composition of the social network and functioning of the social network—we focus in this chapter on (a) the presence or absence of the spousal relationship and (b) quality aspects of the spousal relationship, as determinants of (nuances in) emotional and social loneliness of older adults.

## Defining Couple Relationships: A More Nuanced Approach

The couple relationship, and more particularly marriage, has always been seen as an important avenue for alleviating social isolation and loneliness. Research has repeatedly shown the protective effect of an intimate partner bond on the physical, financial, and mental well-being of both men and women (for an overview, see Waite & Gallagher, 2000). The majority of couple relationships encompass adults currently married in first or subsequent marriages, living as a couple in a two-person household or sharing their household with dependent biological and/or stepchildren. However, other types of couple-centered households also occur. In several regions of the world, coresidence of older adults and one or more of their adult children is high, although decreasing. In Japan, for example, 58% of adults ages 60 and over coreside with at least one of their children (Grundy, 2000; Takagi, Silverstein, & Crimmins, 2007). In Bulgaria and Georgia, coresidence is 25% and 50%, respectively (De Jong Gierveld, Dykstra, & Schenk, 2012). In contrast, in the United States and Western Europe, coresidence is much lower, varying between 5% and 15% (Pilkauskas, 2012; Ruggles, 2007).

In Northern and Western Europe and the United States, an increasing percentage of middle-aged and older adults live as cohabiting couples, not officially married but sharing the household, either with or without children and others (Chevan, 1996; de Graaf & Kalmijn, 2003; Sassler, 2010; Seltzer, 2004). In the absence of a legal civic framework, this type of relationship is characterized by less strict rules and the possibility of less commitment compared with their married peers (Rhoades, Stanley, & Markman, 2012; Skinner et al., 2002). Brown and Kawamura (2010) showed, however, that cohabitors and married persons do not significantly differ in their reports of emotional satisfaction, time spent together, criticism, and demands. They concluded that, overall, cohabitation nowadays may operate as an alternative to marriage for middle-aged and older adults. A third type of couple relationships, emerging in several Western countries, is the intimate relationship without permanently living together, referred to as the living-apart-together (LAT) relationship (see also Chapter 4, this volume). Men and women involved in an LAT relationship continue to live in a one-person household, intermittently (e.g., several days a week or on weekends) sharing the household with their partner. In most cases it is based on specific wishes for independence and privacy, and as such it is an example of modern attitudes (De Jong Gierveld, 2004; De Jong Gierveld & Merz, 2013; Duncan, Carter, Phillips, Roseneil, & Stoilova, 2013; Haskey, 2005; Moustgaard & Martikainen, 2009; Stevens,

2002; Strohm, Seltzer, Cochran, & Mays, 2009). Opting for an LAT relationship is especially favored by older widows and divorcees, either for reasons of shielding their children or to stay independent for as long as possible (De Jong Gierveld & Merz, 2013; Upton-Davis, 2015).

Up until now, in discussing partner relationships we have not differentiated between heterosexual and same-sex couples. The number of same-sex partner bonds is increasing, and these bonds are realized in either a marriage-type relationship, in cohabitation, or in LAT relationships. Note that living arrangements such as consensual unions and all types of same-sex relationships may have become a realistic option starting only in the late second half of the 20th century, when sociocultural changes allowed people to move away from traditional patterns of behavior, resulting in a reduction in behavioral conformation (Inglehart, 1997; Kane, 2013; Van de Kaa, 1987).

It goes without saying that the formal legal bond is present only in married couples. Those cohabiting are characterized by either a civil notarial bond or the absence of any formal arrangement underlying their living together. The LAT relationship is the type of couple relationship in which there is no formalized bond, no living together, and no legalized set of reciprocal support arrangements. Social expectations regarding caring and support between the partners differs accordingly: being most concrete for those in marriage, possibly less concrete for those involved in cohabitation, and more vague for LAT partners, although outcomes varied between countries as related to varying social contexts (Lee & Ono, 2012). (See Chapter 4, this volume, for a more comprehensive discussion of care obligations in LAT relationships and changing societal norms' potential implications for these obligations using Swedish society as a case study.)

### Is the Couple Bond Decisive for Alleviating Loneliness?

Older people's strategies to maintain an optimal level of social well-being are addressed in the socioemotional selectivity theory (Carstensen, 1992). In this theory, the primacy of social goals is expected to be related to time constraints. When time is perceived to be limited, as is the case for many older adults, emotional goals assume primacy. Empirical research has shown that "older couples regulate emotion in a way that should help preserve what is a very important late-life relationship—marriage" (Carstensen, 1995, p. 155).

Persons in a couple relationship tend to be better protected from emotional loneliness than persons without a partner bond (Peters & Liefbroer, 1997). Feelings of emotional loneliness in older adults without a partner are associated with living alone, a restricted network, the desire for more friends (Wenger et al., 1996), and unfulfilled expectations of contacts with friends (Routasalo, Savikko, Tilvis, Strandberg, & Pitkälä, 2006). Several mechanisms can explain why the absence of a partner in the household makes people more vulnerable to emotional loneliness. First, a key structuring influence is the size of the social network of kin and nonkin; a larger social network increases the possibilities for including a confidant and network members who are willing to be involved in exchanges of emotional and instrumental support. Most older adults have a significant number of relationships; the modal network size ranges between 10 and 14 using a network identification method based on frequency of contact and perceived importance in seven domains of relationships (Van Tilburg, 1998). The smallest networks were found for males who lived alone and were unmarried (mean size 7.8) or divorced (mean size 9.2). In the middle were unmarried and divorced females who lived alone (mean size 12.1 and 10.6, respectively). Males and females who lived alone and were widowed (mean network sizes 12.0 and 13.3, respectively) are characterized by, over time, strongly varying network sizes: During the stressful period following the death of the spouse, widows and widowers have more contacts with others. However, contacts and support return to preloss levels or lower in the long run (Guiaux et al., 2007). The networks of older adults who lived with a spouse were the largest. There was no difference between the males and females in this category (mean network size 14.5 and 14.3, respectively; Van Tilburg, 1995). Second, when help is needed, persons living alone lack in-house support and, by definition, have to orient themselves toward others outside the household. This orientation requires additional time, energy, and perseverance, and consequently many older adults living alone do not always receive the support needed. However, support receipt as well as contact frequency with network members are strongly associated with the partner history of those living alone: Contact frequency with children, children-in-law, and siblings is lowest for those living alone after divorce and more regular for those living alone after widowhood (De Jong Gierveld & Peeters, 2003). Third, gender in combination with partner history is important in explaining loneliness risks of older adults living alone. In accordance with the asymmetric gratification principle, men are more likely to find fulfillment of emotional needs in marriage than women. Consequently, widowed, divorced, and never married older men living alone are emotionally lonelier than widows and divorced or never married women living alone (Dykstra & De Jong Gierveld, 2004). "Outside of marriage, men are more likely to have unmet emotional needs because of their greater inclination towards an exclusive partner relationship" (Dykstra & De Jong Gierveld, 2004, p. 148). In contrast, women are known to have more complex affective needs than men, and this is reflected in older women's desire for and realization of a network of intimate and supportive relationships with a wider circle of personal relationships than their male peers. Being a member of a wider social network of friends, women living alone are better protected and experience less intense feelings of social loneliness compared with men living alone. It has to be noted that the same mechanism is responsible for the higher levels of social loneliness among married men than among married women. Recent research has shown that of the married older women and men, 18% and 16% are emotionally lonely and that social loneliness is reported by 18% and 26%, respectively (De Jong Gierveld et al., 2009).

Research that investigates the association between loneliness and remarriage, cohabitation without marriage, and LAT relationships started after widowhood or divorce is still rather scarce. Remarriage is significantly associated with higher levels of emotional loneliness, compared with men and women in first marriage (De Jong Gierveld et al., 2009). But further research is needed to clarify the association between repartnering after widowhood or divorce and experiencing emotional and social loneliness. To conclude, married persons are better protected against loneliness; those without a spouse and living alone are significantly lonelier. However, the dichotomy of married versus not married masks differences within the respective groups; marital history and gender have to be taken into account to nuance loneliness experiences among those living alone. In the next section, we investigate the quality of the couple relationship to nuance loneliness experiences among married men and women.

## The Quality of the Couple Relationship Is Most Important

Carstensen, Fung, and Charles (2003) showed that in older age, strong emotional bonds are maintained or even increased between spouses, as is the satisfaction they engender. However, a partner in older age does not always provide protection against loneliness. Negative interactions and experiences in the partner relationship increase the risks for higher levels of loneliness (Stevens & Westerhof, 2006). Older persons who do not identify their spouse or partner as their most supportive network member tend to be significantly lonelier than peers who evaluate the partner as their first confidant (Van Tilburg, 1988). A lower amount of perceived social support received from the spouse or partner also is significantly associated with higher levels of loneliness (Segrin, 2003), and the evaluation of the spousal sexual relationship as not (very) pleasant or as nonexistent is associated with higher levels of loneliness, emotional loneliness in particular (De Jong Gierveld et al., 2009). In sum, the evaluation of the quality of the spousal relationship as positive is decisive for experiencing lower levels of (emotional) loneliness, and the evaluation of the spousal bond as negative is associated with higher levels of (emotional) loneliness.

In contrast to the ideas of Weiss (1973), who connected the presence and functioning of the partner exclusively to emotional loneliness, recent research in the Netherlands has shown that the presence and functioning of the partner bond is also crucial in determining the risks of social loneliness. A higher degree of agreement between spouses in several aspects of daily life, a higher frequency of good conversations, and the identification of the spouse as first confidant are significantly associated with lower levels of social loneliness (De Jong Gierveld et al., 2009). In particular, having fewer good conversations with one's spouse, experiencing a lack of spousal support, and evaluating one's current sex life as "not applicable" or not pleasant was associated with higher levels of social loneliness.

Marriage history is of importance for the quality of the spousal relationship, too (Dykstra & De Jong Gierveld, 2004; Peters & Liefbroer, 1997; Wenger et al., 1996). The problems people faced in their marriage do not end after divorce but can linger on during remarriage (De Jong Gierveld & Merz, 2013; Kalmijn & Monden, 2006), especially because repartnering encompasses many changes (moving to a new home, adapting to new household rules, reorganizing the bonds with dependent and older children). Remarried persons confronted with all these changes and possible stressful situations may thus be involved in extra, time-consuming activities to manage the new situation; consequently, they may not be that successful in rebuilding a social network encompassing the networks of both the original and new partner, resulting in higher levels of social loneliness. If so, differences between social networks of the married and remarried may decrease with the duration of the spousal relationship of remarried individuals, which may explain why few differences are found between social networks of the married and the remarried in the general and older population (Dykstra & Fokkema, 2007; Kalmijn & Broese van Groenou, 2005).

In conclusion, an optimal functioning bond with the spouse (in first or subsequent marriage) decreases both the risks of emotional and social loneliness.

## POLICY IMPLICATIONS AND RECOMMENDATIONS

Drawing on the cognitive perspective of loneliness, this chapter provides an overview of the proximal and distal determinants of loneliness in couples in later life. Proximal determinants refer to the social network, notably the couple relationship, and the subjective evaluations regarding these personal relationships. Distal determinants are gender, living conditions, and health that influence loneliness either directly or via these personal relationships. We conclude that it is the quality of the partner relationship that matters most regarding feelings of loneliness, and that relationship quality may vary by partner type, marital history, gender, living conditions, and health of the spouse. In addition, the cultural value placed on the marital relationship differs across countries and depends on the importance placed on gender, family, and living arrangements of older adults. This overview brings us to specific groups at risk of loneliness that could be the focus of intervention programs. For intervention programs to be successful, it is crucial that there is optimal coherence between the causes and types of loneliness on the one hand and the type of intervention selected on the other hand (De Jong Gierveld, Fokkema, & Van Tilburg, 2011). In general, three types of interventions for alleviating loneliness are possible: (a) reducing the perceived discrepancy between actual and desired relationships by increasing the number and quality of the relationships to the desired level; (b) reducing the perceived discrepancy by decreasing the standards held for relationships to the level of reality; and (c) reducing the perceived discrepancy by reducing the effect of the discrepancy, for example, by accepting these feelings or by seeing loneliness in perspective. Next, we connect two groups at risk for loneliness with specific types of interventions.

The first group at risk for emotional and social loneliness includes those who are remarried in late life, cohabiting with a partner, or engaged in an LAT relationship. Their social network may not be as well developed as for those in a long-lasting first marriage, calling for more effort by the couple themselves to build new and mutual social relationships, in particular when their own children, friends, and acquaintances do not show much approval of the new relationship. In addition, it may be beneficial to lower the standards of relationship quality in a new relationship in later life, as it may not compare favorably with the first marriage, in particular for widowed persons (De Jong Gierveld et al., 2009; Stevens & Westerhof, 2006). For those in cohabitation and LAT relationships, there is no formalized bond, and there are fewer concrete social expectations regarding caring and support between the partners and within their social network. This may contribute to unfulfilled wishes regarding support in times of illness and need. Professional and voluntary support organizations need to recognize these issues associated with relationships developed later in life and help older couples to increase their social network and discuss relationship standards and expectations regarding care and support.

The second group at risk is older couples in which one or both of the spouses suffer from health problems. In particular, spousal health problems increase the risk for social and emotional loneliness. Nondisabled spouses are likely to enter a long-lasting care trajectory in which care demands and care provision increase over the years and decrease their social life, well-being and own health. Many communities have developed social service programs for caregivers, but spousal caregivers may be reluctant to ask for help from their social network and from professional caregivers (Broese van Groenou, De Boer, & Iedema, 2013), and this may explain why many spouses are sole caregivers (Keating & Dosman, 2009). Interventions for this group should be focused on asking and accepting help, sharing care responsibilities with others, and psychological processes of accepting a lower quality of the relationship. Within this group, men and those in deprived living conditions in particular should receive additional attention, as their capacities for mobilizing social networks and help are lower compared with women and those with better living conditions.

## CONCLUSION

Because of extended life expectancy, many people remain in their first marriage until late in life. For others, the opportunities to engage in new partner relationships after widowhood or divorce increase significantly. This is a positive development, as being single is the most important determinant of loneliness. With the increased variety of couple relationships, a more nuanced view of the benefits of these relationships is needed. Social embedding of the couple and the quality of the relationship are more important than just being in the relationship. Partnered older adults whose spousal relationship quality is hampered have an increased risk of emotional and social loneliness.

## REFERENCES

Aartsen, M., & Jylhä, M. (2011). Onset of loneliness in older adults: Results of a 28 year prospective study. *European Journal of Ageing, 8*, 31–38. http://dx.doi.org/10.1007/s10433-011-0175-7

Aartsen, M. J., Van Tilburg, T. G., Smits, C. H. M., & Knipscheer, C. P. (2004). A longitudinal study on the impact of physical and cognitive decline on the personal network in old age. *Journal of Social and Personal Relationships, 21*, 249–266. http://dx.doi.org/10.1177/0265407504041386

Ajrouch, K. J., Blandon, A. Y., & Antonucci, T. C. (2005). Social networks among men and women: The effects of age and socioeconomic status. *The Journals of Gerontology: Series B. Psychological Sciences and Social Sciences, 60*, S311–S317. http://dx.doi.org/10.1093/geronb/60.6.S311

Ben-Zur, H. (2012). Loneliness, optimism, and well-being among married, divorced, and widowed individuals. *The Journal of Psychology: Interdisciplinary and Applied, 146*, 23–36. http://dx.doi.org/10.1080/00223980.2010.548414

Bookwala, J., & Schulz, R. (1996). Spousal similarity in subjective well-being: The Cardiovascular Health Study. *Psychology and Aging, 11*, 582–590. http://dx.doi.org/10.1037/0882-7974.11.4.582

Broese van Groenou, M. I., De Boer, A., & Iedema, J. (2013). Positive and negative evaluation of caregiving among three different types of informal care relationships. *European Journal of Ageing, 10*, 301–311. http://dx.doi.org/10.1007/s10433-013-0276-6

Broese van Groenou, M., Hoogendijk, E. O., & Van Tilburg, T. G. (2013). Continued and new personal relationships in later life: Differential effects of health. *Journal of Aging and Health, 25*, 274–295. http://dx.doi.org/10.1177/0898264312468033

Brown, S. L., & Kawamura, S. (2010). Relationship quality among cohabitors and marrieds in older adulthood. *Social Science Research, 39*, 777–786. http://dx.doi.org/10.1016/j.ssresearch.2010.04.010

Carstensen, L. L. (1992). Social and emotional patterns in adulthood: Support for socioemotional selectivity theory. *Psychology and Aging, 7*, 331–338. http://dx.doi.org/10.1037/0882-7974.7.3.331

Carstensen, L. L. (1995). Evidence for a life-span theory of socioemotional selectivity. *Current Directions in Psychological Science, 4*, 151–156. http://dx.doi.org/10.1111/1467-8721.ep11512261

Carstensen, L. L., Fung, H. H., & Charles, S. T. (2003). Socioemotional selectivity theory and the regulation of emotion in the second half of life. *Motivation and Emotion, 27*, 103–123. http://dx.doi.org/10.1023/A:1024569803230

Chevan, A. (1996). As cheaply as one: Cohabitation in the older population. *Journal of Marriage and the Family, 58*, 656–667. http://dx.doi.org/10.2307/353726

Chodorow, N. (1978). *The reproduction of mothering: Psychoanalysis and the sociology of gender*. Berkeley: University of California Press.

de Graaf, P. M., & Kalmijn, M. (2003). Alternative routes in the remarriage market: Competing-risk analyses of union formation after divorce. *Social Forces, 81*, 1459–1498. http://dx.doi.org/10.1353/sof.2003.0052

De Jong Gierveld, J. (2004). Remarriage, unmarried cohabitation, living apart together: Partner relationships following bereavement or divorce. *Journal of Marriage and Family, 66*, 236–243. http://dx.doi.org/10.1111/j.0022-2445.2004.00017.x

De Jong Gierveld, J., Broese van Groenou, M., Hoogendoorn, A. W., & Smit, J. H. (2009). Quality of marriages in later life and emotional and social loneliness. *Journal of Gerontology: Series B. Psychological Sciences and Social Sciences, 64*, 497–506. http://dx.doi.org/10.1093/geronb/gbn043

De Jong Gierveld, J., Dykstra, P. A., & Schenk, N. (2012). Living arrangements, intergenerational support types and older adult loneliness in Eastern and Western Europe. *Demographic Research, 27*, 167–200. http://dx.doi.org/10.4054/DemRes.2012.27.7

De Jong Gierveld, J., Fokkema, T., & Van Tilburg, T. (2011). Alleviating loneliness among older adults: Possibilities and constraints of interventions. In *Safeguarding the convoy: A call to action from the campaign to end loneliness* (pp. 41–45). Abingdon, Oxfordshire, England: Age UK Oxfordshire.

De Jong Gierveld, J., & Kamphuis, F. (1985). The development of a Rasch-type loneliness scale. *Applied Psychological Measurement, 9*, 289–299. http://dx.doi.org/10.1177/014662168500900307

De Jong Gierveld, J., Keating, N., & Fast, J. E. (2015). Determinants of loneliness among older adults in Canada. *Canadian Journal on Aging / La Revue canadienne du vieillissement, 34*, 125–136. http://dx.doi.org/10.1017/S0714980815000070

De Jong Gierveld, J., & Merz, E.-M. (2013). Parents' partnership decision making after divorce or widowhood: The role of (step)children. *Journal of Marriage and Family, 75*, 1098–1113. http://dx.doi.org/10.1111/jomf.12061

De Jong Gierveld, J., & Peeters, A. (2003). The interweaving of repartnered older adults' lives with their children and siblings. *Ageing and Society, 23*, 187–205. http://dx.doi.org/10.1017/S0144686X02001095

De Jong Gierveld, J., & Tesch-Römer, C. (2012). Loneliness in old age in Eastern and Western European societies: Theoretical perspectives. *European Journal of Ageing, 9*, 285–295. http://dx.doi.org/10.1007/s10433-012-0248-2

De Jong Gierveld, J., & Van Tilburg, T. (1999). *Manual of the Loneliness Scale*. Amsterdam, the Netherlands: Vrije Universiteit.

De Jong Gierveld, J., & Van Tilburg, T. (2006). A six-item scale for overall, emotional, and social loneliness: Confirmative tests on new survey data. *Research on Aging, 28*, 582–598. http://dx.doi.org/10.1177/0164027506289723

De Jong Gierveld, J., & Van Tilburg, T. (2010). The De Jong Gierveld short scales for emotional and social loneliness: Tested on data from 7 countries in the UN generations and gender surveys. *European Journal of Ageing, 7*, 121–130. http://dx.doi.org/10.1007/s10433-010-0144-6

De Jong Gierveld, J., Van Tilburg, T., & Dykstra, P. A. (2006). Loneliness and social isolation. In A. Vangelisti & D. Perlman (Eds.), *Cambridge handbook of personal relationships* (pp. 485–500). Cambridge, England: Cambridge University Press. http://dx.doi.org/10.1017/CBO9780511606632.027

Duncan, S., Carter, J., Phillips, M., Roseneil, S., & Stoilova, M. (2013). Why do people live apart together? *Families, Relationships and Societies, 2*, 323–338. http://dx.doi.org/10.1332/204674313X673419

Dykstra, P. A., & De Jong Gierveld, J. (1994). The theory of mental incongruity, with a specific application to loneliness among widowed men and women. In R. Erber & R. Gilmour (Eds.), *Theoretical frameworks for personal relationships* (pp. 235–259). Hillsdale, NJ: Erlbaum.

Dykstra, P. A., & De Jong Gierveld, J. (2004). Gender and marital-history differences in emotional and social loneliness among Dutch older adults. *Canadian Journal on Aging / La Revue canadienne du vieillissement, 23*, 141–155. http://dx.doi.org/10.1353/cja.2004.0018

Dykstra, P. A., & Fokkema, T. (2007). Social and emotional loneliness among divorced and married men and women: Comparing the deficit and cognitive perspectives. *Basic and Applied Social Psychology, 29*, 1–12. http://dx.doi.org/10.1080/01973530701330843

Dykstra, P. A., Van Tilburg, T. G., & De Jong Gierveld, J. (2005). Changes in older adult loneliness: Results from a seven-year longitudinal study. *Research on Aging, 27*, 725–747. http://dx.doi.org/10.1177/0164027505279712

Ferraro, K. F., & Shippee, T. P. (2009). Aging and cumulative inequality: How does inequality get under the skin? *The Gerontologist, 49*, 333–343. http://dx.doi.org/10.1093/geront/gnp034

Fokkema, T., De Jong Gierveld, J., & Dykstra, P. A. (2012). Cross-national differences in older adult loneliness. *The Journal of Psychology: Interdisciplinary and Applied, 146*, 201–228. http://dx.doi.org/10.1080/00223980.2011.631612

Grundy, E. (2000). Co-residence of mid-life children with their elderly parents in England and Wales: Changes between 1981 and 1991. *Population Studies, 54*, 193–206. http://dx.doi.org/10.1080/713779085

Guiaux, M., Van Tilburg, T., & Broese van Groenou, M. (2007). Changes in contact and support exchange in personal networks after widowhood. *Personal Relationships, 14*, 457–473. http://dx.doi.org/10.1111/j.1475-6811.2007.00165.x

Haskey, J. (2005). Living arrangements in contemporary Britain: Having a partner who usually lives elsewhere and living apart together (LAT). *Population Trends, 122*, 35–45.

Hawkley, L. C., Hughes, M. E., Waite, L. J., Masi, C. M., Thisted, R. A., & Cacioppo, J. T. (2008). From social structural factors to perceptions of relationship quality and loneliness: The Chicago Health, Aging, and Social Relations study. *The Journals of Gerontology: Series B. Psychological Sciences and Social Sciences, 63*, S375–S384. http://dx.doi.org/10.1093/geronb/63.6.S375

Holt-Lunstad, J., Smith, T. B., & Layton, J. B. (2010). Social relationships and mortality risk: A meta-analytic review. *PLoS Medicine, 7*, e1000316. http://dx.doi.org/10.1371/journal.pmed.1000316

Inglehart, R. (1997). *Modernization and postmodernization: Cultural, economic and political change in 43 societies*. Princeton, NJ: Princeton University Press.

Kalmijn, M., & Broese van Groenou, M. I. (2005). Differential effects of divorce on social integration. *Journal of Social and Personal Relationships, 22*, 455–476. http://dx.doi.org/10.1177/0265407505054516

Kalmijn, M., & Monden, C. W. S. (2006). Are the negative effects of divorce on well-being dependent on marital quality? *Journal of Marriage and Family, 68*, 1197–1213. http://dx.doi.org/10.1111/j.1741-3737.2006.00323.x

Kane, J. B. (2013). A closer look at the second demographic transition in the US: Evidence of bidirectionality from a cohort perspective (1982–2006). *Population Research and Policy Review, 32*, 47–80. http://dx.doi.org/10.1007/s11113-012-9257-2

Keating, N., & Dosman, D. (2009). Social capital and the care networks of frail seniors. *Canadian Review of Sociology, 46*, 301–318. http://dx.doi.org/10.1111/j.1755-618X.2009.01216.x

Korporaal, M., Broese van Groenou, M. I., & Van Tilburg, T. G. (2008). Effects of own and spousal disability on loneliness among older adults. *Journal of Aging and Health, 20*, 306–325. http://dx.doi.org/10.1177/0898264308315431

Korporaal, M., Broese van Groenou, M. I., & Van Tilburg, T. G. (2013). Health problems and marital satisfaction among older couples. *Journal of Aging and Health, 25*, 1279–1298. http://dx.doi.org/10.1177/0898264313501387

Lee, K. S., & Ono, H. (2012). Marriage, cohabitation, and happiness: A cross-national analysis of 27 countries. *Journal of Marriage and Family, 74*, 953–972. http://dx.doi.org/10.1111/j.1741-3737.2012.01001.x

Leung, G. T. Y., De Jong Gierveld, J., & Lam, L. C. W. (2008). Validation of the Chinese translation of the 6-item De Jong Gierveld Loneliness Scale in elderly Chinese. *International Psychogeriatrics, 20*, 1262–1272. http://dx.doi.org/10.1017/S1041610208007552

Lopata, H. Z. (1980). Loneliness in widowhood. In J. Hartog (Ed.), *The anatomy of loneliness* (pp. 237–258). New York, NY: International Universities Press.

Lopata, H. Z. (1996). *Current widowhood: Myths and realities.* Thousand Oaks, CA: Sage.

Lyons, R. F., Sullivan, M. J. L., Ritvo, P. G., & Coyne, J. C. (1995). *Relationships in chronic illness and disability.* Thousand Oaks, CA: Sage.

Moustgaard, H., & Martikainen, P. (2009). Nonmarital cohabitation among older Finnish men and women: Socioeconomic characteristics and forms of union dissolution. *The Journals of Gerontology: Series B. Psychological Sciences and Social Sciences, 64*, 507–516. http://dx.doi.org/10.1093/geronb/gbp024

Penning, M. J., Liu, G., & Chou, P. H. B. (2014). Measuring loneliness among middle-aged and older adults: The UCLA and De Jong Gierveld Loneliness Scales. *Social Indicators Research, 118*, 1147–1166. http://dx.doi.org/10.1007/s11205-013-0461-1

Perlman, D., & Peplau, L. A. (1981). Toward a social psychology of loneliness. In R. Gilmour & S. Duck (Eds.), *Personal relationships 3: Personal relationships in disorder* (pp. 31–43). London, England: Academic Press.

Peters, A., & Liefbroer, A. C. (1997). Beyond marital status: Partner history and well-being in old age. *Journal of Marriage and Family, 59*, 687–699. http://dx.doi.org/10.2307/353954

Phillipson, C. (2004). Review article: Urbanisation and ageing: Towards a new environmental gerontology. *Ageing and Society, 24*, 963–972. http://dx.doi.org/10.1017/S0144686X04002405

Pilkauskas, N. V. (2012). Three-generation family households: Differences by family structure at birth. *Journal of Marriage and Family, 74*, 931–943. http://dx.doi.org/10.1111/j.1741-3737.2012.01008.x

Pinquart, M., & Sörensen, S. (2001). Influences on loneliness in older adults: A meta-analysis. *Basic and Applied Social Psychology, 23*, 245–266. http://dx.doi.org/10.1207/S15324834BASP2304_2

Rhoades, G. K., Stanley, S. M., & Markman, H. J. (2012). A longitudinal investigation of commitment dynamics in cohabiting relationships. *Journal of Family Issues, 33*, 369–390. http://dx.doi.org/10.1177/0192513X11420940

Routasalo, P. E., Savikko, N., Tilvis, R. S., Strandberg, T. E., & Pitkälä, K. H. (2006). Social contacts and their relationship to loneliness among aged people—a population-based study. *Gerontology, 52*, 181–187. http://dx.doi.org/10.1159/000091828

Ruggles, S. (2007). The decline of intergenerational coresidence in the United States, 1850 to 2000. *American Sociological Review, 72*, 964–989. http://dx.doi.org/10.1177/000312240707200606

Russell, D., Peplau, L. A., & Ferguson, M. L. (1978). Developing a measure of loneliness. *Journal of Personality Assessment, 42*, 290–294. http://dx.doi.org/10.1207/s15327752jpa4203_11

Russell, D. W. (1996). UCLA Loneliness Scale (Version 3): Reliability, validity, and factor structure. *Journal of Personality Assessment, 66*, 20–40. http://dx.doi.org/10.1207/s15327752jpa6601_2

Russell, D. W., Cutrona, C. E., de la Mora, A., & Wallace, R. B. (1997). Loneliness and nursing home admission among rural older adults. *Psychology and Aging, 12*, 574–589. http://dx.doi.org/10.1037/0882-7974.12.4.574

Sassler, S. (2010). Partnering across the life course: Sex, relationships, and mate selection. *Journal of Marriage and Family, 72*, 557–575. http://dx.doi.org/10.1111/j.1741-3737.2010.00718.x

Scharf, T., & De Jong Gierveld, J. (2008). Loneliness in urban neighbourhoods: An Anglo-Dutch comparison. *European Journal of Ageing, 5*, 103–115. http://dx.doi.org/10.1007/s10433-008-0080-x

Segrin, C. (2003). Age moderates the relationship between social support and psychosocial problems. *Human Communication Research, 29*, 317–342. http://dx.doi.org/10.1111/j.1468-2958.2003.tb00842.x

Seltzer, J. (2004). Cohabitation in the United States and Britain: Demography, kinship, and the future. *Journal of Marriage and Family, 66*, 921–928. http://dx.doi.org/10.1111/j.0022-2445.2004.00062.x

Siegel, M. J., Bradley, E. H., Gallo, W. T., & Kasl, S. V. (2004). The effect of spousal mental and physical health on husbands' and wives' depressive symptoms, among older adults: Longitudinal evidence from the Health and Retirement Survey. *Journal of Aging and Health, 16*, 398–425. http://dx.doi.org/10.1177/0898264304264208

Skinner, K. B., Bahr, S. J., Crane, D. R., & Call, V. R. (2002). Cohabitation, marriage and remarriage: A comparison of relationships quality over time. *Journal of Family Issues, 23*, 74–90. http://dx.doi.org/10.1177/0192513X02023001004

Stevens, N. (2002). Re-engaging: New partnerships in late-life widowhood. *Ageing International, 27*, 27–42. http://dx.doi.org/10.1007/s12126-002-1013-1

Stevens, N., & Westerhof, G. J. (2006). Partners and others: Social provisions and loneliness among married Dutch men and women in the second half of life. *Journal of Social and Personal Relationships, 23*, 921–941. http://dx.doi.org/10.1177/0265407506070474

Strohm, C. Q., Seltzer, J. A., Cochran, S. D., & Mays, V. M. (2009). "Living Apart Together" relationships in the United States. *Demographic Research, 21,* 177–214. http://dx.doi.org/10.4054/DemRes.2009.21.7

Takagi, E., Silverstein, M., & Crimmins, E. (2007). Intergenerational coresidence of older adults in Japan: Conditions for cultural plasticity. *The Journals of Gerontology: Series B. Psychological Sciences and Social Sciences, 62,* S330–S339. http://dx.doi.org/10.1093/geronb/62.5.S330

Theeke, L. A., & Mallow, J. (2013). Original research: Loneliness and quality of life in chronically ill rural older adults. *The American Journal of Nursing, 113,* 28–37. http://dx.doi.org/10.1097/01.NAJ.0000434169.53750.14

Upton-Davis, K. (2015). Subverting gendered norms of cohabitation: Living Apart Together for women over 45. *Journal of Gender Studies, 24,* 104–116. http://dx.doi.org/10.1080/09589236.2013.861346

Van de Kaa, D. J. (1987). Europe's second demographic transition. *Population Bulletin, 42,* 1–59.

van Nes, F., Jonsson, H., Abma, T., & Deeg, D. (2013). Changing everyday activities of couples in late life: Converging and keeping up. *Journal of Aging Studies, 27,* 82–91. http://dx.doi.org/10.1016/j.jaging.2012.09.002

Van Tilburg, T. (1988). *Verkregen en gewenste ondersteuning in het licht van eenzaamheidservaringen* [Obtained and desired social support in association with loneliness]. Doctoral dissertation, Free University, Amsterdam, the Netherlands.

Van Tilburg, T. (1995). Delineation of the social network and differences in network size. In C. P. M. Knipscheer, J. De Jong Gierveld, T. Van Tilburg, & P. A. Dykstra (Eds.), *Living arrangements and social networks of older adults* (pp. 83–96). Amsterdam, the Netherlands: VU University Press.

Van Tilburg, T. (1998). Losing and gaining in old age: Changes in personal network size and social support in a four-year longitudinal study. *The Journals of Gerontology: Series B. Psychological Sciences and Social Sciences, 53,* S313–S323. http://dx.doi.org/10.1093/geronb/53B.6.S313

Van Tilburg, T., & De Jong Gierveld, J. (2007). *Zicht op eenzaamheid: achtergronden, oorzaken en aanpak* [Loneliness, causes and interventions]. Assen, the Netherlands: Van Gorcum.

Van Tilburg, T., & De Leeuw, E. (1991). Stability of scale quality under various data collection procedures: A mode comparison on the 'De Jong-Gierveld Loneliness Scale.' *International Journal of Public Opinion Research, 3,* 69–85. http://dx.doi.org/10.1093/ijpor/3.1.69

Victor, C., Scambler, S. J., Marston, L., Bond, J., & Bowling, A. (2006). Older people's experiences of loneliness in the UK: Does gender matter? *Social Policy and Society, 5,* 27–38. http://dx.doi.org/10.1017/S1474746405002733

Waite, L. J., & Gallagher, M. (2000). *The case for marriage: Why married people are happier, healthier and better off financially.* New York, NY: Doubleday.

Walker, R. B., & Luszcz, M. A. (2009). The health and relationship dynamics of late-life couples: A systematic review of the literature. *Ageing and Society, 29,* 455–480. http://dx.doi.org/10.1017/S0144686X08007903

Warner, D. F., & Kelley-Moore, J. (2012). The social context of disablement among older adults: Does marital quality matter for loneliness? *Journal of Health and Social Behavior, 53,* 50–66. http://dx.doi.org/10.1177/0022146512439540

Weiss, R. S. (1973). *Loneliness: The experience of emotional and social isolation.* Cambridge, MA: The MIT Press.

Wenger, G. C., & Burholt, V. (2004). Changes in levels of social isolation and loneliness among older people in a rural area: A twenty-year longitudinal study. *Canadian Journal on Aging / La Revue canadienne du vieillissement, 23,* 115–127. http://dx.doi.org/10.1353/cja.2004.0028

Wenger, C. G., Davies, R., Shahtahmasebi, S., & Scott, A. (1996). Social isolation and loneliness in old age: Review and model refinement. *Ageing and Society, 16,* 333–358. http://dx.doi.org/10.1017/S0144686X00003457

# 4

# INTIMACY AND OBLIGATIONS IN LAT RELATIONSHIPS IN LATE LIFE

SOFIE GHAZANFAREEON KARLSSON AND MAJEN ESPVALL

Burgess (1926) long ago argued that urbanization, increased individualism, and the emancipation of women would transform social relations and functions within the family. Since Burgess's pioneering work, families have been transformed both in terms of form and meaning, and a wide range of external, environmental factors and changes in society—beyond the relationship itself—have affected how people interact with each other. There have been two noticeable trends: toward an increasing individualization and toward increasing diversity in relationship practices (Daly, 2005; Giddens, 1992). Personal relationships have, to some extent, lost their roots in social and economic conditions—previously linked to the traditional family—resulting in increased opportunities for people to give priority to love and to move in and out of social relations on freer and more reflection-based premises (Beck, 1998; Castells, 2011).

http://dx.doi.org/10.1037/14897-005
*Couple Relationships in the Middle and Later Years: Their Nature, Complexity, and Role in Health and Illness,*
J. Bookwala (Editor)

Changes in family structures also mean that the traditional division of obligations and reciprocity norms in close relationships are in a state of flux. In comparison with previous periods, modern families today are arguably more complex and more heterogeneous, which also implies that the norms relating to responsibilities for giving care and support are currently under challenge. Hand in hand with changes in family structure, new conditions for other types of close and intimate relationships have emerged. Contemporary intimate relations challenge the view of human relationships governed by social convention and instead idealize love selected by the heart. The romantic view of close relations also applies to older generations' living conditions and social organization of intimacy and sociability.

Older adults live longer, the number of divorces has increased, and it has become more typical for older adults to live alone (Robards, Evandrou, Falkingham, & Vlachantoni, 2012; Sundström & Ángeles Tortosa, 2010). The increasing number of older adults living alone as a result of divorce illustrates the fact that they are no longer simply indirectly influenced by the current changes in family life (e.g., their children's divorces) but are increasingly becoming actors in the process of change (Borell & Ghazanfareeon Karlsson, 2003). An example of these changes in family life and intimate relationships in late life is the emergence of living-apart-together relationships (LAT), that is, long-term intimate relationships that are, by choice, not based on a common home and that provide an alternative to cohabitation, within or outside wedlock. The LAT relationship gives older women and men the possibility of having an emotionally satisfying intimate relationship while retaining their autonomy (Ghazanfareeon Karlsson, 2006). Living "apart together," compared with living together in a shared home, involves radically different demands on the coordination of time, activities, resources, and care.

In this chapter, we discuss how new forms of intimate relationships among older adults, exemplified by LAT relationships, challenge family obligations, especially under Swedish conditions and its welfare state arrangement of eldercare. By analyzing motives and social constructions of LAT relationships, the overall aim is to explore how expectations of informal caring affect intimacy and obligations in older adults' LAT relations. Consistent with our aim we give particular emphasis to strategies involved when partners are dealing with expectations of care and support.

## LAT: DEFINITIONS AND PREVALENCE

LAT relationships among older adults have been the focus of a number of studies in recent years, in particular, in the Netherlands (De Jong Gierveld, 2004), Sweden (Ghazanfareeon Karlsson, 2006; Ghazanfareeon Karlsson &

Borell, 2002, 2005), and Canada (Funk & Kobayashi, 2014). As these studies have demonstrated, LAT relationships in this age group are primarily a vehicle for giving and receiving emotional support and are less concerned with the duties and obligations that are traditionally associated with marriage.

In comparison with marriage, LAT relationships in late life provide better opportunities for combining intimacy with autonomy. The first studies of LAT relationships among older adults in Sweden (Ghazanfareeon Karlsson, 2006) showed that it is primarily women who take the initiative in choosing this type of relationship. They want to have an intimate relationship but also want to have time for a life of their own. Their own home represents a key resource in their search for independence and allows women, in particular, to establish boundaries to their commitment to social life and the degree of adaptation to their partner. According to Duncan and Phillips (2011), LAT relationships are seen by the majority in Great Britain as a "good enough" partnership and reveal the same expectations about commitment and fidelity as marriage or cohabitation.

An LAT couple does not share a common home. However, they are defined by close others and by themselves as a couple, and the relationship contains intimacy and love. The term *LAT relationship* was first mentioned in 1978 by a Dutch journalist. In Sweden, and in other Scandinavian countries, the term *särbo* (living apart together) is nowadays well known. In other European countries, such as France and Germany, different terms are used, including *cohabitation intermittente* (Caradec, 1996) and *partners in different households* (Schneider, 1996). The discussion of the LAT concept is developed to different degrees in different countries. In some countries, the term *commuter marriage* is used interchangeably with *dual-households* or *dual-residence living* (Winfield, 1985) to refer to LAT relationships. The distinction between those two concepts and LAT relationships is connected to the issue of one's home. If the couple has a shared home and one of them stays away from that home because of work circumstances, as in a commuter marriage, then this is different from an LAT relationship where each partner has his or her own home (i.e., they have two separate residences). Publicly, the acronym LAT may be unfamiliar because there are different terms in different countries, but the understanding and acceptance of the relationship seem common.

Studies around Europe (Caradec, 1996; Haskey, 2005; Haskey & Lewis, 2006) have shown that between 5% and 10% of the population are in an LAT relationship. Studies from Canada, Australia, and Japan estimate their LAT population to be of very similar scale (Iwasawa, 2004; Milan & Peters, 2003; Reimondos, Evans, & Grey, 2011). Among those in their later years, estimates reveal that 12% of Canadians over the age of 50 live as LATs (Milan & Peters, 2003), and in Sweden, Holland, and Australia around 4% of those over 65 years of age are committed to this kind of relationship (De Jong

Gierveld, 2004; Ghazanfareeon Karlsson, 2006; Upton-Davis, 2012). These numbers are rising in accordance with demographic changes and changes connected to family and intimate relations norms.

Recent studies around the world have shown that those under the age of 24 who are engaged in an LAT relationship often consider the relationship to be a step toward cohabitation or marriage (see, e.g., Ermisch & Seidler, 2009; Haskey, 2005). Among LATs over the age of 24, however, the relationship is most often not seen as a stage in a relationship, and it lasts over a longer period of time. This is especially evident when older adults, over the age of 55, live in LAT relationships (Ghazanfareeon Karlsson, 2006). Our studies of LAT partners (over the age of 60) in Sweden show that they see their relationship as long term, but the length of time they say they have been LAT partners varies widely, from 1 to 28 years (with a median length of 6 years; Ghazanfareeon Karlsson, 2006; Ghazanfareeon Karlsson & Borell, 2002, 2005; Ghazanfareeon Karlsson, Johansson, Gerdner, & Borell, 2007). The partners may live on the same block or far apart. They keep in touch with each other by telephone on a more or less daily basis, but the time actually spent together varies: 36% meet almost every day, 51% a couple of times a week, and 12% twice a month or even more seldom.

Even in the mid-1990s, one third of the adults in the EU who were engaged in an intimate relationship but were not married or cohabiting unmarried were in an LAT relationship. In the age group 20 to 34, as many as 46% of Italians, 37% of Spanish, and 32% of Germans lived in an LAT relationship (Gonzales-Lopez & Solsona-Pairo, 2000). A majority of the Spanish LATs in the age group stated that this was an involuntary arrangement, because the reason for not being able to live together typically had to do with job and housing circumstances. Among Italians and Germans, however, the choice to live in an LAT relationship was more of a voluntarily adopted decision.

These trends show that LAT is a widespread way of conducting relationships in different countries and at different stages of life. Why partners live apart may vary according to their age, gender, stage of life, and financial reasons and may be based on varying contexts of country and family norms.

## THE SWEDISH CONTEXT AND LAT RELATIONSHIPS IN LATE LIFE

Swedish conditions provide a unique context for understanding LAT relationships among older adults, given that Sweden has one of the oldest populations in the world; more than 18% of the total population is 65 years of age or older (Lennartsson & Heimerson, 2012), and a relatively large number, approximately 4% of the Swedish elderly population, live in LAT relationships (Ghazanfareeon Karlsson, 2006; Levin, 2004). Sweden is also of interest in this context because many Swedish LAT relationships have been facilitated by the country's welfare model. The Swedish welfare model is a highly individualistic model where individuals, regardless of marital status, are expected to support themselves on the basis of a strong social norm concerning autonomy and self-sufficiency (i.e., not being a burden on others). The ideology behind the Swedish welfare state is that public services are regarded as conditional social rights, and the state bears the primary responsibility for eldercare provision for individuals when they are unable to provide for themselves.

Nevertheless, the political and economic situation of the Swedish welfare state has been subject to trends toward market orientation, privatization, and cutbacks in public spending in the past 2 decades (Palme et al., 2003). These economic trends mean that the boundaries between those areas that are the state's obligation and responsibility and those that lie within the personal/social domain are subject to serious challenges (SOU, 2000:3). Within this new political context, the traditionally conservative ideology of a "caring society," where family, friends, and other close relations are expected to a greater extent to participate in informal caring relations, has regained popularity (Espvall & Dellgran, 2010; Larsson & Thorslund, 2002).

Contrary to the expectations of those who cherish this ideology, research has shown that strategies designed to reactivate support capacities within social network relationships, as a means of compensating for cutbacks in the welfare system, may be problematic (Espvall & Dellgran, 2008). And, there are reasons to assume that it will be particularly challenging in older adults' LAT relationships when care needs are large, the support capacity limited, and the nature of the relationship still tentative and in a stage of negotiation.


## LAT IN LATE LIFE: MOTIVES AND CONSTRUCTIONS

In older adults' LAT relationships, both intimacy and security can be found in combination with personal freedom, and a typical feature of this type of relationship is that it can be seen in different ways by those involved in them. Some LAT partners, usually men, choose to see it as a conventional, more or less marriage-like relationship, whereas others, usually women, see this type of relationship as more open and experimental (Ghazanfareeon Karlsson & Borell, 2002).

We conducted a larger study of intimacy, autonomy, and commitment in LAT relations among older adults in Sweden to understand the motives for choosing to live in an LAT relationship and the rules and roles implied by the relationship (Ghazanfareeon Karlsson, 2006; Ghazanfareeon Karlsson & Borell, 2002, 2005; Ghazanfareeon Karlsson et al., 2007). The study included a large quantitative survey to LAT partners over the age of 60 (n = 116) and three qualitative in-depth studies with LATs over the age of 60 (n = 20) who participated in the larger quantitative survey; in two of the three qualitative studies, only women participated. These studies showed that LAT relationships among older men and women in Sweden vary greatly, but that it is nevertheless possible to identify relatively clear and common patterns. Before describing the findings, however, it is important to note that because individuals who form LAT relationships are not listed in any register, the exact size of the population is unknown. In view of this, it is extremely difficult to attain a statistically representative sample. Participants were recruited through advertising in nine local newspapers in three regions of Sweden, which together represent both rural and urban areas. The advertisements invited individuals aged 60 or older to take part in a study of LAT relationships among older adults.

A total of 116 individuals participated in the quantitative survey. The sample included slightly more women (57%) than men, varying in age from 60 to 90 years; the majority, 52%, fell into the category described as the young-old (65–74 years). Approximately half were divorced, and 40% were widows or widowers. A clear majority had both children and grandchildren of their own. The majority had established the LAT relationship after a divorce or widowhood; only 6% were living apart with their former spouse. Participants were highly educated (high school diploma or higher) and claimed to have good or excellent health. Thus, it is possible that self-selection bias is at play or that the sample does not adequately represent all older adults living apart together.

Our results showed that the emotional content of the relationship is brought into focus in LAT relationships among older adults. This makes the LAT relationship well suited to this age group, given the increased value of emotional aspects of relationships with age (Carstensen, Isaacowitz, & Charles, 1999). Furthermore, the results showed that older LAT partners, both those participating in the quantitative and in the qualitative studies, saw their relationship as deeply intimate, representing mutual trust, understanding, and sharing of confidences. One participant stated that,

> When I became older I felt a need for a close relationship even more than ever before. Of course I wanted a relationship that could provide an intimate relation between a man and a woman, not just a friendship. I think that one needs one another even more when you are old . . . my partner is my support in everything and yes, I think he feels the same way about me. (Carin, age 75)

Faithfulness is also a central question for the LAT partners participating in our studies. Erik put it like this:

> Some women, especially at the dance on Thursdays, show a certain interest in me but no, me and my LAT partner have made a promise to each other: if we go out with another that will be it! And it would really be a disaster for both of us. You see we meet every day and we support each other in every way. (Erik, age 78)

A balance between intimacy and independence is maintained by participants through having access to a home of their own. The data from the survey show that separate homes usually mean separate private economies. Joint saving and ownership is unusual and does not seem to increase with time, that is, LAT relationships do not seem to become more "marriage like" over time.

## LAT: DIFFERENT GENDER AGENDAS

A pattern appears that indicates a considerable difference between the answers of older LAT men and women concerning their motives for living in this kind of relationship. In general, one can say that the women tend to have more clear motives for choosing LAT relationships (Ghazanfareeon Karlsson, 2006; Ghazanfareeon Karlsson & Borell, 2002; Ghazanfareeon Karlsson et al., 2007). This pattern makes us understand that it is women who are the primary driving force behind the choice of the relationship. Significantly more women than men mentioned experiencing difficulties in adapting to the habits or ways of a new partner or that both of them find their separate housing very suitable (one is a heavy smoker or one has pets and the other one is allergic; or none of them wanted to move to the other's home). The men in our studies were more unclear in their motives for choosing this kind of relationship, and those participating in our interviews said that the LAT relationship suited them more because of different obligations they had toward their own children and grandchildren. Some men said they would have preferred cohabitation instead of living in an LAT relationship, but that that was not only up to them to decide. The gender disparity is especially evident regarding two motives: the importance of having a home of one's own and the importance of being freed of duties that would arise if one shared a common home, both revolving largely around autonomy. In our face-to-face interviews, women emphasized that the LAT relationship enables them to combine intimacy with what they refer to as a strong desire to "be themselves" and "live their own lives." One of the women in our studies put it like this:

> Having a home of my own lets me feel I am deciding for myself and that I don't have to consider other people. It wouldn't work if we lived together. Then I couldn't say: "It's time for you to go!" (Patricia, age 62)

Retaining a home of one's own is, thus, an essential factor in shaping LAT relationships in late life. It is a place in which personal control is ensured and optimized: a boundary-making resource that these women draw on to balance their need for privacy and time alone with their need for intimacy and closeness. Older LAT women describe their own home and their self-imposed single status as a privilege and marriage or other forms of cohabitation as a loss of this privilege. Marianne put it like this:

> I want to be with my family alone from time to time because we have so much else to talk about. He is quite talkative and he can be dominant. I have not wanted to get married or move in together because then there is someone who comes home and yells and checks on you: "what have you done with the money!" or so. (Marianne, age 76)

When examining older women's ways of setting boundaries in their LAT relationships, the most striking result was the variety in boundary setting that exists. Having their own homes allows those women that wish to, to segment their social relationships in time and space—that is, they can have independent relationships with their partners, children, grandchildren, friends, and other relations. But LAT relationships also allow older adults to integrate these relationships in different ways and give them the flexibility to alternate between meeting their friends and relatives together with their partner or separately, depending on the situation. Although individual LAT strategies range from relatively segmented to relatively integrated, it seems that the ability to control the way in which these relationships are organized is of primary importance for women in LAT relationships. This pattern is not evident among the men who participated in our studies; intimacy, security, and trust seemed to be of most importance to them when choosing a close relationship. As noted previously, many men in our studies also would have preferred to live in another, more marriage-like relationship instead of in an LAT relationship.

In their interview responses, older LAT women also described, from a comparative and analytical perspective, how social patterns and conditions based on norms and concepts of gender have either enabled them to achieve, or prevented them from achieving, autonomy in different relationships and periods of their lives (Ghazanfareeon Karlsson, 2006). The nature of their relationships, and the context in which they have been formed, has major significance for whether it is possible to change, challenge, or question the gender norms and how this can create different opportunities for achieving autonomy. This possibility—of being able to challenge gender norms of different sorts and to achieve autonomy in a relationship—is described by the women interviewees as a crucial factor in defining how they currently see their lives, comparatively speaking, in a more positive light.

# INTIMACY AND SOCIAL OBLIGATIONS

Bengtson, Rosenthal, and Burton (1990) claimed that the age structure in many families has changed from "a pyramid to a beanpole" (p. 3), by which they mean that family structures have a shape that is now long and thin, with more generations alive within families, but with fewer members alive in each generation. The metaphor of the beanpole highlights the remarkable changes in the demographics of age and the important implications, not only for family functions, but also for intimacy and social obligations in other forms of close relations. For example, as a consequence of the restructuring of families, there are reasons to assume that older adults who have fewer children and grandchildren seek and construct intimate relations with others outside the family to a higher degree, potentially to experience emotional closeness and the exchange of different kinds of social support.

Intimacy theories propose that intimate adult relationships are experienced when a person feels understood, valued, and cared for through a partner's response (Reis & Patrick, 1996). Reis (2001) described intimacy as an interactive process with three components: one person's expressions of thoughts and feelings; the partner's response; and the perceptions of the partner's response. Intimacy also implies reciprocity, meaning that these two roles are typically alternated (i.e., the understanding that when one party receives something from another, this requires something in return).

The idea is often advanced that kin relationships have a distinctive characteristic that sets them apart from other, nonbiological relationships. This characteristic can be defined in terms of moral rules concerned with duty and obligations, that is, who should help whom, in which situations, and under what conditions. However, it is difficult to actually identify clear rules about what someone should do for a relative in defined circumstances and what motives underpin the provision of support in different types of relationships. Kohli and Künemund (2003) argued that the motivation for giving support consists of a complex array of reasons with a large amount of overlap and interaction between different motives. The motives are significant not only for the frequencies and extent of support, but also for the recipients' experiences of support. It certainly makes a difference whether support is motivated by self-interest, by love, or by generosity or is executed out of a sense of personal obligation. People seem to interpret and negotiate their exchanges within the scope of certain guidelines with reference to the context in which they find themselves, which means that different motives or preferences can result in different evaluations of similar situations.

Other research has confirmed that the quality of the relationship, joint history of support exchange, and whether the receipt of assistance would disturb the balance between dependence and independence in the relationship are factors that affect decisions of social support and care (Espvall, 2008). Furthermore, for many persons illness means a great need for support both practically and emotionally, but there are indications of a gap between the patient's hopes for aid and close relatives' ability to live up to those expectations (Dunkel-Schetter & Bennett, 1990). The causes of and motives for the lack of support are varied. One reason may be that family and friends do not understand or misjudge the need for aid. Another explanation could be the donor's lack of capacity to provide effective support in the given situation. It may be that the prospective provider feels uncertain about how best to provide the support or experiences feelings of fear, guilt, and helplessness in doing so. A third reason is that the support provider and recipient may have diverging views on how the current situation should be handled and what support is functional.

Finch and Mason (1993) argued that people operate with a concept of family obligation that is much more fluid than is implied by the ideas of moral imperatives associated with genealogical positions. They contended that the obligation to give help is conceptualized as a result of a "process of negotiation, in which people are giving and receiving, balancing out one kind of assistance against another, maintaining an appropriate independence from each other as well as mutual interdependence" (Finch & Mason, 1993, p. 167). These types of negotiations of care in LAT relations among older adults presuppose that both partners have somewhat consistent opportunities to give and receive support and assistance.

We can assume that the processes and conditions of reciprocity and responsibility in LAT relations among older adults in several respects involve clashes between, on the one hand, older morals in the form of structurally and culturally accepted norms surrounding care obligations and, on the other, new codes that govern social action and interaction in LAT relationships. Furthermore, it is reasonable to assume that people interpret and negotiate their exchanges of care and support within the scope of certain guidelines with reference to the context in which they find themselves.


## CARE AND SUPPORT AMONG OLDER LAT INDIVIDUALS

Irrespective of the kind of relationship we live in, in our old age, the issue of care will sooner or later emerge. In this situation, we may find ourselves obliged to take responsibility for providing care against our will, or we may find ourselves without someone to care for us when we need it.

When expectations and attitudes of older adults in LAT relationships concerning giving and receiving care and support, within as well as outside the relationship, were investigated (Ghazanfareeon Karlsson et al., 2007), both men and women ranked their LAT partner as their main provider of support, in comparison with other members of their network, although this was particularly prevalent among men. Within the LAT relationship, men reported that they received more services than women did, although previously married men also reported a greater decrease in services than women when compared with their former relationship. Men also agreed more with conventional relationship norms compared with women, whereas women reported stronger motives for living apart together.

In interviews with older LAT women assessing their responsibility for their partner in the case of his illness (Ghazanfareeon Karlsson, 2006; Ghazanfareeon Karlsson & Borell, 2002, 2005), health and housing were strongly connected to each other. The question of living together because of care needs was discussed in detail in two of the interviews, and the conflict between care and personal autonomy was clear. The following quotation illustrates this:

> Then of course if he gets ill . . . well then I don't know . . . I want to help him as much as possible of course . . . really we should get a shared apartment, but I don't want that either. No way, then I wouldn't be free any longer. No, I think you should have separate homes. Now, when we meet, it's very pleasant and that wouldn't be the case if we lived together. (Christina, age 76)

However, it is not only the individual's way of seeing their LAT relationship that influences expectations about care in the future. Older LAT partners, like other older adults in Sweden, still expect good care services in their old age to be provided by the public sector. The question of care also varies according to the gender perspective. Naturally, the ideas we have about men and women affect how our expectations and demands of care are formed. More care options are open to men, and they also receive more support than women do from those around them when they are caring for a spouse, which affects both their experience of and attitude toward care (Ghazanfareeon Karlsson, 2006; Ghazanfareeon Karlsson et al., 2007). Moreover, the aging process for men means that they become more care oriented than younger men (Kaye & Applegate, 1990). They feel greater self-assurance, their psychological well-being improves, and their definition of masculinity becomes more flexible (Tornstam, 1996). Thus, a combination of personal, structural, and social factors appears to underlie the attitudes toward care of men and women in LAT relationships.

As mentioned before, older LAT men and women see these relationships in different ways, and it is therefore interesting to examine how gender influences the motives for choosing an LAT relationship and the way in which this relationship is maintained.

# DIFFERENT BUT ALIKE

New norms around marriage, cohabitation, premarital sex, gender equality, and rapidly increasing divorce rates have opened up opportunities to create new intimate relationships on freer and more reflection-based premises at all ages, including in late life. The increased prevalence of LAT relationships among older adults can be regarded in some ways as a historically new family form where partners can, at the same time, experience intimacy and preserve personal autonomy.

The main difference between LAT relations and other forms of love relationships is the lack of fixed standards and established conventions for how these relationships can be constructed. This translates into many opportunities for older couples to combine intimacy, love, and autonomy; the latter is a primary motive for choosing an LAT relationship, especially among older women. The LAT relationship is also flexible in that partners can choose, depending on the context, how they wish to appear—for example, as singles, married, or LATs. One of the women who participated in our study mentioned that she and her partner introduce themselves as a married couple when they travel abroad and in situations where they feel uncertain about how new acquaintances would regard their LAT relationship. In other situations it may be more convenient to present oneself as single.

Sharing an LAT relationship means that the partners dare to challenge conventional forms of living and communicate how the relationship can be maintained and developed in relation to the personal needs of each partner and other external causes. Because of different desires, backgrounds, ages, ethnicity, and social relationships to others, the construction of the LAT relationship can vary greatly across couples. Despite these variations, there are some common traits. The need for intimacy is reconciled with the need for having one's own home, a private life, and the ability to segment relationships with others. The separate home also creates opportunities to keep belongings and memories related to a past life.

Furthermore, an LAT relationship is also a vehicle for giving and receiving emotional and other forms of support; however, our interviews show that women and men have different references in the negotiations of various forms of support exchanges. Men more often see the relationship as a conventional, more or less marriage-like relationship, whereas women see this type of relationship as more open and experimental. One reason for this gender difference may be that women do not wish to risk the autonomy they already have gained. The cohorts of aging women of today are the same cohorts of women who restructured family life in the last 50 or 60 years. They have experienced the ideal of the nuclear family in the 1950s, and they also belong to the cohort of women who gradually participated in a shift from unpaid work to wage labor. The altered position of women did not bring an equivalent change in the domestic sphere, and women typically experienced a double workload: paid labor as well as housework and child care (Hochschild & Machung, 1989). The rising divorce rates, from the 1960s onward, can be seen as the first indication of strains arising in a largely unaltered family model that was ill-adapted to women's increasing participation in paid work outside the home. Women both initiated divorces to a greater extent than men did and were instrumental in efforts to create more autonomous and equal relationships both outside and inside the framework of marriage.

## CHALLENGES FOR THE SWEDISH WELFARE STATE

Because of the fact that people live longer and divorces among older adults have started to increase (Sundström & Ángeles Tortosa, 2010), more and more people create new intimate relationships in old age. In the case of Sweden in particular, there also are expectations for social support and care in LAT relationships within the context of the welfare state. The majority of older Swedish LATs in our studies find it crucial that the legal system does not equate the LAT relationship with cohabitation or marriage (Ghazanfareeon Karlsson, 2006; Ghazanfareeon Karlsson et al., 2007). This is vital because the relationship is seen, especially by women, as a safeguard against demands of care for the LAT partner.

Economic and demographic trends in the past 2 decades, with cuts in public spending and increasing numbers of older people, have challenged the universal care model in Sweden. As a consequence the care system has become weaker, and there has been a substantial reduction in the proportion of older people who receive formal care; the service has become more selective and resources have been concentrated to persons with the greatest medical needs. Informal care/support as a substitute for public care services leaves relatives with few opportunities to abstain from help giving, and the increased informal care is typically provided by middle-aged daughters and older wives (Szebehely, 2005).

This transformation of the eldercare network in Sweden, from formal to informal support, has been carried out despite the fact that adult children in Sweden have no legal obligation to provide care or financial support for their parents (Esping-Andersen, 1990); only married and cohabiting persons have the legal obligation to assist each other. Although help and support from children and other relatives is large and growing, there are still high expectations on the welfare state as a provider for eldercare. The reason for this is that older adults do not want to bear the burden of care to family—or to be dependent on care provided by the family—especially not when it comes to extensive, long-term, or intimate assistance (Svallfors, 2011).

The ideological foundations of the Swedish welfare model, where living autonomously has been emphasized, has enabled women (and men) to choose a new way of living in old age. Women who choose an LAT relationship see their own home as a protection against potential claims and expectations for providing care and support to the male partner. They express that as long as they do not live under the same roof as the partner, they expect that the public sector offers the partner necessary care in time of need.

It is reasonable to assume that in the future Sweden will see an increasing number of older people who choose different forms of relationships based on factors such as ethnicity, class, sexuality, and personal preferences. As new forms of relationships, such as LAT relationships, become more common among older adults, other forms of social network relations and interactions also will change. New intimate relations and altered obligations in family relationships will constitute new demands for the welfare state in terms of health care and support. It is not likely that the generation of women who fought for and achieved a certain level of gender equality will, in their late-life years, accept cuts in universal welfare systems. In an LAT relationship in Sweden, one cannot demand that a partner provide care in old age because the relationship is based more on voluntary commitments than on institutionalized commitments between partners. Politicians, social workers, and other government officials may need to reconsider their conventional—perhaps stereotyped—views on the intimate relationships of older adults and their gendered expectations of informal care. Exploiting LAT relationships could be counterproductive if it leads to termination of the relationship or, in other cases, challenges the pursuit of gender equality.

## CONCLUSION

The aim of this chapter was to examine the preferences of intimacy and obligations of older people in their construction of LAT relationships. The study results show that, in addition to the importance of having a home of their own, the coordination of time, activities, resources, and social relations are of vital significance for older adults in LAT relationships. The labeling of the LAT relationship is flexible, which means that partners can choose based on the context how they would like to appear, as singles or married. The relationship also enables the partners to actively establish limits for the relationship and recreate them continuously. Furthermore, the study shows how important autonomy is in the relationship, especially for women, and how varied this protection of boundaries can be.

The LAT relations of older people contain considerable potential for support and care, though in comparison with more institutionalized relationships, such as marriage, the caring contract cannot be taken for granted. The LAT partner is the highest rated provider of care and support, especially by men, but because the relationship is based on more voluntary commitments between partners, one cannot demand or assume that the partner will provide care in old age. This poses particular challenges to the welfare state in terms of opportunities to demand care efforts from relatives.

Our empirical material is based on interviews and questionnaires with older people living in Sweden. This of course restricts our conclusions in terms of generalizability. The Swedish welfare model is, as mentioned earlier, highly individualistic, and the state bears the primary responsibility for elderly care provision, which is of crucial importance for older people's courses of action. Therefore, there is a need for wider comparative studies examining LAT relations in different sociopolitical contexts and how LAT partners negotiate illness, disability, and care based on available formal support and care options. Future research also must incorporate longitudinal study designs and dyadic approaches to investigate how LAT relationships are established and negotiated, how long they typically last, and what causes them to be terminated.

Older people have for a long time been left out of the extensive research on changes in intimate relationships and family life. This applies not only to new forms of close relationships, such as LAT relations, but also to changes in these established relationship forms. It is highly likely that future generations will place new demands on the reconciliation of intimacy and autonomy also within the context of marital relations, and therefore there is reason to assume that we can learn a lot from how LAT partners construct their relations

# REFERENCES

Beck, U. (1998). The cosmopolitan manifesto. *New Statesman, 127*, 28–31.

Bengtson, V. L., Rosenthal, C., & Burton, L. (1990). Families and aging: Diversity and heterogeneity. In R. H. Binstock & L. K. George (Eds.), *Handbook of aging and the social sciences* (3rd ed., pp. 263–287). New York, NY: Academic Press.

Borell, K., & Ghazanfareeon Karlsson, S. (2003). Reconceptualising intimacy and ageing: Living apart together. In S. Arber, K. Davidson & J. Ginn (Eds.), *Gender and ageing: Changing roles and relationships* (pp. 47–62). Buckingham, England: Open University Press.

Burgess, E. W. (1926). The family as a unity of interacting personalities. *The Family, 7*, 3–9.

Caradec, V. (1996). *Les formes de la vie conjugale des "jeunes" couple "âgés"* [The forms of conjugal life of young couples ages]. *Population, 51*, 897–928. http://dx.doi. org/10.2307/1534359

Carstensen, L. L., Isaacowitz, D. M., & Charles, S. T. (1999). Taking time seriously. A theory of socioemotional selectivity. *American Psychologist, 54*, 165–181. http://dx.doi.org/10.1037/0003-066X.54.3.165

Castells, M. (2011). *The power of identity: The information age: Economy, society and culture* (Vol. 2). Chichester, England: Wiley-Blackwell.

Daly, M. (2005). Changing family life in Europe: Significance for state and society. *European Societies, 7*, 379–398. http://dx.doi.org/10.1080/14616690500194001

De Jong Gierveld, J. (2004). Remarriage, unmarried cohabitation, living apart together: Partner relationships following bereavement or divorce. *Journal of Marriage and Family, 66*, 236–243. http://dx.doi.org/10.1111/j.0022-2445.2004.00017.x

Duncan, S., & Phillips, M. (2011). People who live apart together (LATs): New family form or just a stage? *International Review of Sociology, 21*, 513–532. http://dx.doi.org/10.1080/03906701.2011.625660

Dunkel-Schetter, C., & Bennett, T. L. (1990). Differentiating the cognitive and behavioral aspects of social support. In B. R. Sarason, G. Sarason, & G. R. Pierce (Eds.), *Social support: An interactional view* (pp. 297–318). New York, NY: Wiley.

Ermisch, J., & Seidler, T. (2009). Living apart together. In M. Brynin & J. Ermisch (Eds.), *Changing relationships* (pp. 28–42). London, England: Routledge.

Esping-Andersen, G. (1990). *Three worlds of welfare capitalism*. Cambridge, England: Polity Press.

Espvall, M. (2008). From obligations to negotiations: Reciprocity and reflexivity in informal financial support. *European Journal of Social Work, 11*, 355–367. http://dx.doi.org/10.1080/13691450802075717

Espvall, M., & Dellgran, P. (2008). I skuggan av välfärdsstaten [In the shadow of the welfare state]. In B. Halleröd & A. Grönlund (Eds.), *Jämställdhetens pris* [The price of gender equality] (pp. 247–264). Umeå, Sweden: Borea.

Espvall, M., & Dellgran, P. (2010). Can we count on each other? Reciprocity and conflicts in financial support in Sweden. *International Journal of Social Welfare, 19*, 84–94. http://dx.doi.org/10.1111/j.1468-2397.2008.00615.x

Finch, J., & Mason, J. (1993). *Negotiating family responsibilities*. New York, NY: Tavistock/Routledge. http://dx.doi.org/10.4324/9780203393208

Funk, L. M., & Kobayashi, K. M. (2014). From motivations to accounts: An interpretive analysis of "living apart together" relationships in mid- to later-life couples. *Journal of Family Issues*. Advance online publication. http://dx.doi.org/10.1177/0192513X14529432

Ghazanfareeon Karlsson, S. (2006). *Tillsammans men var för sig—Om särboendere- lationer bland äldre kvinnor och män i Sverige* [Together but still apart. On LAT-relations among older women and men in Sweden]. Doctoral dissertation, Umeå Universitet, Umeå, Sweden.

Ghazanfareeon Karlsson, S., & Borell, K. (2002). Intimacy and autonomy, gender and ageing: Living apart together. *Ageing International, 27*, 11–26. http://dx.doi.org/10.1007/s12126-002-1012-2

Ghazanfareeon Karlsson, S., & Borell, K. (2005). A home of their own: Women's boundary work in LAT-relationships. *Journal of Aging Studies, 19*, 73–84. http://dx.doi.org/10.1016/j.jaging.2004.03.008

Ghazanfareeon Karlsson, S., Johansson, S., Gerdner, A., & Borell, K. (2007). Caring while living apart. *Journal of Gerontological Social Work, 49*, 3–27. http://dx.doi.org/10.1300/J083v49n04_02

Giddens, A. (1992). *The transformation of intimacy: Sexuality, love and eroticism in modern societies.* Cambridge, England: Polity Press.

Gonzales-Lopez, M., & Solsona-Pairo, M. (2000). Households and families: Changing living arrangements and gender relations. In S. Duncan & B. Pfau-Effinger (Eds.), *Gender, economy and culture in the European Union* (pp. 49–86). London, England: Routledge.

Haskey, J. (2005). Living arrangements in contemporary Britain: Having a partner who usually lives elsewhere and living apart together (LAT). *Population Trends, 122*, 35–45.

Haskey, J., & Lewis, J. (2006). Living apart together in Britain: context and meaning. *International Journal of Law in Context, 2*, 37–48. http://dx.doi.org/10.1017/S1744552306001030

Hochschild, A., & Machung, A. (1989). *The second shift: Working parents and the revolutions at home.* New York, NY: Viking.

Iwasawa, M. (2004). Partnership transition in contemporary Japan: Prevalence of childless non-cohabiting couples. *The Japanese Journal of Population, 2*, 76–92.

Kaye, L. W., & Applegate, J. S. (1990). *Men as caregivers to the elderly. Understanding and aiding unrecognized family support.* Lexington, MA: Lexington Books.

Kohli, M., & Künemund, H. (2003). Intergenerational transfers in the family. In V. L. Bengtson & A. Lowenstein (Eds.), *Global aging and challenges to families* (pp. 123–142). New York, NY: Walter deGruyter.

Larsson, K., & Thorslund, M. (2002). Does gender matter? Differences in patterns of informal support and formal services in a Swedish urban elderly population. *Research on Aging, 24*, 308–336. http://dx.doi.org/10.1177/0164027502243002

Lennartsson, C., & Heimerson, I. (2012). Elderly people's health. Health in Sweden: The National Public Health Report 2012. Chapter 5. *Scandinavian Journal of Public Health, 40*(Suppl. 9), 95–120. http://dx.doi.org/10.1177/1403494812459468

Levin, I. (2004). Living apart together: A new family form. *Current Sociology, 52*, 223–240. http://dx.doi.org/10.1177/0011392104041809

Milan, A., & Peters, A. (2003). Couples living apart. *Canadian Social Trends, 69*, 2–6.

Palme, J., Bergmark, A., Bäckman, O., Estrada, F., Fritzell, J., Lundberg, O., . . . Szebehely, M., & the Swedish Welfare Commission. (2003). A welfare balance sheet for the 1990s. Final report of the Swedish Welfare Commission. *Scandinavian Journal of Public Health, 60*(Suppl.), 7–143.

Reimondos, A., Evans, A., & Grey, E. (2011). Living-apart-together (LAT) relationships in Australia. *Family Matters, 87*, 43–55.

Reis, H. T. (2001). Relationship experiences and emotional well-being. In C. D. Ryff & B. H. Singer (Eds.), *Emotion, social relationships, and health* (pp. 56–86). New York, NY: Oxford University Press. http://dx.doi.org/10.1093/acprof:oso/9780195145410.003.0003

Reis, H. T., & Patrick, B. C. (1996). Attachment and intimacy: Component processes. In E. T. Higgins & A. W. Kruglanski (Eds.), *Social psychology: Handbook of basic principles* (pp. 523–563). New York, NY: Guilford Press.

Robards, J., Evandrou, M., Falkingham, J., & Vlachantoni, A. (2012). Marital status, health and mortality. *Maturitas, 73*, 295–299. http://dx.doi.org/10.1016/j.maturitas.2012.08.007

Schneider, N. F. (1996). Partnerschaften mit getrennten Haushalten in den neuen und alten Bundesländern [Partnerships with separate households in the new and old states]. In W. Bien (Ed.), *Familie an der Schwelle zum neuen Jahrtausend* [Family at the dawn of the new millennium] (pp. 88–97). Opladen, Germany: Leske und Budrich.

SOU. (2000:3). *Välfärd vid vägskäl* [Welfare at crossroads]. Stockholm, Sweden: Socialdepartementet.

Sundström, G., & Ángeles Tortosa, M. (2010). Tills döden skiljer oss åt—eller? [Till death do us part—or?]. *Välfärd, 4*, 16–18.

Svallfors, S. (2011). A bedrock of support? Trends in welfare state attitudes in Sweden, 1981–2010. *Social Policy and Administration, 45*, 806–825. http://dx.doi.org/10.1111/j.1467-9515.2011.00796.x

Szebehely, M. (2005). *Anhörigas betalda och obetalda äldreomsorgsinsatser. Forskarrapport till Jämställdhetspolitiska utredningen* [Paid and unpaid informal care. Research Report 66 to Government Commission on Gender Equity]. Stockholm, Sweden: Fritzes.

Tornstam, L. (1996). Caring for the elderly: Introducing the theory of gerotranscendence as a supplementary frame of reference for caring for the elderly. *Scandinavian Journal of Caring Sciences, 10*, 144–150. http://dx.doi.org/10.1111/j.1471-6712.1996.tb00327.x

Upton-Davis, K. (2012). Living apart together relationships (LAT): Severing intimacy from obligation. *Gender Issues, 29*, 25–38. http://dx.doi.org/10.1007/s12147-012-9110-2

Winfield, F. (1985). *Commuter marriages: Living together, apart.* New York, NY: Columbia University Press.

# 5

# SAME-SEX RELATIONSHIPS IN MIDDLE AND LATE ADULTHOOD

BOZENA ZDANIUK AND CHRISTINE SMITH

Close and intimate relationships become increasingly important as we age (AARP, 2004; Li & Fung, 2011). However, developmental models of midlife do not tend to address the experiences of lesbians and gay men that could strengthen or weaken their relationships (Howell & Beth, 2004). Howell and Beth (2004) suggested, for example, that earlier experiences of coming out may help lesbians and gay men develop strengths such as personal awareness and independence that they use in the aging process. King and Orel (2012), however, posited that gay men over 50 who experienced stigma and marginalization and have internalized these messages are more hidden and hard to reach, while Gurevitch (2000) indicated that midlife lesbians may have community support for visibility and authenticity but also suffer the loss of heterosexual privilege. Thus, the experiences of lesbians and gay men at midlife may be unique—both from the heterosexual population and from one another.

The extant scholarship on older lesbian and gay Americans has focused on aspects unrelated to their romantic relationships and has been summarized

http://dx.doi.org/10.1037/14897-006
*Couple Relationships in the Middle and Later Years: Their Nature, Complexity, and Role in Health and Illness*,
J. Bookwala (Editor)

in a variety of sources (e.g., Averett & Jenkins, 2012; Grant, Koskovich, Frazer, & Bjerk, 2010; Hunter, 2005; Kimmel, Rose, & David, 2006). Concurrently, research on same-sex couples has been increasingly published since the mid-1990s (see Kurdek, 1995, 2005; Peplau & Fingerhut, 2007) but seldom has examined specific age groups. Consequently, research on mid- and late-life same-sex couples is still scarce. In this chapter, we summarize what is known specifically about older same-sex couples' relationships while incorporating the findings about aging lesbians and gay men as well as findings from broader same-sex couples' research to inform our analysis.

## PREVALENCE AND INCREASED VISIBILITY OF MID- AND LATE-LIFE SAME-SEX COUPLES

It is estimated that there are 1 million to 3 million LGB (lesbian, gay, and bisexual) people age 65 or older (Fredriksen-Goldsen & Muraco, 2010; Jacobson & Grossman, 1996) and 2 million to 8 million LGB baby boomers age 50 or older (Lee & Quam, 2013) in the United States. Additionally, estimates suggest that approximately 44% of lesbians and 28% of gay men cohabit in same-sex partnerships (Black, Gates, Sanders, & Taylor, 2000). The 2000 U.S. Census reported almost 600,000 households of same-sex couples in the United States with about the same number of male–male and female–female relationships (Gates & Ost, 2004). About 14% of such couples included at least one Black partner and 16% at least one Hispanic partner. The number of census-reported same-sex couples grew by 30% in the following 5 years, which is a sharp increase when compared with the increase of the general population of only 6% in the same time span (Gates, 2006). Gates attributed this increase to same-sex couples becoming more visible and more willing to report their relationship as the social attitudes toward them change. In light of the growing visibility of same-sex couples, it is vital to study this important demographic.

## COMPARING SAME-SEX AND HETEROSEXUAL COUPLES

A growing body of research has examined lesbian and gay male couples, much of it comparing them with heterosexual couples (Kitzinger & Coyle, 1995). The comparison with heterosexual couples is often used to normalize lesbian and gay relationships as similar to heterosexual relationships. However, no matter how similar, lesbian and gay couples lack the social, legal, and religious support that heterosexual couples receive (Kitzinger & Coyle, 1995). They may receive less family support as well (Kurdek, 2004a, 2005). Additionally, lesbians and gay males may lack role models, both as individuals regarding how to function as a sexual minority in the world, and as members of a healthy couple (Read, 2009). There are few media images of midlife or older gay and lesbian couples, and unless one is immersed in a gay or lesbian community, there may be few opportunities to interact with other same-sex couples. With a number of states legalizing marriage equality, and with the recent U.S. Supreme Court ruling, attitudes and experiences may be changing. Thus, this area of research is an evolving one.

## Relationship Formation

Studies on the qualities lesbian and gay people seek in potential partners are generally similar to studies of the heterosexual population. All three groups seek shared values, affection, and trustworthiness. Regardless of sexual orientation, women emphasize more the importance of personality, whereas men emphasize the importance of physical characteristics (for reviews, see Peplau & Fingerhut, 2007; Peplau & Spalding, 2000). Very few studies have analyzed age as a factor or looked specifically at midlife or older lesbians and gay men who seek sexual/romantic partners. One study indicated that as lesbians grow older, they are less likely to offer and ask for physical attractiveness in their personal ads (Smith, 2006). The same study also found that lesbians over 40 were most likely to offer honesty and tend to seek partners who are of similar age or younger. In their study of lesbian dating and courtship, Rose and Zand (2002) interviewed women in their twenties and thirties and in midlife (40–65 years) and concluded that midlife lesbians did not like to waste time on prolonged aimless dating. Compared with younger lesbians, they were more likely to ask for a date and to initiate physical intimacy because they viewed dating as having a goal of an ensuing serious relationship, and with this goal in mind, they expressed concern about the "attachment worthiness" of potential partners.

Green (2004) listed a number of risk factors affecting the development of same-sex relationships: (a) homophobia (internalized and external), (b) lack of a normative and legal template for same-sex couples, and (c) lower levels of family support. In fact, in a qualitative study of 40 committed same-sex couples of various ages (Rostosky, Riggle, Gray, & Hatton, 2007), only one third perceived their family as supportive of their sexual orientation and as welcoming to their partner. Because of the cohort effect (middle-aged and older couples belonging to cohorts characterized by higher experiences of homophobia), older couples are more likely to experience such additional burdens.

## Coming Out Later in Life

Although precise rates are difficult to establish, there are some indications that a substantive number of lesbians and gay men come out in midlife or later, many of them after being in previous heterosexual marriages. A study using a large national sample (Bryant & Demian, 1994) reported that 27% of lesbians and 19% of gay men were formerly in heterosexual marriages. In studies with smaller samples, 27% of the older lesbians (Kehoe, 1989) and 20% of gay men (Berger, 1982) reported being previously married. There is also evidence that women arrive at the milestones toward lesbian self-identification later in their lives than gay men (Floyd & Bakeman, 2006). In a study of 73 lesbians who were at least 50 years old, Tully (1988) found that one in five (22%) reported being over 40 years of age when they first had sex with another woman. Recent work on sexual fluidity in women would suggest that same-sex attraction as a new development in midlife is more likely to be associated with lesbian women's than gay men's coming out (Diamond, 2012). Thus, one or both partners in the lesbian mid- or late-life relationship may be undergoing not only the aftermath of divorce, but also an intense process of new sexual identity formation (Jensen, 1999; Kitzinger & Wilkinson, 1995).

**Relationship Maintenance**

Research has suggested that same-sex couples are largely similar to heterosexual couples in their development and maintenance of commitment (Kurdek, 2005; Peplau & Fingerhut, 2007). To what degree such similarities hold for midlife and older couples requires further research. Blando (2003) argues that older gay and lesbian couples might face some unique circumstances. For example, when both partners are equally out, they can use their "outing" behavior and seek out gay/lesbian networks as a means to strengthen their relationship (Haas & Stafford, 1998; Lasala, 2000). Furthermore, the lack of well-established social scripts for older same-sex couples provides opportunity for more within-couple bonding while facing social stigma and more flexibility in roles and relationship functioning (de Vries, 2007).

**Relationship Satisfaction, Role Allocation, and Conflict Resolution**

Some studies have found that self-reported relationship quality and satisfaction are similar among lesbian, gay male, and heterosexual couples (Kurdek, 2005; Roisman, Clausell, Holland, Fortuna, & Elieff, 2008). Others have found that lesbian couples report higher levels of relationship satisfaction, less conflict, and more partner support than either heterosexual or gay male couples (Metz, Rosser, & Strapko, 1994; Meuwly, Feinstein, Davila, Nunez, & Bodenmann, 2013). In a five-year longitudinal study of predictors of relationship outcomes, lesbian couples reported higher levels of intimacy than did heterosexual and gay male couples (Kurdek 1998). Because this study was longitudinal, many of the couples at Year 5 were in midlife, given that the heterosexual participants were in their middle 30s and the lesbian and gay participants were in their early 40s when the study began.

One area of particular interest for research in examining lesbian and gay male relationships has been the issue of gender equality. Because both members of the couple are of the same sex, partners typically do not fall into traditional gender roles. Gay male and lesbian couples are more likely to value equality in the relationship than are heterosexual couples (Kurdek, 2004b); this is especially true for lesbian couples. Additionally, gay male and lesbian couples are more likely to divide household labor evenly (Goldberg, 2013; Kurdek, 2005, 2006). However, Sutphin (2010) found that similar to heterosexual couples, factors such as education, income, and hours worked outside the home impacted the division of labor.

Several studies have examined conflict resolution in couples across the lifespan. Same-sex couples tend to use more positive and effective communication styles during a conflict than their heterosexual counterparts (Gottman et al., 2003; Kurdek, 2005; Metz et al., 1994). Focusing specifically on midlife couples, Mackey, Diemer, and O'Brien (2000) studied gay male, lesbian, and heterosexual couples with a mean age of 57 who had been together an average of 30 years. They found that lesbian couples reported more openness and honesty in talking to partners than did heterosexual or gay male couples. For all couples, expression of physical affection, absence of major conflict, and a sense of fairness in the relationship predicted better relationship quality.

A number of studies have examined partner violence in same-sex couples. More research exists on interpersonal violence in lesbian relationships than in gay male relationships (Baker, Buick, Kim, Moniz, & Nava, 2013). For example, Balsam and Szymanski (2005) found that 40% of their sample of lesbian and bisexual women had been physically or sexually violent toward a female partner and 44% had experienced physical or sexual violence from a female partner in their lifetime. In addition, over 25% of women currently in a romantic relationship were victims of physical or sexual violence in the past year. In a study of gay men, Landolt and Dutton (1997) found that 40% reported one member of the couple had committed one or more acts of violence in the past year. A more recent study that included both gay men and lesbians found lower rates of violence, with about 17% of the sample reporting that they had been victims of same-sex partner violence and approximately 9% reporting that they perpetrated violence against a same-sex partner in their lifetime (Carvalho, Lewis, Derlega, Winstead, & Viggiano, 2011).

Studies that have compared rates of interpersonal violence among same-sex and heterosexual couples generally find similar or higher rates among same-sex couples (Balsam, Rothblum, & Beauchaine, 2005; Drabble, Trocki, Hughes, Korcha, & Lown, 2013; Messinger, 2011). Reasons for the higher levels may be increased alcohol use and abuse among lesbians and gay men (Drabble et al., 2013; Klostermann, Kelley, Milletich, & Mignone, 2011), minority stress (Carvalho et al., 2011), higher rates of childhood abuse (Fortunata & Kohn, 2003), and feelings of disempowerment that may result in attempts to control those who may expose vulnerabilities (McKenry, Serovich, Mason, & Mosack, 2006).

## Sexuality

Sexual satisfaction tends to be related to overall relationship satisfaction in lesbian and gay male couples (Biss & Horne, 2005; Eldridge & Gilbert, 1990; Mackey et al., 2000). However, what might lead to sexual satisfaction may differ for gay male and lesbian couples. As Kitzinger and Coyle (1995) noted, lesbian and gay males' sexual relationships may not conform to a heterosexual model, with gay men having more frequent sex and lesbians less frequent. A number of studies suggest gay male couples may be less likely to be monogamous than lesbian or heterosexual couples, and these findings seem to hold for gay male couples in midlife and late life (Gotta et al., 2011; Green, Bettinger, & Zacks, 1996). Bonello and Cross (2009) interviewed eight gay men (average age of 42) who have sex outside of their primary romantic relationship and found that it satisfied their need for sexual variety, while emotional bonding was reserved for their partners. Parsons, Starks, Gamarel, and Grov (2012) found that 52.8% of the gay male couples in their study, many of whom were in midlife, had monogamous relationships, with the rest having varied nonmonogamous patterns. They found that sexual arrangement was not related to sexual satisfaction or communication in the couples, although monogamous men had higher rates of sexual jealousy. Hoff, Beougher, Chakravarty, Darbes, and Neilands (2010) found no differences in relationship satisfaction among monogamous and nonmonogamous gay male couples with an average age of 41 and found their sexual arrangements were created to strengthen their relationship.

As Peplau and Fingerhut (2007) reported, much discussion has ensued regarding the low level of sex in lesbian relationships. Research in the 1980s documented the experience of "lesbian bed death," the idea that over time, lesbian couples have decreasing amounts of sex and, eventually, no sex at all (Nichols, 2004). This suggests that midlife lesbian couples are having increasingly infrequent sexual activity. Nichols discussed a survey of lesbian and heterosexual women (no ages reported) that found that lesbian couples did have a slightly lower level of frequency of sex than did heterosexual couples, although both had sex on average about once a week. As Bridges and Horne (2007) noted, decrease in sexual desire or frequency does not necessarily mean decrease in overall sexual satisfaction in a relationship. They found that a discrepancy between partners in the amount of sex desired, rather than frequency, predicted lower sexual satisfaction. Their findings also suggest that being in the earlier stages of a relationship was related to greater sexual satisfaction, suggesting that sexual satisfaction may be lower for women who are older or are in long-term relationships. Indeed, Bridges and Horne found that for their coupled lesbian participants ages 18 to 70, sexual satisfaction decreased with age.

For all couples, having children tends to decrease frequency of sexual activity and sexual satisfaction. Huebner, Mandic, Mackaronis, Beougher, and Hoff (2012) interviewed gay male couples (mean age of 45) who were actively parenting and found that the importance of sex declined when they became parents, as did the number of extrarelationship partners. Farr, Forssell, and Patterson (2010) reported that lesbian parents have the least amount of sex and gay male parents the most, with heterosexual parents in the middle. However, gay fathers have less sex than do gay men who are not fathers (Huebner et al., 2012).

## Factors Affecting Relationship Longevity

On the basis of the Rusbult (1983) identity model, research on the longevity of heterosexual couples has identified several main predictors of lasting relationships: positive feelings of love and relationship satisfaction, level of investment into the relationship, social and legal barriers to relationship dissolution, and availability of better alternatives. In general, same-sex couples' longevity is predicted by the same set of factors. For example, Beals, Impett, and Peplau (2002) found that all those factors predicted relationship stability among lesbian couples, although less variance was explained by the model than in heterosexual couples. It should be noted, however, that the study included a wide range of ages, and so it is unclear how this model fits midlife and older couples.

## Relationship Dissolution

Even though divorce statistics are not available for same-sex couples, research has indicated that, in general, same-sex couples are more likely to break up than heterosexual couples (Blumstein & Schwartz, 1983; Lau, 2012). Kurdek (1998) reported that in his prospective study spanning 5 years, 7% of heterosexual married couples, 14% of gay couples, and 16% of lesbian couples dissolved their relationship. These higher rates of relationship dissolution are at least in part attributable to same-sex couples reporting fewer barriers to breaking up than heterosexual couples (Kurdek, 1998, 2004a). Ongoing normalization of same-sex couples may lead to increased similarity to heterosexual couples in all aspects, including social structures that keep partners together. A more recent study, using longitudinal data to compare heterosexual married couples and same-sex couples who are married or in marriage-like committed relationships, found no difference in breakup rates for couples (M. J. Rosenfeld, 2014).

A unique outcome of same-sex couples' breakup is keeping an ex-partner as a close friend. Harkless and Fowers (2005) compared heterosexual males and females, gay men, and lesbians, the majority of whom were 35 or older, on their attitudes toward postbreakup connectedness and actual interactions with ex-partners. They found that both lesbians and gay men were more interested in keeping connection with their ex-partners and maintained more interactions and close ties with their ex-partners than heterosexual women and men. The authors explain this phenomenon as motivated by strong desire to maintain powerful bonds created during past relationships as a protection against surrounding homophobia and heterosexism.

## CAREGIVING

As couples age, there is an increasing likelihood that one member of the partnership may become a caregiver for the other partner who has become seriously ill or disabled. Cohen and Murray (2007) suggested that lesbian and gay caregivers might be less likely to use community agencies providing formal care because of real or perceived homophobia from those agencies. Coon (2007) reported that caregivers of gays and lesbians who are middle-aged or older might face increased stress and experience lower quality of life as a result of discriminatory policies. Fredriksen-Goldsen, Kim, Muraco, and Mincer (2009) studied older lesbian, gay, and bisexual chronically ill care recipients and their caregivers (36 dyads), half of whom were same-sex couples. They found that the perceived social discrimination predicted levels of depression for both the care recipient and caregiver; this link was mitigated by better relationship quality (but only for the care recipient). In examining caregiving by partners in gay male, lesbian, and heterosexual couples, Leppel (2008) found that women with disabled female partners and men with disabled partners (male or female) worked fewer hours than those without a disabled partner, whereas women with a disabled male partner worked more hours. The number of hours worked may reflect the gendered economic realities of caregiving—that men tend to make more money, so male caregivers can reduce hours, whereas female caregivers must increase hours to make up for lost male income. For lesbian couples, caregivers may be less dependent on the income of their partner, so they may also reduce their own hours of work for caregiving. In terms of health and well-being, Hash (2006) found that midlife and older gay and lesbian caregivers of chronically ill partners reported physical and emotional strain during caregiving as well as loneliness and depression during postcaregiving bereavement.

As D. Rosenfeld, Bartlam, and Smith (2012) noted, many gay men died during the height of the HIV/AIDS crisis in the late 1980s, and as a result, current gay male baby boomers lost many in their cohort. These experiences have had a profound impact on their life course. Additionally, many of these men are now aging with HIV, given the high incidence of infection among gay men 47 to 65 years old; some have been living with HIV for years, whereas others are newly infected. Karpiak (2008) reported that in 2005, about one third of all AIDS cases in major cities such as Los Angeles, San Francisco, and New York were men 50 years of age and older. Thus, some midlife men may be caring for partners who have HIV/AIDS. Wight, Aneshensel, and LeBlanc (2003) examined gay men who were caring for a friend or partner with HIV. Forty-one percent of caregivers were also living with HIV. Caregivers were likely to experience emotional distress if they felt overloaded by caregiving demands, experienced high levels of AIDS alienation/stigma, and were concerned about finances. Among HIV-positive caregivers, their own poor health influenced their emotional distress. Land, Hudson, and Stiefel (2003) found that caregivers with HIV had higher levels of depression than caregivers without HIV. Rosengard and Folkman (1997) found that when caregivers of partners with HIV perceived little social support for caregiving, they felt less socially integrated, felt highly burdened, and reported the most suicidal ideation.

## CLINICAL AND POLICY APPLICATIONS

Midlife and late-life same-sex couples are uniquely shaped by social policies and attitudes. Progress in legalizing same-sex marriages is likely to affect such couples in ways that will not be fully known for quite some time. The majority of gay men and lesbians are strongly in favor of extending legal rights to marry to same-sex couples. In a 2001 national survey (Kaiser Family Foundation, 2001), three quarters of lesbian and gay respondents said that they would like to be able to marry. A more recent survey of LGBT (lesbian, gay, bisexual, and transgender) individuals in the United States by the Pew Research Center (2013) found that 94% of LGBT adults favored same-sex marriage. The impact of age on such attitudes was not assessed, however. In the 2013 Pew Research Center survey, 39% of LGBT respondents also reported that the issue of marriage has drawn attention from other issues relevant to the LGBT community. In Averett, Yoon, and Jenkins's (2012) study of older lesbians' sexuality, the majority of those participants who expressed their opinion had negative attitudes toward marriage while asserting that same-sex couples should have a right to marry if they choose. Despite such diverse ideological approaches to the institution of marriage, there is already some indication that same-sex legal marriage may benefit middle-aged and older aged spouses. For example, marriage may provide health protection beyond that provided by domestic partnership or other forms of close relationships. In a sample of middle-aged and older gay men, Wight, LeBlanc, de Vries, and Detels (2012) found that being legally married significantly protected members of the couple from the adverse mental health impact of minority stress (in this case, stigma related to perceived sexual orientation and excessive HIV bereavements) in combination with aging stress (loss of independence and financial concerns).

## Couples' Counseling

It is critical that counselors make themselves aware of the toll that social stigmatization and discrimination exert on the relationship functioning in same-sex couples. Bepko and Johnson (2000) listed four factors influencing same-sex couples' functioning: (a) homophobia and heterosexism, (b) gender norms, (c) issues around coming out to others, and (d) social support from family of origin and family of choice. With these factors in mind, counselors must have knowledge about possible cohort effects when addressing the internalized and external homophobia affecting couples seeking help, with late-life couples being possibly more and differently affected by homophobia than midlife couples. For example, awareness of gender norms may help when addressing the uniquely lesbian issue of "fusion," defined as excessive closeness. Even though fusion is less of an issue with older coupled lesbians (Greene, Causby, & Miller, 1999), it may still need to be addressed in middle-aged lesbian couples. It is important to remember that norms for closeness are largely based on heterosexual standards, and greater closeness between two female lovers may not be dysfunctional. Ackbar and Senn (2010) proposed dividing closeness into positive (intimacy and caregiving) and negative (intrusiveness) and only consider excessive intrusiveness as problematic in lesbian relationships.

## Relationship Violence

Midlife and older gays and lesbians in abusive relationships may have little access to counseling because services for domestic violence victims are aimed primarily at heterosexual women. Lesbians who are victims of interpersonal violence may have access to those services. However, as Simpson and Helfrich (2007) noted, lesbians may experience barriers to services including heterosexist attitudes by service providers and a lack of commitment to serving lesbian clients. Gay men who experience domestic violence also may have fewer options for services such as shelter, counseling, and legal services (Hines & Douglas, 2011).

No specific research exists on relationship violence in midlife same-sex couples. A small but increasing literature exists on domestic violence in midlife relationships for heterosexual couples that may be applicable, although most of it focuses on heterosexual women. In Vickerman and Margolin's (2008) community sample of heterosexuals, physical violence decreased over time. Bookwala, Sobin, and Zdaniuk (2005) examined aggression in marital couples across the lifespan and found that with age, couples were less likely to argue heatedly and shout at each other and to hit and throw things at each other. Conversely, Akers and Kaukinen (2009) suggested that reports of domestic violence (but not necessarily the frequency of abuse) increase with victim age and may peak in midlife. They suggested that this peaking during midlife may be evident because younger victims may not trust the police, whereas older victims may have learned to cope with long-term abuse.

Domestic violence among gay elders also could be underreported. According to Peterman and Dixon (2003), many gay men and lesbians have developed high rates of independence as a result of dealing with a homophobic society, and this may lead gay elders to be isolated from the larger community and potential resources. They may fear opening up their personal lives to a hostile society, may be reluctant to seek assistance from domestic violence shelters and law enforcement, and may feel financially vulnerable if they leave a long-term abusive relationship because of the lack of legal couple protections. Gay elders may also fear that they will not be able to find another partner and so may remain with their abusers and thus in abusive relationships. Clearly, the dearth of research on interpersonal violence in long-term and midlife gay and lesbian relationships underscores the need for further research on this important issue.

## CURRENT THEORETICAL AND METHODOLOGICAL ISSUES AND FUTURE DIRECTIONS

Many studies on same-sex couples still rely on small convenience samples (Kurdek, 2005). Typically, they include all ages and provide only descriptive statistics on age. Occasionally, researchers control for age in the analyses but seldom do they examine age as a main factor. To gain better knowledge about middle-aged and older same-sex couples, this particular population needs to be targeted and studies need to use larger, more representative samples. The increasing visibility of same-sex couples that is due to the legalization of marriage and the accelerated change in societal attitudes toward same-sex relationships may allow the recruitment of larger samples in research. Moreover, the increasing ubiquity of the Internet may allow for the use of online-based methodologies to reach large numbers of middle-aged and older people involved in same-sex relationships, especially given the greater facility with technology in recent cohorts of middle-aged and older adults. Online research may also allow the recruitment of subgroups of same-sex couples, such as those belonging to ethnic minority groups or couples residing in rural area and small towns, who are typically underrepresented in research on middle-aged and older same-sex couples.

More research is needed on the impact of parenting on relationship functioning among middle-aged same-sex couples. Although midlife may be a time when heterosexual couples experience the "empty nest" or become grandparents, lesbian and gay couples may be becoming parents for the first time or may still have children living with them because many same-sex couples become parents later than heterosexual couples (Bos, Van Balen, & Van Den Boom, 2004; Gates, Badgett, Macomber, & Chambers, 2007). Current research on LGBT parenting focuses mostly on the child–parent relationship and the impact of LGBT parenting on children (Tasker, 2005), but we know very little about the impact of parenting on the relationship between the same-sex coparents. Some initial findings signal that parenting at midlife may provide opportunities to both strengthen and weaken lesbian and gay relationships in some unique ways. Biblarz and Stacey (2010) reported that lesbian and gay parents share their household, parenting, and income-earning responsibilities more equally than heterosexual couples. Same-sex couples also report more compatibility with division of labor with the partner as coparent as well as more relationship satisfaction than heterosexual coparenting couples. On the other hand, lesbian coparenting couples might be more likely to dissolve their relationship while parenting than their heterosexual counterparts (Biblarz & Stacey, 2010). A pressure to serve as role models for all same-sex families and feelings of being closely scrutinized as parents may be another source of strain on the relationship of lesbian and gay coparents (Barber, 2012; Fitzgerald, 2010). More work is needed to understand the potential positive and negative impact of parenting on relationship quality in same-sex midlife couples.

Finally, research on midlife and older same-sex couples would greatly benefit from the infusion of available life-span theories applicable to the couple experience, such as the lifespan theory of control (Heckhausen & Schulz, 1995), the socioemotional selectivity theory (Carstensen, 1995), and the theory of love over the lifespan (Bierhoff & Schmohr, 2004). The benefits may be bidirectional, allowing for a better understanding of same-sex couples as well as leading to the verification and further development of theoretical approaches.

## REFERENCES

AARP. (2004). *Boomers at midlife: The AARP life stage study, wave 3*. Washington, DC: Author. Retrieved from http://assets.aarp.org/rgcenter/general/boomers_midlife_2004.pdf

Ackbar, S., & Senn, C. Y. (2010). What's the confusion about fusion?—Differentiating positive and negative closeness in lesbian relationships. *Journal of Marital and Family Therapy, 36*, 416–430. http://dx.doi.org/10.1111/j.1752-0606.2010.00219.x

Akers, C., & Kaukinen, C. (2009). The police reporting behavior of intimate part-ner violence victims. *Journal of Family Violence, 24*, 159–171. http://dx.doi.org/10.1007/s10896-008-9213-4

Averett, P., & Jenkins, C. (2012). Review of the literature on older lesbians: Implica-tions for education, practice, and research. *Journal of Applied Gerontology, 31*, 537–561. http://dx.doi.org/10.1177/0733464810392555

Averett, P., Yoon, I., & Jenkins, C. L. (2012). Older lesbian sexuality: Identity, sexual behavior, and the impact of aging. *Journal of Sex Research, 49*, 495–507. http://dx.doi.org/10.1080/00224499.2011.582543

Baker, N. L., Buick, J. D., Kim, S. R., Moniz, S., & Nava, K. L. (2013). Lessons from examining same-sex intimate partner violence. *Sex Roles, 69*, 182–192. http://dx.doi.org/10.1007/s11199-012-0218-3

Balsam, K. F., Rothblum, E. D., & Beauchaine, T. P. (2005). Victimization over the life span: A comparison of lesbian, gay, bisexual, and heterosexual siblings. *Journal of Consulting and Clinical Psychology, 73*, 477–487. http://dx.doi.org/10.1037/0022-006X.73.3.477

Balsam, K. F., & Szymanski, D. M. (2005). Relationship quality and domestic violence in women's same-sex relationships: The role of minority stress. *Psychology of Women Quarterly, 29*, 258–269. http://dx.doi.org/10.1111/j.1471-6402.2005.00220.x

Barber, M. E. (2012). LGBT parenting. In P. Levounis, J. Drescher, & M. E. Barber (Eds.), *The LGBT casebook* (pp. 59–71). Arlington, VA: American Psychiatric Publishing.

Beals, K. P., Impett, E. A., & Peplau, L. A. (2002). Lesbians in love. *Journal of Lesbian Studies, 6*, 53–63. http://dx.doi.org/10.1300/J155v06n01_06

Bepko, C., & Johnson, T. (2000). Gay and lesbian couples in therapy: Perspectives for the contemporary family therapist. *Journal of Marital and Family Therapy, 26*, 409–419. http://dx.doi.org/10.1111/j.1752-0606.2000.tb00312.x

Berger, R. M. (1982). *Gay and gray: The older homosexual man*. Champaign: University of Illinois Press.

Biblarz, T. J., & Stacey, J. (2010). How does the gender of parents matter? *Jour-nal of Marriage and Family, 72*, 3–22. http://dx.doi.org/10.1111/j.1741-3737.2009.00678.x

Bierhoff, H., & Schmohr, M. (2004). Romantic and marital relationships. In F. R. Lang & K. L. Fingerman (Eds.), *Growing together: Personal relationships across the lifespan* (pp. 103–129). New York, NY: Cambridge University Press.

Biss, W. J., & Horne, S. G. (2005). Sexual satisfaction as more than a gendered con-cept: The roles of psychological well-being and sexual orientation. *Journal of Con-structivist Psychology, 18*, 25–38. http://dx.doi.org/10.1080/10720530590523044

Black, D., Gates, G., Sanders, S., & Taylor, L. (2000). Demographics of the gay and lesbian population in the United States: Evidence from available systematic data sources. *Demography, 37*, 139–154. http://dx.doi.org/10.2307/2648117

Blando, J. A. (2003). Twice hidden: Older gay and lesbian couples, friends, and intimacy. *Generations, 25*, 87–89.

Blumstein, P., & Schwartz, P. (1983). *American couple: Money, work, sex*. New York, NY: William Morrow.

Bonello, K., & Cross, M. C. (2009). Gay monogamy: I love you but I can't have sex with only you. *Journal of Homosexuality, 57*, 117–139. http://dx.doi.org/10.1080/00918360903445962

Bookwala, J., Sobin, J., & Zdaniuk, B. (2005). Gender and aggression in marital relationships: A life-span perspective. *Sex Roles, 52*, 797–806. http://dx.doi.org/10.1007/s11199-005-4200-1

Bos, H. M., Van Balen, F., & Van Den Boom, D. C. (2004). Experience of parenthood, couple relationship, social support, and child-rearing goals in planned lesbian mother families. *Journal of Child Psychology and Psychiatry, 45*, 755–764. http://dx.doi.org/10.1111/j.1469-7610.2004.00269.x

Bridges, S. K., & Horne, S. G. (2007). Sexual satisfaction and desire discrepancy in same sex women's relationships. *Journal of Sex & Marital Therapy, 33*, 41–53. http://dx.doi.org/10.1080/00926230600998466

Bryant, A. S., & Demian. (1994). Relationship characteristics of American gay and lesbian couples: Findings from a national survey. *Journal of Gay & Lesbian Social Services, 1*, 101–117. http://dx.doi.org/10.1300/J041v01n02_06

Carstensen, L. L. (1995). Evidence for a life-span theory of socioemotional selectivity. *Current Directions in Psychological Science, 4*, 151–156. http://dx.doi.org/10.1111/1467-8721.ep11512261

Carvalho, A. F., Lewis, R. J., Derlega, V. J., Winstead, B. A., & Viggiano, D. (2011). Internalized sexual minority stressors and same-sex intimate partner violence. *Journal of Family Violence, 26*, 501–509. http://dx.doi.org/10.1007/s10896-011-9384-2

Cohen, H. L., & Murray, Y. (2007). Older lesbian and gay caregivers: Caring for families of choice and caring for families of origin. *Journal of Human Behavior in the Social Environment, 14*, 275–298. http://dx.doi.org/10.1300/J137v14n01_14

Coon, D. W. (2007). Exploring interventions for LGBT caregivers: Issues and examples. *Journal of Gay & Lesbian Social Services, 18*, 109–128. http://dx.doi.org/10.1300/J041v18n03_07

de Vries, B. (2007). LGBT couples in later life: A study in diversity. *Generations, 31*, 18–23.

Diamond, L. M. (2012). The desire disorder in research on sexual orientation in women: Contributions of dynamical systems theory. *Archives of Sexual Behavior, 41*, 73–83. http://dx.doi.org/10.1007/s10508-012-9909-7

Drabble, L., Trocki, K. F., Hughes, T. L., Korcha, R. A., & Lown, A. E. (2013). Sexual orientation differences in the relationship between victimization and hazardous drinking among women in the National Alcohol Survey. *Psychology of Addictive Behaviors, 27*, 639–648. http://dx.doi.org/10.1037/a0031486

Eldridge, N. S., & Gilbert, L. A. (1990). Correlates of relationship satisfaction in lesbian couples. *Psychology of Women Quarterly, 14,* 43–62. http://dx.doi.org/10.1111/j.1471-6402.1990.tb00004.x

Farr, R. H., Forssell, S. L., & Patterson, C. J. (2010). Gay, lesbian, and heterosexual adoptive parents: Couple and relationship issues. *Journal of GLBT Family Studies, 6,* 199–213. http://dx.doi.org/10.1080/15504281003705436

Fitzgerald, T. (2010). Queerspawn and their families: Psychotherapy with LGBTQ families. *Journal of Gay & Lesbian Mental Health, 14,* 155–162. http://dx.doi.org/10.1080/19359700903433276

Floyd, F. J., & Bakeman, R. (2006). Coming-out across the life course: Implications of age and historical context. *Archives of Sexual Behavior, 35,* 287–296. http://dx.doi.org/10.1007/s10508-006-9022-x

Fortunata, B., & Kohn, C. S. (2003). Demographic, psychosocial, and personality characteristics of lesbian batterers. *Violence and Victims, 18,* 557–568. http://dx.doi.org/10.1891/vivi.2003.18.5.557

Fredriksen-Goldsen, K. I., Kim, H., Muraco, A., & Mincer, S. (2009). Chronically ill midlife and older lesbians, gay men, and bisexuals and their informal caregivers: The impact of the social context. *Sexuality Research & Social Policy: A Journal of the NSRC, 6,* 52–64.

Fredriksen-Goldsen, K. I., & Muraco, A. (2010). Aging and sexual orientation: A 25-year review of the literature. *Research on Aging, 32,* 372–413. http://dx.doi.org/10.1177/0164027509360355

Gates, G. J. (2006). *Same-sex couples and the gay, lesbian, bisexual population: New estimates from the American Community Survey.* Los Angeles, CA: UCLA School of Law, Williams Institute. Retrieved from http://escholarship.org/uc/item/8h08t0zf

Gates, G. J., Badgett, M. V. L., Macomber, J. E., & Chambers, K. (2007). *Adoption and foster care by gay and lesbian parents in the United States.* Los Angeles, CA: UCLA School of Law, Williams Institute. http://dx.doi.org/10.1037/e690872011-001

Gates, G. J., & Ost, J. (2004). *The gay and lesbian atlas.* Washington, DC: Urban Institute Press.

Goldberg, A. (2013). "Doing" and "undoing" gender: The meaning and division of housework in same-sex couples. *Journal of Family Theory & Review, 5,* 85–104. http://dx.doi.org/10.1111/jftr.12009

Gotta, G., Green, R. J., Rothblum, E., Solomon, S., Balsam, K., & Schwartz, P. (2011). Heterosexual, lesbian, and gay male relationships: A comparison of couples in 1975 and 2000. *Family Process, 50,* 353–376. http://dx.doi.org/10.1111/j.1545-5300.2011.01365.x

Gottman, J. M., Levenson, R. W., Swanson, C., Swanson, K., Tyson, R., & Yoshimoto, D. (2003). Observing gay, lesbian and heterosexual couples' relationships: Mathematical modeling of conflict interaction. *Journal of Homosexuality, 45,* 65–91. http://dx.doi.org/10.1300/J082v45n01_04

Grant, J. M., Koskovich, G., Frazer, M. S., & Bjerk, S. (2010). *Outing age 2010: Public policy issues affecting gay, lesbian, bisexual, and transgender elders*. New York, NY: National Gay and Lesbian Task Force Policy Institute. Retrieved from http://www.thetaskforce.org/reports

Green, R.-J. (2004). Risk and resilience in lesbian and gay couples: Comment on Solomon, Rothblum, and Balsam (2004). *Journal of Family Psychology, 18*, 290–292. http://dx.doi.org/10.1037/0893-3200.18.2.290

Green, R.-J., Bettinger, M., & Zacks, E. (1996). Are lesbian couples fused and gay male couples disengaged? Questioning gender straightjackets. In J. Laird & R.-J. Green (Eds.), *Lesbians and gays in couples and families: A handbook for therapists* (pp. 185–230). San Francisco, CA: Jossey-Bass.

Greene, K., Causby, V., & Miller, D. H. (1999). The nature and function of fusion in the dynamics of lesbian relationships. *Affilia, 14*, 78–97. http://dx.doi.org/10.1177/08861099922093527

Gurevitch, J. (2000). Filial bereavement: Midlife lesbian daughters and intersubjective thoughts. In M. R. Adelman (Ed.), *Midlife lesbian relationships: Friends, lovers, children, and parents* (pp. 49–76). New York, NY: Harrington Park Press. http://dx.doi.org/10.1300/J041v11n02_03

Haas, S. M., & Stafford, L. (1998). An initial examination of maintenance behaviors in gay and lesbian relationships. *Journal of Social and Personal Relationships, 15*, 846–855. http://dx.doi.org/10.1177/0265407598156008

Harkless, L. E., & Fowers, B. J. (2005). Similarities and differences in relational boundaries among heterosexuals, gay men, and lesbians. *Psychology of Women Quarterly, 29*, 167–176. http://dx.doi.org/10.1111/j.1471-6402.2005.00179.x

Hash, K. (2006). Caregiving and post-caregiving experiences of midlife and older gay men and lesbians. *Journal of Gerontological Social Work, 47*, 121–138. http://dx.doi.org/10.1300/J083v47n03_08

Heckhausen, J., & Schulz, R. (1995). A life-span theory of control. *Psychological Review, 102*, 284–304. http://dx.doi.org/10.1037/0033-295X.102.2.284

Hines, D. A., & Douglas, E. M. (2011). The reported availability of U.S. domestic violence services to victims who vary by age, sexual orientation, and gender. *Partner Abuse, 2*, 3–30. http://dx.doi.org/10.1891/1946-6560.2.1.3

Hoff, C. C., Beougher, S. C., Chakravarty, D., Darbes, L. A., & Neilands, T. B. (2010). Relationship characteristics and motivations behind agreements among gay male couples: Differences by agreement type and couple serostatus. *AIDS Care, 22*, 827–835. http://dx.doi.org/10.1080/09540120903443384

Howell, L. C., & Beth, A. (2004). Pioneers in our own lives: Grounded theory of lesbians' midlife development. *Journal of Women & Aging, 16*, 133–147. http://dx.doi.org/10.1300/J074v16n03_10

Huebner, D. M., Mandic, C. G., Mackaronis, J. E., Beougher, S. C., & Hoff, C. C. (2012). The impact of parenting on gay male couples' relationships, sexuality, and HIV risk. *Couple and Family Psychology: Research and Practice, 1*, 106–119. http://dx.doi.org/10.1037/a0028687

Hunter, S. (2005). *Midlife and older LGBT adults: Knowledge and affirmative practice for the social services*. New York, NY: Haworth Press.

Jacobson, S., & Grossman, A. H. (1996). Older lesbians and gay men: Old myths, new images, and future directions. In R. C. Savin-Williams & K. M. Cohen (Eds.), *The lives of lesbians, gays, and bisexuals: Children to adults* (pp. 345–373). Orlando, FL: Harcourt Brace College.

Jensen, K. L. (1999). *Lesbian epiphanies: Women coming out in later life*. New York, NY: Harrington Park Press.

Kaiser Family Foundation. (2001). *Inside-out: A report on the experiences of lesbians, gays and bisexuals in America and the public's view on issues and policies related to sexual orientation*. Menlo Park, CA: Author.

Karpiak, S. (2008). *An in-depth examination of an emerging population: Who are these older adults living with HIV?* Retrieved from http://www.health.ny.gov/diseases/aids/conferences/plenaries/docs/whoaretheseolderadults.pdf

Kehoe, M. (1989). *Lesbians over sixty speak for themselves*. New York, NY: Haworth Press.

Kimmel, D., Rose, T., & David, S. (2006). *Lesbian, gay, bisexual, and transgender aging: Research and clinical perspectives*. New York, NY: Columbia University Press.

King, S. D., & Orel, N. (2012). Midlife and older gay men living with HIV/AIDS: The influence of resiliency and psychosocial stress factors on health needs. *Journal of Gay & Lesbian Social Services, 24*, 346–370. http://dx.doi.org/10.1080/10538720.2012.721669

Kitzinger, C., & Coyle, A. (1995). Lesbian and gay couples: Speaking of difference. *The Psychologist, 6*, 64–69.

Kitzinger, C., & Wilkinson, S. (1995). Transitions from heterosexuality to lesbianism: The discursive production of lesbian identities. *Developmental Psychology, 31*, 95–104. http://dx.doi.org/10.1037/0012-1649.31.1.95

Klostermann, K., Kelley, M. L., Milletich, R. J., & Mignone, T. (2011). Alcohol and partner aggression among gay and lesbian couples. *Aggression and Violent Behavior, 16*, 115–119.

Kurdek, L. A. (1995). Lesbian and gay couples. In A. R. D'Augelli & C. J. Patterson (Eds.), *Lesbian, gay, and bisexual identities over the lifespan: Psychological perspectives* (pp. 243–261). New York, NY: Oxford University Press. http://dx.doi.org/10.1093/acprof:oso/9780195082319.003.0010

Kurdek, L. A. (1998). Relationship outcomes and their predictors: Longitudinal evidence from heterosexual married, gay cohabiting, and lesbian cohabiting couples. *Journal of Marriage and Family, 60*, 553–568. http://dx.doi.org/10.2307/353528

Kurdek, L. A. (2004a). Are gay and lesbian cohabiting couples really different from heterosexual married couples? *Journal of Marriage and Family, 66*, 880–900. http://dx.doi.org/10.1111/j.0022-2445.2004.00060.x

Kurdek, L. A. (2004b). Gay men and lesbians: The family context. In M. Coleman & L. H. Ganong (Eds.), *Handbook of contemporary families: Considering the past, contemplating the future* (pp. 96–115). Thousand Oaks, CA: Sage. http://dx.doi.org/10.4135/9781412976022.n6

Kurdek, L. A. (2005). What do we know about gay and lesbian couples? *Current Directions in Psychological Science, 14,* 251–254. http://dx.doi.org/10.1111/j.0963-7214.2005.00375.x

Kurdek, L. A. (2006). Differences between partners from heterosexual, gay, and lesbian cohabitating couples. *Journal of Marriage and Family, 68,* 509–528. http://dx.doi.org/10.1111/j.1741-3737.2006.00268.x

Land, H., Hudson, S. M., & Stiefel, B. (2003). Stress and depression among HIV-positive and HIV-negative gay and bisexual AIDS caregivers. *AIDS and Behavior, 7,* 41–53. http://dx.doi.org/10.1023/A:1022509306761

Landolt, M. A., & Dutton, D. G. (1997). Power and personality: An analysis of gay male intimate abuse. *Sex Roles, 37,* 335–359. http://dx.doi.org/10.1023/A:1025649306193

Lasala, M. C. (2000). Gay male couples. *Journal of Homosexuality, 39,* 47–71. http://dx.doi.org/10.1300/J082v39n02_03

Lau, C. W. (2012). The stability of same-sex cohabitation, different sex cohabitation, and marriage. *Journal of Marriage and Family, 74,* 973–988. http://dx.doi.org/10.1111/j.1741-3737.2012.01000.x

Lee, M. G., & Quam, J. K. (2013). Comparing supports for LGBT aging in rural versus urban areas. *Journal of Gerontological Social Work, 56,* 112–126. http://dx.doi.org/10.1080/01634372.2012.747580

Leppel, K. (2008). The relationship between hours worked and partner's disability in opposite- and same-sex couples. *Culture, Health & Sexuality, 10,* 773–785. http://dx.doi.org/10.1080/13691050802254641

Li, T., & Fung, H. (2011). The dynamic goal theory of marital satisfaction. *Review of General Psychology, 15,* 246–254. http://dx.doi.org/10.1037/a0024694

Mackey, R. A., Diemer, M. A., & O'Brien, B. A. (2000). Psychological intimacy in the lasting relationships of heterosexual and same gendered couples. *Sex Roles, 43,* 201–227. http://dx.doi.org/10.1023/A:1007028930658

McKenry, P. C., Serovich, J. M., Mason, T. L., & Mosack, K. (2006). Perpetration of gay and lesbian partner violence: A disempowerment perspective. *Journal of Family Violence, 21,* 233–243. http://dx.doi.org/10.1007/s10896-006-9020-8

Messinger, A. M. (2011). Invisible victims: Same-sex IPV in the National Violence Against Women Survey. *Journal of Interpersonal Violence, 26,* 2228–2243. http://dx.doi.org/10.1177/0886260510383023

Metz, M. E., Rosser, B. R., & Strapko, N. (1994). Differences in conflict-resolution styles among heterosexual, gay, and lesbian couples. *Journal of Sex Research, 31,* 293–308. http://dx.doi.org/10.1080/00224499409551764

Meuwly, N., Feinstein, B. A., Davila, J., Nunez, D. G., & Bodenmann, G. (2013). Relationship quality among Swiss women in opposite-sex versus same-sex romantic relationships. *Swiss Journal of Psychology, 72,* 229–233. http://dx.doi.org/10.1024/1421-0185/a000115

Nichols, M. (2004). Lesbian sexuality/female sexuality: Rethinking 'lesbian bed death.' *Sexual and Relationship Therapy*, 19, 363–371. http://dx.doi.org/10.1080/14681990412331298036

Parsons, J. T., Starks, T. J., Gamarel, K. E., & Grov, C. (2012). Non-monogamy and sexual relationship quality among same-sex male couples. *Journal of Family Psychology*, 26, 669–677. http://dx.doi.org/10.1037/a0029561

Peplau, L. A., & Fingerhut, A. W. (2007). The close relationships of lesbians and gay men. *Annual Review of Psychology*, 58, 405–424. http://dx.doi.org/10.1146/annurev.psych.58.110405.085701

Peplau, L. A., & Spalding, L. R. (2000). The close relationships of lesbians, gay men, and bisexuals. In C. Hendrick & S. S. Hendrick (Eds.), *Close relationships: A sourcebook* (pp. 110–123). Thousand Oaks, CA: Sage. http://dx.doi.org/10.4135/9781452220437.n9

Peterman, L. M., & Dixon, C. G. (2003). Domestic violence between same-sex partners: Implications for counseling. *Journal of Counseling & Development*, 81, 40–47. http://dx.doi.org/10.1002/j.1556-6678.2003.tb00223.x

Pew Research Center. (2013). *A survey of LGBT Americans: Attitudes, experiences, and values in changing times*. Retrieved from http://www.pewsocialtrends.org/2013/06/13/a-survey-of-lgbt-americans/

Read, M. M. (2009). Midlife lesbian lifeworlds: Narrative theory and sexual identity. In P. L. Hammack & B. J. Cohler (Eds.), *The story of sexual identity: Narrative perspectives on the gay and lesbian life course* (pp. 347–374). New York, NY: Oxford University Press. http://dx.doi.org/10.1093/acprof:oso/9780195326789.003.0015

Roisman, G. I., Clausell, E., Holland, A., Fortuna, K., & Elieff, C. (2008). Adult romantic relationships as contexts of human development: A multimethod comparison of same-sex couples with opposite-sex dating, engaged, and married dyads. *Developmental Psychology*, 44, 91–101. http://dx.doi.org/10.1037/0012-1649.44.1.91

Rose, S. M., & Zand, D. (2002). Lesbian dating and courtship from young adulthood to midlife. *Journal of Lesbian Studies*, 6, 85–109. http://dx.doi.org/10.1300/J155v06n01_09

Rosenfeld, D., Bartlam, B., & Smith, R. D. (2012). Out of the closet and into the trenches: Gay male baby boomers, aging, and HIV/AIDS. *The Gerontologist*, 52, 255–264. http://dx.doi.org/10.1093/geront/gnr138

Rosenfeld, M. J. (2014). Couple longevity in the era of same-sex marriage in the United States. *Journal of Marriage and Family*, 76, 905–918. http://dx.doi.org/10.1111/jomf.12141

Rosengard, C., & Folkman, S. (1997). Suicidal ideation, bereavement, HIV serostatus and psychosocial variables in partners of men with AIDS. *AIDS Care*, 9, 373–384. http://dx.doi.org/10.1080/713613168

Rostosky, S., Riggle, E. B., Gray, B. E., & Hatton, R. L. (2007). Minority stress experiences in committed same-sex couple relationships. *Professional Psychology: Research and Practice*, 38, 392–400. http://dx.doi.org/10.1037/0735-7028.38.4.392

Rusbult, C. E. (1983). A longitudinal test of the investment model: The development (and deterioration) of satisfaction and commitment in heterosexual involvements. *Journal of Personality and Social Psychology, 45*, 101–117. http://dx.doi.org/10.1037/0022-3514.45.1.101

Simpson, E. K., & Helfrich, C. A. (2007). Lesbian survivors of intimate partner violence. *Journal of Gay & Lesbian Social Services, 18*, 39–59. http://dx.doi.org/10.1300/J041v18n02_03

Smith, C. A. (2006, August). *Long walks on the beaches of Provincetown: Does age impact partner preferences in lesbians?* Paper presented at the annual convention of the American Psychological Association, New Orleans, Louisiana.

Sutphin, S. T. (2010). Social exchange theory and the division of labor in same-sex couples. *Marriage & Family Review, 46*, 191–206. http://dx.doi.org/10.1080/01494929.2010.490102

Tasker, F. (2005). Lesbian mothers, gay fathers, and their children: A review. *Journal of Developmental and Behavioral Pediatrics, 26*, 224–240. http://dx.doi.org/10.1097/00004703-200506000-00012

Tully, C. (1988). Caregiving: What do midlife lesbians view as important? *Journal of Gay & Lesbian Psychotherapy, 1*, 87–104. http://dx.doi.org/10.1300/J236v01n01_10

Vickerman, K. A., & Margolin, G. (2008). Trajectories of physical and emotional marital aggression in midlife couples. *Violence and Victims, 23*, 18–34. http://dx.doi.org/10.1891/0886-6708.23.1.18

Wight, R. G., Aneshensel, C. S., & LeBlanc, A. J. (2003). Stress buffering effects of family support in AIDS caregiving. *AIDS Care, 15*, 595–613. http://dx.doi.org/10.1080/09540120310001595096

Wight, R. G., LeBlanc, A. J., de Vries, B., & Detels, R. (2012). Stress and mental health among midlife and older gay-identified men. *American Journal of Public Health, 102*, 503–510. http://dx.doi.org/10.2105/AJPH.2011.300384

# 6

# SEXUAL INTIMACY IN MID- AND LATE-LIFE COUPLES

AMY C. LODGE AND DEBRA UMBERSON

Sex is both an integral component of—as well as a key contributor to—well-being and relationship quality in midlife and late life (DeLamater, Hyde, & Fong, 2008; Laumann et al., 2005). Thus, as Western countries experience a "graying" of their populations (Kingsberg, 2000), sexuality is particularly important for the overall quality of life of aging populations. There is little consensus in the literature, however, on how to define sexual behavior in middle and late adulthood. Whereas some research has suggested that most heterosexual mid- and late-life adults consider only penetrative, vaginal intercourse to be "real sex" (Lodge & Umberson, 2012; Waite & Das, 2010), other research has suggested that when vaginal intercourse is either not possible or desired, mid- and late-life adults redefine the meaning of sexuality to include other physically intimate experiences (e.g., kissing, holding hands, cuddling; Gott & Hinchliff, 2003b, 2003c; Lodge & Umberson, 2012). Most research, however, has measured sexuality vis-à-vis vaginal intercourse, and as a result,

http://dx.doi.org/10.1037/14897-007
*Couple Relationships in the Middle and Later Years: Their Nature, Complexity, and Role in Health and Illness,*
J. Bookwala (Editor)

we know little about other forms of sexuality in midlife and late life, including nonheterosexualities (de Vries, 2009). In this chapter we provide a broad overview of key areas of research on sexuality in midlife and late life.[1]

## OVERVIEW OF PREVIOUS LITERATURE

Sexual behavior is an important topic for several reasons. Sexual frequency (DeLamater et al., 2008; DeLamater & Moorman, 2007), sexual satisfaction (DeLamater et al., 2008; Gott & Hinchliff, 2003c), and sexual desire (Skultety, 2007), and an absence of sexual dysfunction (Laumann & Waite, 2008) are positively associated with higher levels of marital quality and relationship satisfaction. The association is likely bidirectional: Longitudinal evidence has suggested that sexual satisfaction positively influences marital quality (Yeh, Lorenz, Wickrama, Conger, & Elder, 2006), whereas individuals with higher levels of marital dissatisfaction are more likely to experience sexual dysfunction and a lack of sexual interest (Laumann & Waite, 2008).

The link between sex and mental/physical well-being is well documented. Worse mental and physical health is associated with lower levels of sexual frequency (DeLamater & Moorman, 2007), sexual satisfaction (Laumann et al., 2005), and sexual desire (Kontula & Haavio-Mannila, 2009), and more sexual dysfunction (Bancroft, 2007; Laumann & Waite, 2008). The relationship between sex and well-being is likely bidirectional: Sexual dysfunctions, for example, may both cause or exacerbate depressive symptoms at the same time that depressive symptoms may cause or exacerbate sexual dysfunction (Araujo, Durante, Feldman, Goldstein, & McKinlay, 1998). Laumann and Waite (2008) argued that one mechanism linking physical health and sexual dysfunction in midlife and late life is mental health. Poor physical health is highly correlated with diminished psychological well-being, which in turn reduces sexual desire.

### Sexual Activity and Frequency in Midlife and Late Life

Most adults continue to have sexual intercourse into late life (Gott & Hinchliff, 2003c; Lindau et al., 2007). A number of factors are predictive of sexual activity in midlife and late life, including male gender (Karraker, DeLamater, & Schwartz, 2011; Kontula & Haavio-Mannila, 2009); younger

---

[1]Unless otherwise noted, key findings and themes presented in this chapter apply to both mid- and late-life individuals, given that the distinction between the two periods of life is fluid and varies considerably across studies.

age (Karraker et al., 2011; Waite & Das, 2010); being married or partnered (Kontula & Haavio-Mannila, 2009); higher levels of education (Matthias, Lubben, Atchison, & Schweitzer, 1997); younger cohort (i.e., generation; Beckman, Waern, Gustafson, & Skoog, 2008); and for couples, male physical health (Lindau et al., 2007; Waite & Das, 2010).

Many of the factors that predict sexual activity also predict sexual frequency. For example, sexual frequency declines with age (DeLamater & Moorman, 2007; Kontula & Haavio-Mannila, 2009; Lindau et al., 2007), and longitudinal data suggest that age has a negative effect on sexual frequency beyond the effect of cohort or generation (DeLamater & Moorman, 2007), although cohort differences do matter, with more recent or younger cohorts having higher rates of sexual frequency in midlife and late life (Edwards & Booth, 1994). Some research, however, has revealed that although age is associated with a decline in vaginal and oral sex, age is not associated with frequency of kissing, hugging, caressing, and sexual touching (AARP, 2005). There is also disagreement in the literature as to whether masturbation frequency increases or decreases with age (Araujo, Mohr, & McKinlay, 2004). Physical health problems—either personal or in the partner—are also associated with lower levels of sexual frequency (DeLamater et al., 2008; DeLamater & Moorman, 2007).

Individuals with a committed partner have higher levels of sexual frequency (Kontula & Haavio-Mannila, 2009), although levels are lower for married couples compared with unmarried, committed couples (AARP, 2010). This may be because marital duration is negatively correlated with sexual frequency (Call, Sprecher, & Schwartz, 1995). Relationship and marital satisfaction are also positively associated with sexual frequency (DeLamater et al., 2008; DeLamater & Moorman, 2007). There are relatively large gender differences in sexual frequency in midlife and late life (Kontula & Haavio-Mannila, 2009), with men reporting greater frequency than women (DeLamater & Moorman, 2007). One possible reason for this gender difference is that among heterosexual couples, the male partner tends to be older and therefore may be more likely to face age-related barriers to sexual activity, negatively impacting women's sexual frequency regardless of personal age. Further, unbalanced sex ratios in late life, combined with the fact that men tend to have younger partners than women, also may mean that women are less likely to have access to a sexual partner. Men's higher rates of partnership (AARP, 2010) and gender differences in reporting (whereby men may overestimate sexual frequency and/or women may underestimate sexual frequency; Willetts, Sprecher, & Beck, 2004) may explain some of the gender difference in sexual frequency; however, these gender differences in sexual frequency hold regardless of marital or partnership status (Karraker et al., 2011).

## Sexual Attitudes in Midlife and Late Life

Traditionally, older adults have been framed as asexual or their sexual experiences have been depicted as humorous and/or repugnant (Gott, Hinchliff, & Galena, 2004). As a result, mid- and late-life individuals may view themselves as asexual and/or experience shame about their sexual desires and behaviors (Gott & Hinchliff, 2003a). However, research generally has suggested that mid- and late-life adults have positive attitudes toward sexual activity and regard sex as natural, normal, and important for personal well-being and relationship quality (AARP, 2010; Gott & Hinchliff, 2003b, 2003c). Relationship status matters for sexual attitudes: Individuals without a sexual partner are more likely to say sex is not important to them (Gott & Hinchliff, 2003b), and most mid- and late-life adults prefer to have sex within the context of a relationship, generally reporting no interest in casual sex or one-night stands (Gott & Hinchliff, 2003b).

There may be gender differences in sexual attitudes: Men are more likely than women to report that sex is important for quality of life and relationship satisfaction (AARP, 2010). Men's and women's views on sexual activity may converge with age, however. One study found that as men age they place less importance on sexual activity and more importance on emotional intimacy, whereas women consistently rate emotional intimacy as more important than sex (Wiley & Bortz, 1996). Individuals who face barriers to sexual activity (e.g., health problems) are less likely to view sex as important, although this may not be attributable to age per se, but may stem from age-related barriers to sexual activity that result in a reprioritization of sex (Gott & Hinchliff, 2003b). Finally, research on Swedish 70-year-olds has revealed that more recent or younger cohorts of older adults have more positive attitudes toward sexuality than earlier born or older cohorts (Beckman et al., 2008), which may in part reflect a shift away from cultural discourses that define older adults as asexual to cultural discourses that emphasize the importance of remaining sexually active as a marker of healthy and successful aging (Gott, 2005; Katz & Marshall, 2003).

## Sexual Satisfaction in Midlife and Late Life

Research on sexual satisfaction and sexual quality in midlife to late life has produced mixed results. Some studies have found that sexual satisfaction levels remain stable over the life course (McKinlay & Feldman, 1994), others have suggested that sex improves with age (Gullette, 2011; Vares, Potts, Gavey, & Grace, 2007), and still others have suggested that sexual satisfaction deteriorates with age (AARP, 2010). Some research has revealed that women experience declines in sexual satisfaction but men do not (Kontula

& Haavio-Mannila, 2009), whereas other research has suggested that women experience heightened levels of sexual satisfaction with age because of greater experience and a shift from sex focused on reproduction or wifely duty to sex focused on pleasure (Gott & Hinchliff, 2003c). These inconsistencies may be due to age/cohort confounds (Araujo et al., 2004); some scholars have suggested that cohort differences—not age—explain declines in sexual satisfaction (Carpenter, Nathanson, & Kim, 2009). Younger cohorts tend to use a wider range of sexual techniques than older cohorts (Edwards & Booth, 1994), and this may be adaptive as people experience age-related physical changes that interfere with the ability to have sexual intercourse. Research on Swedish 70-year-olds revealed that later born cohorts have higher levels of sexual satisfaction than earlier born cohorts (Beckman et al., 2008). Cohort differences may also explain gender differences in sexual satisfaction in late life, as women in earlier cohorts are more likely to conceptualize sex as a marital duty rather than a source of pleasure (Gott & Hinchliff, 2003c).

Other factors positively associated with sexual satisfaction include sexual frequency (AARP, 2010), relationship satisfaction (DeLamater et al., 2008), better physical and mental health (Laumann et al., 2005), and a lack of financial problems (Laumann et al., 2005). Some studies have further suggested that married people have higher levels of sexual satisfaction than single people, because married people are more likely to have the knowledge and ability needed to sexually satisfy their partner (Laumann et al., 1994).

### Sexual Desire in Midlife and Late Life

Sexual desire is a complex phenomenon that encompasses biological drives; psychological motivations; and personal and social expectations, beliefs, and values (Kingsberg, 2000). Research on sexual desire is far from definitive: Although some research has suggested that age has a negative effect on levels of sexual desire (DeLamater & Sill, 2005; Laumann et al., 2005), other research has suggested that sexual desire remains relatively constant throughout the adult life course (even into deep old age), but that a variety of social, psychological, and physical factors may prevent sexual desire from finding expression in midlife and late life (Davidson & Fennell, 2002; Kontula & Haavio-Mannila, 2009; Skultety, 2007). Kontula and Haavio-Mannila (2009) found that the "negative effect of biological aging on sexual desire disappears when people are satisfied with their sexual experience, are sexually functioning, and healthy" (p. 54).

Some research has suggested that the negative relationship between age and sexual desire is stronger for men (DeLamater & Sill, 2005) or holds only for men (Laumann et al., 2005). However, women may have lower levels of sexual desire than men (Kontula & Haavio-Mannila, 2009). Women also experience a decreased level of desire during the menopausal transition (Basson, 2005). However, it remains unclear whether these decreased levels of desire are attributable solely to menopause. For example, a loss of reproductive capacities may negatively affect women's sense of femininity and sexual identity, and thus levels of sexual desire (Kingsberg, 2000). Moreover, women who believe that the physical signs of aging make them unattractive may experience a reduced level of sexual desire (Kingsberg, 2000). Beliefs about age and appropriateness of sexual activity may also be important: For women a lack of interest in sex is associated with the belief that aging reduces sexual desire and activity (Laumann et al., 2005).

Relationship characteristics are also important for sexual desire in midlife and late life. For example, Kontula and Haavio-Mannila (2009) found that relationship duration is negatively correlated with women's sexual desire. Yet, women (DeLamater & Sill, 2005) and men (Skoog, 1996) with partners have higher levels of sexual desire than those who lack partners. This may be partly due to cultural norms about the appropriateness of sexual activity outside of relationships (Davidson & Fennell, 2002). Wood, Mansfield, and Koch (2007) found that relationship quality also matters: Postmenopausal women who are able to talk to their partners about how to facilitate their sexual desire report having more sexual desire. A lack of sexual desire is also associated with low expectations about the future viability of their current relationship for mid- and late-life women, but not men (Laumann et al., 2005). Other relationship characteristics, such as conflict and partner discrepancies in desire, may also affect levels of sexual desire (Skultety, 2007). Additional factors that have a negative effect on sexual desire include poor health (Kontula & Haavio-Mannila, 2009; Laumann et al., 2005), high blood pressure (DeLamater & Sill, 2005), depression (Laumann et al., 2005), and low income (DeLamater & Sill, 2005). Many social factors that are likely to affect sexual desire in midlife to late life have not been explored (e.g., ageism, body image and concerns about the appearance of the aging body, cultural beliefs about older adults' sexuality); qualitative research is uniquely situated to uncovering those factors, which can then be measured in future quantitative research.

**Sexual Dysfunction in Midlife and Late Life**

As part of a broader shift in the medicalization of sexuality (Tiefer, 1996), a great deal of research has focused on sexual dysfunction. Sexual dysfunction may cause depression (Araujo et al., 1998) as well as marital and relationship conflict (Rust, Golombok, & Collier, 1988) and is associated with diminished quality of life (Laumann, Paik, & Rosen, 1999). Moreover, one type of sexual dysfunction may precipitate another type: Men who experience erectile dysfunction (ED) are more likely to later report low levels of sexual desire

(Kingsberg, 2000). Many adults, however, do not discuss sexual concerns or problems with medical practitioners due to shame, embarrassment, or the belief that sexual dysfunctions are a normal part of aging (Gott et al., 2004). Further, when postmenopausal women do discuss sexual concerns with their doctors, they are typically given little useful information (Wood et al., 2007).

Data from the National Social Life, Health and Aging Project, a nationally representative sample of American adults ages 57 to 85, found that half of sexually active mid- to late-life adults experience some type of sexual problem (Lindau et al., 2007). Men are most likely to report problems maintaining an erection, lack of interest in sex, climaxing too quickly, anxiety about sexual performance, and inability to climax. For women the most commonly reported problems are lack of interest in sex, difficulty with lubrication, inability to climax, finding sex not pleasurable, and pain.

The relationship between age and sexual dysfunction is complex and differs by gender. Longitudinal analyses have revealed that for men aging is associated with an increased inability to achieve orgasm, trouble maintaining an erection, and a lack of sexual desire (Araujo et al., 2004; Feldman, Goldstein, Hatzichristou, Krane, & McKinlay, 1994; Laumann et al., 2005; Laumann & Waite, 2008). Age is less closely related to sexual dysfunction for women; lubrication difficulties become more common with advancing age for women (Laumann et al., 2005), but other sexual dysfunctions (e.g., inability to orgasm, pain, or arousal disorders) are more common among younger women (Kingsberg, 2000; Laumann et al., 2005; Laumann et al., 1999). Further, more recent cohorts of late-life men and women report fewer sexual dysfunctions than earlier born cohorts, which may be due to changes in cultural attitudes about sexuality and the liberalization of sexual conduct, among other factors (Beckman et al., 2008).

It is unclear why some types of sexual dysfunction are more prevalent with age. Although some have argued that declining testosterone levels in both men and women lead to lower levels of sexual desire (and ED for men; Bancroft, 2007) and declines in estrogen during menopause lead to decreased vaginal lubrication for women (Kingsberg, 2002), others have suggested that social factors are more important than biological factors (Laumann & Waite, 2008). For example, Laumann and Waite (2008) argued that sexual problems in midlife to late life primarily stem from stressors in multiple life domains. Further, given evidence that postmenopausal women who internalize ageist beliefs that older women are unattractive experience reductions in sexual desire (Kingsberg, 2000), similar processes may contribute to decreased vaginal lubrication. Cross-cultural research has also supported this latter position; prevalence of sexual dysfunctions varies globally (Kontula & Haavio-Mannila, 2009; Laumann et al., 2005). For example, in a global study of sexual dysfunctions among 40–80-year-olds, the prevalence of erectile and lubrication difficulties were twice as high in East and Southeast Asia as in other regions of the world (Laumann et al., 2005).

Further, Lindau et al. (2007) found that physical health is a better predictor of sexual problems than age per se. A number of studies have found that physical health problems are predictive of sexual dysfunction (Laumann & Waite, 2008; Laumann et al., 2005; McKinlay & Feldman, 1994; Wood et al., 2007). Cardiovascular disease, diabetes, prostate and breast cancers, lower urinary tract symptoms, incontinence, hypertension, and other physical health problems interfere with sexual functioning (Skultety, 2007). Medications used to treat health problems as well as surgical interventions may further interfere with sexual functioning, and some adults are reluctant to engage in sexual intercourse because of uncertainty about their abilities and whether sex will exacerbate health conditions (Steinke, 2005).

A great deal of research has demonstrated that mental health is an important predictor of sexual functioning (Bancroft, 2007; Laumann & Waite, 2008; Laumann et al., 2005). Happiness (Laumann et al., 1999) and emotional well-being (Rosen & Bachmann, 2008) are positively associated with sexual functioning, whereas depression (Laumann & Waite, 2008; McKinlay & Feldman, 1994), anger (McKinlay & Feldman, 1994), stress, anxiety, and poor self-rated mental health (Laumann & Waite, 2008) are all predictive of a range of sexual dysfunctions, including ED, lubrication difficulties, inability to orgasm, a lack of sexual interest, and sexual pain. Additionally, antidepressant medications have been linked to sexual problems, including low levels of sexual desire, ED, and inability to orgasm (Csoka & Shipko, 2006). Although the causal direction between mental health and sexual functioning is unclear, it is likely that sexual problems are both a cause and consequence of lower levels of well-being (Araujo et al., 1998).

Finally, relationship characteristics are also important for sexual functioning. Sexual dysfunctions are less common among individuals who are married or in committed relationships (Laumann & Waite, 2008; Laumann et al., 1999, 2005). For example, among 57- to 85-year-olds, married men are less likely than widowed or never married men to experience a lack of sexual pleasure and less likely to experience performance anxiety in comparison with separated or divorced men (Laumann & Waite, 2008). Among 40- to 80-year-old men, being in an uncommitted relationship is associated with erectile difficulties (Laumann et al., 2005). Similarly, among women ages 40 through 80, those who believe or worry that their current intimate relationship is unlikely to last are more likely to report an inability to orgasm (Laumann et al., 2005). Relationship satisfaction is also predictive of sexual functioning (Laumann & Waite, 2008). Women who are dissatisfied with their relationship are more likely to experience a lack of sexual pleasure and inability to orgasm, whereas men who are dissatisfied with their relationship are more likely to experience a lack of sexual interest

(Laumann & Waite, 2008). However, leaving an unsatisfactory relationship for a new, satisfying relationship may positively impact sexual functioning for both men and women (Kontula & Haavio-Mannila, 2009).

Although the literature on sexual dysfunction frames a lack of sexual desire or the inability to have sex as problematic, mid- and late-life adults may not regard these sexual changes as problematic. They may, in fact, welcome these changes, especially if sex earlier in life was not enjoyable or was coercive. Alternatively, men and women may regard sexual change as a normal part of aging. For example, Gott and Hinchliff (2003b) found that although men in their sixties regarded ED as very problematic, men in their 70s viewed ED as a normal part of aging. Thus, some mid- and late-life adults may attribute different meanings to different types of sexual "dysfunctions" than researchers do. Moreover, these meanings may vary by age, gender, and race/ethnicity. We need more research on how mid- and late-life adults experience sexual "problems" and the various meanings they attach to those experiences.

### Relationships in Midlife and Late Life

Another strand of research has focused on relationships in midlife to late life, although this research has largely ignored sexuality. In the past few decades there has been a substantial increase in the number of mid- to late-life adults who are unmarried—both due to an increase in divorce and an increase in the proportion of never-married individuals (Cooney & Dunne, 2001; Sassler, 2010). Older adults are also increasingly likely to cohabit as an alternative to marriage as well as to engage in other nonmarital intimate relationships (e.g., living-apart-together [LAT] relationships, wherein partners maintain separate residences and finances, but frequently spend the night with one another; Calasanti & Kiecolt, 2007; Sassler, 2010). Thus, the 21st century will be characterized by greater heterogeneity in relationship statuses in midlife and late life (Cooney & Dunne, 2001). However, little is known about dating and (re)partnering in midlife and late life (Sassler, 2010) or the role of sex outside of nonmarital relationships.

We do know that there are gender differences in repartnering with men more likely to want to date and repartner following divorce and widowhood (Carr, 2004; Davidson, 2002) as well as to do so (De Jong Gierveld, 2004). Indeed, some widows report a newfound sense of freedom following their spouse's death and are reluctant to repartner because they do not wish to lose this new sense of independence or to take on caregiving responsibilities again (Davidson, 2001). Women often desire companionship, however, and many women prefer to date someone rather than to marry a new partner, particularly in late life, which allows them to simultaneously maintain a level of independence and companionship (Carr, 2004; Davidson, 2002).

Some research has suggested that mid- and late-life adults who are interested in repartnering and dating are primarily motivated to seek emotional rather than sexual intimacy (Moore & Stratton, 2002) and place primary emphasis on the companionate aspect of relationships (Bulcroft & O'Connor, 1986). One qualitative study from the 1980s found that for adults aged 60 and older who were dating, sex and romance were generally not key to the relationship, but rather were described as "frosting on the cake" or "nice but not essential" (Bulcroft & O'Connor, 1986). This may not be true for more recent cohorts, however. Further, this desexualized view of mid- to late-life adults (whether articulated by respondents or researchers) may reflect cultural discourses that position older adults as asexual, and thus these findings should be interpreted in light of this cultural context. Given the importance of sex for intimate relationships, the experiences and meanings of sexuality outside of traditional marriages need to be further examined. Research should also examine relationship histories (Cooney & Dunne, 2001) and how these map onto sexual experiences and meanings over the life course.

## CRITIQUE OF PREVIOUS RESEARCH

Most research on this topic has been from a medical perspective, and as such it has largely been atheoretical and has failed to examine how social, cultural, and psychological factors (Burgess, 2004; DeLamater & Hyde 2004; Gott, 2005; Lodge & Umberson, 2012) matter for sex in midlife and late life. Rather, previous research on this topic has generally been descriptive and focused on quantifying specific sexual acts (Burgess, 2004; Gott & Hinchliff, 2003b). Some scholars, however, have suggested the usefulness of applying various perspectives and theories to understanding sex in midlife to late life including script theory (Marsiglio & Greer, 1994), a life course perspective (Carpenter, 2010; Lodge & Umberson, 2012), a biopsychosocial perspective (DeLamater & Moorman, 2007; DeLamater & Sill, 2005), an age relations framework (Connidis & Walker, 2009), and intersectionality theory (Connidis & Walker, 2009; Lodge & Umberson, 2012).

Carpenter (2010) further extended a life course perspective to advocate the use of a "gendered sexuality over the life course" perspective. Drawing on life course, gender, and scripting theories, Carpenter (2010) proposed that "sexual beliefs and behaviors result from individuals' lifelong accumulation of advantageous and disadvantageous experiences, and their adoption and rejection of sexual scripts, within specific socio-historical contexts" (p. 157). Further, Carpenter posited that gender-specific experiences and scripts give rise to gendered trajectories of sexuality, and these gendered processes intersect with race/ethnicity, social class, and sexual identity. Applying this perspective to the topic of sex in midlife and late life would require longitudinal or retrospective data to examine how earlier life course experiences of gendered sexuality matter for late-life experiences of gendered sexuality and how those experiences are inflected by race/ethnicity, social class, and sexual identity.

Indeed, although scholars have proposed a number of theoretical perspectives with which to study this topic, few empirical studies have done so. Notable exceptions exist, however, including Lodge and Umberson's (2012) research on sex in mid- and late-life couples, which integrated life course and intersectionality perspectives to examine how gender and age (as both structural locations and cultural systems of meaning) intersect to shape husbands' and wives' experiences of sex within marriage and how this changes over the life course. DeLamater and colleagues have fruitfully applied a biopsychosocial perspective to examine how biological, psychological, and social factors simultaneously shape sexual desire (DeLamater & Sill, 2005) and sexual frequency (DeLamater & Moorman, 2007). There is a need, however, for more theoretically motivated and informed studies on this topic.

Aging and sexuality will be most fruitfully understood through a synthesis of theories. As illustrated by Carpenter (2010) and Lodge and Umberson (2012), the synthesis of life course and gender and intersectionality theories are one particularly promising avenue. Another useful synthesis, particularly for studying nonheterosexualities, is the synthesis of queer and gerontology theories (e.g., critical feminist gerontology, life course theory; Brown, 2009). Brown (2009), for example, delineated how integrating queer and gerontology theories could be used to study the lives of LGBT (lesbian, gay, bisexual, and transgender) older adults. Queer theory could be integrated with a life course perspective to disrupt the heteronormative assumptions that life course theory is based on (e.g., assumptions of marriage) to examine how relationship and sexual histories over the life course intersect to shape the sexual experiences of mid- and late-life LGBT adults and couples.

## Research on Nonheterosexual Sexualities

Previous research on this topic has largely focused on heterosexual individuals or couples or failed to examine how sexual identity may matter for sexual experiences (de Vries, 2009). This omission likely stems from the fact that queer theorists have largely ignored older adults, and gerontologists have typically failed to examine sexuality (Brown, 2009). And although there is a small literature on sexual minority populations in midlife to late life, this literature largely ignores expressions of sexuality per se (de Vries,

2009; Scherrer, 2009), which may be in response to stereotypes that sexual minorities (particularly men) are hypersexual or otherwise sexually deviant (Peplau, Fingerhut, & Beals, 2004).

Focus groups with gay men have revealed that sexuality remains a very important component of men's identities, and gay men view sex as integral to quality intimate relationships, although sex may be more important for middle-aged than older gay men (with the latter more likely to emphasize a greater appreciation of nonsexual aspects of life as they age, such as spirituality; Asencio, Blank, Descartes, & Crawford, 2009). Further, although both part-nered midlife gay and straight men emphasize that perceived declines in sex-ual functioning are distressing, midlife gay men also emphasize that perceived declines in physical attractiveness are distressing and that this may adversely affect their levels of sexual desire and frequency (Lodge & Umberson, 2013). In contrast, menopause may have little impact on lesbians' sexuality (unlike heterosexual women), possibly because lesbian sexuality is less focused on intercourse and penetration (Cole & Rothblum, 1991).

Finally, a few studies have compared the sexual experiences of gay, les-bian, and heterosexual couples. For example, several studies have found that regardless of age, lesbian couples have the lowest levels of sexual frequency, gay couples the highest levels of sexual frequency, and heterosexual couples occupy an intermediate position (Peplau et al., 2004). Like heterosexual cou-ples, however, same-sex couples experience declines in sexual frequency with age (although the negative effect of relationship duration on sexual frequency is stronger than the negative effect of age for all couple types; Peplau et al., 2004). Further, for all couple types, higher levels of sexual frequency are asso-ciated with higher levels of sexual and relationship satisfaction over the life course (Peplau et al., 2004).

Recent research on long-term same-sex and different-sex midlife couples reveals that whereas gay male couples typically separate sexual and emotional intimacy, lesbian couples view sexual intimacy as integral to emotional inti-macy (Umberson, Thomeer, & Lodge, 2015). This study also found that like gay men, heterosexual men are more likely to separate sex from emotional intimacy, whereas like lesbian women, heterosexual women are more likely to see emotional and sexual intimacy as connected. Moreover, among different-sex couples, gendered views lead to conflict and tension in relationships, whereas same-sex partners tend to be on the same page in terms of sexual and emotional intimacy (Umberson et al., 2015). In summary, there is a greater need for research on nonheterosexualities in midlife and late life, including research on the sexual experiences of bisexual and transgendered individuals (Brown, 2009; de Vries, 2009; Heaphy et al., 2004), as well as how experiences of sex may vary for racially, ethnically, and socioeconomically diverse LGBT individuals and couples.

## Racial/Ethnic and Socioeconomic Differences

We know very little about how race/ethnicity and social class matter for sex in midlife to late life (Cooney & Dunne, 2001; DeLamater & Hyde, 2004). In terms of race/ethnicity, limited information exists on differences in levels of sexual satisfaction, sexual attitudes, and rates of dysfunction, but it remains largely unclear why these differences exist. Research on sexual satisfaction has revealed that Asian Americans have lower levels of sexual satisfaction than Whites, Blacks, and Hispanics (AARP, 2005). Further, partnered Blacks and Hispanics are more likely than Whites and Asian Americans to believe that their partner is very satisfied with their sexual relationship and to discuss sexual satisfaction with their partner (AARP, 2005). Whites and Asian Americans are also more likely than Blacks and Hispanics to agree with the statement "Sex becomes less important to people as they age" (AARP, 2005). Again, it is not clear why these racial/ethnic differences in sexual satisfaction and attitudes exist.

There are also racial/ethnic differences in the prevalence of sexual dysfunctions. One study found that among adults ages 57 to 85, Black men are significantly more likely to report a lack of sexual interest, premature climax, and a lack of sexual pleasure than White men; Black women are significantly less likely to report lubrication problems than White and Hispanic women; and Hispanic women are more likely to report sexual pain than White and Black women (Laumann & Waite, 2008). Another nationally representative study that examined the prevalence of sexual dysfunctions among 18- to 59-year-olds found that overall Hispanics are less likely to have sexual problems than Whites and Blacks (Laumann et al., 1999). This study further found that Black women are more likely to experience low levels of sexual desire and less sexual pleasure than White women, whereas White women are more likely to experience sexual pain than Black women (1999). It is not clear why different racial and ethnic groups in the United States are more likely to experience particular sexual dysfunctions or why these patterns differ by age.

Socioeconomic status (SES) is also associated with sexual problems among mid- and late-life adults. Among adults ages 18 to 59, higher levels of education are associated with fewer sexual dysfunctions for both men and women (Laumann et al., 1999). Women with college degrees are significantly less likely to experience problems achieving orgasm, sexual pain, sexual anxiety, and low sexual desire than women with lower levels of education, and men with college degrees are less likely to report premature climax, non-pleasurable sex, and sexual anxiety compared with men with lower levels of education (Laumann et al., 1999). Similar patterns have been found among adults ages 57 to 85, with two exceptions: Men with some college education report higher levels of erectile problems than men with lower levels of education (Laumann & Waite, 2008), and women ages 40 to 80 with lower levels of education are less likely to report difficulties with lubrication compared with women with higher levels of education (Laumann et al., 2005).

Among mid- and late-life adults, financial problems are associated with the inability to orgasm for women and ED for men (Laumann et al., 2005). Mid- and late-life Blacks are also more likely than other racial/ethnic groups to say that a better financial situation would increase their levels of sexual satisfaction (AARP, 2005), suggesting the importance of financial stress for sexual problems. Higher levels of other forms of stress are also related to greater likelihood of experiencing sexual dysfunctions (Laumann et al., 1999), and lower SES individuals and racial/ethnic minorities are more likely to experience higher rates of stress (Turner & Avison, 2003), suggesting one possible explanation for racial/ethnic and SES differences in levels of sexual dysfunction. Finally, one of the few studies to examine socioeconomic variation among mid- and late-life gay men found that lower SES men were more likely than affluent men to emphasize the importance of sex (Asencio et al., 2009). Clearly, more research on racial/ethnic and SES differences in sexual experiences in midlife and late life is needed.

## RESEARCH AND CLINICAL IMPLICATIONS

One of the most important areas for future research on sexuality in midlife and late life is the development of empirically grounded theory. In particular, synthesizing life course, intersectionality, and queer theories may provide great utility in studying the diversity of sexual experiences and expression. For example, Carpenter (2010) argued that a life course perspective and gender theory can be usefully integrated to examine how sexual histories and trajectories vary at the intersection of gender, race, social/ class, and sexual identity. A life course perspective is also useful for examining relationship histories (Cooney & Dunne, 2001) and how they intersect with sexual histories. Life course theory emphasizes the importance of linked lives—that individuals' lived experiences are grounded in relationships with others—and future research should examine how sexuality is experienced in relational contexts across the lifespan. This concept further points to the importance of collecting dyadic data to assess and compare both partners' sexual experiences (Cooney & Dunne, 2001). Further, queer theory has the potential to disrupt the heteronormative assumptions of life course theory (Brown, 2009) and demonstrate how relationship and sexual histories may intersect to shape the sexual experiences of mid- and late-life LGBT adults. The application of such theories has the potential to develop a greater empirical understanding of sexuality in midlife and late life that goes beyond the quantification of sexual acts. The failure of previous research to examine how race/ethnicity, social class, and sexual identity matter for sexual experiences in midlife and late life has likely hampered theoretical development. Thus, future data collections should focus on more diverse populations (both individuals and dyads).

Clinicians who work with mid- and late-life adults and couples should not assume that older adults are asexual but rather should be prepared to discuss sexuality as an important component of physical and mental well-being. For example, clinicians should discuss how prescription drugs and other medical interventions might impact sexuality, ask patients about any sexual concerns or problems that they may be experiencing, and openly discuss the links between sex and aging. Mental health practitioners should be prepared to attend to the important links between sex and well-being and relationship satisfaction. In particular, given that age-related physical changes that impact individuals' and couples' sex lives (e.g., ED) are often distressing (Lodge & Umberson, 2012), clinicians should work with patients to address this distress to develop positive self-concepts and experiences of sex. It is also important for clinicians to attend to the ways that relationship and sexual experiences earlier in life may matter for relationships and sexuality in midlife and late life. Finally, the provision of anti-ageist training to clinicians regarding sexual behavior, needs, and desires in midlife and late life is also needed.

In summary, the bulk of what we know about sex in midlife and late life comes from research examining the correlates of sexual frequency, satisfaction, desire, and dysfunction. Although this research is pathbreaking in that it has examined sexuality among mid- and late-life adults (in a context where they have often been defined as asexual), there are several limitations of this research. Most important, this research has been atheoretical and has failed to examine racial/ethnic and social class diversity, the experiences of sexual minorities, and how sexual experiences intersect with relationship histories. Attending to these issues will drive forward a greater theoretical and empirical understanding of the diversity of sexual experiences in midlife and late life.

## REFERENCES

AARP. (2005). *Sexuality at midlife and beyond: 2004 updated of attitudes and behaviors*. Washington, DC: Author. Retrieved from http://assets.aarp.org/rgcenter/general/2004_sexuality.pdf

AARP. (2010). *Sex, romance, and relationships: AARP survey of midlife and older adults*. Washington, DC: Author. Retrieved from http://assets.aarp.org/rgcenter/general/srr_09.pdf

Araujo, A. B., Durante, R., Feldman, H. A., Goldstein, I., & McKinlay, J. B. (1998). The relationship between depressive symptoms and male erectile dysfunction: Cross-sectional results from the Massachusetts Male Aging Study. *Psychosomatic Medicine, 60*, 458–465. http://dx.doi.org/10.1097/00006842-199807000-00011

Araujo, A. B., Mohr, B. A., & McKinlay, J. B. (2004). Changes in sexual function in middle-aged and older men: Longitudinal data from the Massachusetts Male Aging Study. *Journal of the American Geriatrics Society, 52*, 1502–1509. http://dx.doi.org/10.1111/j.0002-8614.2004.52413.x

Asencio, M., Blank, T., Descartes, L., & Crawford, A. (2009). The prospect of prostate cancer: A challenge for gay men's sexualities as they age. *Sexuality Research & Social Policy, 6*, 38–51. http://dx.doi.org/10.1525/srsp.2009.6.4.38

Bancroft, J. H. J. (2007). Sex and aging. *The New England Journal of Medicine, 357*, 820–822. http://dx.doi.org/10.1056/NEJMe078137

Basson, R. (2005). Women's sexual dysfunction: Revised and expanded definitions. *Canadian Medical Association Journal, 172*, 1327–1333. http://dx.doi.org/10.1503/cmaj.1020174

Beckman, N., Waern, M., Gustafson, D., & Skoog, I. (2008). Secular trends in self reported sexual activity and satisfaction in Swedish 70 year olds: Cross sectional survey of four populations, 1971–2001. *British Medical Journal, 337*, a279. http://dx.doi.org/10.1136/bmj.a279

Brown, M. T. (2009). LGBT aging and rhetorical silence. *Sexuality Research & Social Policy, 6*, 65–78. http://dx.doi.org/10.1525/srsp.2009.6.4.65

Bulcroft, K., & O'Connor, M. (1986). The importance of dating relationships on quality of life for older persons. *Family Relations, 35*, 397–401. http://dx.doi.org/10.2307/584367

Burgess, E. O. (2004). Sexuality in midlife and later life couples. In J. H. Harvey, A. Wenzel, & S. Sprecher (Eds.), *The handbook of sexuality in close relationships* (pp. 437–454). Mahwah, NJ: Erlbaum.

Calasanti, T., & Kiecolt, K. J. (2007). Diversity among late-life couples. *Generations, 3*, 10–17.

Call, V., Sprecher, S., & Schwartz, P. (1995). The incidence and frequency of marital sex in a national sample. *Journal of Marriage and Family, 57*, 639–652. http://dx.doi.org/10.2307/353919

Carpenter, L. M. (2010). Gendered sexuality over the life course: A conceptual framework. *Sociological Perspectives, 53*, 155–178. http://dx.doi.org/10.1525/sop.2010.53.2.155

Carpenter, L. M., Nathanson, C. A., & Kim, Y. J. (2009). Physical women, emotional men: Gender and sexual satisfaction in midlife. *Archives of Sexual Behavior, 38*, 87–107. http://dx.doi.org/10.1007/s10508-007-9215-y

Carr, D. (2004). The desire to date and remarry among older widows and widowers. *Journal of Marriage and Family, 66*, 1051–1068. http://dx.doi.org/10.1111/j.0022-2445.2004.00078.x

Cole, E., & Rothblum, E. D. (1991). Lesbian sex at menopause: As good as ever, or better than ever. In B. Sang, J. Warshow, & A. J. Smith (Eds.), *Lesbians at midlife* (pp. 184–193). San Francisco, CA: Spinsters Book Company.

Connidis, I. A., & Walker, A. J. (2009). (Re)Visioning gender, age, and aging in families. In S. A. Lloyd, A. L. Few, & K. R. Allen (Eds.), *Handbook of feminist family studies* (pp. 147–159). Los Angeles, CA: Sage. http://dx.doi.org/10.4135/9781412982801.n12

Cooney, T. M., & Dunne, K. (2001). Intimate relationships in later life: Current realities, future prospects. *Journal of Family Issues, 22*, 838–858. http://dx.doi.org/10.1177/019251301022007003

Csoka, A. B., & Shipko, S. (2006). Persistent sexual side effects after SSRI discontinuation. *Psychotherapy and Psychosomatics, 75*, 187–188. http://dx.doi.org/10.1159/000091777

Davidson, K. (2001). Late life widowhood, selfishness and new partnership choices: A gendered perspective. *Ageing and Society, 21*, 297–318. http://dx.doi.org/10.1017/S0144686X01008169

Davidson, K. (2002). Gender differences in new partnership choices and constraints for older widows and widowers. *Ageing International, 27*, 43–60. http://dx.doi.org/10.1007/s12126-002-1014-0

Davidson, K., & Fennell, G. (2002). New intimate relationships in later life. *Ageing International, 27*, 3–10. http://dx.doi.org/10.1007/s12126-002-1011-3

De Jong Gierveld, J. (2004). Remarriage, unmarried cohabitation, living apart together: Partner relationships following bereavement or divorce. *Journal of Marriage and Family, 66*, 236–243. http://dx.doi.org/10.1111/j.0022-2445.2004.00017.x

DeLamater, J., & Hyde, J. S. (2004). Conceptual and theoretical issues in studying sexuality in close relationships. In J. H. Harvey, A. Wenzel, & S. Sprecher (Eds.), *The handbook of sexuality in close relationships* (pp. 7–30). Hillsdale, NJ: Erlbaum.

DeLamater, J., Hyde, J. S., & Fong, M.-C. (2008). Sexual satisfaction in the seventh decade of life. *Journal of Sex & Marital Therapy, 34*, 439–454. http://dx.doi.org/10.1080/00926230802156251

DeLamater, J., & Moorman, S. M. (2007). Sexual behavior in later life. *Journal of Aging and Health, 19*, 921–945. http://dx.doi.org/10.1177/0898264307308342

DeLamater, J. D., & Sill, M. (2005). Sexual desire in later life. *Journal of Sex Research, 42*, 138–149. http://dx.doi.org/10.1080/00224490509552267

de Vries, B. (2009). Introduction to special issue sexuality and aging: A late-blooming relationship. *Sexuality Research & Social Policy, 6*, 1–4. http://dx.doi.org/10.1007/BF03179195

Edwards, J. N., & Booth, A. (1994). Sexuality, marriage, and well-being: The middle years. In A. S. Rossi (Ed.), *Sexuality across the life course* (pp. 233–259). Chicago, IL: University of Chicago Press.

Feldman, H. A., Goldstein, I., Hatzichristou, D. G., Krane, R. J., & McKinlay, J. B. (1994). Impotence and its medical and psychosocial correlates: Results of the Massachusetts Male Aging Study. *The Journal of Urology, 151*, 54–61.

Gott, M. (2005). *Sexuality, sexual health, and ageing*. Maidenhead, Berkshire, England: Open University Press.

Gott, M., & Hinchliff, S. (2003a). Barriers to seeking treatment for sexual problems in primary care: A qualitative study with older people. *Family Practice, 20*, 690–695. http://dx.doi.org/10.1093/fampra/cmg612

Gott, M., & Hinchliff, S. (2003b). How important is sex in later life? The views of older people. *Social Science & Medicine, 56*, 1617–1628. http://dx.doi.org/10.1016/S0277-9536(02)00180-6

Gott, M., & Hinchliff, S. (2003c). Sex and ageing: A gendered issue. In S. Arber, K. Davidson, & J. Ginn (Eds.), *Gender and ageing: Changing roles and relationships* (pp. 63–78). Buckingham, England: Open University Press.

Gott, M., Hinchliff, S., & Galena, E. (2004). General practitioner attitudes to discussing sexual health issues with older people. *Social Science & Medicine, 58*, 2093–2103. http://dx.doi.org/10.1016/j.soc scimed.2003.08.025

Gullette, M. M. (2011). *Agewise: Fighting the new ageism in America*. Chicago, IL: University of Chicago Press. http://dx.doi.org/10.7208/chicago/9780226310756.001.0001

Heaphy, B., Yip, A. K. T., & Thompson, D. (2004). Aging in a non-heterosexual context. *Ageing and Society, 24*, 881–902. http://dx.doi.org/10.1017/S0144686X03001600

Karraker, A., DeLamater, J., & Schwartz, C. R. (2011). Sexual frequency decline from midlife to later life. *The Journals of Gerontology: Series B. Psychological Sciences and Social Sciences, 66*, 502–512. http://dx.doi.org/10.1093/geronb/gbr058

Katz, S., & Marshall, M. (2003). New sex for old: Lifestyle, consumerism, and the ethics of aging well. *Journal of Aging Studies, 17*, 3–16. http://dx.doi.org/10.1016/S0890-4065(02)00086-5

Kingsberg, S. A. (2000). The psychological impact of aging on sexuality and relationships. *Journal of Women's Health & Gender-Based Medicine, 9*(Suppl. 1), S33–S38. http://dx.doi.org/10.1089/152460900318849

Kingsberg, S. A. (2002). The impact of aging on sexual function in women and their partners. *Archives of Sexual Behavior, 31*, 431–437. http://dx.doi.org/10.1023/A:1019844209233

Kontula, O., & Haavio-Mannila, E. (2009). The impact of aging on human sexual activity and sexual desire. *Journal of Sex Research, 46*, 46–56. http://dx.doi.org/10.1080/00224490802624414

Laumann, E. O., Gagnon, J. H., Michael, R. T., & Michaels, S. (1994). *The social organization of sexuality: Sexual practices in the United States*. Chicago, IL: University of Chicago Press.

Laumann, E. O., Nicolosi, A., Glasser, D. B., Paik, A., Gingell, C., Moreira, E., Wang, T., & the GSSAB Investigators' Group. (2005). Sexual problems among women and men aged 40–80 y: Prevalence and correlates identified in the Global Study of Sexual Attitudes and Behaviors. *International Journal of Impotence Research,* *17,* 39–57. http://dx.doi.org/10.1038/sj.ijir.3901250

Laumann, E. O., Paik, A., & Rosen, R. C. (1999). Sexual dysfunction in the United States: Prevalence and predictors. *JAMA, 281,* 537–544. http://dx.doi.org/10.1001/jama.281.6.537

Laumann, E. O., & Waite, L. J. (2008). Sexual dysfunction among older adults: Prevalence and risk factors from a nationally representative U.S. probability sample of men and women 57–85 years of age. *Journal of Sexual Medicine, 5,* 2300–2311.

Lindau, S. T., Schumm, L. P., Laumann, E. O., Levinson, W., O'Muircheartaigh, C. A., & Waite, L. J. (2007). A study of sexuality and health among older adults in the United States. *The New England Journal of Medicine, 357,* 762–774. http://dx.doi.org/10.1056/NEJMoa067423

Lodge, A. C., & Umberson, D. (2012). All shook up: Sexuality of mid- to later life married couples. *Journal of Marriage and Family, 74,* 428–443. http://dx.doi.org/10.1111/j.1741-3737.2012.00969.x

Lodge, A. C., & Umberson, D. (2013). Age and embodied masculinities: Midlife gay and straight men talk about their bodies. *Journal of Aging Studies, 27,* 225–232. http://dx.doi.org/10.1016/j.jaging.2013.03.004

Marsiglio, W., & Greer, R. A. (1994). A gender analysis of older men's sexuality. In J. Edward, H. Thompson, & M. S. Kimmel (Eds.), *Older men's lives* (pp. 122–140). Thousand Oaks, CA: Sage. http://dx.doi.org/10.4135/9781452243474.n7

Matthias, R. E., Lubben, J. E., Atchison, K. A., & Schweitzer, S. O. (1997). Sexual activity and satisfaction among very old adults: Results from a community-dwelling Medicare population survey. *The Gerontologist, 37,* 6–14. http://dx.doi.org/10.1093/geront/37.1.6

McKinlay, J. B., & Feldman, H. A. (1994). Age-related variation in sexual activity and interest in normal men: Results from the Massachusetts Male Aging Study. In A. S. Rossi (Ed.), *Sexuality across the life course* (pp. 261–286). Chicago, IL: University of Chicago Press.

Moore, A. J., & Stratton, D. C. (2002). *Resilient widowers: Older men speak for themselves.* New York, NY: Springer.

Peplau, L. A., Fingerhut, A. W., & Beals, K. P. (2004). Sexuality in the relationships of lesbians and gay men. In J. H. Harvey, A. Wenzel, & S. Spretcher (Eds.), *Handbook of sexuality in close relationships* (pp. 349–369). Mahwah, NJ: Erlbaum. http://dx.doi.org/10.4324/9781410610249

Rosen, R. C., & Bachmann, G. A. (2008). Sexual well-being, happiness, and satisfaction, in women: The case for a new conceptual paradigm. *Journal of Sex & Marital Therapy, 34,* 291–297. http://dx.doi.org/10.1080/00926230802096234

Rust, J., Golombok, S., & Collier, J. (1988). Marital problems and sexual dysfunction: How are they related? *The British Journal of Psychiatry, 152,* 629–631. http://dx.doi.org/10.1192/bjp.152.5.629

Sassler, S. (2010). Partnering across the life course: Sex, relationships, and mate selection. *Journal of Marriage and Family, 72*, 557–575. http://dx.doi.org/10.1111/j.1741-3737.2010.00718.x

Scherrer, K. S. (2009). Images of sexuality and aging in gerontological literature. *Sexuality Research & Social Policy, 6*, 5–12. http://dx.doi.org/10.1525/srsp.2009.6.4.5

Skoog, I. (1996). Sex and Swedish 85-year-olds. *The New England Journal of Medicine, 334*, 1140–1141. http://dx.doi.org/10.1056/NEJM199604253341718

Skultety, K. (2007). Addressing issues of sexuality with older couples. *Generations, 3*, 31–37.

Steinke, E. E. (2005). Intimacy needs and chronic illness: Strategies for sexual counseling and self-management. *Journal of Gerontological Nursing, 31*, 40–50. http://dx.doi.org/10.3928/0098-9134-20050501-08

Tiefer, L. (1996). The medicalization of sexuality: Conceptual, normative, and professional issues. *Annual Review of Sex Research, 7*, 252–282.

Turner, R. J., & Avison, W. R. (2003). Status variations in stress exposure: Implications for the interpretation of research on race, socioeconomic status, and gender. *Journal of Health and Social Behavior, 44*, 488–505. http://dx.doi.org/10.2307/1519795

Umberson, D., Thomeer, M. B., & Lodge, A. C. (2015). Intimacy and emotion work in lesbian, gay, and heterosexual relationships. *Journal of Marriage and Family, 77*, 542–556. http://dx.doi.org/10.1111/jomf.12178

Vares, T., Potts, A., Gavey, N., & Grace, V. M. (2007). Reconceptualizing cultural narratives of mature women's sexuality in the Viagra era. *Journal of Aging Studies, 21*, 153–164. http://dx.doi.org/10.1016/j.jaging.2006.08.002

Waite, L., & Das, A. (2010). Families, social life, and well-being at older ages. *Demography, 47*(Suppl.), S87–S109. http://dx.doi.org/10.1353/dem.2010.0009

Wiley, D., & Bortz, W. M., II. (1996). Sexuality and aging—usual and successful. *The Journals of Gerontology: Series A: Biological Sciences and Medical Sciences, 51*, M142–M146. http://dx.doi.org/10.1093/gerona/51A.3.M142

Willetts, M. C., Sprecher, S., & Beck, F. D. (2004). Overview of sexual practices and attitudes within relational contexts. In J. H. Harvey, A. Wenzel, & S. Sprecher (Eds.), *Handbook of sexuality in close relationships* (pp. 57–85). Mahwah, NJ: Erlbaum.

Wood, J. M., Mansfield, P. K., & Koch, P. B. (2007). Negotiating sexual agency: Postmenopausal women's meaning and experience of sexual desire. *Qualitative Health Research, 17*, 189–200. http://dx.doi.org/10.1177/1049732306297415

Yeh, H. C., Lorenz, F. O., Wickrama, K. A. S., Conger, R. D., & Elder, G. H., Jr. (2006). Relationships among sexual satisfaction, marital quality, and marital instability at midlife. *Journal of Family Psychology, 20*, 339–343. http://dx.doi.org/10.1037/0893-3200.20.2.339

# 7

# SPOUSAL ROLE ALLOCATION AND EQUITY IN OLDER COUPLES

LIAT KULIK

The issue of equality and equity in spousal role allocation has been one of the most popular topics examined by researchers over the years, especially following the massive entry of women into the labor force in Western countries. For the term *equality in spousal role allocation*, some definitions adopt a pragmatic instrumental orientation and define equality in spousal life as a situation in which the man and the woman participate equally in the housework (Hochshild, 1989) or their contributions are more or less equal (Brannen & Moss, 1991). These definitions of equality in spousal role allocation are measured by minutes and hours, tasks, or overall responsibility. The concept of *spousal equity*, on the other hand, emphasizes symbolic and relational meanings and actually refers to perceived equality; it argues that feelings of (in)-equity are based on subjective evaluations of outcomes, the degree to which outcomes are valued, and that perceptions of fairness and equity are the result

http://dx.doi.org/10.1037/14897-008
*Couple Relationships in the Middle and Later Years: Their Nature, Complexity, and Role in Health and Illness,*
J. Bookwala (Editor)

of comparison with others (Greenstein, 1996). However, these two terms are used interchangeably in much of the academic literature.

Interest in examining the nature of household task allocation stems from findings indicating that in Western societies, equality and equity in household tasks are related to marital satisfaction and marital quality (e.g., Stanik & Bryant, 2012). However, most of the studies on this topic have focused on parents with young children living at home, and there is a relative dearth of research on allocation of household tasks in midlife and late adulthood. The lack of research attention to these life periods may be attributed to findings indicating that the burden of household chores declines significantly in midlife and late adulthood, especially after the empty nest stage (for a review, see Anderson & Sabatelli, 2007). Hence, it has been assumed that the examination of equity in household role allocation and its impact on the spousal relationship in later stages of the life cycle is not as relevant as it is in earlier stages. However, equity in role allocation among spouses in midlife and late adulthood has become a highly relevant issue in light of recent normative changes and developments in different domains. For example, medical advancements that have increased life expectancy (Saraceno & Keck, 2010) have prolonged the stage of late adulthood. Long-lasting marriages have consequently become more prevalent today than in the past, and research on household task allocation over the entire lifespan, including midlife and late adulthood, has become highly relevant.

When examining the nature and sources of spousal role allocation in the later stages of marriage, it is important to take into account several major transitions in midlife and late adulthood that may affect the dyadic unit as well as the division of labor at home (Bookwala, 2012). These transitions include the empty nest and retirement (of one or both partners), as well as becoming a caregiver to one or more ill family members. In this chapter, I focus on how each of these transitions affects spousal role allocation and equity in household tasks in the later stages of life, that is, in midlife and late adulthood.

## THEORETICAL APPROACHES TO EXPLAINING
## SPOUSAL ROLE ALLOCATION

Over the years, researchers have offered a variety of theories to explain spousal role allocation, which can be applied to the early as well as to later stages of spousal life. According to one of the most popular approaches, allocation of household tasks is determined by the partners' gender role ideology (e.g., Katz-Wise, Priess, & Hyde, 2010). Hence, among couples who maintain traditional gender role norms, the man is responsible for supporting the family, whereas the woman is responsible for household chores. In contradistinction, among couples who maintain a more egalitarian perspective of gender roles, the man participates more in household chores and child care, and spousal role allocation is more equal (Kamo, 1994). According to the gender role ideology approach, cohort effects are reflected in an increasing trend toward egalitarianism. That is, role allocation among spouses in the younger generation is more equal than in the older generation (Artis & Pavalko, 2003).

According to another well-known approach, the relative resource theory, spousal role allocation is determined primarily by the relative resources available to each partner (Blood & Wolfe, 1960). Therefore, the partner with more resources (e.g., money, socioeconomic status, occupational prestige) is more powerful and may assume less responsibility for household tasks, which are considered to be less desirable. Finally, according to the time-available approach (e.g., Bittman, England, Sayer, Folbre, & Matheson, 2003), paid work outside the home imposes constraints on the amount of time available for housework. It can therefore be expected that hours of work outside the home will be negatively associated with participation in household chores. Thus, from the perspective of time availability, the spouses' employment patterns may have a direct effect on the time they devote to housework.

In contradistinction to the previously mentioned theories, which argue that household task allocation is based on one aspect of spousal life (i.e., the spouses' gender role ideology, their relative resources, or the time they have at their disposal), the family life-cycle approach to spousal role allocation integrates several perspectives, which reflect developments that take place in the life of family members, including parents as well as their children (Coltrane, 2000). Specifically, it has been argued that the stages of the family life cycle reflect events related to the aging of spouses and maturation of their children and are thus associated with different economic and household labor needs of each of the partners (Duvall & Miller, 1985). According to this perspective, the amount of household labor for mothers is much greater in the child-rearing stages of family life than in the later stages (Gordon & Whelan-Berry, 2005; Pleck, 1985). For husbands, the family life-cycle perspective relates to fluctuations in occupational involvement, which in turn affect the extent of their involvement in household tasks (Anderson & Sabatelli, 2007). This approach was generally adopted by researchers in early studies (Rexroat & Shehan, 1987), as well as in more recent studies (Coltrane & Shih, 2010) that attempted to explain fluctuations in household task allocation in different stages of the family life cycle.

On the basis of this approach, in this chapter I analyze changes in allocation of household tasks among spouses resulting from transitions in family life. As mentioned, emphasis will be placed on three transition points in midlife and late adulthood: the empty nest, retirement, and becoming a caregiver to an ill family member.

# SPOUSAL ROLE ALLOCATION IN MIDLIFE
## AND THE EMPTY NEST STAGE

Researchers in the field consider midlife to be a period of biological, psychological, and social changes (for a review, see Muhlbauer & Chrisler, 2007). It is marked by an increased risk for health consequences, as well as by shifts in the responsibilities assumed by individuals (Bromberger & Matthews, 1996). These developments in midlife are accompanied by changes in the priority that individuals give to performing social roles. For example, the middle years are also a time when the husband's work frequently demands change. According to early scholars, some men may continue in their occupation with the same intensity as in earlier stages, whereas others may slow down after achieving their occupational aspirations (Bakan, 1966).

One of the important transition points in midlife is the children leaving home, a life stage that begins when the first child leaves home (the *launching* stage) and ends when the last child leaves home (the *empty nest* stage). Various definitions have been offered for this stage in the parental life cycle, but the empty nest usually refers to the postparenthood phase (Barber, 1989). In light of the changes that take place in this life stage, early as well as more recent studies have revealed that many couples reallocate the responsibilities they assumed when the children were at home. Consistent with these findings, a well-known early study by Rexroat and Shehan (1987) found that women in the empty nest stage spend 10 hours less on housework per week than do women with children living at home. There has been criticism, however, about the methodology used in early research dealing with the impact of the empty nest on individuals and on spousal life. For example, it has been argued that these studies were based on small convenience or clinical samples (Pillay, 1988) or that there were uncontrolled cohort effects (Adelmann & Zajonc, 1989).

In contrast to earlier assertions that associated the empty nest stage with marital crises (e.g., Back, 1971), more recent studies have shown that the empty nest is an event that parents look forward to, prepare for, and do not find stressful. Consistent with these findings, an Australian study revealed that the event of the last child leaving home does not adversely affect women's quality of life (Dennerstein, Dudley, & Guthrie, 2002). On the contrary, a significant improvement was found in the participants' experiences of happiness and well-being, and there was a substantial decline in the experience of daily hassles during the empty nest years. Hence, the findings indicate that the physical and emotional burden of household responsibilities for husbands and wives is alleviated to some extent in this stage of the family life cycle. This provides both partners with more freedom to engage in additional roles in the areas of community activity and self-development (e.g., volunteer work, continuing education, hobbies), which they may not have been able to do while raising their children. In this connection, a recent Israeli study found that beginning with the empty nest stage, spouses tend to occupy more social roles than they did in earlier and later stages of the family life cycle (Kulik, Shilo-Levin, & Liberman, 2014). In the same study, it was also found that during the empty nest stage, husbands and wives experience less work–home role conflict (both interference of work responsibilities with family demands and interference of family demands with work) compared with earlier stages of marriage. Moreover, Gordon and Whelan-Berry (2005) found that in midlife, husbands make some contribution to family and household activities, although this contribution is usually limited. Thus, the examination of early and recent research findings indicates that despite the general trend toward continuity in the patterns of spousal task allocation that have been established over the years, there is a certain shift toward more equality in this domain in midlife and after the empty nest stage.

## RETIREMENT AND SPOUSAL ROLE ALLOCATION

Retirement is a major transition in the life cycle, marking the end of one of the most important social roles in human life, that is, the role of worker. This event is accompanied by numerous changes in many life spheres. In the economic sphere, the drop in income levels might affect the lifestyle of retired individuals (Gratton & Rotondo, 1992). On the social level, relationships and contacts originating in the workplace often dissolve, including ties with colleagues, customers, and union members, as well as participation in leisure groups based on work connections (Bossé, Aldwin, Levenson, Workman-Daniels, & Ekerdt, 1990). From a psychological perspective, scholars have pointed to changes in life goals after retirement. Whereas working individuals tend to have achievement-oriented goals, retirees tend to focus on family life, which they hope will be a source of support, love, and friendship (Kulik, 2004). Although the previously mentioned changes occur at the individual level, they may also be reflected in the dyadic unit (see Chapter 8, this volume, for a discussion of the role of retirement in marital quality). Thus, retirement is not only a personal event but also can be considered a spousal event that impacts the allocation of household roles. Most of the studies dealing with the impact of retirement on spousal role allocation have focused on men's retirement, whereas very few have considered the impact of women's retirement (e.g., Brubaker & Brubaker, 1992; Calasanti, 1996; Kulik, 2004). The dearth of research on women's retirement has been attributed to women's relatively late entry into the labor force, as well as to the commonly held assumption that work life is less central to women than men.

Two main theoretical approaches have been used by researchers to explain changes in task allocation among spouses after retirement: the relative resource theory (Blood & Wolfe, 1960) and the time-available approach (Bittman et al., 2003). According to the relative resource theory, because some resources are lost after retirement, the retired spouse will participate more in household tasks that are considered undesirable. According to the time-available approach (Aldous, Mulligan, & Bjarnason, 1998), after retirement the retired spouse (husband or wife) has more free time and will participate more in household tasks. The clear-cut predictions of these two theories notwithstanding, research on spousal role allocation after retirement has also revealed inconsistent findings: Some studies have shown continuity in patterns of spousal role allocation after retirement, whereas others have revealed changes in the general frame of continuity. In line with the continuity approach, irrespective of which partner has retired (husband, wife, or both partners), studies have shown a general trend toward maintaining the division of tasks that existed before retirement (for a review, see Szinovacz, Ekerdt, Butt, Barton, & Oala, 2012). However, other studies have shown that despite the general trend toward continuity in spousal power relations, changes take place after retirement. For example, a study conducted in Israel (Kulik & Zuckerman-Bareli, 1997) indicated that although general spousal power relations remained stable after the husband's retirement, men tended to become more involved in making decisions about social aspects of family life than they were before retirement (e.g., decisions about taking vacations and leisure time). In the same vein, Szinovacz (2000) reported that after retirement, husbands participate more in household work and help more when their wives are in poor health. Kulik (2004) found that elderly husbands with working wives maintained more liberal gender role attitudes regardless of their employment status (working or retired) than did husbands of nonworking wives. Among husbands with a liberal gender role ideology, social and psychological resources (e.g., emotional strength, ability to cope with crises) were the main factors that explained decision-making patterns. However, among husbands with a traditional gender role ideology, the spousal advantage in economic resources was the most salient factor that contributed to decision-making patterns (Kulik, 1999). Gender role attitudes apparently reflect the importance that retired husbands attribute to spousal resources and are thus a key factor in explaining spousal power relations. Husbands with a traditional view of gender roles may have more rigid perceptions of family life and attribute importance to the most concrete resources, that is, economic resources that enable them to make decisions about matters such as engagement in household tasks. However, husbands with liberal gender role attitudes and a more flexible perception of family life may attribute importance to less concrete spousal resources such as hardiness, coping with crises, and emotional coping as a means of gaining an advantage in decision making in the household.

Regarding women's retirement, findings revealed that because they have more time at their disposal after retirement, formerly working wives engage more in household chores and in maintenance than they did during the employment stage (Szinovacz, 1989), and as they grow older and become more susceptible to health problems, their ability to invest efforts in these tasks declines (Hafstrom & Schram, 1983). In addition, Kulik (2001a) found that the division of household tasks in the retirement stage depends on gender stereotypes. Feminine tasks such as cooking, ironing, and laundry were found to be more egalitarian in later stages of marital life, whereas masculine tasks such as repairs and gardening continued to be performed by men regardless of their employment status (employed or retired). Moreover, Kulik (2001a) showed that the impact of retirement on marital relations is similar for men and women in most aspects of marriage. This includes power relations as reflected in major decisions such as decisions about the family budget and major purchases, as well as in minor decisions such as purchasing household items and renovations. In these areas, it was found that the decision-making patterns do not change appreciably before and after retirement and tend to be egalitarian regardless of whether the retired spouse is the husband or the wife. However, despite similarities in the impact of men's and women's retirement on marital relations, differences were found among retired men and women in two areas: involvement in decisions about domestic affairs and participation in feminine household tasks. In both of these areas, the men became more involved after retirement, whereas the women indicated that they maintained the same levels of involvement in these domains (Kulik, 2001a).

Taking a broader perspective that assumes that the joint employment status of the spouses, rather than the employment status of each individual partner, affects spousal role allocation during retirement, Kulik (2001b) compared spousal role allocation among four types of preretired and retired couples. The comparison was based on the participant's as well as the spouse's employment status (employed–near retirement vs. retired). A distinction was made between two types of synchronous couples: preretired couples (both partners employed but approaching retirement) and retired couples (both partners retired), and two types of asynchronous couples (employed husband–retired wife and retired husband–employed wife). In general, decision-making patterns and role allocation were found to be egalitarian among all four types of couples. Nevertheless, the distinctions relating to feminine tasks (e.g., cooking and cleaning) and general tasks (e.g., running errands) across the four types of couples are noteworthy. In both types of tasks, the synchronous retired couples (both spouses retired) were more egalitarian than the synchronous preretired and asynchronous couples. Masculine tasks, however, as reflected in technical jobs that require physical strength and appropriate skills, were performed to a greater extent by the husband, regardless of couple type (synchronous vs. asynchronous).

## CAREGIVING AND ROLE ALLOCATION

Caregiving represents a broad range of activities, including providing personal care, doing household chores, preparing meals, shopping, taking care of finances, providing companionship, checking up regularly, arranging and supervising activities and outside services, and coordinating medical care (Roberto & Jarrott, 2008). Scholars have argued that becoming a caregiver to a family member is a life transition, which is accompanied by many changes (Bookwala, 2012). Contrary to other life transitions experienced by individuals in middle and late adulthood (e.g., empty nest, retirement), the event of becoming a caregiver to a family member usually occurs without any preparation or training.

Modern theories of caregiving are based on the underlying premise that the intensive involvement with the care recipient over an extended period of time creates a physical and psychological strain for the caregiver (Pinquart & Sörensen, 2006). Moreover, becoming a caregiver is accompanied by high levels of unpredictability and uncontrollability and can affect the caregiver's relations with the partner, as reflected in role allocation (for a review, see Pruchno & Gitlin, 2013). During late adulthood, couples can experience caregiving mainly from two perspectives: They can care for needy elderly family members, especially parents, and they can care for their ill spouses. In this context, the question that arises is: How does the fact that one spouse becomes a caregiver in late adulthood affect spousal role allocation?

## CAREGIVING FOR AGING PARENTS
## AND SPOUSAL ROLE ALLOCATION

Caregivers for aging parents in midlife or late adulthood may experience stress created by physical and psychological demands. Researchers have identified these demands as primary stressors (stemming directly from the needs of the care recipient) and secondary stressors (stemming from the primary stressors, including role strain, interpersonal conflict, and intrapsychic strain; Pearlin, Mullan, Semple, & Skaff, 1990). Although both women and men feel a sense of obligation to their aging parents, there is some evidence for gender inequality in this domain (Silverstein, Gans, & Yang, 2006). Several studies have shown that, in general, women are more likely to care for sick and handicapped family members than men (Pope, Kolomer, & Glass, 2012), daughters are more likely to care for parents than sons, and sisters are more likely to care for siblings than brothers (Coward, Horne, & Dwyer, 1992). A meta-analysis conducted by Pinquart and Sörensen (2006) demonstrated that women provide more hours of caregiving, engage in more caregiving tasks, and provide more personal care. A Chinese study revealed that married daughters, especially those living with their parents, provide more financial support to parents than married sons (Xie & Zhu, 2009). Some scholars have argued that women provide more care to their aging parents and tend to perform more caregiving tasks than men because they are trained to perform these roles and are used to engaging in tasks that are unskilled, repetitious, monotonous, have no boundaries, and yield few tangible rewards (Stoller, 1990).

Caregiving for older parents or parents-in-law is a potential source of conflict in marital relations in middle and late life (Connidis & Kemp, 2008). It can interfere with marital roles by reducing the time and energy available for interaction with the spouse and can create feelings of neglect or inequity in the allocation of spousal roles (Suitor & Pillemer, 1990). Bookwala (2009) found that middle-aged married daughters caring for a parent were more likely to report inequities in role allocation in their marital relationship than their male counterparts in the sample. There may also be economic costs to the caregiver role, especially for wives who care for older parents and devote less time to their paid work (Kingson & O'Grady-LeShane, 1993). According to the relative resource theory, the decline in resources as a result of caregiving can indirectly affect allocation of tasks in the home by lowering the wife's negotiation power. In this context, Suitor and Pillemer (1990) examined how husbands can assist their wives in caregiving to older family members and revealed a diverse range of instrumental tasks that can relieve the caregiver of her responsibilities to her ill parent. The husbands' support to caregiving wives includes direct care to the ill parent, running errands that the wife–caregiver would otherwise have to run, staying with the parent, and contributing more to household chores to reduce the caregiver's overall responsibilities.

With reference to the relationship between caregiving and marital satisfaction, Bookwala (2009) found that the decline in marital quality may not occur immediately after one spouse becomes a caregiver. Rather, it may accumulate over several years before it becomes evident. In the same study, long-term caregivers (daughters and sons) were found to be significantly less happy in their marriage than recent caregivers and to feel significantly greater marital role inequity.

Besides these effects of caregiving to aging parents, some optimistic aspects can be mentioned when taking a lifespan approach to the care of elder family members. In this vein, emerging literature on caregivers has demonstrated a clear and positive impact of caregiving, including improvements in problem-solving abilities, increased self-understanding, and a growing sense of competence among caregivers (Roberto & Jarrott, 2008).

## CAREGIVING SPOUSES AND ROLE ALLOCATION

Researchers have indicated that the responsibility of becoming the primary caregiver for one's spouse in late adulthood goes beyond the responsibility of caring for offspring and other family members (Haberkern & Szydlik, 2010). The four most demanding caregiving activities perceived by spousal caregivers were, in the following order: providing transportation, doing additional household tasks, providing emotional support, and monitoring symptoms and additional tasks outside the home (Park et al., 2013). Furthermore, Pinquart and Sörensen's (2006) meta-analysis of gender differences in spousal caregiver outcomes found that wives generally experienced greater caregiver burden and depression than husbands, but gender differences were smaller for spouses than for other caregiver relationship types. The smaller gender differential for spousal caregivers was attributed to the relatively strong responsibility that spouses feel for their partners. The experience of spousal caregiving also has roots in the precaregiving period of marriage. Spouses who had higher levels of marital disagreement prior to caregiving reported a greater decrease in happiness and a greater increase in depression following their assumption of caregiving responsibilities than spouses with more favorable marital experiences. Caregivers who reported lower quality marital relationships were also more likely to end their caregiving activities than were those who reported higher quality marital relationships (Choi & Marks, 2006). Dwyer and Seccombe (1991) found that husbands report devoting more time to caregiving and perform more tasks than caregiving wives. In this context, they suggested that caregivers may not report tasks for which they have been responsible throughout their married lives. Hence, wives who usually do housework and laundry may not have reported these tasks as part of their caregiving routine because they consider them to be normative responsibilities (Walker, Pratt, & Eddy, 1995), whereas husbands who perform these tasks generally report them as caregiving tasks. There is some evidence that male and female caregivers are significantly more likely to help with tasks that are typically gender stereotyped. For example, in an early study, Young and Kahana (1989) found that wives provide significantly more assistance and help with laundry, whereas husbands are the major helpers with maintenance and repairs. Contrary to caregiving wives who may feel that they are obligated to provide care to their spouses (Williamson & Schulz, 1990), husbands may regard caregiving as part of their set of tasks (Miller, 1990) but are more likely to supplement caregiving with formal services than wives (Pruchno & Resch, 1989).

## ROLE ALLOCATION AMONG COHABITING HETEROSEXUAL AND SAME-SEX COUPLES

In light of the growing proportion of cohabiting couples (heterosexual and same-sex) in midlife and late adulthood in recent decades, the issue of role allocation in the later stages of life has become highly relevant to this population. Cohabitation is similar to marriage in that it is a monogamous relationship, and when it occurs at a later stage in the couple's life it is usually based on the hope for continuity. Notwithstanding the prevalence of heterosexual and same-sex cohabiting couples today, there is a modest body of research that compares the division of housework among lesbian, gay, and heterosexual cohabiting couples and even less among aging couples. Therefore, with regard to equity in household allocation among heterosexual versus same-sex couples in later stages of life, we must extrapolate on the basis of comparative studies on earlier life stages. This literature is consistent in suggesting that same-sex couples divide housework more equally than heterosexual couples (Goldberg, Smith, & Perry-Jenkins, 2012). This finding has been explained by empirical findings that lesbians, gays, and bisexuals (LGB) have a more flexible gender identity (Lippa, 2008). It has been argued that these couples would therefore also be more flexible in their approach to the division of housework (Julien, Arellano, & Turgeon, 1997). Moreover, there are empirical findings that same-sex couples may be more attuned and sensitive to the issue of equality and inequality in their relationship. It can thus be argued that such sensitivity should, theoretically, predispose same-sex couples toward greater equality in the division of housework (Dunne, 2000). Some scholars have referred to the equal sharing of housework among same-sex couples as the "egalitarian ethic" (Downing & Goldberg, 2011). Although these data seem to suggest that a commitment to egalitarianism may be sufficient to essentially "degender" (and therefore enable equal sharing of housework), some scholars have emphasized that conclusions about an egalitarian ethic among same-sex couples are oversimplified and serve to obscure the diversity inherent in same-sex families (Goldberg, 2013). Thus, differences in time availability and resources between partners may ultimately influence who does what, thus challenging the notion that same-sex couples are not influenced by status and power differences (Goldberg, 2013).

Even though it has been found that most gays and lesbians view equality in spousal life as an ideal situation, lesbian women have shown a greater tendency than gay men to evaluate equality in their spousal relationship as a desirable situation (for a review, see Rose, 2015). Moreover, lesbian women actively discourage hierarchical relationships with their partners and tend to believe that differences in authority within the family should not be determined by differences in the amount of financial resources that each partner brings to the relationship (Sullivan, 2004). Thus, many highly educated lesbians use the feminist egalitarian framework as a model for organizing their family lives (Sullivan, 2004). The finding that lesbians show a greater tendency toward egalitarian relationships than gay men may be attributed to differences in the degree of importance that gay men and lesbians ascribe to equality in spousal role allocation. Specifically, women feel less comfortable dominating or being dominated. They report higher levels of affection and trust in their partners and tend to foster a more empowering relationship than men (Ferree, 1990). However, some studies have found that the distribution of tasks in lesbian households is less than equal (Carrington, 1999), especially when the lesbian parent is the biological mother. The biological mother spends more time on child care and household chores, particularly during the months immediately after birth (Gartrell, Deck, Rodas, Peyser, & Banks, 2005).

## ROLE ALLOCATION AND MARITAL SATISFACTION IN LATE ADULTHOOD

The previously mentioned changes in midlife and late adulthood may cause a realignment of activities within the household, which in turn can affect spouses' evaluations of fairness and equity (Hagedoorn et al., 2006). The equity theory is consistent with this perspective (Walster, Walster, & Berscheid, 1978). An early study conducted by Keith and Schafer (1985) found that middle-aged and older wives who perceive the allocation of tasks such as cooking and housekeeping as unequal are more depressed and dissatisfied with their roles than wives who perceive the allocation of tasks as egalitarian. Furthermore, Kulik (2002) revealed that equality in minor decisions (e.g., about spending time) as well as equality in carrying out general tasks (e.g., paying bills) is related to higher marital satisfaction among retirees. It was also found that equality in different types of tasks has a differential impact on wives and husbands. In late adulthood, perceived equality in allocation of domestic tasks is a more significant predictor of high marital quality for women, whereas equality in maintenance tasks, which are typically considered masculine, plays a more significant role in predicting higher marital quality for men. Perceived equality in performing feminine tasks for women and masculine tasks for men was also found to be related to lower marital tension (Kulik, 2004). The same study also found that besides the contribution of equality in task allocation to explaining marital quality in late adulthood, the contribution of equality in other aspects of marital life, such as decision making and income, is also significant: The more the participants perceive each partner's contribution to the family income and participation in decision making as equitable, the higher their marital satisfaction.

## SUMMARY

In late adulthood and midlife, men and women attribute considerable importance to their spousal role. The role of spouse is considered to be most important in these life stages, after the role of parent. Moreover, satisfaction with the spousal role in late adulthood is related to a sense of well-being and a sense of meaning in life among men and women (Kulik et al., 2014). The extent of perceived equality in household role allocation during this life stage is an important aspect of spousal life that can be a source of tension and conflict on the one hand and a source of enjoyment on the other hand.

The review of the research literature presented here indicates that despite the changes that take place in spousal relationships as a result of life transitions, the overall division of household roles does not change substantially in middle and late adulthood. Moreover, a gendered division of labor in which women devote more time to household chores is maintained in later stages of the spousal relationship, regardless of life transitions. Thus, following the transition to the empty nest and retirement phases, and following the transition to becoming caregivers in the later stages of marital life, women continue to bear the burden of household tasks as they did in the earlier stages of life. It appears that in this respect, the impact of life transitions on household role allocation in the later stages of life is greater for husbands than for wives. Specifically, when the husband retires (whether or not the wife continues to work), he tends to participate more in household tasks. In contradistinction, the woman's retirement has less of an impact because she remains in the territory of the home that she had dominated before. Furthermore, the role of caregiver to elderly and ill family members has traditionally been considered a feminine role, and in late adulthood it replaces the role of caring for young children that women assumed in early adulthood. As such, it can be concluded that the gendered allocation of roles that characterized the earlier stages of the spousal relationship continues in late adulthood. However, minor changes occur as reflected in the nature of task allocation as well as in decision-making patterns. Research has also suggested that same-sex couples are more egalitarian than heterosexual couples, with the allocation of roles being more equal among lesbian couples than among gay men.

Finally, the potential cohort effect is noteworthy when generalizing findings on spousal role allocation in midlife and late life. The studies presented in this chapter relate to people who have undergone a process of early socialization to gender roles that were prevalent in previous generations. However, younger generations are experiencing more egalitarian processes of socialization to gender roles with a greater emphasis on the value of equality in spousal or partnered life. It is therefore possible that there will be more equality in spousal role allocation when more recent cohorts reach midlife and late adulthood and that the impact of role equality on marital satisfaction will be greater than seen in today's generation of middle-aged and older adults.

## RECOMMENDATIONS FOR FUTURE RESEARCH

Notwithstanding major developments in research on dyadic relations in midlife and late adulthood in recent years, there is a need for further research on the topic. Because existing studies on spousal role allocation are dated, and in light of the major changes that have occurred in gender roles and family life in the contemporary era, research in the field of aging should focus more on examining the determinants of spousal role allocation among aging couples today. Moreover, most of the existing studies on spousal task allocation focused on husbands and wives. Thus, efforts should be invested in examining spousal task allocation among older couples in different types of relationships. In particular, the increasing legal recognition of same-sex marriage makes these unions an important focus for future research.

In light of the increased life expectancy, future studies on spousal task allocation should take into account the impact of the longer duration of marriages today. Notably, researchers have emphasized substages of late adulthood, and a distinction has been made between the "young-old," "old-old," and "oldest-old" (Riediger, Freund, & Baltes, 2005). Thus, each of these substages should be examined separately, rather than examining role allocation for the entire period of late adulthood.

Similarly, researchers have identified different stages in the transition to retirement, beginning with the stage of euphoria through the stage of disillusionment and until the stage of reconciliation (Reitzes & Mutran, 2004). Because these stages differ from each other in the way that retirees use the time at their disposal following retirement, task allocation should be examined separately in each stage of late adulthood. Another possible direction of research relates to the inclusion of cultural perspectives in the analysis of spousal role allocation in late adulthood. Most studies on role allocation in the late stage of the spousal relationship were conducted in Western cultures.

It would be interesting to examine spousal role allocation at later ages among non-Western cultures and to compare the findings with Western cultures. Finally, an attempt should be made to shed light on the determinants of role allocation from a broader perspective that integrates qualitative aspects of the spousal relationship in the face of transitions in later ages of life. This recommendation raises the questions: Does the quality of spousal relationship at transition points in marriage affect spousal role allocation? Do enjoyable relationships versus conflictual spousal relationships at each transition point in midlife and late life create different contexts for spousal role allocation? Undoubtedly, examining spousal role allocation in late adulthood remains an important area of continued empirical inquiry for researchers today.

The conclusions that can be derived from the findings presented in this chapter have some practical implications. Family therapists working with couples in the later stages of marriage should be aware of the changes that may occur in spousal role allocation at major transition points in late adulthood and should take these changes into account in developing professional interventions. Family therapists should also be aware that individuals are prepared for some normative changes (e.g., empty nest, retirement) but may not be sufficiently prepared for other changes, such as becoming the primary caregiver to a family member, which may last for many years over the spousal life cycle and may affect spousal interaction as well as task allocation. Counselors should also emphasize to their clients the importance of spousal task allocation, which was found to be a major determinant of marital quality in the process of aging. In so doing, they should describe the potential changes in task allocation following the transitions in late adulthood and prepare older couples to cope effectively with the changes in an attempt to alleviate stress and promote marital quality.

## REFERENCES

Adelmann, P. K., & Zajonc, R. B. (1989). Facial efference and the experience of emotion. *Annual Review of Psychology, 40*, 249–280. http://dx.doi.org/10.1146/annurev.ps.40.020189.001341

Aldous, J., Mulligan, G. M., & Bjarnason, T. (1998). Fathering over time: What makes the difference? *Journal of Marriage and Family, 60*, 809–820. http://dx.doi.org/10.2307/353626

Anderson, S. A., & Sabatelli, R. M. (2007). *Family interaction: A multigenerational development perspective.* Boston, MA: Pearson Education.

Artis, J. E., & Pavalko, E. K. (2003). Explaining the decline in women's household labor: Individual change and cohort differences. *Journal of Marriage and Family, 65*, 746–761. http://dx.doi.org/10.1111/j.1741-3737.2003.00746.x

Back, K. W. (1971). Transition to aging and the self-image. *International Journal of Aging & Human Development, 2,* 296–304. http://dx.doi.org/10.2190/AG.2.4.g

Bakan, D. (1966). *The duality of human existence: An essay on psychology and religion.* Oxford, England: Rand McNally.

Barber, C. E. (1989). Transition to the empty nest. In S. J. Bahr & E. T. Peterson (Eds.), *Aging and the family* (pp. 15–32). Lexington, MA: D.C. Heath & Co.

Bittman, M., England, P., Sayer, L. C., Folbre, N., & Matheson, G. (2003). When does gender trump money? Bargaining and time in household work. *American Journal of Sociology, 109,* 186–214. http://dx.doi.org/10.1086/378341

Blood, R., & Wolfe, D. (1960). *Husbands and wives.* New York, NY: Free Press.

Bookwala, J. (2009). The impact of parent care on marital quality and well-being in adult daughters and sons. *Journals of Gerontology: Series B. Psychological Sciences and Social Sciences, 64,* 339–347. http://dx.doi.org/10.1093/geronb/gbp018

Bookwala, J. (2012). Marriage and other partnered relationships in middle and late adulthood. In R. Blieszner & V. Bedford (Eds.), *Handbook of families and aging* (pp. 91–123). Santa Barbara, CA: Praeger.

Bossé, R., Aldwin, C. M., Levenson, M. R., Workman-Daniels, K., & Ekerdt, D. J. (1990). Differences in social support among retirees and workers: Findings from the Normative Aging Study. *Psychology and Aging, 5,* 41–47. http://dx.doi.org/10.1037/0882-7974.5.1.41

Brannen, J., & Moss, P. (1991). *Managing mothers: Dual earner households after maternity leave.* London, England: Unwin Hyman.

Bromberger, J. T., & Matthews, K. A. (1996). A longitudinal study of the effects of pessimism, trait anxiety, and life stress on depressive symptoms in middle-aged women. *Psychology and Aging, 11,* 207–213. http://dx.doi.org/10.1037/0882-7974.11.2.207

Brubaker, E., & Brubaker, T. H. (1992). The context of retired women as caregivers. In M. Szinovacz, D. J. Ekerdt, & B. H. Vinick (Eds.), *Families and retirement: Conceptual and methodological issues* (pp. 222–235). Newbury Park, CA: Sage. http://dx.doi.org/10.4135/9781483325354.n14

Calasanti, T. M. (1996). Gender and life satisfaction in retirement: An assessment of the male model. *The Journals of Gerontology: Series B. Psychological Sciences and Social Sciences, 51,* S18–S29. http://dx.doi.org/10.1093/geronb/51B.1.S18

Carrington, C. (1999). *No place like home: Relationships and family life among lesbians and gay men.* Chicago, IL: University of Chicago Press. http://dx.doi.org/10.7208/chicago/9780226094847.001.0001

Choi, H., & Marks, N. F. (2006). Transition to caregiving, marital disagreement, and psychological well-being: A prospective U.S. national study. *Journal of Family Issues, 27,* 1701–1722. http://dx.doi.org/10.1177/0192513X06291523

Coltrane, S. (2000). Research on household labor: Modeling and measuring the social embeddedness of routine family work. *Journal of Marriage and Family, 62,* 1247–1268. http://dx.doi.org/10.1111/j.1741-3737.2000.01208.x

Coltrane, S., & Shih, K. Y. (2010). Gender and the division of labor. In J. Chrisler & D. R. McCreary (Eds.), *Handbook of gender research in psychology* (pp. 401–422). New York, NY: Springer. http://dx.doi.org/10.1007/978-1-4419-1467-5_17

Connidis, I. A., & Kemp, C. L. (2008). Negotiating actual and anticipated parental support: Multiple sibling voices in three-generation families. *Journal of Aging Studies, 22,* 229–238. http://dx.doi.org/10.1016/j.jaging.2007.06.002

Coward, R. T., Horne, C., & Dwyer, J. W. (1992). Demographic perspectives on gender and family caregiving. In J. W. Dwyer & R. T. Coward (Eds.), *Gender, family and elder care* (pp. 18–33). Newbury Park, CA: Sage.

Dennerstein, L., Dudley, E., & Guthrie, J. (2002). Empty nest or revolving door? A prospective study of women's quality of life in midlife during the phase of children leaving and re-entering the home. *Psychological Medicine, 32,* 545–550. http://dx.doi.org/10.1017/S0033291701004810

Downing, J. B., & Goldberg, A. E. (2011). Lesbian mothers' constructions of the division of paid and unpaid labor. *Feminism & Psychology, 21,* 100–120. http://dx.doi.org/10.1177/0959353510375869

Dunne, G. A. (2000). Opting into motherhood: Lesbians blurring the boundaries and transforming the meaning of parenthood and kinship. *Gender & Society, 14,* 11–35. http://dx.doi.org/10.1177/089124300014001003

Duvall, E. M., & Miller, B. C. (1985). *Marriage and family development.* New York, NY: Harper and Row.

Dwyer, J. W., & Seccombe, K. (1991). Elder care as family labor: The influence of gender and family position. *Journal of Family Issues, 12,* 229–247. http://dx.doi.org/10.1177/019251391012002006

Ferree, M. M. (1990). Beyond separate spheres: Feminism and family research. *Journal of Marriage and Family, 52,* 866–884. http://dx.doi.org/10.2307/353307

Gartrell, N., Deck, A., Rodas, C., Peyser, H., & Banks, A. (2005). The National Lesbian Family Study: 4. Interviews with the 10-year-old children. *American Journal of Orthopsychiatry, 75,* 518–524. http://dx.doi.org/10.1037/0002-9432.75.4.518

Goldberg, A. E. (2013). "Doing" and "undoing" gender: The meaning and division of housework in same-sex couples. *Journal of Family Theory & Review, 5*(2), 85–104. http://dx.doi.org/10.1111/jftr.12009

Goldberg, A. E., Smith, J. Z., & Perry-Jenkins, M. (2012). The division of labor in lesbian, gay, and heterosexual new adoptive parents. *Journal of Marriage and Family, 74,* 812–828. http://dx.doi.org/10.1111/j.1741-3737.2012.00992.x

Gordon, J. R., & Whelan-Berry, K. S. (2005). Contributions to family and household activities by the husbands of midlife professional women. *Journal of Family Issues, 26,* 899–923. http://dx.doi.org/10.1177/0192513X04273590

Gratton, B., & Rotondo, F. M. (1992). The "family fund": Strategies for security in old age in the industrial era. In M. Szinovacz, D. J. Ekerdt, & B. H. Vinick (Eds.), *Families and retirement: Conceptual and methodological issues* (pp. 51–63). Newbury Park, CA: Sage. http://dx.doi.org/10.4135/9781483325354.n3

Greenstein, T. N. (1996). Husbands' participation in domestic labor: Interactive effects of wives' and husbands' gender ideologies. *Journal of Marriage and Family*, 58, 585–595. http://dx.doi.org/10.2307/353719

Haberkern, K., & Szydlik, M. (2010). State care provision, societal opinion and children's care of older parents in 11 European countries. *Ageing and Society*, 30, 299–323. http://dx.doi.org/10.1017/S0144686X09990316

Hafstrom, J. L., & Schram, V. R. (1983). Housework time of wives: Pressure, facilitators, constraints. *Home Economics Research Journal*, 11, 245–254. http://dx.doi.org/10.1177/1077727X8301100306

Hagedoorn, M., Van Yperen, N. W., Coyne, J. C., van Jaarsveld, C. H., Ranchor, A. V., van Sonderen, E., & Sanderman, R. (2006). Does marriage protect older people from distress? The role of equity and recency of bereavement. *Psychology and Aging*, 21, 611–620. http://dx.doi.org/10.1037/0882-7974.21.3.611

Hochschild, A. (1989). *The second shift: Working parents and the revolution at home*. New York, NY: Viking.

Julien, D., Arellano, C., & Turgeon, L. (1997). *Gender issues in heterosexual, gay and lesbian couples*. Hoboken, NJ: Wiley.

Kamo, Y. (1994). Division of household work in the United States and Japan. *Journal of Family Issues*, 15, 348–378. http://dx.doi.org/10.1177/019251394015003002

Katz-Wise, S. L., Priess, H. A., & Hyde, J. S. (2010). Gender-role attitudes and behavior across the transition to parenthood. *Developmental Psychology*, 46, 18–28. http://dx.doi.org/10.1037/a0017820

Keith, P. M., & Schafer, R. B. (1985). Equity, role strains, and depression among middle-aged and older men and women. In W. A. Peterson & J. S. Quadango (Eds.), *Social bonds in later life* (pp. 37–49). Beverly Hills, CA: Sage.

Kingson, E. R., & O'Grady-LeShane, R. (1993). The effects of caregiving on women's Social Security benefits. *The Gerontologist*, 33, 230–239. http://dx.doi.org/10.1093/geront/33.2.230

Kulik, L. (1999). Marital power relations, resources and gender role ideology: A multivariate model of assessing effects. *Journal of Comparative Family Studies*, 30, 189–206.

Kulik, L. (2001a). Marital relations in late adulthood, throughout the retirement process. *Ageing and Society*, 21, 447–469. http://dx.doi.org/10.1017/S0144686X01008273

Kulik, L. (2001b). Marital relationship in late adulthood: Synchronous versus asynchronous couples. *International Journal of Aging & Human Development*, 52, 323–339. http://dx.doi.org/10.2190/7N22-5MUC-4MVC-NCQQ

Kulik, L. (2002). Equality in marriage, marital satisfaction, and life satisfaction: A comparative analysis of pre-retired and retired men and women in Israel. *Families in Society*, 83, 197–207. http://dx.doi.org/10.1606/1044-3894.32

Kulik, L. (2004). Perceived equality in spousal relations, marital quality, and life satisfaction: Comparison of elderly Israeli wives and husbands. *Families in Society*, 85, 243–250.

Kulik, L., Shilo-Levin, S., & Liberman, G. (2014, February). *Differences in performing roles and in the experience of role conflict along the life cycle*. Paper presented at the 20th Gerontological Conference, Tel-Aviv, Israel.

Kulik, L., & Zuckerman-Bareli, H. (1997). Continuity and discontinuity in attitudes toward marital power relations: Pre-retired versus retired husbands. *Ageing and Society*, 17, 571–595. http://dx.doi.org/10.1017/S0144686X97006491

Lippa, R. A. (2008). Sex differences and sexual orientation differences in personality: Findings from the BBC Internet survey. *Archives of Sexual Behavior, 37*, 173–187. http://dx.doi.org/10.1007/s10508-007-9267-z

Miller, D. M. (1990). *Caregiving in chronic illness: The experience of married persons whose spouses have MS*. Unpublished doctoral dissertation, Case Western Reserve University, Cleveland, OH.

Muhlbauer, V., & Chrisler, J. C. (Eds.). (2007). *Women over 50: Psychological perspectives*. New York, NY: Springer. http://dx.doi.org/10.1007/978-0-387-46341-4

Park, E. O., Yates, B. C., Schumacher, K. L., Meza, J., Kosloski, K., & Pullen, C. (2013). Caregiving demand and difficulty in older adult spousal caregivers after coronary artery bypass surgery. *Geriatric Nursing, 34*, 383–387. http://dx.doi.org/10.1016/j.gerinurse.2013.05.007

Pearlin, L. I., Mullan, J. T., Semple, S. J., & Skaff, M. M. (1990). Caregiving and the stress process: An overview of concepts and their measures. *The Gerontologist*, 30, 583–594. http://dx.doi.org/10.1093/geront/30.5.583

Pillay, A. L. (1988). Midlife depression and the "empty nest" syndrome in Indian women. *Psychological Reports, 63*, 591–594. http://dx.doi.org/10.2466/pr0.1988.63.2.591

Pinquart, M., & Sörensen, S. (2006). Gender differences in caregiver stressors, social resources, and health: An updated meta-analysis. *Journals of Gerontology: Series B. Psychological Sciences and Social Sciences, 61*, 33–45. http://dx.doi.org/10.1093/geronb/61.1.P33

Pleck, J. H. (1985). *Working wives, working husbands*. Beverly Hills, CA: Sage.

Pope, N. D., Kolomer, S., & Glass, A. P. (2012). How women in late midlife become caregivers for their aging parents. *Journal of Women & Aging, 24*, 242–261. http://dx.doi.org/10.1080/08952841.2012.639676

Pruchno, R. A., & Gitlin, L. N. (2013). Family caregiving in late life: Shifting paradigms. In R. Blieszner & V. Bedford (Eds.), *Handbook of families and aging* (pp. 514–541). Santa Barbara, CA: Praeger.

Pruchno, R. A., & Resch, N. L. (1989). Aberrant behaviors and Alzheimer's disease: Mental health effects on spouse caregivers. *Journal of Gerontology, 44*, S177–S182. http://dx.doi.org/10.1093/geronj/44.5.S177

Reitzes, D. C., & Mutran, E. J. (2004). The transition to retirement: Stages and factors that influence retirement adjustment. *International Journal of Aging & Human Development, 59,* 63–84. http://dx.doi.org/10.2190/NYPP-RFFP-5RFK-8EB8

Rexroat, C., & Shehan, C. (1987). The life cycle and spouses' time in housework. *Journal of Marriage and Family, 49,* 737–750. http://dx.doi.org/10.2307/351968

Riediger, M., Freund, A. M., & Baltes, P. B. (2005). Managing life through personal goals: Intergoal facilitation and intensity of goal pursuit in younger and older adulthood. *Journals of Gerontology: Series B. Psychological Sciences and Social Sciences, 60,* 84–91. http://dx.doi.org/10.1093/geronb/60.2.P84

Roberto, K. A., & Jarrott, S. E. (2008). Family caregivers of older adults: A life span perspective. *Family Relations, 57,* 100–111. http://dx.doi.org/10.1111/j.1741-3729.2007.00486.x

Rose, S. M. (2015). Lesbians over 60: Newer every day. In V. Muhlbauer, J. C. Chrisler, & F. L. Denmark (Eds.), *Women and aging: An international, intersectional power perspective* (pp. 117–146). New York, NY: Springer.

Saraceno, C., & Keck, W. (2010). Can we identify intergenerational policy regimes in Europe? *European Societies, 12,* 675–696. http://dx.doi.org/10.1080/14616696.2010.483006

Silverstein, M., Gans, D., & Yang, F. M. (2006). Intergenerational support to aging parents the role of norms and needs. *Journal of Family Issues, 27,* 1068–1084. http://dx.doi.org/10.1177/0192513X06288120

Stanik, C. E., & Bryant, C. M. (2012). Marital quality of newlywed African American couples: Implications of egalitarian gender role dynamics. *Sex Roles, 66*(3–4), 256–267. http://dx.doi.org/10.1007/s11199-012-0117-7

Stoller, E. P. (1990). Males as helpers: The role of sons, relatives, and friends. *The Gerontologist, 30,* 228–235. http://dx.doi.org/10.1093/geront/30.2.228

Suitor, J. J., & Pillemer, K. (1990). Transition to the status of family caregiver: A new framework for studying social support and well-being. In S. M. Stahl (Ed.), *The legacy of longevity: Health, and health care in later life* (pp. 310–320). Beverly Hills, CA: Sage.

Sullivan, M. (2004). *The family of woman: Lesbian mothers, their children, and the undoing of gender.* Berkeley, CA: University of California Press.

Szinovacz, M. (1989). Decision-making on retirement timing. In D. Brinberg & J. Jaccard (Eds.), *Dyadic decision making* (pp. 286–310). New York, NY: Springer. http://dx.doi.org/10.1007/978-1-4612-3516-3_12

Szinovacz, M. E. (2000). Changes in housework after retirement: A panel analysis. *Journal of Marriage and Family, 62,* 78–92. http://dx.doi.org/10.1111/j.1741-3737.2000.00078.x

Szinovacz, M. E., Ekerdt, D., Butt, A., Barton, K., & Oala, C. R. (2012). Families and retirement. In R. Blieszner & V. H. Bedford (Eds.), *Handbook of families and aging* (pp. 461–488). Santa Barbara, CA: Praeger.

Walker, A. J., Pratt, C. C., & Eddy, L. (1995). Informal caregiving to aging family members: A critical review. *Family Relations, 44,* 402–411. http://dx.doi.org/10.2307/584996

Walster, E., Walster, G. W., & Berscheid, E. (1978). *Equity: Theory and research.* Boston, MA: Allyn & Bacon.

Williamson, G. M., & Schulz, R. (1990). Relationship orientation, quality of prior relationship, and distress among caregivers of Alzheimer's patients. *Psychology and Aging, 5,* 502–509. http://dx.doi.org/10.1037/0882-7974.5.4.502

Xie, Y., & Zhu, H. (2009). Do sons or daughters give more money to parents in urban China? *Journal of Marriage and Family, 71,* 174–186. http://dx.doi.org/10.1111/j.1741-3737.2008.00588.x

Young, R. F., & Kahana, E. (1989). Specifying caregiver outcomes: Gender and relationship aspects of caregiving strain. *The Gerontologist, 29,* 660–666. http://dx.doi.org/10.1093/geront/29.5.660

# 8

# THESE HAPPY GOLDEN YEARS? THE ROLE OF RETIREMENT IN MARITAL QUALITY

AMY RAUER AND JAKOB F. JENSEN

Retirement has often been referred to as "the golden years"—a wonderful, relaxing time when individuals can shed the responsibilities and burdens of the previous decades and focus on rediscovering themselves and their spouses (Marson & Zebley, 2000). Implicit within this conceptualization of retirement is the notion that this is a time of life characterized by uniformly positive changes within the individual and within family relationships, particularly within marriage. Research has found, however, that individuals' experience of the transition to retirement is varied (Wang, 2007), with many retirees experiencing little, if any, change in well-being on retiring, others experiencing distress, and still others experiencing benefits. If older adults do not follow a uniform adjustment pattern during the retirement process, then it is unlikely uniformity would exist in the effects of retirement on marital quality, which captures a spouse's global evaluation of the positive and negative dimensions of the marriage. Although couples' experiences are intricately linked across

http://dx.doi.org/10.1037/14897-009
*Couple Relationships in the Middle and Later Years: Their Nature, Complexity, and Role in Health and Illness,*
J. Bookwala (Editor)

the lifespan, particularly when it comes to retirement decisions and adjustment (Pienta & Hayward, 2002; Szinovacz & Davey, 2005), recent theoretical advances underscore the heterogeneity of the effects of marriage on
retirement both within and between couples (Wickrama, O'Neal, & Lorenz,
2013). This heterogeneity is likely to increase in the future as a response to
the unique nature of the baby boomer cohort as well as changes to the retirement process itself, with a growing number of individuals transitioning into
and back out of retirement in response to changing personal, family, and
financial demands (Maestas, 2010; Pleau & Shauman, 2013). Accordingly,
the goal of the current chapter is to review how retirement has been linked to
marital quality, with careful consideration of how recent sociohistorical trends
may alter these links over the coming decades and the implications of these
changes.

## MARITAL QUALITY AND RETIREMENT: A MIXED BAG

The study of the effects of retirement on marriage has undergone dramatic changes over the past century or so. First, the increase in life expectancy
means that most people are living long enough to experience retirement, and
the period of retirement has lengthened considerably (Settersten & Trauten,
2010). Second, because of the unprecedented size of the baby boomer cohort,
the number of individuals retiring each year is fast outpacing any other segment
of the population (Rowe, 2007). Finally, women's increased workforce participation in the 20th century means that both spouses now have to adjust to
exiting the workforce on retirement (Miller & Yorgason, 2009). To understand
the effects of these changes, we draw on Wickrama and colleagues' (2013)
life course–stress process framework. This framework suggests that to understand the level and change of marital functioning during retirement, one must
consider how an individual's and his or her spouse's cumulative chronic life
experiences (e.g., preretirement marital quality), personal characteristics (e.g.,
health), and genotype jointly impact their marriage directly and indirectly via
their effects on mid- and late-life transitions (e.g., retirement timing). In light
of this complexity, it is not surprising that the literature on the effects of retirement on marital quality is inconsistent, with many studies finding no effects
on the marriage, others finding declines in marital quality, and a few finding
couples benefit from this transition.

### Lack of Support for a Link Between Retirement and Marital Quality

In a pioneering review of the literature, Atchley (1992) concluded that
retirement posed "little threat to marital quality" (p. 146). More recent and

methodologically sophisticated work supports Atchley's conclusion that the transition to retirement has minimal, if any, effects on the marriage (Davey & Szinovacz, 2004). Instead, stability in marital quality dominates across this transition (Miller & Yorgason, 2009). Interestingly, much of the work supporting the lack of change in marriage across the retirement transition is derived from studies testing the oft-cited U-shaped curve of marital quality, which states that changes should occur (Miller, 2000). The U-shaped curve proposed that couples experience a steep decline in quality in the early years, followed by a plateau in the middle years, and eventually a modest upturn in the later years. This upturn was thought to be a result of both retirement and the launching of children, revealing the assumption that the improvements in the marital relationship during the later years are a result of having reduced responsibilities and thus more time for the marriage (Orbuch, House, Mero, & Webster, 1996; VanLaningham, Johnson, & Amato, 2001).

Though cross-sectional studies have found evidence of this curve, Bookwala (2012) suggested that this may be due to methodological artifacts (e.g., cross-sectional designs, cohort effects, attrition of divorced couples), as more advanced, longitudinal studies have failed to find this pattern (Vaillant & Vaillant, 1993; VanLaningham et al., 2001). Miller (2000) concluded that couples tend to adapt to changes in their circumstances, such as retirement, as a result of an underlying tendency toward stability. As a potential explanation, Fitzpatrick, Bushfield, and Vinick (2005) found that contrary to the couples' own expectations, there was significant stability in couples' individual and couple activities. Thus, although many couples expect their lives to be different after retirement, their lives are remarkably similar to when they were still working.

### Support for the Negative Impact of Retirement on Marital Quality

Although most studies continue to find minimal effects of retirement on marital quality, those that are found tend to be negative. To note, the negative effects that emerge appear to be mostly time limited, which may explain why the aforementioned studies that focused on longer time frames did not catch difficulties immediately following the transition to retirement (Vaillant & Vaillant, 1993; VanLaningham et al., 2001). For example, Moen, Kim, and Hofmeister (2001) found decreased marital quality for both men and women who had just transitioned to retirement in comparison to those who were still employed. Those who had been retired over two years, however, had comparable marital quality to those who were still employed. These findings suggest that there is something about the transition itself, perhaps the temporary declines in psychological well-being and life satisfaction that accompany the transition for some (Pinquart & Schindler, 2007; Wang, 2007), that negatively affects the marriage, but the actual state of retirement does not.

As to why the transition might initially be difficult, several explanations exist. First, the increased time together that naturally occurs in retirement may be problematic for some, as Bushfield, Fitzpatrick, and Vinick (2008) found that in single-earner households, some women were bothered by their husbands' intrusion into their activities on his retirement. Further, Kulik (2001) found retirement was associated with less marital enjoyment for both retiring husbands and retiring wives, suggesting that both spouses may perceive this increased time together as excessive. Second, men may initiate sex less frequently after retirement than they had before because of a perceived decline of social status and less confidence in their masculinity (Papaharitou et al., 2008; Trudel, Turgeon, & Piché, 2000), resulting in diminished sexual and marital satisfaction for both spouses. Finally, husbands and wives may have different attitudes about how to manage their finances in their later years, underscoring the potential moderating role that financial well-being may play in affecting marital quality in retirement. For example, Lundberg, Startz, and Stillman (2003) found wives prefer to save more than husbands do, which may explain why Dew and Yorgason (2010) found financial pressure during the retirement transition to exert a negative impact on the marriage. To note, the distress caused by economic difficulties was not present for those who had retired prior to the study. These findings indicate that although some couples may take a little time to reestablish their preretirement marital quality, stability in marital quality is the predominant experience of most retired couples (Miller & Yorgason, 2009).

## Support for the Benefits of Retirement for Marital Quality

Though there is little empirical support for the benefits of retirement, most couples anticipate that it will positively affect their marriage (Rosenkoetter & Garris, 2001). Of the few studies that did find benefits, these appear to be more in enhancements to specific marital processes, rather than to general evaluations of marital quality. For example, Trudel and colleagues (2000) suggested that couples' sexual intimacy is enriched by retirement, as many of the occupational and childrearing activities that previously precluded sexual activity are no longer present. This increased intimacy may explain why retired couples report fewer marital complaints than working couples (Kulik, 2001). Similarly, Szinovacz and Schaffer (2000) found that husbands, but not wives, perceived a decline in heated arguments on the wives' retirement, especially if both spouses retired. A husband's own retirement, on the other hand, appeared to enhance his perceptions of calm discussions if he or his wife was strongly invested in the marriage. Spouses who are less attached to their relationship may seek outside engagements or interests to avoid interacting with each other, thus they have fewer opportunities for either confrontations or calm discussions. Finally, Fitzpatrick and Vinick (2003) found that wives felt an increase in their marital cohesion when their husbands retired, with minimal effects of her own employment status on perceptions of cohesion. Even among studies finding enhancements to the marriage as a result of retirement, these benefits appear to be contingent on a number of factors, ranging from the preretirement quality of the marriage to which spouse is retiring or if they both are and when.

Miller and Yorgason (2009) suggested that researchers continue to find mixed evidence because the increased time couples spend together postretirement amplifies their preretirement marital characteristics and tendencies. Although this explanation highlights the inherent heterogeneity that exists within couples, it only focuses on differences in how couples interact with each other. Per life course–stress theory (Wickrama et al., 2013), however, there are a variety of additional individual, couple, and contextual factors that precede the retirement transition as well as those that are concurrent with the transition that are likely to also affect the couples' experience of retirement and in turn their evaluations of their marriage and thus must be considered.

## POTENTIAL MODERATORS OF THE TRANSITION TO RETIREMENT: A MORE NUANCED APPROACH

The effects of the transition to retirement on marital quality are not uniform across couples or even within the same couple. However, although some partners may be more likely to experience difficulties across this transition because of their particular configuration of individual, couple, and contextual circumstances, many of these factors precede the transition to retirement, thus offering potential points of entry for smoothing the transition to retirement well before it occurs.

### Preretirement Job Characteristics and Timing

The effects of the transition to retirement on marital quality may be shaped largely by what happens at the workplace and when. For example, individuals who are in stressful jobs may benefit greatly from retiring. Given how much the marital climate is affected by an individual's work stress (N. A. Roberts & Levenson, 2001), removing this stressor should enhance marital quality for couples that had a higher quality relationship prior to the work environment stress. But if the job was rewarding, then retirement may simultaneously remove a critical resource for the couple while adding a stressor. This latter case is more likely if the decision to retire was not entirely one's own, as spouses who feel forced into retirement have more adjustment difficulties (Szinovacz & Davey, 2005; van Solinge & Henkens, 2005), which in turn is likely to negatively impact the marital relationship.

When one retires, be it voluntary or forced, also shapes the retirement experience, with off-time events, those that deviate from the normative timing of life events, being especially consequential for functioning (Wickrama et al., 2013). Retiring too early could leave individuals struggling and thus negatively impact the marriage. Further complicating the effects of timing is that couples must jointly negotiate the timing of retirement, deciding whether to retire together or to stagger their retirements and in which direction. Although some evidence suggests that men's preferences are weighted more heavily, particularly in traditional male-breadwinner families (Denaeghel, Mortelmans, & Borghgraef, 2011), most husbands and wives prefer retiring together, and it appears to be better for their marriage than a staggered retirement (Davey & Szinovacz, 2004). Of couples who do stagger retirement, the most problematic pairings are those in which the husbands retired first (Moen et al., 2001). These effects may depend though on couples' views of gender roles in the marriage. Szinovacz (1996) found that the husband retired/wife employed pattern was associated with lower marital quality for those with traditional views of gender, but couples with those views in the employed husband/retired wife pattern had higher marital quality. These findings suggest that couples' perspectives on their job and the nature and timing of retirement may portend important differences in how they will adjust to retirement.

## Preretirement Marital Characteristics and Expectations

Much of the heterogeneity that exists in how couples adjust to retirement appears to be forecast by differences in their preretirement relationship and expectations. This is not surprising as the quality of the marriage even impacts the decision whether to retire and when (Miller & Yorgason, 2009; Mock & Cornelius, 2007), with happier couples retiring earlier to spend more time together and unhappier couples delaying this togetherness by staying in the workforce for longer periods (Szinovacz & DeViney, 2000). Interestingly though, the same characteristics of a couple that benefit them earlier in their marriage may prove challenging during the retirement years. Spousal similarity in personality, for example, benefits marital satisfaction earlier in the lifespan (Gaunt, 2006), but Shiota and Levenson (2007) found this not to be the case for older couples. The reduction of couples' responsibilities during retirement and subsequent increases in time together may result in couples becoming bored with each other because of too much overlap.

One area in which couples often appreciate greater overlap in their marriage during the retirement years is in their marital role allocation (see Chapter 7, this volume). Although women traditionally bear the brunt of household responsibilities when both spouses are working (Bartley, Blanton, & Gilliard, 2005), men take on a larger role during retirement (Kulik, 2001). Although greater equity predicts marital satisfaction in most couples (Kulik, 2002), the extent to which couples embrace this equity depends on their pre-retirement gender role attitudes. Wives with more egalitarian beliefs appreciated husbands' increased participation in housework, viewing their husbands as more supportive, thus increasing their perceptions of marital quality (Piña & Bengtson, 1993). On the other hand, wives with more conservative gender role attitudes may perceive husbands' increased participation as intrusive. For example, Bushfield, Fitzpatrick, and Vinick (2008) found that wives of retired husbands reported more perceptions of impingement.

Not only do one's preretirement relational beliefs affect the transition to retirement, but Van Solinge and Henkens (2005) suggested that one's beliefs about the *transition* to retirement itself can also shape how a couple adjusts during this time. Drawing on longitudinal data from a large sample of Dutch couples, the authors found that older adults who had negative preretirement expectations (e.g., concerns about marital conflict) coupled with low scores on self-efficacy reported a more difficult retirement adjustment. Thus, groundwork for couples' adjustment to retirement is laid much earlier in the marriage. The mixed effects of retirement on marriage will likely persist in light of the varied experiences and expectations couples bring to this transition.

## Couples' Marital History

This variety is likely to grow, as dramatic changes in family composition in the United States over the past few decades, in particular rising divorce rates, mean that a growing number of older adults are entering their later years having accumulated a diverse history of relationship experiences. It is projected that the 21st century will be characterized by even greater heterogeneity in relationships for the older population (Cooney & Dunne, 2001). This heterogeneity is important to consider when looking at the transition to retirement because the differential resources couples have accumulated as a result of their marital experiences are likely to impact their adjustment as a couple. Divorce, in particular, has been found to compromise financial resource accumulation across the lifespan (Zissimopoulos, Karney, & Rauer, 2015), meaning that remarried older adults may need to delay retirement because of greater financial need. Given that financial pressures increase marital stress for all couples prior to and during the retirement transition (Dew & Yorgason, 2010), remarried couples may be at additional risk for marital stress during this transition compared with continuously married individuals resulting from disparities in their wealth accumulation.

Remarried individuals could face fewer general adjustment difficulties than their continuously married counterparts though, as transitioning to both spouses being at home could represent a larger adjustment for couples who have been continuously married for decades and had most of their time and activities structured by one or both spouses working. Indeed, Pienta, Hayward, and Jenkins (2000) found that older adults married less than 10 years had fewer health problems relative to persons with a long-standing marriage. This suggests that marital history may have a complicated relationship with a couple's retirement adjustment—benefiting couples in some areas and providing additional challenges in others.

### Couples' Health

Although being married is generally associated with better health during the retirement years (Bookwala, 2005; Pienta et al., 2000), normative health declines could affect the timing of and adjustment to retirement. Older adults in poor health may have to retire early and against their own desires, which could diminish their satisfaction with their retirement and in turn their marriage (Higginbottom, Barling, & Kelloway, 1993). The decision to retire, however, is not only impacted by one's own health, but also by the health of one's partner, with some evidence suggesting the latter might be a more powerful predictor of retirement decisions. Szinovacz and DeViney (2000) found that husbands were more likely to retire if their wives were in poor health, though they did not find wives' decision to retire was related to husbands' health. In contrast, Pienta and Hayward (2002) found wives were more likely to retire based on their husbands' health. This inconsistency may be related to how health was measured—Szinovacz and DeViney assessed self-reported health, whereas Pienta and Hayward examined work disabilities. The latter likely requires a more concerted caregiving effort, thus having a greater impact on wives' decision whether to continue working.

Retiring because of health concerns, be it one's own or one's spouse's, could accentuate the negative effects of the retirement transition on marital quality as individuals may shift from a fulfilling career to a time of either dependence (when one's own health was at issue) or intensive caregiving (when the spouse's health was at issue). This may become a larger issue in the future as Peluso, Parsons, and Watts (2013) suggested that many individuals are now postponing retirement because of financial issues. The effects of these delays in retirement may mean that health will begin to play a larger role in both spouses' retirement decisions, with fewer couples able to actually enjoy their golden years together as a result of declining health during this time.

# FUTURE DIRECTIONS FOR THEORY AND RESEARCH

Although recent research has enhanced our understanding of how marriages are impacted by retirement, several issues warrant further consideration. First, research must expand beyond its current conceptualization of the marital relationship. Most frequently, studies have focused on how the transition to retirement affects overall evaluations of the marriage (e.g., marital quality, satisfaction) using retrospective reports of preretirement marital functioning. The first challenge of using this approach is that the accuracy of retrospective reports is questionable, particularly for recollections of changes in marital quality (Karney & Frye, 2002).

The second challenge is that measures traditionally used to gauge these evaluations were developed and tested with younger populations, which is problematic as measures often contain items not relevant for older populations (e.g., childrearing) and omit items that are (e.g., spouse's health; Haynes et al., 1992). Even if these measures show retrospective or prospective changes in mean levels of marital quality, Davey and Szinovacz (2004) suggested that we should not be constrained to assessing marriage in this manner, as spouses' retirement experiences have different consequences for the marital relationship beyond overall evaluations of quality. For example, aspects of marriage that were either beneficial or neutral preretirement may become sources of conflict on the transition to retirement as they become more salient (e.g., leisure activities; Miller & Yorgason, 2009). Interestingly, although Davey and Szinovacz (2004) found that marital conflict was not affected by either spouse's retirement, time spent together became less central to both spouses' meaning of marital solidarity on husbands' retirement.

To better capture these changing marital dynamics, researchers may want to consider including observational assessments of older couples. Although observational work of conflict in older couples was embraced by some researchers (Carstensen, Gottman, & Levenson, 1995; Heffner et al., 2006), there has been surprisingly little other observational work. This dearth is important to consider as the literature on observing marriages has itself undergone a transformation during this time, acknowledging the importance of looking beyond conflict to understand how couples interact in other settings (Weiss & Heyman, 2004). This shift in focus may be particularly important when considering the experiences of retired couples. For example, providing effective support to one's spouse may be more difficult during the retirement years. Whereas spouses may have previously been supporting each other through the difficulty of a stressful job, they may now need to transition to helping one another deal with the loss of said job as well as new challenges in other domains (e.g., health, loss of social contacts). There are additional challenges for spouses as support providers in older adulthood, as even the most well-intentioned support can exacerbate older adults' fears of dependence, which inspires feelings of incompetence or unsuccessful aging (Knight & Ricciardelli, 2003). In their review, L. J. Roberts and Greenberg (2002) concluded that the standard support paradigm in observational research may not reveal this vulnerable side to couples and proposed a new task paradigm. They found that asking couples to discuss a personal vulnerability (e.g., things they felt insecure about) successfully elicited more naturalistic, emotionally rich interactions between the partners. Using the vulnerability paradigm in observational studies of retired couples may be particularly powerful at detecting important differences in how couples handle their own and each other's adjustment to retirement.

Another way to capture how retirement affects couples is to move beyond structured laboratory paradigms to focus on more naturally occurring conversations between couples. Observing couples for 10 minutes during dinnertime conversations in an apartment laboratory, Driver and Gottman (2004) found that couples' positive everyday moments appeared to influence their ability to access humor during their arguments more so than in the standard laboratory setting. Given the likely changes that occur in couple communication across the transition to retirement, with couples no longer discussing work and instead possibly discussing their shared daily activities, it may be informative to see how the content of their dialogue shifts across this transition.

Perhaps the best way to uncover these nuances is to use a multimethod approach that includes both quantitative and qualitative components. Though there have been a few qualitative studies asking individuals to reflect on how retirement affected their gender identities and roles (Barnes & Parry, 2004), little has been done to examine how couples perceive changes in their marriage across this transition. A paradigm that might be useful in this endeavor comes from Holmberg, Orbuch, and Veroff (2004), who asked newlywed couples to tell their relationship histories. This more emic approach might reveal nuances in how the marriage changed versus stayed the same across the transition to retirement, as well as suggest how this transition compared with previous ones (e.g., parenthood, empty nest). Further, Hilbourne (1999) found that using more qualitative approaches enables researchers to develop a more holistic perspective on retirement, one that acknowledges the diversity of couples' experiences during this time.

To fully capture this variability that exists both within and between couples across the retirement transition, a number of methodological limitations of the literature must be addressed. First, despite the fact that retirement is a couple phenomenon, most research has only begun to capture the interdependencies of couples' retirement experiences. The work on gender provides a preliminary step to elucidating how these dependencies affect the marriage, but we need to go beyond gender differences as those can mask other important couple dynamics, such as the processes by which key factors influence evaluations of marriage for both partners (Bookwala, 2012). A dyadic approach is especially critical later in life as the strength of cross-spouse effects may intensify as the couples accumulate more shared history (Wickrama et al., 2013).

Second, though longitudinal studies are more prevalent in this area of research than in others focusing on later life marriage (Bookwala, 2012), cross-sectional studies dominate, and the longitudinal studies are often limited in scope. The former limits our ability to examine how marriage changes during retirement and to capture bidirectional associations therein, as cross-sectional studies rely on retrospective reports or comparisons with currently working individuals (Atchley, 1992), and the latter often only compare individuals at two time points—immediately following the transition to retirement and years later when the "honeymoon phase" has ended (Bushfield et al., 2008). Even prospective longitudinal studies tend to focus on couples at two time points—shortly before and after retirement (Fitzpatrick & Vinick, 2003; Moen et al., 2001). Longer term, prospective studies are critical moving forward as retirement is no longer a static, unidirectional change for many couples. The recent recession has created financial strain that not only led many couples to delay retirement, but also forced others to reenter the workforce after they retire, a phenomenon known as *unretirement* (Maestas, 2010; Pleau & Shauman, 2013). The challenges that couples face when one or both partners transition back to full- or part-time work (e.g., relationship related, financial, psychological, emotional) clearly merit study.

Appreciating the growing heterogeneity of couples represents the next area ripe for future research. A growing number of older adults are enjoying cohabiting relationships (Brown, Lee, & Bulanda, 2006), and the effect of retirement on their relationships remains to be seen. Focusing on cohabitation may also enable researchers to understand the effects of retirement on same-sex couples, an understudied but important population. Older cohorts of same-sex couples have been found to be more comparable to cohabiting couples with regards to their retirement planning, though lesbian couples benefit in particular from planning their retirement together (Mock & Cornelius, 2007). Another key facet of couples' lives is whether they have children and grandchildren. Some older couples take on primary caregiving responsibilities for adult children and grandchildren, leaving much less time for self-care, exercising, socializing, and personal hobbies after retirement (Hughes, Waite, LaPierre, & Luo, 2007). On the other hand, couples may see the opportunity to spend time with grandchildren as one of the joys of retirement (Marson & Zebley, 2000). This depends though on whether they can enjoy their grandchildren from afar, as custodial grandparents report a greater strain on their marital quality and financial resources during retirement (Hayslip & Kaminski, 2005). Despite theoretical support linking financial strain to greater marital strain during retirement (Wickrama et al., 2013), the study of socioeconomic differences with regards to couples' adjustment to retirement has been relatively limited. Finally, research on racial and ethnic differences in this area has been limited (Miller & Yorgason, 2009), despite evidence from Szinovacz, DeViney, and Davey (2001) suggesting that African Americans have a unique and complex set of factors that predict their retirement decisions.

Amplifying this heterogeneity in couple relationships is the fact that marriages exist within a complex network of friends, family, neighbors, and coworkers (Huston, 2000). As they age, individuals prune their networks, resulting in greater emotional dependence and potential burden on the spouse (Luong, Charles, & Fingerman, 2011). Retirement may hasten this process, as retirees report smaller support networks than those who are working (Van Tilburg, 2003). On the other hand, using a cross-sequential design, Cozijnsen, Stevens, and Van Tilburg (2010) found recent cohorts of retirees want to reestablish their work-related ties after losing touch on retirement. Further, although work-related ties may drop off early in retirement, these gaps in the network tend to be replaced by other relationships (e.g., neighbors; Van Tilburg, 2003). But the extent to which retirees maintain a strong network and how much it includes coworkers likely varies across individuals and couples, as large differences exist in the composition of older adults' social networks (Fiori, Smith, & Antonucci, 2007). Given the powerful role social networks can play in determining intimate relationship quality (Helms, Crouter, & McHale, 2003; Jensen & Rauer, 2014), further consideration is clearly warranted of how changes that occur within the social network as a result of retirement affect marital quality.

## CLINICAL AND POLICY IMPLICATIONS AND RECOMMENDATIONS

Given that marital quality buffers the health impact of age-related stressors, among which is included retirement (Bookwala, 2012), society has a vested interest in enhancing the marital quality of couples across the transition to retirement. The importance of these efforts is underscored given that the divorce rate among individuals over 50 has risen substantially in recent years (Brown & Lin, 2012). The challenge is that the traditional approach to enhancing marital quality is via therapy, but older adults tend to avoid therapy in part because of a perceived stigma of psychological counseling and a concern about the lack of efficacy of therapeutic interventions (Ellin, 2013; Goldstein & Preston, 1984). Thus, seeking therapy in older adulthood first needs to be normalized. Medical practitioners, who are more likely to be in contact with older adults and to have their advice heeded, should ask about patients' marital functioning and recommend therapy for those who indicate problems. The benefits of doing so are considerable, as marital quality has been related to both faster recovery from surgery and greater treatment adherence (Kulik & Mahler, 2006; Trief, Ploutz-Snyder, Britton, & Weinstock, 2004).

This proposal, however, hinges on the efficacy of these marital interventions, which may be a potential concern. Perhaps in part because of older adults' reluctance to seek therapy, there is a lack of research within the marriage and family therapy field on aging issues (Lambert-Shute & Fruhauf, 2011), leaving therapists feeling less confident about how well prepared they are to work with older clients (Yorgason, Miller, & White, 2009). Yorgason and colleagues (2009) suggested that therapists should be provided with more specialized gerontological training to help older couples navigate the difficulties associated with aging, including the transition to retirement. Further, it is necessary to evaluate if traditional approaches to marital therapy will be as effective for older populations, as previous research has found that relationship processes (e.g., conflict, support) may operate differently in older couples (Carstensen et al., 1995; Rauer, Sabey, & Jensen, 2014).

A strategy without as many barriers is to enhance marital quality before retirement occurs (Peluso et al., 2013). Family therapists can engage in preretirement counseling/coaching to help couples prepare for retirement. For example, ensuring that family therapists be more financially minded could help younger couples better financially prepare for retirement, helping ease some of the stresses traditionally associated with this transition. Relatedly, seminars offered to preretirees in the workplace could focus on providing information about family life in older adulthood (Dorfman, 2002). For example, they could help future retirees anticipate that there may be some adjustment issues in their marriage during the postretirement transition but that these will likely diminish in significance over time. The workplace also may be an especially appropriate place to target individuals planning to postpone retirement because of the recent recession. Postponing retirement may add further complications to the transition to retirement, given that the delay in retirement could co-occur with a number of other aging-related issues (e.g., caregiving). Indeed, such consideration of how experiencing multiple transitions affects marriage in later life has been largely overlooked (Wickrama et al., 2013). As a result, practitioners may be less well equipped to provide effective support and counseling to couples dealing simultaneously with multiple transitions. If these delays in retirement are financially driven, one solution may be to better educate spouses on retirement savings incentives earlier in the lifespan so that they are not compelled to work until their health is the determining factor in their retirement decisions. These programs should be especially targeted toward remarried individuals, who are most likely to have experienced financial setbacks because of their complicated marital histories (Zissimopoulos et al., 2015).

Bringing these lines of thought together, the need for protecting and promoting the quality of couples' relationships across the retirement transition is clear and critical. If couples' relationships suffer across this transition, individuals and their families pay a price. Further, if this results in divorce postretirement, individuals will be forced to turn to institutional rather than familial sources of support (Brown & Lin, 2012), especially if the loss of spousal support exacerbates aging-related health declines. Therefore, efforts to promote relationship quality are clearly warranted, and it appears that targeting the years during the retirement transition may be most effective, as these seem to be the most difficult to navigate. Helping couples prepare for the relational, emotional, financial, and social changes that accompany the transition to retirement will go a long way to ensuring their successful transition both as individuals and as a couple.

To accomplish this, we need additional research that is grounded in developmental theories and the life course–stress process frameworks, as these will help researchers take into account the heterogeneity of couples' experiences related to retirement—before, during, and after the transition. As this heterogeneity is only likely to increase as the number and proportion of older adults retiring grows over the coming years, it will be critical to provide practitioners and policymakers with a more nuanced understanding of marital quality during the retirement years and its predictors and consequences. By doing so, we can enhance the efficacy of their efforts to promote the quality of marriages in all phases of the transition to retirement and, in turn, ensure that more older adults are able to fully enjoy their golden years together.

## REFERENCES

Atchley, R. C. (1992). Retirement and marital satisfaction. In M. Szinovacz, D. J. Ekerdt, & B. H. Vinick (Eds.), *Families and retirement* (pp. 145–159). Newbury Park, CA: Sage. http://dx.doi.org/10.4135/9781483325354.n9

Barnes, H., & Parry, J. (2004). Renegotiating identity and relationships: Men and women's adjustments to retirement. *Ageing and Society, 24*, 213–233. http://dx.doi.org/10.1017/S0144686X0300148X

Bartley, S., Blanton, P., & Gilliard, J. (2005). Husbands and wives in dual-earner marriages: Decision-making, gender role attitudes, division of household labor, and equity. *Marriage & Family Review, 37*, 69–94. http://dx.doi.org/10.1300/J002v37n04_05

Bookwala, J. (2005). The role of marital quality in physical health during the mature years. *Journal of Aging and Health, 17*, 85–104. http://dx.doi.org/10.1177/0898264304272794

Bookwala, J. (2012). Marriage and other partnered relationships in middle and late adulthood. In R. Blieszner & V. H. Bedford (Eds.), *Handbook of families and aging* (pp. 91–123). Santa Barbara, CA: Praeger.

Brown, S. L., Lee, G. R., & Bulanda, J. R. (2006). Cohabitation among older adults: A national portrait. *The Journals of Gerontology: Series B. Psychological Sciences and Social Sciences, 61*, S71–S79. http://dx.doi.org/10.1093/geronb/61.2.S71

Brown, S. L., & Lin, I. F. (2012). The gray divorce revolution: Rising divorce among middle-aged and older adults, 1990–2010. *The Journals of Gerontology: Series B. Psychological Sciences and Social Sciences, 67*, 731–741. http://dx.doi.org/10.1093/geronb/gbs089

Bushfield, S. Y., Fitzpatrick, T. R., & Vinick, B. H. (2008). Perceptions of "impingement" and marital satisfaction among wives of retired husbands. *Journal of Women & Aging, 20*, 199–213. http://dx.doi.org/10.1080/08952840801984469

Carstensen, L. L., Gottman, J. M., & Levenson, R. W. (1995). Emotional behavior in long-term marriage. *Psychology and Aging, 10*, 140–149. http://dx.doi.org/10.1037/0882-7974.10.1.140

Cooney, T. M., & Dunne, K. (2001). Intimate relationships in later life: Current realities, future prospects. *Journal of Family Issues, 22*, 838–858. http://dx.doi.org/10.1177/019251301022007003

Cozijnsen, R., Stevens, N. L., & Van Tilburg, T. G. (2010). Maintaining work-related personal ties following retirement. *Personal Relationships, 17*, 345–356. http://dx.doi.org/10.1111/j.1475-6811.2010.01283.x

Davey, A., & Szinovacz, M. E. (2004). Dimensions if marital quality and retirement. *Journal of Family Issues, 25*, 431–464. http://dx.doi.org/10.1177/0192513X03257698

Denaeghel, K., Mortelmans, D., & Borghgraef, A. (2011). Spousal influence on the retirement decisions of single-earner and dual-earner couples. *Advances in Life Course Research, 16*, 112–123. http://dx.doi.org/10.1016/j.alcr.2011.06.001

Dew, J., & Yorgason, J. (2010). Economic pressure and marital conflict in retirement-aged couples. *Journal of Family Issues, 31*, 164–188. http://dx.doi.org/10.1177/0192513X09344168

Dorfman, L. T. (2002). Retirement and family relationships: An opportunity in later life. *Generations, 26*, 74–79.

Driver, J. L., & Gottman, J. M. (2004). Daily marital interactions and positive affect during marital conflict among newlywed couples. *Family Process, 43*, 301–314. http://dx.doi.org/10.1111/j.1545-5300.2004.00024.x

Ellin, A. (2013, April 22). How therapy can help in the golden years. *The New York Times*. Retrieved from http://well.blogs.nytimes.com/2013/04/22/how-therapy-can-help-in-the-golden-years/?nl=todaysheadlines&emc=edit_th_20130423

Fiori, K. L., Smith, J., & Antonucci, T. C. (2007). Social network types among older adults: A multidimensional approach. *The Journals of Gerontology: Series B. Psychological Sciences and Social Sciences, 62*, 322–330. http://dx.doi.org/10.1093/geronb/62.6.P322

Fitzpatrick, T. R., Bushfield, S., & Vinick, B. H. (2005). Anticipated and experienced changes in activities after husbands retire. *Journal of Gerontological Social Work, 46,* 69–84. http://dx.doi.org/10.1300/J083v46n02_06

Fitzpatrick, T. R., & Vinick, B. H. (2003). The impact of husbands' retirement on wives' marital quality. *Journal of Family Social Work, 7,* 83–100. http://dx.doi.org/10.1300/J039v07n01_06

Gaunt, R. (2006). Couple similarity and marital satisfaction: Are similar spouses happier? *Journal of Personality, 74,* 1401–1420. http://dx.doi.org/10.1111/j.1467-6494.2006.00414.x

Goldstein, S., & Preston, J. (1984). Marital therapy for the elderly. *Canadian Medical Association Journal, 130,* 1551–1553.

Haynes, S. N., Floyd, F. J., Lemsky, C., Rogers, E., Winemiller, D., Heilman, N., . . . Cardone, L. (1992). The Marital Satisfaction Questionnaire for Older Persons. *Psychological Assessment, 4,* 473–482. http://dx.doi.org/10.1037/1040-3590.4.4.473

Hayslip, B., Jr., & Kaminski, P. L. (2005). Grandparents raising their grandchildren: A review of the literature and suggestions for practice. *The Gerontologist, 45,* 262–269. http://dx.doi.org/10.1093/geront/45.2.262

Heffner, K. L., Loving, T. J., Kiecolt-Glaser, J. K., Himawan, L. K., Glaser, R., & Malarkey, W. B. (2006). Older spouses' cortisol responses to marital conflict: Associations with demand/withdraw communication patterns. *Journal of Behavioral Medicine, 29,* 317–325. http://dx.doi.org/10.1007/s10865-006-9058-3

Helms, H. M., Crouter, C., & McHale, S. M. (2003). Marital quality and spouses' marriage work with close friends and each other. *Journal of Marriage and Family, 65,* 963–977. http://dx.doi.org/10.1111/j.1741-3737.2003.00963.x

Hilbourne, M. (1999). Living together full time? Middle-class couples approaching retirement. *Ageing and Society, 19,* 161–183. http://dx.doi.org/10.1017/S0144686X99007230

Higginbottom, S. F., Barling, J., & Kelloway, E. K. (1993). Linking retirement experiences and marital satisfaction: A mediational model. *Psychology and Aging, 8,* 508–516. http://dx.doi.org/10.1037/0882-7974.8.4.508

Holmberg, D., Orbuch, T. L., & Veroff, J. (2004). *Thrice told tales: Married couples tell their stories.* Mahwah, NJ: Erlbaum.

Hughes, M. E., Waite, L. J., LaPierre, T. A., & Luo, Y. (2007). All in the family: The impact of caring for grandchildren on grandparents' health. *The Journals of Gerontology: Series B. Psychological Sciences and Social Sciences, 62,* S108–S119. http://dx.doi.org/10.1093/geronb/62.2.S108

Huston, T. (2000). The social ecology of marriage and other intimate unions. *Journal of Marriage and Family, 62,* 298–320. http://dx.doi.org/10.1111/j.1741-3737.2000.00298.x

Jensen, J., & Rauer, A. J. (2014). Turning inward versus outward: Relationship work in young adults and romantic functioning. *Personal Relationships, 21,* 451–467. http://dx.doi.org/10.1111/pere.12042

Karney, B. R., & Frye, N. E. (2002). "But we've been getting better lately": Comparing prospective and retrospective views of relationship development. *Journal of Personality and Social Psychology, 82*, 222–238. http://dx.doi.org/10.1037/0022-3514.82.2.222

Knight, T., & Ricciardelli, L. A. (2003). Successful aging: Perceptions of adults aged between 70 and 101 years. *International Journal of Aging & Human Development, 56*, 223–245. http://dx.doi.org/10.2190/CG1A-4Y73-WEW8-44QY

Kulik, L. (2001). The impact of men's and women's retirement on marital relations: A comparative analysis. *Journal of Women & Aging, 13*, 21–37. http://dx.doi.org/10.1300/J074v13n02_03

Kulik, L. (2002). Marital equality and the quality of long-term marriage in later life. *Ageing and Society, 22*, 459–481. http://dx.doi.org/10.1017/S0144686X02008772

Kulik, J. A., & Mahler, H. I. (2006). Marital quality predicts hospital stay following coronary artery bypass surgery for women but not men. *Social Science & Medicine, 63*, 2031–2040. http://dx.doi.org/10.1016/j.socscimed.2006.05.022

Lambert-Shute, J., & Fruhauf, C. A. (2011). Aging issues: Unanswered questions in marital and family therapy literature. *Journal of Marital and Family Therapy, 37*, 27–36. http://dx.doi.org/10.1111/j.1752-0606.2009.00152.x

Lundberg, S., Startz, R., & Stillman, S. (2003). The retirement-consumption puzzle: A marital bargaining approach. *Journal of Public Economics, 87*, 1199–1218. http://dx.doi.org/10.1016/S0047-2727(01)00169-4

Luong, G., Charles, S. T., & Fingerman, K. L. (2011). Better with age: Social relationships across adulthood. *Journal of Social and Personal Relationships, 28*, 9–23. http://dx.doi.org/10.1177/0265407510391362

Maestas, N. (2010). Back to work: Expectations and realizations of work after retirement. *The Journal of Human Resources, 45*, 718–748. http://dx.doi.org/10.1353/jhr.2010.0011

Marson, D., & Zebley, L. (2000). The other side of the retirement years: Cognitive decline, dementia, and loss of financial capacity. *Journal of Retirement Planning, 4*, 30–39.

Miller, R. B. (2000). Misconceptions about the U-shaped curve of marital satisfaction over the life course. *Family Science Review, 13*, 60–73.

Miller, R. B., & Yorgason, J. B. (2009). The interaction between marital relationships and retirement. In R. Crane & E. J. Hill (Eds.), *Handbook of families and work: Interdisciplinary perspectives* (pp. 392–408). Lanham, MD: University Press of America.

Mock, S. E., & Cornelius, S. W. (2007). Profiles of interdependence: The retirement planning of married, cohabiting, and lesbian couples. *Sex Roles, 56*, 793–800. http://dx.doi.org/10.1007/s11199-007-9243-z

Moen, P., Kim, J. E., & Hofmeister, H. (2001). Couples' work/retirement transitions, gender, and marital quality. *Social Psychology Quarterly, 64*, 55–71. http://dx.doi.org/10.2307/3090150

Orbuch, T., House, J., Mero, R., & Webster, P. (1996). Marital quality over the life course. *Social Psychology Quarterly, 59,* 162–171. http://dx.doi.org/10.2307/2787050

Papaharitou, S., Nakopoulou, E., Kirana, P., Giaglis, G., Moraitou, M., & Hatzichristou, D. (2008). Factors associated with sexuality in later life: An exploratory study in a group of Greek married older adults. *Archives of Gerontology and Geriatrics, 46,* 191–201. http://dx.doi.org/10.1016/j.archger.2007.03.008

Peluso, P. R., Parsons, M., & Watts, R. E. (2013). Work and financial issues related to living longer. In P. R. Peluso, R. E. Watts, & M. Parsons (Eds.), *Changing aging, changing family therapy: Practicing with 21st century realities* (pp. 127–150). New York, NY: Routledge.

Pienta, A. M., & Hayward, M. D. (2002). Who expects to continue working after age 62? The retirement plans of couples. *The Journals of Gerontology: Series B. Psychological Sciences and Social Sciences, 57,* S199–S208. http://dx.doi.org/10.1093/geronb/57.4.S199

Pienta, A. M., Hayward, M. D., & Jenkins, K. R. (2000). Health consequences of marriage for the retirement years. *Journal of Family Issues, 21,* 559–586. http://dx.doi.org/10.1177/019251300021005003

Piña, D. L., & Bengtson, V. L. (1993). The division of household labor and wives' happiness: Ideology, employment, and perceptions of support. *Journal of Marriage and Family, 55,* 901–912. http://dx.doi.org/10.2307/352771

Pinquart, M., & Schindler, I. (2007). Changes of life satisfaction in the transition to retirement: A latent-class approach. *Psychology and Aging, 22,* 442–455. http://dx.doi.org/10.1037/0882-7974.22.3.442

Pleau, R., & Shauman, K. (2013). Trends and correlates of post-retirement employment, 1977–2009. *Human Relations, 66,* 113–141. http://dx.doi.org/10.1177/0018726712447003

Rauer, A. J., Sabey, A. S., & Jensen, J. F. (2014). Growing old together: Compassionate love and health in older adulthood. *Journal of Social and Personal Relationships, 31,* 677–697. http://dx.doi.org/10.1177/0265407513503596

Roberts, L. J., & Greenberg, D. R. (2002). Observational "windows" to intimacy processes in marriage. In P. Noller & J. A. Feeney (Eds.), *Understanding marriage: Developments in the study of couple interaction* (pp. 118–149). Cambridge, England: Cambridge University Press. http://dx.doi.org/10.1017/CBO9780511500077.008

Roberts, N. A., & Levenson, R. W. (2001). The remains of the workday: Impact of job stress and exhaustion on marital interaction in police couples. *Journal of Marriage and Family, 63,* 1052–1067. http://dx.doi.org/10.1111/j.1741-3737.2001.01052.x

Rosenkoetter, M. M., & Garris, J. M. (2001). Retirement planning, use of time, and psychosocial adjustment. *Issues in Mental Health Nursing, 22,* 703–722. http://dx.doi.org/10.1080/016128401750434491

Rowe, J. (2007). *Opportunities and challenges of an aging society.* Presentation given at the Institute for Survey Research at the University of Michigan.

Settersten, R. A., & Trauten, M. E. (2010). On time and ties: Why the life course matters for old age policies. In R. B. Hudson (Ed.), *The new politics of old age policy* (pp. 141–159). Baltimore, MD: Johns Hopkins University Press.

Shiota, M. N., & Levenson, R. W. (2007). Birds of a feather don't always fly farthest: Similarity in Big Five personality predicts more negative marital satisfaction trajectories in long-term marriages. *Psychology and Aging, 22,* 666–675. http://dx.doi.org/10.1037/0882-7974.22.4.666

Szinovacz, M. E. (1996). Couples' employment/retirement patterns and perceptions of marital quality. *Research on Aging, 18,* 243–268. http://dx.doi.org/10.1177/0164027596182005

Szinovacz, M. E., & Davey, A. (2005). Retirement and marital decision making: Effects on retirement satisfaction. *Journal of Marriage and Family, 67,* 387–398. http://dx.doi.org/10.1111/j.0022-2445.2005.00123.x

Szinovacz, M. E., & DeViney, S. (2000). Marital characteristics and retirement decisions. *Research on Aging, 22,* 470–498. http://dx.doi.org/10.1177/0164027500225002

Szinovacz, M. E., DeViney, S., & Davey, A. (2001). Influences of family obligations and relationships on retirement: Variations by gender, race, and marital status. *The Journals of Gerontology: Series B. Psychological Sciences and Social Sciences, 56,* S20–S27. http://dx.doi.org/10.1093/geronb/56.1.S20

Szinovacz, M. E., & Schaffer, A. M. (2000). Effects of retirement on marital conflict tactics. *Journal of Family Issues, 21,* 367–389. http://dx.doi.org/10.1177/019251300021003005

Trief, P. M., Ploutz-Snyder, R., Britton, K. D., & Weinstock, R. S. (2004). The relationship between marital quality and adherence to the diabetes care regimen. *Annals of Behavioral Medicine, 27,* 148–154. http://dx.doi.org/10.1207/s15324796abm2703_2

Trudel, G., Turgeon, L., & Piché, L. (2000). Marital and sexual aspects of old age. *Sexual and Relationship Therapy, 15,* 381–406. http://dx.doi.org/10.1080/713697433

Vaillant, C. O., & Vaillant, G. E. (1993). Is the U-curve of marital satisfaction an illusion? A 40-year study of marriage. *Journal of Marriage and Family, 55,* 230–239. http://dx.doi.org/10.2307/352971

VanLaningham, J., Johnson, D. R., & Amato, P. (2001). Marital happiness, marital duration, and the U-shaped curve: Evidence from a five-wave panel study. *Social Forces, 79,* 1313–1341. http://dx.doi.org/10.1353/sof.2001.0055

van Solinge, H., & Henkens, K. (2005). Couples' adjustment to retirement: A multi-actor panel study. *The Journals of Gerontology: Series B. Psychological Sciences and Social Sciences, 60,* S11–S20. http://dx.doi.org/10.1093/geronb/60.1.S11

Van Tilburg, T. (2003). Consequences of men's retirement for the continuation of work-related personal relationships. *Ageing International, 28,* 345–358. http://dx.doi.org/10.1007/s12126-003-1008-6

Wang, M. (2007). Profiling retirees in the retirement transition and adjustment process: Examining the longitudinal change patterns of retirees' psychological well-being. *Journal of Applied Psychology, 92,* 455–474. http://dx.doi.org/10.1037/0021-9010.92.2.455

Weiss, R. L., & Heyman, R. E. (2004). Couples observational research: An impertinent, critical overview. In P. K. Kerig & D. H. Baucom (Eds.), *Couple observational coding systems* (pp. 11–26). Mahwah, NJ: Erlbaum.

Wickrama, K. A. S., O'Neal, C., & Lorenz, F. (2013). Marital functioning from middle to later years: A life course-stress process framework. *Journal of Family Theory & Review, 5,* 15–34. http://dx.doi.org/10.1111/jftr.12000

Yorgason, J., Miller, R., & White, M. (2009). Aging and family therapy: Exploring the training and knowledge of family therapists. *The American Journal of Family Therapy, 37,* 28–47. http://dx.doi.org/10.1080/01926180701804600

Zissimopoulos, J., Karney, B., & Rauer, A. (2015). Marriage and economic well-being at older ages. *Review of Economics of the Household, 13,* 1–35. http://dx.doi.org/10.1007/s11150-013-9205-x

# 9

# HEALTH CONTRIBUTIONS TO MARITAL QUALITY: EXPECTED AND UNEXPECTED LINKS

JEREMY B. YORGASON AND HEEJEONG CHOI

A growing body of research has examined associations between health and marital relationships. A substantial portion of that research examines health benefits of being married, having positive marital quality, or the detrimental effects of conflict in marriage (see McFarland, Hayward, & Brown, 2013; Waite & Gallagher, 2000). In contrast, there are times when married persons have age-associated or various other health problems relatively independent of the quality of their relationships, generally in midlife and later life, the development of which can then have an impact on their future marital quality (Booth & Johnson, 1994; Yorgason, Booth, & Johnson, 2008). Such research involves both general health as well as specific health problems, with findings often indicating health problems as a stressor to marriage. Other less-anticipated findings, however, suggest a strengthening of marital relationships in response to being confronted with one partner's health decline.

http://dx.doi.org/10.1037/14897-010
*Couple Relationships in the Middle and Later Years: Their Nature, Complexity, and Role in Health and Illness,*
J. Bookwala (Editor)

During the past several years, research related to ways that health problems affect marital quality has increased, with many studies addressing couple relationships in the context of specific illnesses. We define *marital quality* as a multidimensional indicator of relationship quality comprising, but not limited to, marital happiness/marital satisfaction, marital interactions, marital problems, marital conflict, and marital stability (Johnson, White, Edwards, & Booth, 1986). Table 9.1 contains examples of such studies, including a brief summary of findings in relation to the leading causes of death in the United States: cancer, cardiovascular disease (e.g., coronary artery disease), chronic obstructive pulmonary disease (COPD), diabetes, cerebral vascular accidents (i.e., stroke), dementia, and accidents (e.g., traumatic brain injuries). Further, other studies have examined marital relationships in the context of health-related sensory impairments (e.g., Strawbridge, Wallhagen, & Shema, 2007; Yorgason, Piercy, & Piercy, 2007) and other less common illnesses such as fibromyalgia and multiple sclerosis (Bigatti & Cronan, 2002; Pakenham, 1998). These and many other studies attest to the expanding literature in this area.

Many recent studies in this area have assumed the perspective that couples define the illness of one partner as a *couple experience*. That is, the articles imply that couples "react as an emotional system rather than as individuals" (Hagedoorn, Sanderman, Bolks, Tuinstra, & Coyne, 2008). For example, consider the titles of the following articles: "Marital Satisfaction in Couples With Rheumatoid Arthritis" (Bermas, Tucker, Winkelman, & Katz, 2000), "Distress in Couples Coping With Cancer" (Hagedoorn et al., 2008), "Collaborative Coping and Daily Mood in Couples Dealing With Prostate Cancer" (Berg et al., 2008), and "Chronic Illness and Marital Relationships: The Influence of Osteoporosis on the Lives of Older Couples" (Roberto, Gold, & Yorgason, 2004). It is noteworthy that these articles suggest that an illness belongs to the couple and not to one spouse.

The broad scope of research involving the effects of health problems on marital relationships encompasses various foci including general and specific health effects on marital satisfaction, marital quality, and marital stability; dyadic appraisal, dyadic coping, and illness-specific spousal support that may mediate the health to marriage association; and marital quality as a context where dyadic appraisal, coping, and illness-specific spousal support is enacted. Existing research also highlights gender as a significant moderator of the health–marriage linkage.

The purpose of the current chapter is to organize themes in the previously mentioned literature in ways that demonstrate expected associations between health and marital quality, as well as findings in the literature that are less anticipated. We integrate the vulnerability–stress–adaptation model (Karney & Bradbury, 1995), the developmental contextual model of dyadic

TABLE 9.1
Effects of Illness (the Leading Causes of Death
in the United States) on Marital Relationships

| Study | Illness | Sample size, marital measure | Findings |
|---|---|---|---|
| Blais & Boisvert (2005) | Traumatic brain injury (TBI) | Literature review of studies examining the psychological and marital outcomes among couples that have had a TBI, as well as important covariates | Couple experiences following TBI suggest great variability, with emphasis made to role changes, loss of sexual intimacy, loss of empathic communication, and the effects of trauma. |
| Iida, Stephens, Franks, & Rook (2013) | Diabetes (Type 2) | Daily diary study involving 127 couples across 24 days | Higher diabetes symptoms were associated with lower relationship enjoyment and increased tension for both patients and spouses. A longer duration of having diabetes compounded these effects. |
| Kazemi-Saleh, Pishgou, Assari, & Tavallaii (2007) | Coronary artery disease | 87 married patients (65 males, 22 females); Dyadic Adjustment Scale | One third of the sample reported sexual fear. Higher sexual fear was associated with lower marital satisfaction. |
| Meier, Bodenmann, Moergeli, Peter-Write, Martin, Buechi, & Jenewein (2012) | Chronic obstructive pulmonary disease (COPD) | 43 couples with COPD, 138 healthy couples, all in a committed relationship, living together, and between the ages of 40 and 85 | Couples with COPD reported more negative and less positive dyadic coping than their healthy counterparts. |
| Préau, Bouhnik, Rey, Mancini, & the ALD Cancer Study Group (2011) | Cancer | 3,221 persons with cancer (1,719 males, 1,502 females); patients reported whether cancer "brought them closer to their partner" | Approximately 33% of males and 42% of females with cancer reported that cancer had brought them closer to their partner. |
| Thommessen, Aarsland, Braekhus, Oksengaard, Engedal, & Laake (2002) | Stroke, dementia, and Parkinson's disease | Three studies involving couples with stroke ($n = 36$), dementia ($n = 92$), and Parkinson's disease ($n = 58$) | Common challenges included disrupted household routines, social activity restrictions, sleep disturbances, and problems with holiday travel. Cognitive functioning was linked with spouse burden. |

appraisal and coping (Berg & Upchurch, 2007), and the stress process model (Pearlin, Mullan, Semple, & Skaff, 1990) to consider research findings (see Figure 9.1). As a guiding and organizing framework, the integrated model is described first. We then summarize literature reporting expected findings, followed by unanticipated findings and possible interpretations. Gender is described as a potential moderator linking health to marital relationship outcomes, followed by directions for future study.

## THEORETICAL FRAMEWORK

As seen in Figure 9.1, primary health stressors predict adaptive processes and secondary stressors, which then are linked with relationship outcomes. *Enduring characteristics* (called *vulnerabilities* by Karney & Bradbury, 1995) may be manifested either as vulnerabilities, strengths, or characteristics that moderate the effects of health stressors or adaptive processes on relationship outcomes. For example, high marital quality may be an enduring characteristic that moderates the effects of health challenges on psychological distress or conflict surrounding division of household chores (Brosseau, McDonald, & Stephen, 2011; Dalton, Nelson, Brobst, Lindsay, & Friedman, 2007; Roper & Yorgason, 2009).

Within this adapted model, *dyadic appraisal* is made through similarity of illness representations by partners (e.g., to what extent does each partner see the illness as controllable?) and shared versus unique illness ownership (is this his, her, or our illness?). Also, *dyadic coping* and *illness-specific spousal support* occur along a continuum, ranging from spouse uninvolvement to being supportive, collaborative, and on the extreme, controlling. The degree to which couples cope in collaborative fashion, or the ways that they interact with each other to adapt to an illness, may be associated with relationship outcomes.

*Primary health stressors* are those that stem directly from health problems, such as illness symptoms. *Secondary stressors* may be health related, or they may simply result from primary health stressors, and may include experiences such as role shifts in marriage because of health limitations in one partner or financial difficulties associated with paying medical bills. As seen in Figure 9.1, secondary stressors are placed as mediators between primary health stressors and relationship outcomes, yet they are separate from adaptive processes as such stressors operate differently from how couples respond to illness. Gender is not explicitly represented in the figure but is linked to aspects of each part of the model (stressors, adaptive processes, and outcomes).

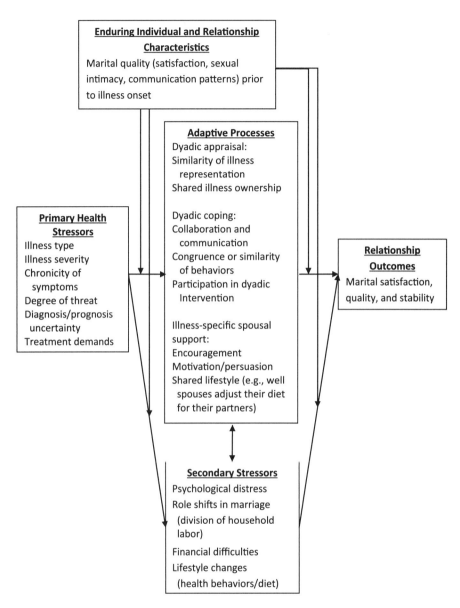

*Figure 9.1.* Model of illness and marriage integrating the vulnerability–stress–adaptation model, the developmental contextual model of dyadic coping, and the stress process model. Data from Berg and Upchurch (2007); Karney and Bradbury (1995); and Pearlin, Mullan, Semple, and Skaff (1990).

# EXPECTED CONTRIBUTIONS OF HEALTH
# TO MARITAL QUALITY

According to the adapted model presented in Figure 9.1, health challenges likely take a toll on marital relationships. Further, according to this model, couple processes in response to illness stressors play a prominent role in predicting how couples will fare. Research examining the effects of health problems within marriage has provided support for both of these propositions. Health links with marital outcomes is first considered, followed by a discussion of potential mechanisms involved.

First, research has consistently linked health challenges with marital outcomes. Declines in global health outcomes, such as self-rated health, functional impairment, and the existence of chronic illnesses, have been associated with decreases in marital relationship quality (Booth & Johnson, 1994; Hafstrom & Schram, 1984). For example, data from nonoverlapping waves of the Marital Instability Over the Life Course study have shown that declines in self-rated health were associated with declines in marital happiness (Booth & Johnson, 1994; Yorgason et al., 2008). The earlier of these studies indicated that poorer spousal health was linked to higher divorce proneness and that the health to marital happiness link may have been accounted for by money problems, the division of household labor, changes in marital activities, and respondents' problem behaviors. The later of these studies found that the impact of health declines on marital happiness was stronger for younger and middle-aged couples and that the link was accounted for by psychological distress.

Some studies have suggested that the marital quality of spouses in better health may be more adversely affected by a partner's poor health (Booth & Johnson, 1994; Ferri & Pruchno, 2009; Melton, Hersen, Van Sickle, & Van Hasselt, 1995; Yorgason et al., 2008). That is, declines in a spouse's health tend to have a larger impact on marital quality than if a person's own health declines. Health mismatch between marital partners may cause the healthier partner to take on increasingly greater responsibilities as couples continue to negotiate marital roles. Further, ill partners may receive greater benefits from marriage than healthy partners, such as greater emotional and instrumental support. Some studies have further indicated that a partner's declining health may be more detrimental to women's marital experiences compared with men's (Korporaal, Broese van Groenou, & van Tilburg, 2013; Strawbridge et al., 2007; Yorgason et al., 2008). One reason for this may be linked to the division of household labor. Specifically, when a husband becomes ill, a wife may have an increased amount of work to perform, leading to greater strain. As an example of this possibility, based on a convenience sample of 216 couples (43 had a husband with a chronic illness, 26 had a wife with a chronic illness, and 147 were healthy comparisons), Hafstrom and Schram (1984) examined wives' marital satisfaction in relation to their own and their husbands' chronic illness. Results indicated that husbands' chronic illnesses were associated with lower wives' marital quality, but wives' own poor health was not.

In contrast to studies about general health declines, findings from studies linking specific illnesses to marital quality are not as consistent in terms of the effects of illness onset and progression on the ways marital partners perceive their relationships. For example, in a study involving 127 couples, Iida, Stephens, Franks, and Rook (2013) found that daily diabetes symptoms and distress were linked with lower enjoyment and higher tension in marital interactions. In contrast, in a meta-analytic review of couples coping with cancer, Hagedoorn, Sanderman, Bolks, Tuinstra, and Coyne (2008) cautioned readers that patients with cancer, compared with healthy controls (persons with no cancer), did not necessarily experience heightened risks of marital distress and marital dissolution.

Second, research has started to uncover various mechanisms that link health to marital relationships. Mechanisms fall into three main categories: primary health stressors, secondary stressors, and adaptive processes. Regarding primary health stressors, illness factors such as illness type, severity, chronicity, degree of threat, diagnosis and prognosis uncertainty, and increasing treatment demands on time may determine to some degree how couples are affected (Burman & Margolin, 1992). For example, some illnesses present greater strain than others, such as when comparing the treatment and prognosis of cancer to those of an acquired hearing loss. Also, some illnesses are more ambiguous in nature, such as with the diagnosis, prognosis, and treatment of autoimmune illnesses or dementia, compared with those that are more straightforward, such as having a broken bone or Type 2 diabetes.

Secondary stressors serve as a pathway through which primary health stressors affect couple relationships. These effects may manifest as reactions to or results from the ill spouse's health problems. For example, physical health challenges of a spouse may trigger a decline in the quality of the marital relationship through the occurrence of psychological distress (Yorgason et al., 2008), changes in the division of household chores (Booth & Johnson, 1994), health care costs or financial difficulties since diagnosis (Préau, Bouhnik, Rey, Mancini, & the ALD Cancer Study Group, 2011), and resulting lifestyle changes such as health behaviors/diet (e.g., diabetes management) and disrupted sleep (Rauer & El-Sheikh, 2012). Disagreements between patients and their well spouses over the severity of illness and the amount and quality of care needed or provided also constitute secondary stressors (Dehle et al., 2001).

In many cases, the ways couples appraise and cope with a specific illness, rather than the illness per se, may be what essentially predicts relationship outcomes (see Chapter 13, on dyadic coping, this volume). For example, researchers have found that fantasy and blame coping methods (Bermas,

Tucker, Winkelman, & Katz, 2000), complementary coping by spouses (Badr, 2004), and social support in marriage (Dehle, Larsen, & Landers, 2001) may play a large role in relation to how couples fare in their marriage when chronic illness occurs. Furthermore, as mentioned earlier in the chapter, some couples appraise health challenges as shared, whereas others perceive health problems as belonging to individuals (Berg & Upchurch, 2007; Yorgason et al., 2010). A shared illness appraisal suggests that both spouses view the illness, as well as its accompanying symptoms and treatment, as conjoint, with both being involved in the illness coping process. In contrast, individualized illness appraisals may be linked with more autonomous coping.

Many researchers have examined aspects of dyadic appraisal and coping that can influence how health problems affect couple relationships. Congruence or similarity in thoughts and behaviors between patients and their partners may best represent their dyadic nature that is distinct from individual appraisal and coping. For instance, Roberto, Gold, and Yorgason (2004) found that when husbands and wives had discrepancies in their reports of wife pain levels associated with osteoporosis, wife relationship adjustment was lower. Some researchers examine couple versus individual pronouns used in qualitative interviews with patient couples. For example, Robbins, Mehl, Smith, and Weihs (2013) examined transcripts of 15-minute family discussions focused on cancer posttreatment with 75 families. When partners used "we-talk" language in that study, they also reported better marital adjustment, whereas couples' use of "you" was related to poorer overall adjustment. Also, Hong et al. (2005) examined congruence in exercise patterns among cardiac patients and their partners. They found that support provided (by both spouses) predicted support received (by both spouses) among couples with similar exercise patterns, suggesting that shared health behaviors may facilitate collaborative coping (see Chapter 16, this volume, on couple-based interventions for illness management).

Finally, although marital quality or other important aspects of couple relationships (e.g., sexual intimacy, communication patterns) can be seen as outcomes of health stressors, they may also sometimes provide a proximal context of dyadic coping by buffering the negative effects of illness on different outcomes. Specifically, a number of studies have shown that various dimensions of marital quality (e.g., marital satisfaction, marital closeness, global spousal support in contrast to illness-specific support) buffered the effects of daily health symptoms on individual and partner affect (Roper & Yorgason, 2009; Yorgason, Almeida, Neupert, Spiro, & Hoffman, 2006), were linked with lower mortality rates among patients postcardiac surgery (Idler, Boulifard, & Contrada, 2012), and were associated with decreased secondary traumatic stress among couples with cancer (Brosseau et al., 2011). In terms of sexual intimacy, Préau and colleagues (2011) examined couples with cancer 2 years after diagnosis and found that reports of regular sexual activity were associated with the couples reporting that the illness had brought them closer together. In another example, Milbury and Badr (2013) examined the effects of sexual problems on depressive symptoms in 191 couples with metastatic breast cancer. Communication patterns were examined as moderators to these links. Results indicated that sexual problems were linked with depression for patients only among couples with low levels of mutual constructive communication or high levels of demand–withdraw communication. Because of the impact of illness on couples' sexual intimacy and the importance of sexual intimacy in dyadic coping, treatment programs addressing such concerns are being developed and tested (see Schover et al., 2012).

In summary, congruence in illness perceptions, shared illness ownership, congruence in coping behaviors, and couple interventions are linked to better relationship outcomes. Marital quality can be negatively influenced by health problems, but in some instances it may mitigate the effects of ineffective dyadic coping on health-related outcomes.

## UNEXPECTED CONTRIBUTIONS OF HEALTH TO MARITAL QUALITY

Findings from a few studies indicate that, contrary to expectations, declining health and illness can have positive impacts on marital quality, and spousal support may have no or negative impacts on relationship outcomes. For example, Yorgason et al. (2008) found that the onset of disability was related to an improvement in marital quality. Male participants in the study further indicated that a spouse's disability was linked to higher marital happiness as well as to higher marital interactions. A health crisis, as an acute stressor, could be an opportunity for spouses to support each other and thereby come closer together. Chronic health conditions, on the other hand, are characterized as a constant drain on the relationship (Karney, Story, & Bradbury, 2005). Yet, a prospective study of couples coping with a wife's diagnosis of breast cancer (a chronic stressor) also reported that illness experience and treatments enhanced marital closeness (Dorval et al., 2005). Specifically, in that study, 282 couples were interviewed 12 months after the start of treatment, and at that time 42% of the couples reported to be closer because of the breast cancer. Dorval and colleagues (2005) found that the increased closeness was due in part to spouses reporting the patient to be a confidant, well spouses getting advice from the ill spouse within 2 weeks of diagnosis, going with the ill spouse to surgery, and increased affection from the well spouse toward the ill spouse.

Spousal support in the context of illness also has been found to have complex associations with marriage, yielding both expected (greater stress) and unexpected (greater marital closeness) findings. Research on social support in health contexts has suggested that although supportive behaviors are often positive, sometimes support that is intended as helpful is considered unhelpful and even detrimental (Gleason, Iida, Shrout, & Bolger, 2008; Revenson, Schiaffino, Majerovitz, & Gibofsky, 1991; see also Chapter 15, this volume). As mentioned earlier, partner involvement can range from uninvolvement, to appropriate support, to controlling involvement, and the former and latter types of support are not always helpful (see Gleason et al., 2008). Various patterns of marital interactions around illness indicate forms of both supportive and unsupportive behaviors.

On the positive end, research has shown evidence of positive effects associated with illness-specific supportive behaviors. Relationship benefits among couples facing diabetes are linked with supportive behaviors including encouragement (as opposed to warnings; Stephens, Rook, Franks, Khan, & Iida, 2010); sharing meals together (as opposed to diet-related pressure; Franks et al., 2012); diet-related support (as opposed to persuasion and pressure; Stephens et al., 2013); and support with diet, medications, and couple teamwork (as opposed to nagging and poor communication; Trief et al., 2003).

Regarding unsupportive behaviors, studies have indicated that some patterns of partner interactions or support are linked with worse relationship outcomes. These might include (a) protective buffering, where a well spouse is not addressing health-sensitive topics in an effort to protect their ill or disabled partner from additional relationship stress (e.g., Lavery & Clarke, 1999); (b) controlling, such as when a well spouse learns more about an illness than the patient spouse and then uses that information to attempt to have greater power in the relationship (e.g., Peyrot, McMurry, & Hedges, 1988); (c) a well spouse being overprotective or making choices for their patient partner such as by determining foods and portion sizes that may benefit or place strain on the relationship (August, Rook, Franks, & Stephens, 2013); or (d) in an effort to benefit or manipulate their relationship, "speaking for" a disabled partner that is slow to speak because of speech difficulty (aphasia; Croteau, Vychytil, Larfeuil, & Le Dorze, 2004).

There appears to be a fine balance between a spouse's being involved and supportive versus overly involved and perhaps controlling. It may be helpful for couples and professionals to consider spousal support as having a curvilinear relationship with health to marital outcome associations. In other words, overly high support (control) and too little support (neglect or isolation) appear less helpful, whereas appropriate support appears linked to the best relationship outcomes (Berg & Upchurch, 2007). For example, a patient spouse who receives too much support (i.e., well spouse is controlling) may not feel appropriately autonomous in his or her relationship, whereas a patient spouse who receives too little support (i.e., well spouse is uninvolved) may be overwhelmed by his or her health challenges and feel isolated or resentful in their relationship. Finding an appropriate balance of interdependence may foster the most adaptive marital outcomes.

Spousal support sometimes has been found to have a complex association with health and marriage. For example, in a review of research examining pain behavior between patients and their spouse caregivers, Newton-John (2002) noted the unique situation wherein patient reports of pain are often reinforced unknowingly by one's spouse. Such "solicitous" responses by a spouse include demonstrations of empathy, taking over household chores for the person, and giving the person pain medication. Newton-John's interpretation of this literature was that persons experiencing pain might more readily report that pain to their partner if/when they expected their spouse would be supportive. That support, in turn, became a "solicitation" for increased future pain reports. From that review, other research has indicated that solicitous responses were more common when a pain diagnosis was ambiguous and generally (although not always) when marital satisfaction was lower and depression was higher. Solicitousness in the case of chronic pain is contextualized as being problematic and detrimental to both patients and their partners (see Newton-John, 2002). However, it might alternatively be viewed as one of the ways health "spills over" to affect a spouse (see Westman & Vinokur, 1998) or one of the ways spouses respond in conjoint couple coping. For example, Yorgason, Roper, Sandberg, and Berg (2012) found a similar type of association, where higher reports of daily positive marital interactions in husbands were predictive of higher wife reports of same-day arthritis concerns. Similar to pain solicitation, it may be that wife arthritis concerns were actually driving higher husband reports of positive marital interactions, rather than vice versa.

The literature on ambivalence also is relevant, demonstrating that family relationships, including marriage, are marked by higher levels of conflicted feelings, or ambivalence, which is inherent in interdependent relationships (Luescher & Pillemer, 1998). Feelings of ambivalence could be further heightened in the context of spousal illness as it necessitates greater mutual dependence. Well spouses, especially wives, may feel pulled in two different directions—feelings of love, concern, and care as well as frustration, exhaustion, resentment, and guilt. Yet, few existing studies on marriage in the context of spousal illness explicitly have explored ambivalence as a marital outcome. One could speculate that the marriage benefits seen with declining health may in fact be indicative of higher levels of ambivalence.

# GENDER-SPECIFIC CONTRIBUTIONS
# OF HEALTH TO MARITAL QUALITY

Specific relationship effects of health problems in marriage sometimes vary by whether the patient is male or female. For example, illness sometimes encourages gender-related role shifts, which may sometimes lead to unexpected research findings. The fact that there might be different marital effects of health challenges on husbands and wives is not too surprising, yet gender-related findings such as the amount of spousal support received and its perceived adequacy and effectiveness in relieving psychological distress (Baider & Bengel, 2001; Gleason et al., 2008) indicated interesting trends in how health problems are experienced differently by husbands and wives.

Two bodies of literatures—gender socialization and social support and coping—are often cited as mechanisms that may explain gender differences in marital outcomes in the context of spousal illness. First, the literature on gender socialization maintains that women are socialized to be more nurturing of others and therefore experience greater exposure and reactivity to stressors experienced by their significant others (Kiecolt-Glaser & Newton, 2001; Wethington, McLeod, & Kessler, 1987). Consistent with this argument, wives are typically found to be on the receiving end of distress that husbands transmit (Larson & Almeida, 1999). Also related to gender socialization, wives often assume a disproportionate share of household chores. As a consequence, the demands of illness on the spousal relationship may vary depending on the gender of the ill spouse. When wives are sick, the gender gap in the division of household labor may be narrowed as husbands engage in more household labor, although wives do not necessarily reduce their commitments. When husbands are sick, on the other hand, the gender gap in the division of household labor may widen even more as patient husbands become unable to perform household responsibilities and wives pick up what is left off (Revenson, Abraido-Lanza, Majerovitz, & Jordan, 2005). Such imbalances may lead to dissatisfaction, resentment, and conflict in marital relationships.

Research on coping with arthritis suggests that well wives may receive more problematic support from husbands with arthritis compared with well husbands whose wives suffer from arthritis (Revenson & Majerovitz, 1990). In addition, existing studies have indicated that although husbands and wives may engage in protective buffering, husbands may do so less often than wives (Badr, 2004; Manne et al., 2007). A spouse in good health may use protective buffering to shield the ill partner from experiencing illness-related stress, but doing so may take a psychological toll on the relationship from the perspective of the well spouse (Badr, 2004). Future research might further explore gender differences in the motives, prevalence, and effects of protective buffering.

That is, it may be that caregiving wives use protective buffering more than caregiving husbands in attempts to avoid conflict. In contrast, caregiving husbands may use protective buffering more than caregiving wives so as to not provide additional stress for their ill spouse over and above the already existing health problems.

The potentially differential effects of illness on the marital relationship for husbands compared with wives suggest complex interactions that are not well understood in the current literature. On the surface, such findings may be anticipated, yet when examined more closely, gender-related associations suggest differences in support, protective buffering, division of household chores, and potentially other areas influenced by gender socialization.

## FUTURE RESEARCH AND CONCLUSIONS

As a first step, future research should expand beyond small convenience samples that are examined at one point in time. Cross-sectional designs using smaller convenience samples are common among studies examining the effects of specific illnesses in marriage (e.g., Bigatti & Cronan, 2002; Yorgason et al., 2010). Although such an approach may be appropriate for newer, less understood health problems, the standard should be raised for more established health concerns. Samples of couples with common health problems can be recruited across multiple sites, and data can often reasonably be gathered across the various stages of an illness from diagnosis and treatment to chronic illness management. For example, for a study of how diabetes may impact marital relations, a sample could be recruited at or shortly following diagnosis. Such a sample could then be followed across time through the acute stage of illness management (e.g., the first year after diagnosis where multiple daily insulin injections are required) and into the ongoing management that occurs once a treatment routine is established (e.g., when an insulin pump is acquired and treatment stabilized). Regarding longitudinal research, studies have linked health to marriage across years and across days, yet few if any studies to date have examined the long-term impact of daily health-related processes on later marriage quality and stability. As an exception to longitudinal designs as a preference, however, some illnesses involve intense treatments and life-threatening prognoses.

Although the current chapter is primarily focused on the effects of health on marriage, future research needs to continue to disentangle the various ways in which links between marriage and health are reciprocal. Few existing studies have explicitly considered bidirectionality between health and marriage (Robles, Slatcher, Trombello, & McGinn, 2014). Two studies based on U.S. representative samples found that marital quality and self-rated health generally have a unidirectional relationship, with marital quality being associated with later self-rated health (Proulx & Snyder-Rivas, 2013; Umberson, Williams, Powers, Liu, & Needham, 2006). In contrast to those findings, some specific health problems are not typically caused by marital problems (e.g., sometimes they are due to aging, such as with cancer or cataracts), and yet they go on to influence the marital relationship. The cycle of health affecting marriage and marriage affecting future health could continue indefinitely. Longitudinal research would greatly assist in understanding such complexities within marriage.

The vulnerability–stress–adaptation model of relationships (Karney & Bradbury, 1995) provides a good framework for understanding how illness stressors are linked to relationship outcomes via relationship processes. Also, the developmental contextual model of dyadic coping (Berg & Upchurch, 2007) provides a frame for understanding couple processes as they relate to responding to illness. However, less theoretical guidance is available for understanding unexpected effects of illness in marriage. It will be important to further develop hypotheses and propositions that attempt to explain, theoretically, unanticipated associations such as illness being linked with higher marital quality, supportive spousal responses being linked with poorer health outcomes, and unsupportive responses being linked with better health outcomes. Empirically, research is needed on (a) whether dyadic appraisal and dyadic coping are linked to situations where greater closeness develops in response to illness; (b) how positive health outcomes develop when beneficial enduring characteristics are in place, such as having higher marital quality, personality characteristics such as optimism, better health care, etc.; and (c) whether degree of health-related stressors are linearly associated with relationship outcomes or curvilinear associations exist.

In research examining health within the marital context, gender and health effects are often confounded. That is, some effects of illness on marriage relations tend to be stronger or weaker depending on whether the patient is male or female, or on whether the healthy spouse/caregiver is male or female. These effects may be complicated by illnesses that are gender specific, such as uterine or prostate cancer, or gender dominant, such as osteoporosis, breast cancer, rheumatoid arthritis, and prostate cancer. On one hand, dyadic appraisal may be a greater challenge when the well spouse cannot easily relate to a gender-specific illness of the patient spouse. On the other hand, couples having knowledge about a gender-specific illness may aid well spouses to be supportive or collaborative in their coping. Future research could address these and other gender-related complications.

In conclusion, when one partner of a couple becomes ill, both spouses are typically affected, and they often work together to manage and treat the health concerns. In some instances, the effects of illness on the marital relationship are anticipated. In other cases, the effects of illness on the marital relationship are unanticipated or simply inconsistent. The current chapter provides unique insights into trends in the literature examining the effects of health on marital relationships. Although much research has examined how health challenges affect midlife and later life marital relationships, many possibilities for future research exist including further explorations of gender differences in marital quality when a spouse becomes ill, as well as longitudinal studies that examine couple relationships across various stages of illness.

# REFERENCES

August, K. J., Rook, K. S., Franks, M. M., & Stephens, M. A. P. (2013). Spouses' involvement in their partners' diabetes management: Associations with spouse stress and perceived marital quality. *Journal of Family Psychology, 27*, 712–721. http://dx.doi.org/10.1037/a0034181

Badr, H. (2004). Coping in marital dyads: A contextual perspective on the role of gender and health. *Personal Relationships, 11*, 197–211. http://dx.doi.org/10.1111/j.1475-6811.2004.00078.x

Baider, L., & Bengel, J. (2001). Cancer and the spouse: Gender-related differences in dealing with health care and illness. *Critical Reviews in Oncology/Hematology, 40*, 115–123. http://dx.doi.org/10.1016/S1040-8428(01)00137-8

Berg, C. A., & Upchurch, R. (2007). A developmental-contextual model of couples coping with chronic illness across the adult life span. *Psychological Bulletin, 133*, 920–954. http://dx.doi.org/10.1037/0033-2909.133.6.920

Berg, C. A., Wiebe, D. J., Butner, J., Bloor, L., Bradstreet, C., Upchurch, R., . . . Patton, G. (2008). Collaborative coping and daily mood in couples dealing with prostate cancer. *Psychology and Aging, 23*, 505–516. http://dx.doi.org/10.1037/a0012687

Bermas, B. L., Tucker, J. S., Winkelman, D. K., & Katz, J. N. (2000). Marital satisfaction in couples with rheumatoid arthritis. *Arthritis Care & Research, 13*, 149–155. http://dx.doi.org/10.1002/1529-0131(200006)13:3<149::AID-ANR4>3.0.CO;2-W

Bigatti, S. M., & Cronan, T. A. (2002). An examination of the physical health, health care use, and psychological well-being of spouses of people with fibromyalgia syndrome. *Health Psychology, 21*, 157–166.

Blais, M. C., & Boisvert, J. (2005). Psychological and marital adjustment in couples following a traumatic brain injury (TBI): A critical review. *Brain Injury, 19*, 1223–1235. http://dx.doi.org/10.1080/02699050500309387

Booth, A., & Johnson, D. R. (1994). Declining health and marital quality. *Journal of Marriage and Family, 56*, 218–223. http://dx.doi.org/10.2307/352716

Brosseau, D. C., McDonald, M. J., & Stephen, J. E. (2011). The moderating effect of relationship quality on partner secondary traumatic stress among couples coping with cancer. *Families, Systems, & Health, 29*, 114–126. http://dx.doi.org/10.1037/a0024155

Burman, B., & Margolin, G. (1992). Analysis of the association between marital relationships and health problems: An interactional perspective. *Psychological Bulletin, 112*, 39–63. http://dx.doi.org/10.1037/0033-2909.112.1.39

Croteau, C., Vychytil, A., Larfeuil, C., & Le Dorze, G. (2004). "Speaking for" behaviours in spouses of people with aphasia: A descriptive study of six couples in an interview situation. *Aphasiology, 18*, 291–312. http://dx.doi.org/10.1080/02687030344000616

Dalton, W. T., III, Nelson, D. V., Brobst, J. B., Lindsay, J. E., & Friedman, L. C. (2007). Psychosocial variables associated with husbands' adjustment three months following wives' diagnosis of breast cancer. *Journal of Cancer Education, 22*, 245–249. http://dx.doi.org/10.1007/BF03174124

Dehle, C., Larsen, D., & Landers, J. E. (2001). Social support in marriage. *The American Journal of Family Therapy, 29*, 307–324. http://dx.doi.org/10.1080/01926180126500

Dorval, M., Guay, S., Mondor, M., Mâsse, B., Falardeau, M., Robidoux, A., . . . Maunsell, E. (2005). Couples who get closer after breast cancer: Frequency and predictors in a prospective investigation. *Journal of Clinical Oncology, 23*, 3588–3596. http://dx.doi.org/10.1200/JCO.2005.01.628

Ferri, C. V., & Pruchno, R. A. (2009). Quality of life in end-stage renal disease patients: Differences in patient and spouse perceptions. *Aging & Mental Health, 13*, 706–714. http://dx.doi.org/10.1080/13607860902845558

Franks, M. M., Sahin, Z. S., Seidel, A. J., Shields, C. G., Oates, S. K., & Boushey, C. J. (2012). Table for two: Diabetes distress and diet-related interactions of married patients with diabetes and their spouses. *Families, Systems, & Health, 30*, 154–165. http://dx.doi.org/10.1037/a0028614

Gleason, M. E., Iida, M., Shrout, P. E., & Bolger, N. (2008). Receiving support as a mixed blessing: Evidence for dual effects of support on psychological outcomes. *Journal of Personality and Social Psychology, 94*, 824–838. http://dx.doi.org/10.1037/0022-3514.94.5.824

Hafstrom, J. L., & Schram, V. R. (1984). Chronic illness in couples: Selected characteristics, including wife's satisfaction with and perception of marital relationships. *Family Relations, 33*, 195–203. http://dx.doi.org/10.2307/584605

Hagedoorn, M., Sanderman, R., Bolks, H. N., Tuinstra, J., & Coyne, J. C. (2008). Distress in couples coping with cancer: A meta-analysis and critical review of role and gender effects. *Psychological Bulletin, 134*, 1–30. http://dx.doi.org/10.1037/0033-2909.134.1.1

Hong, T. B., Franks, M. M., Gonzalez, R., Keteyian, S. J., Franklin, B. A., & Artinian, N. T. (2005). A dyadic investigation of exercise support between cardiac patients and their spouses. *Health Psychology, 24*, 430–434. http://dx.doi.org/10.1037/0278-6133.24.4.430

Idler, E. L., Boulifard, D. A., & Contrada, R. J. (2012). Mending broken hearts: Marriage and survival following cardiac surgery. *Journal of Health and Social Behavior, 53*, 33–49. http://dx.doi.org/10.1177/0022146511432342

Iida, M., Stephens, M. A. P., Franks, M. M., & Rook, K. S. (2013). Daily symptoms, distress and interaction quality among couples coping with type 2 diabetes. *Journal of Social and Personal Relationships, 30*, 293–300. http://dx.doi.org/10.1177/0265407512455308

Johnson, D. R., White, L. K., Edwards, J. N., & Booth, A. (1986). Dimensions of marital quality: Toward methodological and conceptualization refinement. *Journal of Family Issues, 7*, 31–49. http://dx.doi.org/10.1177/019251386007001003

Karney, B. R., & Bradbury, T. N. (1995). The longitudinal course of marital quality and stability: A review of theory, method, and research. *Psychological Bulletin, 118*, 3–34. http://dx.doi.org/10.1037/0033-2909.118.1.3

Karney, B. R., Story, L. B., & Bradbury, T. N. (2005). Marriages in context: Interactions between chronic and acute stress among newlyweds. In T. A. Revenson, K. E. Kayser, & G. E. Bodenmann, (Eds.), *Couples coping with stress: Emerging perspectives on dyadic coping* (pp. 13–32). Washington, DC: American Psychological Association.

Kazemi-Saleh, D., Pishgou, B., Assari, S., & Tavallaii, S. A. (2007). Fear of sexual intercourse in patients with coronary artery disease: A pilot study of associated morbidity. *Journal of Sexual Medicine, 4*, 1619–1625.

Kiecolt-Glaser, J. K., & Newton, T. L. (2001). Marriage and health: His and hers. *Psychological Bulletin, 127*, 472–503. http://dx.doi.org/10.1037/0033-2909.127.4.472

Korporaal, M., Broese van Groenou, M. I., & van Tilburg, T. G. (2013). Health problems and marital satisfaction among older couples. *Journal of Aging and Health, 25*, 1279–1298. http://dx.doi.org/10.1177/0898264313501387

Larson, R. W., & Almeida, D. M. (1999). Emotional transmission in the daily lives of families: A new paradigm for studying family process. *Journal of Marriage and Family, 61*, 5–20. http://dx.doi.org/10.2307/353879

Lavery, J. F., & Clarke, V. A. (1999). Prostate cancer: Patients' and spouses' coping and marital adjustment. *Psychology, Health & Medicine, 4*, 289–302. http://dx.doi.org/10.1080/135485099106225

Luescher, K., & Pillemer, K. (1998). Intergenerational ambivalence: A new approach to the study of parent–child relations in later life. *Journal of Marriage and Family, 60*, 413–425. http://dx.doi.org/10.2307/353858

Manne, S. L., Norton, T. R., Ostroff, J. S., Winkel, G., Fox, K., & Grana, G. (2007). Protective buffering and psychological distress among couples coping with breast cancer: The moderating role of relationship satisfaction. *Journal of Family Psychology, 21*, 380–388. http://dx.doi.org/10.1037/0893-3200.21.3.380

McFarland, M. J., Hayward, M. D., & Brown, D. (2013). I've got you under my skin: Marital biography and biological risk. *Journal of Marriage and Family, 75*, 363–380. http://dx.doi.org/10.1111/jomf.12015

Meier, C., Bodenmann, G., Moergeli, H., Peter-Write, M., Martin, M., Buechi, S., & Jenewein, J. (2012). Dyadic coping among couples with COPD: A pilot study. *Journal of Clinical Psychology in Medical Settings, 19*, 243–254.

Melton, M. A., Hersen, M., Van Sickle, T. D., & Van Hasselt, V. B. (1995). Parameters of marriage in older adults: A review of the literature. *Clinical Psychology Review*, *15*, 891–904. http://dx.doi.org/10.1016/0272-7358(95)00051-8

Milbury, K., & Badr, H. (2013). Sexual problems, communication patterns, and depressive symptoms in couples coping with metastatic breast cancer. *Psycho-Oncology*, *22*, 814–822. http://dx.doi.org/10.1002/pon.3079

Newton-John, T. R. O. (2002). Solicitousness and chronic pain: A critical review. *Pain Reviews*, *9*, 7–27. http://dx.doi.org/10.1191/0968130202pr186ra

Pakenham, K. I. (1998). Couple coping and adjustment to multiple sclerosis in care receiver-carer dyads. *Family Relations*, *47*, 269–277. http://dx.doi.org/10.2307/584977

Pearlin, L. I., Mullan, J. T., Semple, S. J., & Skaff, M. M. (1990). Caregiving and the stress process: An overview of concepts and their measures. *The Gerontologist*, *30*, 583–594. http://dx.doi.org/10.1093/geront/30.5.583

Peyrot, M., McMurry, J. F., Jr., & Hedges, R. (1988). Marital adjustment to adult diabetes: Interpersonal congruence and spouse satisfaction. *Journal of Marriage and Family*, *50*, 363–376. http://dx.doi.org/10.2307/352003

Préau, M., Bouhnik, A. D., Rey, D., Mancini, J., & the ALD Cancer Study Group. (2011). Two years after cancer diagnosis, which couples become closer? *European Journal of Cancer Care*, *20*, 380–388. http://dx.doi.org/10.1111/j.1365-2354.2010.01191.x

Proulx, C. M., & Snyder-Rivas, L. A. (2013). The longitudinal associations between marital happiness, problems, and self-rated health. *Journal of Family Psychology*, *27*, 194–202. http://dx.doi.org/10.1037/a0031877

Rauer, A. J., & El-Sheikh, M. (2012). Reciprocal pathways between intimate partner violence and sleep in men and women. *Journal of Family Psychology*, *26*, 470–477. http://dx.doi.org/10.1037/a0027828

Revenson, T. A., Abraido-Lanza, A. F., Majerovitz, S. D., & Jordan, C. (2005). Couples coping with chronic illness: What's gender got to do with it? In T. A. Revenson, K. E. Kayser, & G. E. Bodenmann, (Eds.), *Couples coping with stress: Emerging perspectives on dyadic coping* (pp. 137–156). Washington, DC: American Psychological Association.

Revenson, T. A., & Majerovitz, S. D. (1990). Spouses' support provision to chronically ill patients. *Journal of Social and Personal Relationships*, *7*, 575–586. http://dx.doi.org/10.1177/0265407590074013

Revenson, T. A., Schiaffino, K. M., Majerovitz, S. D., & Gibofsky, A. (1991). Social support as a double-edged sword: The relation of positive and problematic support to depression among rheumatoid arthritis patients. *Social Science & Medicine*, *33*, 807–813. http://dx.doi.org/10.1016/0277-9536(91)90385-P

Robbins, M. L., Mehl, M. R., Smith, H. L., & Weihs, K. L. (2013). Linguistic indicators of patient, couple, and family adjustment following breast cancer. *Psycho-Oncology*, *22*, 1501–1508. http://dx.doi.org/10.1002/pon.3161

Roberto, K. A., Gold, D. T., & Yorgason, J. B. (2004). The influence of osteoporosis on the lives of older couples. *Journal of Applied Gerontology, 23,* 443–456. http://dx.doi.org/10.1177/0733464804270856

Robles, T. F., Slatcher, R. B., Trombello, J. M., & McGinn, M. M. (2014). Marital quality and health: A meta-analytic review. *Psychological Bulletin, 140,* 140–187. http://dx.doi.org/10.1037/a0031859

Roper, S., & Yorgason, J. B. (2009). Older individuals with diabetes and osteoarthritis and their spouses: Effects of activity limitations, marital happiness, and social contacts on partner's daily mood. *Family Relations, 58,* 460–474. http://dx.doi.org/10.1111/j.1741-3729.2009.00566.x

Schover, L. R., Canada, A. L., Yuan, Y., Sui, D., Neese, L., Jenkins, R., & Rhodes, M. M. (2012). A randomized trial of internet-based versus traditional sexual counseling for couples after localized prostate cancer treatment. *Cancer, 118,* 500–509. http://dx.doi.org/10.1002/cncr.26308

Stephens, M. A. P., Franks, M. M., Rook, K. S., Iida, M., Hemphill, R. C., & Salem, J. K. (2013). Spouses' attempts to regulate day-to-day dietary adherence among patients with type 2 diabetes. *Health Psychology, 32,* 1029–1037. http://dx.doi.org/10.1037/a0030018

Stephens, M. A. P., Rook, K. S., Franks, M. M., Khan, C., & Iida, M. (2010). Spouses' use of social control to improve diabetic patients' dietary adherence. *Families, Systems, & Health, 28,* 199–208. http://dx.doi.org/10.1037/a0020513

Strawbridge, W. J., Wallhagen, M. I., & Shema, S. J. (2007). Impact of spouse vision impairment on partner health and well-being: A longitudinal analysis of couples. *The Journals of Gerontology: Series B. Psychological Sciences and Social Sciences, 62,* S315–S322. http://dx.doi.org/10.1093/geronb/62.5.S315

Thommessen, B., Aarsland, D., Braekhus, A., Oksengaard, A. R., Engedal, K., & Laake, K. (2002). The psychosocial burden on spouses of the elderly with stroke, dementia and Parkinson's disease. *International Journal of Geriatric Psychiatry, 17,* 78–84.

Trief, P. M., Sandberg, J., Greenberg, R. P., Graff, K., Castronova, N., Yoon, M., & Weinstock, R. S. (2003). Describing support: A qualitative study of couples living with diabetes. *Families, Systems, & Health, 21,* 57–67. http://dx.doi.org/10.1037/h0089502

Umberson, D., Williams, K., Powers, D. A., Liu, H., & Needham, B. (2006). You make me sick: Marital quality and health over the life course. *Journal of Health and Social Behavior, 47,* 1–16. http://dx.doi.org/10.1177/002214650604700101

Waite, L. J., & Gallagher, M. (2000). *The case for marriage: Why married people are happier, healthier, and better off financially.* New York, NY: Broadway Books.

Westman, M., & Vinokur, A. (1998). Unraveling the relationship of distress levels within couples: Common stressors, empathic reactions, or crossover via social interaction? *Human Relations, 51,* 137–156. http://dx.doi.org/10.1177/001872679805100202

Wethington, E., McLeod, J., & Kessler, R. C. (1987). The importance of life events for explaining sex differences in psychological distress. In R. C. Barmett, C. Biener, & G. K. Baruch (Eds.), *Gender and stress* (pp. 144–156). New York, NY: Free Press.

Yorgason, J. B., Almeida, D., Neupert, S., Spiro, A., & Hoffman, L. (2006). A dyadic examination of daily health symptoms and emotional well-being in later life couples. *Family Relations, 55,* 613–624. http://dx.doi.org/10.1111/j.1741-3729.2006.00430.x

Yorgason, J. B., Booth, A., & Johnson, D. (2008). Health, disability, and marital quality: Is the association different for younger versus older cohorts? *Research on Aging, 30,* 623–648. http://dx.doi.org/10.1177/0164027508322570

Yorgason, J. B., Piercy, F. P., & Piercy, S. K. (2007). Acquired hearing impairment in older couple relationships: An exploration of couple resilience processes. *Journal of Aging Studies, 21,* 215–228. http://dx.doi.org/10.1016/j.jaging.2006.10.002

Yorgason, J. B., Roper, S. O., Sandberg, J. G., & Berg, C. A. (2012). Stress spillover of health symptoms from healthy spouses to patient spouses in older married couples managing both diabetes and osteoarthritis. *Families, Systems, & Health, 30,* 330–343. http://dx.doi.org/10.1037/a0030670

Yorgason, J. B., Roper, S. O., Wheeler, B., Crane, K., Byron, R., Carpenter, L., . . . Higley, D. (2010). Older couples' management of multiple-chronic illnesses: Individual and shared perceptions and coping in type 2 diabetes and osteoarthritis. *Families, Systems, & Health, 28,* 30–47. http://dx.doi.org/10.1037/a0019396

# II

# MARRIAGE, HEALTH, AND ADAPTATION TO ILLNESS IN MIDDLE AND LATE LIFE

# 10

# MARITAL BIOGRAPHY AND HEALTH IN MIDDLE AND LATE LIFE

ZHENMEI ZHANG, HUI LIU, AND YAN-LIANG YU

A long tradition of research has found that being married is associated with better mental health, lower rates of chronic illness, fewer functioning problems and disabilities, and longer life expectancy in the United States (Pienta, Hayward, & Jenkins, 2000; Umberson, Thomeer, & Williams, 2013; Waite & Gallagher, 2000). More recent research on marriage and health has suggested that health is influenced not only by current marital status but also by marital history (Dupre & Meadows, 2007; Hughes & Waite, 2009; Zhang & Hayward, 2006). Growing interest in how cumulative marital history, or marital biography, impacts health in later life can be attributed both to substantial changes in American family life over the past few decades and to the growing prominence of the life course perspective in health research. This

This research was supported in part by an NICHD center grant to the Population Studies Center at the University of Michigan (R24 HD041028) and a National Institute on Aging grant (K01AG043417, principal investigator, Hui Liu). We are grateful to N. E. Barr for editorial assistance.

http://dx.doi.org/10.1037/14897-011
*Couple Relationships in the Middle and Later Years: Their Nature, Complexity, and Role in Health and Illness,* J. Bookwala (Editor)

perspective posits that the aging process starts in early life and that health at any age is a product of biological, psychological, social, and environmental risk factors "acting independently, cumulatively, or interactively across the whole life course" (Kuh & the New Dynamics of Ageing Preparatory Network, 2007, p. 717).

Over the past 6 decades, the institution of marriage has faced significant changes and challenges. For both men and women, the age at marriage has increased, first-marriage and remarriage rates have declined, and divorce and cohabitation have increased markedly for adults of all ages (Casper & Bianchi, 2002). Recent national data has shown that by age 50, more than one third of Americans have divorced at least once, and approximately one quarter have married two times or more (Kreider & Ellis, 2011). For adults ages 50 and over, S. L. Brown and Lin (2012) found that divorce rates doubled between 1990 and 2010, rising from 4.9 to 10.1 divorced persons per 1,000 married persons, and in 2010 about one in four persons who divorced were ages 50 and over. Given these changes, more and more Americans now enter midlife and late life with complex marital histories. A sharp rise in cohabitation represents another significant change to union formation trends during this period. Although only about 8% of first marriages in the 1960s were preceded by cohabitation, the proportion increased to 56% in the 1990s (Casper & Bianchi, 2002). All of these changes suggest that traditional norms about marriage, divorce, and cohabitation have given way to a variety of union formations and family configurations in the United States. They also provide an ideal context to explore how marital biography influences health among baby boomers, who are the first cohort of Americans to experience these changes in adulthood, and who are now on the cusp of old age.

Since the 1970s, the life course perspective has gained prominence in health research. One of its core principles is that "health at any point in the life course has been shaped not only by recent, proximal circumstances and resources, but also by a lifetime of opportunities and constraints, or more distal influences" (Pavalko & Caputo, 2013, p. 1041). As individuals' marital biographies have become more heterogeneous, current marital status alone is viewed as less informative than measures such as union timing, transition, sequencing, and duration to characterize and investigate associated benefits and risks (Barrett, 2000; Dupre, Beck, & Meadows, 2009; Zhang & Hayward, 2006).

In this chapter, we discuss the use of marital biography to measure an individual's cumulative history of marital transitions and theoretical perspectives linking marital biography and health; review research on marital biography and health in midlife and late life; and discuss gaps in the literature, future directions for research, and clinical and policy implications of findings.

# MARITAL BIOGRAPHY

Family researchers have identified at least five interrelated components of marital biography: marital status, marital transitions, marital timing, marital sequencing, and marital status duration (Barrett, 2000; Dupre & Meadows, 2007; Hughes & Waite, 2009). *Marital status* refers to one's current state of being married, divorced, separated, widowed, or never married. *Marital transitions* include movements into and out of marital statuses. *Marital timing* refers to the ages at which marital transitions occur or sometimes the timing of marital transitions relative to other life events (e.g., widowhood and retirement). *Marital sequencing* refers to the order of marital transitions (e.g., married-divorced-remarried vs. married-widowed-remarried). *Marital status duration* reflects the accumulated time spent in a specific marital status, which may include marriage duration, divorce duration, and widowhood duration. Durations can thus differentiate among those who have the same marital status or those who have experienced the same type and number of marital transitions (Dupre & Meadows, 2007). Using measures of marital biography allows researchers to examine health effects that extend beyond current marital status and to analyze more nuanced questions such as: Is remarriage as protective of health as first marriage? Is widowhood at the age of 70 as damaging to health as widowhood at the age of 40? Are multiple divorces more harmful to health than single divorce? Is being married for 30 years at age 65 more protective than being married for 20 years? (Dupre et al., 2009; Zhang, 2006).

# THEORETICAL PERSPECTIVES ON MARITAL BIOGRAPHY AND HEALTH

The majority of the research on marital biography and health draws from three theoretical models: the marital resource model, the stress model, and the selection model. Increasingly, researchers also integrate the cumulative advantage/disadvantage theory in their studies on marital biography and health (Dupre & Meadows, 2007; Umberson et al., 2013).

## Marital Resource Model

The marital resource model suggests that marriage provides social, psychological, and economic resources, which in turn promote mental/physical health and longevity (Waite & Gallagher, 2000). In terms of social and psychological resources, marriage increases access to social support for both spouses (i.e., providing and receiving love, advice, and care), social integration (i.e., feeling connected to others), and social control of health behaviors (i.e., monitoring a spouse's health and health behaviors; Liu & Umberson, 2008; Umberson, 1992). Social support decreases anxiety and depression and buffers the negative effects of stress and other health hazards, which may in turn improve physical health and survival (Umberson & Montez, 2010). Other psychological benefits of marriage include stronger feelings of meaning and purpose in life, more self-acceptance, and a stronger sense of mastery (Marks, 1996). In terms of economic resources, marriage may lead to an increase in income and wealth through specialization, economies of scale, and the pooling of wealth (Becker, 1981). Economic resources directly enhance health through their positive effects on nutrition, caregiving for illness, and access to medical or other health-enhancing resources (Waite & Gallagher, 2000).

## Stress Model

It is widely acknowledged that divorce and death of the spouse are two of the most stressful events a person can experience (Umberson et al., 2013). In contrast to the marital resource model, which attributes health benefits to the institution of marriage, the stress model suggests that the strains of marital dissolution are the primary factor responsible for undermining the health of the divorced, separated, and widowed (Williams & Umberson, 2004). Stress researchers distinguish short-term stressful life events from chronic strains (Turner, Wheaton, & Lloyd, 1995). A *stressful life event* refers to an undesirable event that occurs in a relatively short period of time (e.g., transition to divorce), whereas *chronic strains* refer to persistent or ongoing sources of stress over prolonged periods of time (e.g., persistent marital conflict). Divorce and widowhood are viewed as life events that entail both short- and long-term stress (Carr & Springer, 2010), including decreased financial resources; disruption in social network; loss of social support; and when children are involved, the strain of either single parenthood or of coparenting with a former spouse (Zhang & Hayward, 2006).

## Selection Model

The selection model suggests that individuals in better health or with more favorable health characteristics are more likely to be selected into marriage, whereas those in worse health or with fewer favorable health characteristics are more likely to be selected out of marriage (Fu & Goldman, 1996; Karraker & Latham, 2015). Healthy individuals may be selected into marriage directly, through individuals' preferences for mentally and physically fit spouses, or indirectly, through selection criteria that are themselves associated with health and well-being such as socioeconomic status, health behaviors, and psychological characteristics (Fu & Goldman, 1996; Musick, Brand, & Davis, 2012). Marriage selection seems to work on health at two levels: first, more healthy individuals are more likely to marry, and second, less healthy people are more likely to divorce. For example, a recent study has found that wife's heart problem onset increases the risk of divorce (Karraker & Latham, 2015). However, what is noteworthy is that researchers have found a significant association between marital status and health even after controlling for selection factors such as education, income, personality, health behaviors, and health before marriage (Carr & Springer, 2010; D. R. Johnson & Wu, 2002).

### Cumulative Advantage/Disadvantage Theory

The cumulative advantage/disadvantage theory provides a useful framework for understanding how duration across marital statuses and multiple marital transitions can influence health and survival over the life course. Morbidity and mortality are often influenced by negative events and exposures (e.g., marital distress, marital dissolution, poverty, unhealthy behaviors) that can accumulate over the life course (Kuh & Ben-Shlomo, 1997). Moreover, early disadvantages can compound over time and set in motion more disadvantages. For example, women with children who divorce in early adulthood may face single parenting, along with limited educational/career opportunities and poor economic outlook. The chronic stress of being a single parent with limited resources may lead to psychological distress and unhealthy coping behaviors such as overeating, smoking, and drinking, which further undermine well-being in later life. On the other hand, the positive effects associated with a happy and stable marriage—such as social support and integration, socioeconomic advantages, and support for healthy behaviors—can also accumulate and have lasting beneficial effects on health (Umberson et al., 2013; Zhang & Hayward, 2006). Therefore, this theory posits that the accumulated duration of exposures to negative or positive marital experiences, and especially the number of negative exposures, act to compound the impact on health and mortality (Zhang, 2006).

## EMPIRICAL FINDINGS ON MARITAL BIOGRAPHY AND HEALTH

A burgeoning literature suggests that marital biography affects morbidity and mortality in later life. In this section, we focus on recent research evidence on the association between different dimensions of marital biography and health outcomes.

## Marital Status and Health

Current marital status, an important dimension of marital biography, is strongly associated with health and survival. Researchers have found that married people, on average, enjoy better mental health, fewer chronic illnesses, and longer life expectancy than the divorced/separated, the widowed, and the never married (e.g., Hughes & Waite, 2009; Rendall, Weden, Favreault, & Waldron, 2011; Simon, 2002). In terms of trends, Liu and Umberson (2008) found that differentials in self-reported health have widened in the past several decades between the married and the formerly married, whereas there is a convergence in the self-reported health between married men and never-married men largely due to reported improvements among the latter. Potential explanations for the divergent trends in health between the married and the formerly married include the increasingly important role of marriage in providing social support in the context of greater geographic mobility and the growing advantage in marriage selection of the healthier individuals (Liu & Zhang, 2013). As for the convergence in health between the married men and the never-married men over time, Liu and Umberson attributed it partly to the changes of family and marriage norms.

## Marital Transitions and Health

In recent years, a burgeoning literature has focused on the impact of marital transitions on health—most often mental health, self-rated health, and mortality. Consistent with the marriage resource model, research has shown that entry into marriages improves psychological well-being and decreases depression (Frech & Williams, 2007; Simon, 2002). A recent study (Musick & Bumpass, 2012) found that, even after controlling for preexisting individual characteristics, getting married is associated with moderate improvement in mental and physical health (although these benefits dissipate over time).

On the other side, much research has found that exiting marriage through divorce or widowhood is associated with significant declines in health and increases in mortality. In terms of psychological well-being, studies have found that divorce and widowhood often lead to declines in mental health, although most people seem to recover over time (Lee & DeMaris, 2007; Lorenz, Wickrama, Conger, & Elder, 2006). The results are less consistent for physical health. It is plausible that because chronic disease develops slowly, the negative effects of divorce on physical health may appear years or decades later (Hughes & Waite, 2009). A growing body of research seems to support this view. For example, although Lorenz and colleagues (2006) saw similar levels of physical health among newly divorced and married women, they found that after 10 years the divorced women had significantly higher levels of illness than their continuously married counterparts. Zhang and Hayward (2006) found that marital loss (separation/divorce or widowhood) is associated with a higher prevalence of cardiovascular disease for both men and women ages 51 to 61 years in 1992. Transitions to divorce or widowhood also increase the risk of dying for both men and women (Rendall et al., 2011). As for the pathways linking marital transitions with physical/mental health and mortality, researchers have found that socioeconomic conditions partially explain health differences between married persons and those who experience marital disruptions (particularly for women), whereas social support and healthy behaviors play smaller roles (more so for women than for men; Umberson et al., 2013; Zhang & Hayward, 2006). More recently, researchers have identified factors that moderate the association between marital transitions and physical health. For example, Bookwala, Marshall, and Manning (2014) found that between 1992 and 2004, respondents who became widowed but had a friend who acted as confidante had similar health outcomes as those continuously married during this period and better health than those widowed without a friend as confidante.

Studies examining the effect of the number of marital transitions on health have indicated that people experiencing multiple divorces or widowhoods have worse health than those with a single disruption (Dupre, George, Liu, & Peterson, 2015; Dupre & Meadows, 2007; Zhang, 2006; see Hughes & Waite, 2009, for an exception). For example, Barrett (2000) found that twice-divorced persons were significantly more depressed than the singly divorced, and those twice widowed reported more symptoms of anxiety and substance abuse than singly widowed persons. In Zhang's (2006) analysis, she found that people with multiple marital losses had a higher risk of cardiovascular disease than those with a single loss. Similarly, Dupre et al. (2009) found a graded relationship between the number of divorces and mortality: Compared with men without a divorce, men with one divorce were 1.30 times more likely to die, and men with two or more divorces were 1.80 times more likely to die during a 14-year follow-up, whereas the comparable risks were 1.68 and 1.72, respectively, among women.

## Marital Status Duration and Health

Relatively few studies have examined the health effects of marital status duration, although research has consistently shown that marriage duration contributes to longevity (Dupre et al., 2009). Lillard and Waite (1995) found subtle gender differences in the marital duration–longevity association: For men, mortality risk drops immediately after marriage and then decreases gradually with each additional year of marriage; for women, mortality risk does not decrease immediately after marriage, but decreases more over marriage duration than it does for men. As expected, widowhood significantly increases the risk of death for both men and women during the first few months of bereavement, and then the effect of widowhood declines monotonically until the second year of widowhood and plateaus thereafter (Elwert & Christakis, 2006). Mortality risk also increases during the first few years after a divorce and then attenuates thereafter (Dupre et al., 2009).

The relationship between marriage duration and physical health is more complex. For example, in a study that looked at the prevalence of chronic conditions among 51- to 61-year-olds, those married 20 to 29 years had fewer conditions than those married for shorter periods, whereas those married 30 and more years did not (Pienta et al., 2000). Zhang and Hayward (2006) found that longer marriages were associated with a slightly higher risk of cardiovascular disease onset for both men and women in later life, in part because longer marriages were associated with less healthy behaviors and an accumulation of chronic conditions, such as hypertension, diabetes, and high cholesterol. In another study that examined marital biography and the onset of chronic diseases (i.e., diabetes, cancer, heart attack, or stroke), Dupre and Meadows (2007) found that the health effects of marital duration were contingent on the number of married years accumulated by a specific age. For example, they found that a woman married 20 years at age 50 had a 24% lower risk of disease onset than a woman married only 10 years at age 50. And in another twist, McFarland, Hayward, and Brown (2013) found evidence of differences in the effects of marital duration on biological risks for disease by gender and type of biological risk. They found that marital duration was protective of cardiovascular health for women but not for men and that marital duration was not significantly associated with metabolic and chronic inflammation risk for either men or women.

Fewer studies have examined the effects of widowhood and divorce duration on physical health, and the results are inconsistent. Whereas Zhang and Hayward (2006) found no association between the duration of divorce or widowhood and cardiovascular disease, Dupre and Meadows (2007) found that longer divorce duration was associated with a higher risk of chronic disease onset for men, but widowhood duration was not associated with disease onset when the number of widowhood transitions was controlled for. Hughes and Waite (2009) found that a higher percentage of time spent in divorce or widowhood was associated with a greater number of chronic conditions and mobility limitations. These mixed findings are particularly difficult to interpret in light of the different health outcomes examined, the different measurements of divorce/widowhood duration (current divorce duration vs. the percentage of years spent in being divorced since first marriage), and the variation in study design (cross-sectional vs. longitudinal).

A significant body of research has analyzed the effects of widowhood duration and divorce duration on mental health. Most studies on widowhood duration have found that widowhood is associated with an initial steep decline in mental health, followed by a gradual recovery to prewidowhood mental health over 2 years (Sasson & Umberson, 2014). As for divorce, research has found that it can have a long-term negative impact on psychological well-being—an impact that is partly reduced only if the divorced remarry or enter a cohabiting relationship (D. R. Johnson & Wu, 2002; Lucas, 2005; Mastekaasa, 1994).

## Marital Timing, Sequencing, and Health

A small but growing number of studies have examined the health implications of marital timing among older men and women. These studies show that age at marriage matters for health in later life (Dupre et al., 2009; Hughes & Waite, 2009; McFarland et al., 2013). For example, Dupre and colleagues (2009) found that getting married before age 19 increased mortality risk for both men and women. Compared with getting married between the ages of 19 and 25, marriage at age 18 or younger has also been associated with a higher risk of disease onset for women (Dupre & Meadows, 2007). A recent study found a negative association between age at first marriage and the risk of chronic inflammation for men (McFarland et al., 2013). Part of the reason that early marriages have pernicious effects on health in later life may be that getting married as a teenager is often associated with poverty, dropping out of school, stress, untimely parental responsibilities, and a high risk for divorce over the life course (Dahl, 2010; Dupre et al., 2009).

Analyses have also found that the timing of marital dissolutions has important implications for health (Sasson & Umberson, 2014; Williams & Umberson, 2004). Liu (2012) recently showed that the negative effects of transitions to divorce on self-reported health decreased with age, whereas the health consequences of transitions to widowhood increased with age. Moreover, Liu (2012) found that health effects of marital transitions varied across birth cohorts—for example, divorce had a larger negative health impact for the 1950s cohort than the 1940s cohort, whereas the negative health impact of widowhood was larger for the 1910s cohort than the 1920s cohort.

Few studies have examined how different sequences of marital transitions are associated with health. Barrett (2000) found that those who remarried following divorce did not differ in mental health from those who remarried following widowhood. However, twice-widowed persons had higher rates of substance abuse symptoms than previously divorced and currently widowed individuals. Although the mechanisms through which different sequences of marital transitions affect heath were not explored in the study, Barrett suggested that "experiencing both divorce and widowhood may provide an individual with enhanced psychological resources that prevent the negative health outcomes that marital loss often brings" (p. 461).

## HETEROGENEITY IN THE EFFECTS OF MARITAL BIOGRAPHY ON HEALTH: GENDER, RACE, AND MARITAL QUALITY

Increasingly, recent research has shown that the effects of marital biography on later health vary by a variety of demographic and relationship characteristics. Here, we highlight the most important of these moderators: gender, race, and marital quality.

### Gender

Although research has established that marriage tends to benefit both men's and women's health, debate continues on whether it benefits men more than women (Simon, 2002; Williams, 2003). For example, some have posited that men derive more from marriage than women because wives are more likely than husbands to nurture their partners' well-being through maintaining social connections, providing emotional support, encouraging the adoption of healthy behaviors, and helping monitor their health. In addition, women's role in marriage may consist of more sacrifices and stresses than men's, especially given their generally larger responsibility for parental and household work (Bernard, 1972). Supporting these arguments, a number of studies have documented greater marital status disparities in mental health, physical health, and mortality for men than for women (Hughes & Waite, 2009; Liu, 2009). For example, using 25 years of data from the 1979 National Longitudinal Study of Youth, Teachman (2010) found that marriage was associated with reduced health limitations for men but increased health limitations for women. Although the reasons for this effect are not entirely clear, Teachman hypothesized that increasing caregiving responsibilities and associated stress over a married woman's life (i.e., caring for spouse, children, and elderly parents) may undermine her health.

Other researchers have questioned whether marriage provides more health benefits to men than to women, especially among more recent birth cohorts. They have argued that gender differences in the benefits of marriage may have attenuated or disappeared in recent years because of the significant changes taking place in American family life including declines in male wages, increases in the rates of women's labor force participation and the proportion of dual-earner couples, and increases in men's participation in child care and household chores (Casper & Bianchi, 2002). Some studies have supported this position, reporting that entry into first marriages imparts equal benefits for men and women, and there were no gender differences in the benefits of marriage for psychological well-being (Simon, 2002; Williams, 2003).

A few studies on marriage and physical health have suggested that divorce in later life may be more detrimental to women than men, especially in terms of cardiovascular disease. Clinical studies of marital strain reveal that marital conflict tends to evoke greater and more persistent physiological changes (e.g., increases in systolic blood pressure and elevated stress hormones) for women than for men. As divorce is often a protracted and stressful process marked by marital conflicts, women's greater sensitivity to marital distress may put them at higher risk for cardiovascular and other stress-related diseases than men (Kiecolt-Glaser & Newton, 2001). For example, Zhang and Hayward (2006) found that the risk of experiencing cardiovascular disease onset was higher for divorced women in midlife but not for divorced men. Given the findings that the effects of marital biography are sensitive to gender and the type of health outcome, it is important for researchers to continue to examine gendered effects of marriage and marital dissolution on a variety of health outcomes for mature adults of different birth cohorts.

## Race

Few studies have specifically examined racial/ethnic differences in the effects of marital biography on health. Some researchers have suggested that the meaning of each marital status may be different by race because of social, economic, historical, and cultural factors. For example, the nonmarried statuses may be less stigmatized and have less detrimental consequences on health among Blacks than Whites because of the more common occurrence of divorce, separation, and never-married status among Blacks (Liu & Zhang, 2013). Marriage may also provide fewer social, psychological, and economic resources for Blacks (especially for Black women) than for Whites because of the relatively disadvantaged socioeconomic status of Blacks and the reported lower marital quality among Black couples (Broman, 1993; Bulanda & Brown, 2007). Evidence on race differences in the link between marital biography and health from cross-sectional and longitudinal studies is limited and varies by the health outcomes examined. For example, Barrett (2003) found that separation has a less adverse effect on depressive symptoms for Blacks than for Whites, but divorced Blacks have more symptoms of substance abuse/dependence than divorced Whites, suggesting that divorce may have a stronger negative effect for Blacks. In terms of widowhood and mortality, largely consistent with theoretical arguments about racial differences in marital cultures and marital contexts, Elwert and Christakis (2006) found that widowhood does not increase the risk of mortality among Blacks, whereas it has a strong effect among Whites. Interestingly, other researchers have found that older Blacks seem to benefit more from marriage than older Whites in terms of nonfatal chronic conditions (e.g., back problems, arthritis), functioning problems, and disability (Pienta et al., 2000).

## Marital Quality

Research has found that the health benefits of marriage largely hinge on marital quality. *Marital quality* often refers to a married person's assessment of his or her marriage in terms of marital happiness and satisfaction, marital conflict and disagreement, marital interactions, attitudes, and behaviors. A growing body of research has shown that whereas a happy and satisfying marriage is related to better mental and physical health (Bookwala, 2005; Gallo, Troxel, Matthews, & Kuller 2003), staying in a poor-quality marriage can undermine health, and its negative effect on health can be similar to or sometimes worse than divorcing or remaining unmarried (Hawkins & Booth, 2005). Marital distress can act like a chronic stressor and lead to psychological distress, which is closely associated with physical health problems. Moreover, the efforts to control and change a spouse's unhealthy behaviors are less likely to be successful in an unhappy marriage than a happy marriage (Robles, Slatcher, Trombello, & McGinn, 2014; see also Chapter 15, this volume). Recent studies on biological pathways between marital quality and health have shown that negative marital interactions (e.g., angry behaviors during marital conflicts, high levels of hostility) can undermine cardiovascular health, elevate inflammatory responses, and depress the immune system—all of which may contribute to the development of chronic diseases in later life (Kiecolt-Glaser et al., 2005; Robles et al., 2014). Prior research has also suggested that negative aspects of marital functioning have stronger effects on health than positive aspects of marital functioning (Bookwala, 2005). It is therefore not surprising that researchers have found that increases in marital quality over time are associated with decreases in the number of physical illnesses (Wickrama, Lorenz, Conger, & Elder, 1997), that marital distress is associated with earlier onset of hypertension among long-time married men and women (Wickrama et al. 2001), and that exiting troubled marriages does not negatively impact health relative to staying in those marriages (Hawkins & Booth, 2005).

In addition, high-quality marriages may help ameliorate the negative effects of functional limitations and disability on older adults' mental health and quality of life, whereas low-quality marriages may exacerbate the negative effects of such conditions (Bookwala, 2011; Bookwala & Franks, 2005; Warner & Kelley-Moore, 2012). For example, Bookwala (2011) found that although poor vision was associated with higher levels of depressive symptoms and functional limitations among older adults in less satisfying marriages, it was not associated with either outcome in more satisfying marriages.

## WHERE DO WE GO FROM HERE?

In the past few decades, researchers have made important strides in the study of marital biography and health, using advanced statistical techniques such as growth curve and structural equation modeling with longitudinal data sets. Still, questions remain about how marital experiences over the life course affect well-being and how to account for the tremendous heterogeneity among people with different marital biographies. Here we discuss what we see as the most promising directions for future research.

### Methodology Issues

Significant research gaps remain in terms of methodologies in the field of marital biography and health. One of the most prominent issues is that researchers rarely look beyond their disciplinary boundaries, despite the importance of intersectional processes of social, biological, psychological, and behavioral mechanisms linking marriage to health (Robles & Kiecolt-Glaser, 2003). For example, most biopsychological studies of marital relationships are clinic-based, relying on small community and cross-sectional data without accounting for other social and behavioral covariates. At the same time, social and demographic researchers analyze national datasets, with a focus on self-rated physical health measures or mental health outcomes but lacking biological measures. A recent development of the biodemographic approach provides an innovative tool to address this issue. The biodemographic approach is usually involved with collecting and analyzing biological risk factors (e.g., systolic blood pressure, diastolic blood pressure, total cholesterol, C-reactive protein) in major longitudinal population-based surveys of older adults, such as the Health and Retirement Study (HRS) and the National Social Life, Health, and Aging Project, which present exciting opportunities for researchers to examine the biological pathways linking marital biography and health. In addition, the HRS just completed genotyping 12,507 respondents, and the addition of genetic data will enable scientists to explore how genes interact with marital transitions to produce different health outcomes.

Moreover, previous investigations of marital biography and health have not fully captured the complexities of marital relationships given their focus on the individual rather than the dyad as the unit of analysis. Most studies, especially population-based ones, model the relationship between marriage and health at the individual level and ignore the dyadic nature of marriage (Carr & Springer, 2010). Thus, we know little about how one's own health is related to spousal/dyadic characteristics. Leading scholars in marriage and health have long emphasized the linked lives of spouses and posited that spouses influence each other's social context and thus health risks (Lillard & Waite, 1995). Recent studies in European countries and the United States found that spouse's education influenced health, net of one's own education (D. C. Brown, Hummer, & Hayward, 2014; Jaffe, Eisenbach, Neumark, & Manor, 2006). Future studies should adopt a dyadic approach in the study of marriage and health and examine how various spousal characteristics (e.g., education, race, health and health behavior, personality, and marital satisfaction) affect one's own health risks.

## Heterogeneity of Intimate Relationships in Later Life

So far, research on marital biography and health among older adults has focused on married heterosexual couples. With the legalization and growing societal acceptance of same-sex marriages, it is important to examine the health implications of marriage for same-sex couples. We also think that as an increasing number of older adults choose to cohabit rather than remarry following a divorce or widowhood, research on marital biography and health should take cohabitation into consideration. Recent studies on cohabitation in older adulthood have shown that cohabiting unions in later life are quite stable and may operate as long-term alternatives to marriage (S. L. Brown, Bulanda, & Lee, 2012). Moreover, older cohabitors and married persons do not differ significantly in their reports of relationship quality including emotional satisfaction, pleasure, time spent together, demands, criticism, etc. (S. L. Brown & Kawamura, 2010). However, other research has also suggested that cohabitors have poorer health than their married peers (S. L. Brown, Bulanda, & Lee, 2005; Zhang, 2006). Future research should examine the same areas studied among married heterosexual couples for same-sex and cohabiting couples in later life, looking at the impact on different health outcomes by marital/cohabitational biography factors and relationship quality.

Last, what we know about marital biography and health in midlife and late life is largely based on samples of the general population, and therefore the results tend to be dominated by the experiences of Whites, the largest racial group in the United States (Koball, Moiduddin, Henderson, Goesling, & Besculides, 2010). As the composition of the U.S. older population becomes more racially diverse, we need more research that examines how marital biography influences health in African American, Hispanic, and Asian American populations. Couples are influenced by their own ethnic and cultural backgrounds, health beliefs and behaviors, and unique migration histories and circumstances, which in turn may influence couple relationships and health.

## CLINICAL AND POLICY IMPLICATIONS

Our review indicates that in midlife and late life, marital biography is significantly associated with health and survival, and the protective effects of marriage vary by gender, race, marital quality, and specific health outcomes. Several groups seem to be particularly disadvantaged: those recently divorced or widowed, those with multiple marital breakups, those married as teenagers, and those in low-quality marriages. Thus, health professionals should understand the dynamic impact of marital biography on health and periodically assess their patients from this perspective. In particular, knowing the stresses associated with marital loss in later life and the importance of various forms of social support will help practitioners provide a range of compassionate and effective services.

Also, given that marital quality is strongly linked to health and moderates the relationship between disability and psychological well-being in later life, older adults in unhappy marriages might be encouraged by health professionals, family members, and friends to try marital therapy. Previous research has shown that marital therapy has been effective in helping some couples to improve communication and interpersonal relationship skills, to cope with spousal and children's health problems, and ultimately to enhance marital functioning and satisfaction (S. M. Johnson, 2003; Mead, 2002).

Our review also shows that more and more Americans are entering old age without a partner or with complex marital histories, and many of these individuals are less healthy than their married counterparts, partly because of their disadvantages in socioeconomic resources and social integration. Divorced and widowed older women have higher poverty rates than their male counterparts. Policies aiming at improving women's economic well-being over the life course (e.g., increasing minimum wages, eliminating the gender gap in pay, granting caregiving credit, increasing Social Security survivor benefits) would help reduce poverty for older women in general and for nonmarried older women in particular (Richardson, 2006). At a local level, municipal governments should assess the needs of the increasingly large nonmarried older population and encourage companies, hospitals, and organizations to provide innovative services and programs that improve the health and well-being of nonmarried older adults.

## REFERENCES

Barrett, A. E. (2000). Marital trajectories and mental health. *Journal of Health and Social Behavior, 41,* 451–464. http://dx.doi.org/10.2307/2676297

Barrett, A. E. (2003). Race differences in the mental health effects of divorce: A reexamination incorporating temporal dimensions of the dissolution process. *Journal of Family Issues, 24,* 995–1019. http://dx.doi.org/10.1177/0192513X03256396

Becker, G. S. (1981). *A treatise on the family*. Cambridge, MA: Harvard University Press.

Bernard, J. S. (1972). *The future of marriage*. New York, NY: World.

Bookwala, J. (2005). The role of marital quality in physical health during the mature years. *Journal of Aging and Health, 17*, 85–104. http://dx.doi.org/10.1177/0898264304272794

Bookwala, J. (2011). Marital quality as a moderator of the effects of poor vision on quality of life among older adults. *The Journals of Gerontology: Series B. Psychological Sciences and Social Sciences, 66*, 605–616. http://dx.doi.org/10.1093/geronb/gbr091

Bookwala, J., & Franks, M. M. (2005). Moderating role of marital quality in older adults' depressed affect: Beyond the main-effects model. *The Journals of Gerontology: Series B. Psychological Sciences and Social Sciences, 60*, P338–P341. http://dx.doi.org/10.1093/geronb/60.6.P338

Bookwala, J., Marshall, K. I., & Manning, S. W. (2014). Who needs a friend? Marital status transitions and physical health outcomes in later life. *Health Psychology, 33*, 505–515. http://dx.doi.org/10.1037/hea0000049

Broman, C. L. (1993). Race differences in marital well-being. *Journal of Marriage and Family, 55*, 724–732. http://dx.doi.org/10.2307/353352

Brown, D. C., Hummer, R. A., & Hayward, M. D. (2014). The importance of spousal education for the self-rated health of married adults in the United States. *Population Research and Policy Review, 33*, 127–151. http://dx.doi.org/10.1007/s11113-013-9305-6

Brown, S. L., Bulanda, J. R., & Lee, G. R. (2005). The significance of nonmarital cohabitation: Marital status and mental health benefits among middle-aged and older adults. *The Journals of Gerontology: Series B. Psychological Sciences and Social Sciences, 60*, S21–S29. http://dx.doi.org/10.1093/geronb/60.1.S21

Brown, S. L., Bulanda, J. R., & Lee, G. R. (2012). Transitions into and out of cohabitation in later life. *Journal of Marriage and Family, 74*, 774–793. http://dx.doi.org/10.1111/j.17413737.2012.00994.x

Brown, S. L., & Kawamura, S. (2010). Relationship quality among cohabitors and marrieds in older adulthood. *Social Science Research, 39*, 777–786. http://dx.doi.org/10.1016/j.ssresearch.2010.04.010

Brown, S. L., & Lin, I. F. (2012). The gray divorce revolution: Rising divorce among middle-aged and older adults, 1990–2010. *The Journals of Gerontology: Series B. Psychological Sciences and Social Sciences, 67*, 731–741. http://dx.doi.org/10.1093/geronb/gbs089

Bulanda, J. R., & Brown, S. L. (2007). Race-ethnic differences in marital quality and divorce. *Social Science Research, 36*, 945–967. http://dx.doi.org/10.1016/j.ssresearch.2006.04.001

Carr, D., & Springer, K. W. (2010). Advances in families and health research in the 21st century. *Journal of Marriage and Family, 72*, 743–761. http://dx.doi.org/10.1111/j.1741-3737.2010.00728.x

Casper, L. M., & Bianchi, S. M. (2002). *Continuity and change in the American family.* Thousand Oaks, CA: Sage.

Dahl, G. B. (2010). Early teen marriage and future poverty. *Demography, 47,* 689–718.

Dupre, M. E., Beck, A. N., & Meadows, S. O. (2009). Marital trajectories and mortality among US adults. *American Journal of Epidemiology, 170,* 546–555. http://dx.doi.org/10.1093/aje/kwp194

Dupre, M. E., George, L. K., Liu, G., & Peterson, E. D. (2015). Association between divorce and risks for acute myocardial infarction. *Circulation: Cardiovascular Quality and Outcomes, 8,* 244–251. http://dx.doi.org/10.1161/CIRCOUTCOMES.114.001291

Dupre, M. E., & Meadows, S. O. (2007). Disaggregating the effects of marital trajectories on health. *Journal of Family Issues, 28,* 623–652. http://dx.doi.org/10.1177/0192513X06296296

Elwert, F., & Christakis, N. A. (2006). Widowhood and race. *American Sociological Review, 71,* 16–41. http://dx.doi.org/10.1177/000312240607100102

Frech, A., & Williams, K. (2007). Depression and the psychological benefits of entering marriage. *Journal of Health and Social Behavior, 48,* 149–163. http://dx.doi.org/10.1177/002214650704800204

Fu, H., & Goldman, N. (1996). Incorporating health into models of marriage choice: Demographic and sociological perspective. *Journal of Marriage and Family, 58,* 740–758. http://dx.doi.org/10.2307/353733

Gallo, L. C., Troxel, W. M., Matthews, K. A., & Kuller, L. H. (2003). Marital status and quality in middle-aged women: Associations with levels and trajectories of cardiovascular risk factors. *Health Psychology, 22,* 453–463. http://dx.doi.org/10.1037/0278-6133.22.5.453

Hawkins, D. N., & Booth, A. (2005). Unhappily ever after: Effects of long-term, low-quality marriages on well-being. *Social Forces, 84,* 451–471. http://dx.doi.org/10.1353/sof.2005.0103

Hughes, M. E., & Waite, L. J. (2009). Marital biography and health at mid-life. *Journal of Health and Social Behavior, 50,* 344–358. http://dx.doi.org/10.1177/002214650905000307

Jaffe, D. H., Eisenbach, Z., Neumark, Y. D., & Manor, O. (2006). Effects of husbands' and wives' education on each other's mortality. *Social Science & Medicine, 62,* 2014–2023. http://dx.doi.org/10.1016/j.socscimed.2005.08.030

Johnson, D. R., & Wu, J. (2002). An empirical test of crisis, social selection, and role explanations of the relationship between marital disruption and psychological distress: A pooled time-series analysis of four-wave panel data. *Journal of Marriage and Family, 64,* 211–224. http://dx.doi.org/10.1111/j.1741-3737.2002.00211.x

Johnson, S. M. (2003). The revolution in couple therapy: A practitioner–scientist perspective. *Journal of Marital and Family Therapy, 29,* 365–384. http://dx.doi.org/10.1111/j.1752-0606.2003.tb01213.x

Karraker, A., & Latham, K. (2015). In sickness and in health? Physical illness as a risk factor for marital dissolution in later life. *Journal of Health and Social Behavior, 56*, 420–435. http://dx.doi.org/10.1177/0022146514568351

Kiecolt-Glaser, J. K., Loving, T. J., Stowell, J. R., Malarkey, W. B., Lemeshow, S., Dickinson, S. L., & Glaser, R. (2005). Hostile marital interactions, proinflammatory cytokine production, and wound healing. *Archives of General Psychiatry, 62*, 1377–1384. http://dx.doi.org/10.1001/archpsyc.62.12.1377

Kiecolt-Glaser, J. K., & Newton, T. L. (2001). Marriage and health: His and hers. *Psychological Bulletin, 127*, 472–503. http://dx.doi.org/0033-2909.127.4.472

Koball, H. L., Moiduddin, E., Henderson, J., Goesling, B., & Besculides, M. (2010). What do we know about the link between marriage and health? *Journal of Family Issues, 31*, 1019–1040. http://dx.doi.org/10.1177/0192513X10365834

Kreider, R. M., & Ellis, R. (2011). Number, timing, and duration of marriages and divorces: 2009. *Current Population Reports*, 70–125. Washington, DC: U.S. Census Bureau.

Kuh, D., & Ben-Shlomo, Y. (1997). *A life course approach to chronic disease epidemiology*. New York, NY: Oxford University Press.

Kuh, D., & the New Dynamics of Ageing (NDA) Preparatory Network. (2007). A life course approach to healthy aging, frailty, and capability. *The Journals of Gerontology: Series A. Biological Sciences and Medical Sciences, 62*, 717–721. http://dx.doi.org/10.1093/gerona/62.7.717

Lee, G. R., & DeMaris, A. (2007). Widowhood, gender, and depression: A longitudinal analysis. *Research on Aging, 29*, 56–72. http://dx.doi.org/10.1177/0164027506294098

Lillard, L. A., & Waite, L. J. (1995). Til death do us part: Marital disruption and mortality. *American Journal of Sociology, 100*, 1131–1156. http://dx.doi.org/10.1086/230634

Liu, H. (2009). Till death do us part: Marital status and mortality trends, 1986–2000. *Journal of Marriage and Family, 71*, 1158–1173. http://dx.doi.org/10.1111/j.1741-3737.2009.00661.x

Liu, H. (2012). Marital dissolution and self-rated health: Age trajectories and birth cohort variations. *Social Science & Medicine, 74*, 1107–1116. http://dx.doi.org/10.1016/j.socscimed.2011.11.037

Liu, H., & Umberson, D. J. (2008). The times they are a changin': Marital status and health differentials from 1972 to 2003. *Journal of Health and Social Behavior, 49*, 239–253. http://dx.doi.org/10.1177/002214650804900301

Liu, H., & Zhang, Z. (2013). Disability trends by marital status among older Americans, 1997–2010: An examination by gender and race. *Population Research and Policy Review, 32*, 103–127. http://dx.doi.org/10.1007/s11113-012-9259-0

Lorenz, F. O., Wickrama, K. A., Conger, R. D., & Elder, G. H., Jr. (2006). The short-term and decade-long effects of divorce on women's midlife health. *Journal of Health and Social Behavior, 47*, 111–125. http://dx.doi.org/10.1177/002214650604700202

Lucas, R. E. (2005). Time does not heal all wounds. *Psychological Science, 16,* 945–950. http://dx.doi.org/10.1111/j.1467-9280.2005.01642.x

Marks, N. F. (1996). Flying solo at midlife: Gender, marital status, and psychological well-being. *Journal of Marriage and Family, 58,* 917–932. http://dx.doi.org/10.2307/353980

Mastekaasa, A. (1994). The subjective well-being of the previously married: The importance of unmarried cohabitation and time since widowhood or divorce. *Social Forces, 73,* 665–692. http://dx.doi.org/10.1093/sf/73.2.665

McFarland, M. J., Hayward, M. D., & Brown, D. (2013). I've got you under my skin: Marital biography and biological risk. *Journal of Marriage and Family, 75,* 363–380. http://dx.doi.org/10.1111/jomf.12015

Mead, D. E. (2002). Marital distress, co-occurring depression, and marital therapy: A review. *Journal of Marital and Family Therapy, 28,* 299–314. http://dx.doi.org/10.1111/j.1752-0606.2002.tb01188.x

Musick, K., Brand, J. E., & Davis, D. (2012). Variation in the relationship between education and marriage: Marriage market mismatch? *Journal of Marriage and Family, 74,* 53–69. http://dx.doi.org/10.1111/j.1741-3737.2011.00879.x

Musick, K., & Bumpass, L. (2012). Reexamining the case for marriage: Union formation and changes in well-being. *Journal of Marriage and Family, 74,* 1–18. http://dx.doi.org/10.1111/j.1741-3737.2011.00873.x

Pavalko, E. K., & Caputo, J. (2013). Social inequality and health across the life course. *American Behavioral Scientist, 57,* 1040–1056. http://dx.doi.org/10.1177/0002764213487344

Pienta, A., Hayward, M. D., & Jenkins, K. R. (2000). Health consequences of marriage for the retirement years. *Journal of Family Issues, 21,* 559–586. http://dx.doi.org/10.1177/019251300021005003

Rendall, M. S., Weden, M. M., Favreault, M. M., & Waldron, H. (2011). The protective effect of marriage for survival: A review and update. *Demography, 48,* 481–506. http://dx.doi.org/10.1007/s13524-011-0032-5

Richardson, V. (2006). Implications for public policies and social services: What social workers and other gerontology practitioners can learn from the Changing Lives of Older Couples Study. In D. S. Carr, R. M. Nesse, & C. B. Wortman (Eds.), *Spousal bereavement in late life* (pp. 279–312). New York, NY: Springer.

Robles, T. F., & Kiecolt-Glaser, J. K. (2003). The physiology of marriage: Pathways to health. *Physiology & Behavior, 79,* 409–416. http://dx.doi.org/10.1016/S0031-9384(03)00160-4

Robles, T. F., Slatcher, R. B., Trombello, J. M., & McGinn, M. M. (2014). Marital quality and health: A meta-analytic review. *Psychological Bulletin, 140,* 140–187. http://dx.doi.org/10.1037/a0031859

Sasson, I., & Umberson, D. J. (2014). Widowhood and depression: New light on gender differences, selection, and psychological adjustment. *The Journals of Gerontology: Series B. Psychological Sciences and Social Sciences, 69,* 135–145. http://dx.doi.org/10.1093/geronb/gbt058

Simon, R. W. (2002). Revisiting the relationships among gender, marital status, and mental health. *American Journal of Sociology, 107,* 1065–1096. http://dx.doi.org/10.1086/339225

Teachman, J. (2010). Family life course statuses and transitions: Relationships with health limitations. *Sociological Perspectives, 53,* 201–219. http://dx.doi.org/10.1525/sop.2010.53.2.201

Turner, R. J., Wheaton, B., & Lloyd, D. A. (1995). The epidemiology of social stress. *American Sociological Review, 60,* 104–125. http://dx.doi.org/10.2307/2096348

Umberson, D. (1992). Gender, marital status and the social control of health behavior. *Social Science & Medicine, 34,* 907–917. http://dx.doi.org/10.1016/0277-9536(92)90259-S

Umberson, D., & Montez, J. K. (2010). Social relationships and health: A flashpoint for health policy. *Journal of Health and Social Behavior, 51*(Suppl. 1), S54–S66. http://dx.doi.org/10.1177/0022146510383501

Umberson, D., Thomeer, M., & Williams, K. (2013). Family status and mental health: Recent advances and future directions. In C. S. Aneshensel, J. C. Phelan, & A. Bierman (Eds.), *Handbook of the sociology of mental health* (pp. 405–431). Dordrecht, the Netherlands: Springer. http://dx.doi.org/10.1007/978-94-007-4276-5_20

Waite, L. J., & Gallagher, M. (2000). *The case for marriage: Why married people are happier, healthier, and better off financially.* New York, NY: Doubleday.

Warner, D. F., & Kelley-Moore, J. (2012). The social context of disablement among older adults: Does marital quality matter for loneliness? *Journal of Health and Social Behavior, 53,* 50–66. http://dx.doi.org/10.1177/0022146512439540

Wickrama, K. A. S., Lorenz, F. O., Conger, R. D., & Elder, G. H. J. (1997). Marital quality and physical illness: A latent growth curve analysis. *Journal of Marriage and Family, 59,* 143–155. http://dx.doi.org/10.2307/353668

Wickrama, K. A. S., Lorenz, F. O., Wallace, L. E., Peiris, L., Conger, R. D., & G. H. Elder, Jr. (2001). Family influence on physical health during the middle years: The case of onset of hypertension. *Journal of Marriage and Family, 63,* 527–539. http://dx.doi.org/10.1111/j.1741-3737.2001.00527.x

Williams, K. (2003). Has the future of marriage arrived? A contemporary examination of gender, marriage, and psychological well-being. *Journal of Health and Social Behavior, 44,* 470–487. http://dx.doi.org/10.2307/1519794

Williams, K., & Umberson, D. (2004). Marital status, marital transitions, and health: A gendered life course perspective. *Journal of Health and Social Behavior, 45,* 81–98. http://dx.doi.org/10.1177/002214650404500106

Zhang, Z. (2006). Marital history and the burden of cardiovascular disease in midlife. *The Gerontologist, 46,* 266–270. http://dx.doi.org/10.1093/geront/46.2.266

Zhang, Z., & Hayward, M. D. (2006). Gender, the marital life course, and cardiovascular disease in late midlife. *Journal of Marriage and Family, 68,* 639–657. http://dx.doi.org/10.1111/j.1741-3737.2006.00280.x

# 11

# COLLABORATIVE COGNITION IN MIDDLE AND LATE LIFE: COUPLE NEGOTIATION OF EVERYDAY TASKS

JENNIFER A. MARGRETT AND CELINDA REESE-MELANCON

Intimate partnerships are prevalent in adulthood, and the vast majority of men and women are likely to cohabit and/or marry during their lifetime (Vespa, Lewis, & Kreider, 2013). This is extremely relevant to adult development and aging research and application as intimate partners are in a unique position to influence development and performance throughout adulthood. Partner influence occurs across a variety of domains including cognition, which is an important component of whole-person wellness and a contributor to optimal aging. Cognitive health underpins functioning in daily life including completion of cognitive tasks such as everyday memory tasks (e.g., grocery items, appointments to keep), as well as more complex instrumental activities of daily living such as financial and medication management (Fong et al., 2015). Middle-aged and older spouses often rely on collaboration to accomplish everyday tasks (Morgan & Berg, 2001; Reese & Cherry, 2004; Strough, Patrick, Swenson, Cheng, & Barnes, 2003), and people tend to hold

http://dx.doi.org/10.1037/14897-012
*Couple Relationships in the Middle and Later Years: Their Nature, Complexity, and Role in Health and Illness,*
J. Bookwala (Editor)

positive beliefs about the effectiveness of working together on cognitive tasks (Henkel & Rajaram, 2011). Collaborating on cognitive tasks has clear implications for everyday functioning, especially as individuals' cognitive abilities change and intimate partners face environmental stressors and disease as they age. Investigation of how intimate partners collaborate on cognitive tasks during middle and later adulthood is particularly important as the number of individuals living with cognitive impairment is expected to dramatically increase, coinciding with the growing number of aging baby boomers (Centers for Disease Control and Prevention, 2011).

An important issue when considering intimate partners' navigation of everyday cognitive tasks is the distinction between normative cognitive change and change that is due to pathology (Cherry & Smith, 1998). Memory is a useful example. Normative memory aging reflects changes in memory performance that are part of the typical or natural maturation process such as forgetting where one's car is parked or the name of an acquaintance. In contrast, pathological memory aging reflects changes that are due to disease and affects nearly half of those over age 85 (Centers for Disease Control and Prevention, 2013). Forgetting how to use a can opener or forgetting the name of a close friend or family member are examples of pathological, nonnormative memory aging. As couples age, it could be the case that both partners experience normative change, both could experience pathological changes, or one partner may change in a normative fashion while the other experiences more rapid, pathological change. The type and balance of cognitive change within a couple is likely to affect the process of collaborative give-and-take as well as the extent to which one partner can be relied on to compensate or share the cognitive load for the other. This chapter examines the extent to which relying on one's spouse or partner as a source of compensation for any individual cognitive deficits can be an effective strategy to promote optimal aging.

## EMPIRICAL INVESTIGATION OF COLLABORATIVE COGNITION IN ADULTHOOD

Collaborative cognition (CC) research stems from a lifespan perspective and is inherently multidisciplinary, reflecting core components from several fields of inquiry including human development and family studies, interpersonal relationships and social psychology, communication, health psychology, cognitive psychology, and neuroscience. Evidence from the early developmental literature demonstrates that partners play an integral role in cognitive development and performance (e.g., Gauvain & Rogoff, 1989; Rogoff, Ellis, & Gardner, 1984). Social context is a vital component of children's cognitive development (Piaget as cited in Miller, 1993) and partner behaviors can serve to "scaffold" performance to reach new heights (Vygotsky, 1934/1986). Extension of the collaborative literature into later life is particularly advantageous, as the paradigm of "interactive minds" (Baltes & Staudinger, 1996) appears to be one mechanism used by older adults to enhance or remediate cognitive performance (Bäckman & Dixon, 1992; Staudinger & Baltes, 1996). The extant CC literature largely reflects social cognition underpinnings with a focus on the ways that task demands, partner characteristics, composition of the collaborating dyad, and the resulting interactive processes affect collaborative outcomes. In the sections that follow, we highlight examples of these works, focusing on middle and later life.

## Cognitive Task Differences

A fundamental factor influencing collaborative outcome is type of cognitive task. Differential performance across cognitive tasks can be related to numerous factors, including task content, familiarity, demands, individual ability, personality, culture, and gender. As a result, the nature of the task appears to be related to whether CC is beneficial or detrimental to performance. We first consider memory tasks, which have important consequences for everyday functioning. Following, we outline collaborative research related to other cognitive tasks and address the ways in which dyadic characteristics can potentially impact collaborative task performance.

### Memory Tasks

Particularly relevant to middle-aged and older couples is the overarching concept of *transactive* memory, which refers to the combined knowledge of a dyad or group (Wegner, 1986). One partner may not know everything his or her intimate partner does, but he or she is aware of the knowledge the spouse has and can rely on him or her as a resource for this information. For example, one partner may not know where a particular store is located but recognizes that the other partner knows the way and can give directions as he or she drives. Johansson, Andersson, and Rönnberg (2000; see also Johansson, Andersson, & Rönnberg, 2005) found that, compared with older couples who did not report using transactive memory in daily life, older couples who reported using transactive memory in daily life were better able to remember information provided to them during a visit to a college campus and were also better at remembering to offer requested reminders to the tour guide. Ideally, transactive memory should reduce cognitive load (e.g., help focus attention and target encoding strategies), as long as the partner is a reliable source of information. If, however, one partner starts to experience cognitive impairment, the other may have to learn tasks for which he or she previously relied on a partner. There is relatively little research regarding the general notion of transactive memory, making this a useful avenue for future research to help us better understand how middle-aged and older couples rely on one another for memory support and how the availability of that support may change over time.

In terms of collaboration on specific memory tasks, several studies relevant to our discussion of middle-aged and later life couples reveal the nuances of CC. For example, episodic memory is the ability to remember personal events and experiences, and in this case, two heads are sometimes worse than one. When unfamiliar partners are asked to work together to recall episodic information they have learned in a laboratory setting, their recall levels are often lower than the combined recall levels of individuals who attempt retrieval alone (for a review, see Blumen, Rajaram, & Henkel, 2013). This finding, termed *collaborative inhibition* (Weldon & Bellinger, 1997), is true for a variety of episodic memory tasks, including recall of photographs of household scenes (Ross, Spencer, Blatz, & Restorick, 2008), items from shopping lists (Ross, Spencer, Linardatos, Lam, & Perunovic, 2004), and word lists (Meade & Roediger, 2009), and it appears to impact older and younger adults similarly (Henkel & Rajaram, 2011). Collaborative inhibition may be lessened by working with a familiar partner such as a spouse; however, the outcome for both familiar and unfamiliar dyads appears to hinge on dyadic characteristics.

The effects of collaboration on episodic memory are not entirely negative, because studies also document that engaging in collaborative retrieval attempts actually benefits later individual recall levels (Blumen & Stern, 2011). That is, people who tried to recall collaboratively benefited from that experience in the long run by recalling more than those who only made individual recall attempts. A number of cognitive mechanisms, such as retrieval disruption (Basden, Basden, Bryner, & Thomas, 1997), cross-cuing (Blumen & Rajaram, 2008), and reexposure to material (Weldon & Bellinger, 1997), have been proposed as explanations for the costs and benefits of collaboration on memory tasks. Blumen et al. (2013) identified cross-cuing and reexposure as potential avenues for using collaboration to improve memory performance in later life. For example, they suggested that cross-cuing, which refers to the provision of retrieval cues by a partner, could benefit memory. Consider a couple trying to recall and describe a recent evening out. Through conversation, they cue each other about the details and sequence of events and ultimately successfully describe their experience. Reexposure to material also benefits long-term memory because it serves as a reinstatement of the information to be recalled. Repeated exposure to information is thought to strengthen the memory trace, increasing the likelihood that the information will be remembered later (Ebbinghaus, 1885/1964). Couples have the potential to strengthen each other's memory by calling to mind events and information that otherwise may have decayed or become irretrievable had one spouse not mentioned it to the other.

Remembering to carry out one's intentions, such as remembering to take medication at a certain time or remembering to turn off the stove after cooking, is another important aspect of everyday memory. Researchers refer to this type of memory as *prospective memory* (PM). Only two prior studies have examined whether collaborating on PM tasks benefits performance among adult couples. Johansson et al. (2000) found that older couples generally performed two naturalistic PM tasks (e.g., offering requested reminders to a tour guide during the course of a campus visit) more poorly than older individuals working alone. However, as mentioned previously, dyads of intimate partners who reported using transactive memory performed as well as individuals and better than unfamiliar dyads. Building on this work, Margrett, Reese-Melancon, and Rendell (2011) conducted a laboratory-based study of PM on younger, middle-aged, and older couples. The couples played a PM board game while their performance and interactions were video recorded. The game simulated a series of days in the life of a busy person where the first square on the board was the start of a day and the last square was the end. Over the course of each day, the participant had to remember to perform a number of different types of PM tasks (Rendell & Craik, 2000). For example, participants had to remember to take virtual medication with breakfast (a regularly occurring event), return a library book to the library (an irregularly occurring event), and check their lung capacity at certain times of day (a time-based task). Individual contributions (i.e., solitary responses without spousal input) were distinguished from responses that incorporated spousal contributions (i.e., help or hindrance). Findings revealed that compared with middle-aged and older couples, younger couples performed very well on the PM tasks, but rarely requested or received collaborative input. Middle-aged and older couples demonstrated much more collaboration than did younger spouses. Middle-aged couples clearly benefitted from working together, perhaps reflecting more effective collaborative communication processes, and this was especially true on tasks that did not have strong retrieval cues (e.g., the time-based tasks). Collaborative input among older couples often had a negative effect on performance, and this was especially true on the time-based tasks. However, it is important to note that some older couples benefitted from collaboration. Those older couples who tried to engage each other in ways to approach the task (i.e., tutoring) and offered help in monitoring for upcoming opportunities to perform the PM tasks fared better than those who either did not collaborate in this way or attempted to but offered inaccurate advice (Margrett, Reese-Melancon, Young, Temple, & Linde, 2010). These findings point to the need to consider the impact that within-dyad factors, such as partner ability, and between-dyad differences, such as age, can have on the collaborative process.

*Other Cognitive Tasks*

CC research also encompasses cognitive tasks that are not memory tasks per se but reflect the complexity of everyday functioning for middle-aged and older adults. For example, collaborative benefit has been documented for structured cognitive tasks, including comprehension of everyday printed materials (e.g., medication labels, rebate forms) and route planning, as well as more ill-defined tasks, such as social problem solving (e.g., Berg, Johnson, Meegan, & Strough, 2003; Cheng & Strough, 2004; Margrett & Marsiske, 2002). However, collaborative benefits were not universally reflected on all performance indicators (e.g., efficiency, all types of errors; Cheng & Strough, 2004).

**Interactive Collaborative Processes**

Given their shared history, intimate partners are likely to develop "interactive expertise" (e.g., Dixon & Gould, 1996), weaving together a pattern of partner knowledge and dyadic behaviors. Inclusion of social partners, particularly intimate partners, in studies of cognitive aging is vital (Dixon, 2011), and thus additional context beyond the cognitive is needed to understand the phenomenon of collaboration. Such understanding of partners and their ensuing collaborative processes can inform practitioners' efforts to shape and reap the benefits of CC in middle and later life. Dixon, Gould, and colleagues have conducted several studies to examine the collaborative nature of interaction during memory tasks involving story and prose recall (e.g., Dixon & Gould, 1996; Gagnon & Dixon, 2008; Gould, Kurzman, & Dixon, 1994; Gould, Trevithick, & Dixon, 1991). This collective work demonstrated the impact of partner familiarity on interactive processes and that some partner behaviors may benefit dyadic rapport (e.g., sociability) but disrupt cognitive processes (e.g., recall memory interference). This work suggests that partner familiarity may be particularly beneficial for older adults; however, other work questions this assertion (Gould, Osborn, Krein, & Mortenson, 2002).

Johansson et al. (2000) proposed examining the process that couples use to collaborate on PM tasks as an area for future research because their informal observations of older couples' interactions during a naturalistic PM task indicated that social factors (e.g., partner dominance) appeared to be related to negative outcomes (e.g., one partner taking over memory responsibilities). When Margrett et al. (2011) examined the process of PM collaboration, transcripts of couples' interactions revealed that couples engaged in a variety of socioemotional behaviors but that spousal input varied in terms of how positive and helpful it was. Some couples encouraged each other's participation and congratulated one another on successes achieved during the experimental task, but others made more negative remarks to one another.

Extending investigation of collaborative processes to nonmemory tasks, Kimbler and Margrett (2009) coded familiar and unfamiliar partners' verbal behaviors during collaboration to solve unambiguous tasks based on printed materials (e.g., transportation schedule, rebate form). Their results demonstrated that older adult partners' interactive behaviors were linked to performance outcomes, and the nature of the behaviors differed (a) over the course of task completion (i.e., beginning, middle, and end) and (b) by composition of the dyad (i.e., partner familiarity, partners' skill level relative to one another). Four groups of interactive styles varying in collaborative benefit were identified. Dyads exhibiting the greatest benefit from collaboration were those in which less-skilled partners encouraged their partner's involvement in the task and better skilled partners engaged in tutoring behaviors. This type of give-and-take resulted in superior gain compared with the other three groups, which were less collaborative, more social, or more diffuse in interactive behaviors. To further explore the social and cognitive backdrop of collaboration, we turn to a detailed discussion of partner collaboration on PM and decision-making tasks.

## MIDLIFE AND LATE-LIFE PARTNER INFLUENCES ON COGNITIVE PERFORMANCE: ILLUSTRATIVE EXAMPLES

Middle-aged and older adults face a range of everyday, developmentally relevant tasks that range from remembering doctors' appointments and turning off the stove to resolving interpersonal dilemmas and decision making about health. At a broad level, performance of an intellectual task involves two components reflecting dynamic cognitive and social processes. In terms of cognitive processes, in particular, several commonalities cut across intellectual tasks, including consideration of task requirements, errors that can occur during task completion, and achievement of an outcome. Additionally, there may be specific cognitive components idiosyncratic to various tasks. To illustrate these points, we highlight two types of tasks relevant to middle and later life couples. The first is PM, representing a well-defined cognitive task, and the second is decision making, which is typically ill defined and incorporates multiple cognitive skills as well as subjective, contextual information. As discussed next, the requisite cognitive skills and socioemotional contexts vary and affect both the collaborative processes and task outcome. Figures 11.1 and 11.2 depict our conceptualization of the cognitive and socioemotional processes of performance across PM and decision-making tasks.

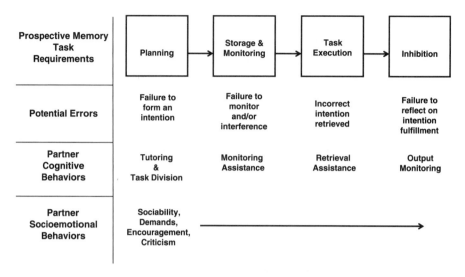

| Prospective Memory Task Requirements | Planning | Storage & Monitoring | Task Execution | Inhibition |
|---|---|---|---|---|
| Potential Errors | Failure to form an intention | Failure to monitor and/or interference | Incorrect intention retrieved | Failure to reflect on intention fulfillment |
| Partner Cognitive Behaviors | Tutoring & Task Division | Monitoring Assistance | Retrieval Assistance | Output Monitoring |
| Partner Socioemotional Behaviors | Sociability, Demands, Encouragement, Criticism | | | |

*Figure 11.1.* Conceptualization of collaborative cognition processes during a prospective memory task. Prospective memory conceptualization data from Kliegel, Mackinlay, and Jäger (2008). Terminology related to collaborative behaviors data from Gould, Kurzman, and Dixon (1994); Kimbler and Margrett (2009); and Margrett, Reese-Melancon, and Rendell (2011).

## Cognitive Collaborative Processes

First, let us consider collaborative cognitive processes and how a partner can contribute to PM performance. As Figure 11.1 reveals, the stages of PM include planning to fulfill an intention, storing and monitoring that intention so that it is not forgotten, fulfilling the intention, and finally inhibiting the intention so that it is not repeated (Kliegel, Mackinlay, & Jäger, 2008). A partner has the opportunity to contribute at each of these stages through a variety of cognitive means. For instance, the partner can help at the planning stage by identifying an intention that needs to be fulfilled, suggesting a strategy that would promote fulfillment, or offering to take the lead on part of the task demands. At the storage and monitoring stage, a partner can contribute by offering reminders of the intention that will soon need to be fulfilled. At the task-execution stage, a partner can contribute by ensuring that the task is actually completed once the opportunity has arisen. Finally, the partner can contribute at the inhibition level, by either asking whether an intention has been fulfilled or reminding that the intention has indeed been fulfilled and should not be repeated. These examples of partner contributions are positive and likely to promote success, but the partner also has the potential to hinder performance, causing prospective memory errors to occur. For instance, at

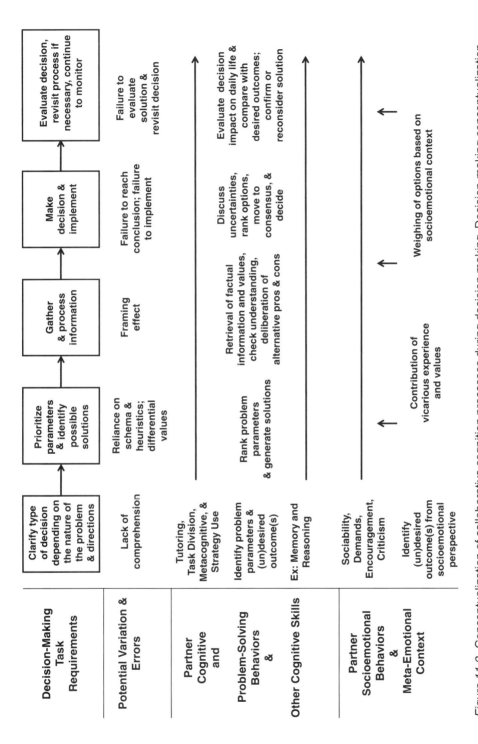

*Figure 11.2.* Conceptualization of collaborative cognition processes during decision making. Decision-making conceptualization data from Gelatt (1962); Epstein and Street (2011); Price, Bereknyei, Kuby, Levinson, and Braddock (2012); and Reyna and Brainerd (2011). Terminology related to partner collaborative behaviors data from Gould, Kurzman, and Dixon (1994); Kimbler and Margrett (2009); and Margrett, Reese-Melancon, and Rendell (2011).

the storage and monitoring stage, a partner may fail to offer reminders of an intention or perhaps more adversely, offer inaccurate reminder information.

A second example of dyadic CC in a specific cognitive domain is provided in Figure 11.2. As depicted, decision making is a cognitive process that involves multiple steps and is iterative in nature. The basic components of the decision-making process are generally a series of steps that include identification of purpose or representation of the problem at hand, data gathering (e.g., retrieval of stored information and values), strategy generation and valuation, reaching of a decision, realization of an outcome, and monitoring and evaluation of the decision and outcome with potential to revisit steps within the process (e.g., Gelatt, 1962; Reyna & Brainerd, 2011).

Decision making is complex for many reasons. First, it relies on memory, but it also incorporates other aspects of cognitive performance and higher level executive functioning. Second, decision making in real-world settings is usually quite messy. Although problems can be well defined, having one correct solution (e.g., completing a tax form), everyday problems are often ill defined and may have several potential solutions. Third, perceptions of and responses to the problem at hand are influenced by many factors, including directions and information provided, the multifaceted nature of problems encountered by middle-aged and older adults (e.g., health challenges, finances), and the problem parameters and values that undergird prioritization of these parameters (e.g., preference for autonomy). As shown in Figure 11.2, intimate partners offer multiple avenues for influencing partner decision making, ranging from task-general behaviors (e.g., tutoring) to task-specific behaviors (e.g., conceptualization of problem parameters).

Across cognitive tasks facing middle-aged and older couples, both the actual and perceived cognitive ability of collaborating spouses have the capacity to influence cognitive task performance. First, actual cognitive ability reflects the capacity for partners to either positively or negatively influence task performance (e.g., whether the partner is a help or a hindrance to task completion, utility, and safety). Second, perceptions of a partner's abilities have the capacity to influence collaborative process (e.g., how much partner input is sought or accepted, tenor of the interaction). The latter point relates to discussion of socioemotional processes, which follows.

## Socioemotional Collaborative Processes

Intimate partners have the potential to influence all stages of cognitive task performance through their socioemotional behaviors (see Figures 11.1 and 11.2). Whereas a partner's cognitive behaviors may have a relatively direct influence on the way a task is carried out, a partner's socioemotional behaviors may have a more diffuse influence by affecting motivation that could impact all aspects of the task, resulting in either benefit or degradation to cognitive performance. On the basis of prior work (i.e., Gould et al., 1994; Kimbler & Margrett, 2009; Margrett et al., 2011), we highlight four interpersonal behaviors observed among middle-aged and older partners. These behaviors reflect socioemotional processes that do not directly incorporate an explicit cognitive component and include sociability, encouragement, demands, and criticism. Through both sociability and encouragement, a partner may offer social support that bolsters a spouse's performance, allowing him or her to attain goals and complete tasks that otherwise may not have been attempted. Additionally, in terms of sociability, partners may exhibit rapport-building behaviors to get to know one another in the event of unfamiliar partnering or to ensure a positive interpersonal experience (e.g., sharing of personal stories, joke telling) with a familiar partner. Although this behavior can create an affirmative working environment, it can also serve to degrade performance (e.g., interference during encoding or retrieval on a memory task; Figure 11.1) or alter the outcome (e.g., introduction of varying experiences and values resulting in differential weighting of options; Figure 11.2). In addition, interpersonally negative behaviors such as demands and criticism can undermine the working environment and dissuade partner participation.

From these illustrations, it is clear that CC is a dynamic process that reflects the synergy between person, collaborator, and environment. Intimate partners serve to influence the process and outcome of CC via cognitive and socioemotional means as well as the interaction between the two. Some commonalities are likely to exist across person-collaborator-task contexts; however, enhanced theoretical work followed by additional empirical investigation is needed to advance understanding of the nuances and mechanisms related to this powerful everyday phenomenon. Next we discuss theoretical implications, including the developmental and socioemotional contexts differing within and between midlife and later life couples.

## ADVANCING THEORETICAL PERSPECTIVES RELEVANT TO APPLIED COLLABORATIVE COGNITION

At the broadest level, our conceptualization of CC rests on the foundation of bioecological theory outlined by Bronfenbrenner and others, which includes person-context-time as important elements to understanding development (e.g., Bronfenbrenner & Ceci, 1994; Tudge, Mokrova, Hatfield, & Karnik, 2009). The inclusion of multiple levels of analysis, from interacting individuals to influential broader systems, is very relevant to our discussion of collaborating minds as we consider individual differences (e.g., neuropsychological development and functioning), collaborative processes (e.g., partner behaviors), and macroinfluences (e.g., gender role socialization). Particular to couples, we concur with Huston (2000; see Figure 11.3) that it is important to consider individual partner beliefs and behaviors, behaviors within the intimate partnership context, as well as the broader environmental niche of the couple. Each partner contributes to individual and dyadic development and has a stake in the outcomes. Specific to developmental change and optimizing aging, we build on the work of Baltes and Baltes (1990) related to "successful aging" and view intimate partners as a source of compensation in critical areas that have already been selected and optimized (e.g., medication adherence or financial planning). The effectiveness of the partner as a source of compensation for everyday cognitive tasks, however, depends on individual differences and dyadic characteristics. Thus, we expect that the conceptual models put forth in Figures 11.1 and 11.2 will function differently for couples in middle and later life who are facing varying normative (e.g., typical cognitive aging, role changes, retirement planning) and nonnormative (e.g., financial hardship, cancer, dementia, depression) challenges to cognitive and emotional well-being. Variation due to individual differences between partners and differences between dyads will influence processes and outcomes for couples.

On the basis of the existing literature and the examples of CC in the two specific domains of prospective memory and decision making described previously, we propose that any theoretical framework for the study and application of CC in middle and older adulthood must integrate several key components. Broadly, it should capitalize on a multidisciplinary perspective and reflect both the process and product of CC. The framework must also be able to (a) address complex everyday tasks that may be ongoing and not have one correct answer; (b) account for partners' individual differences and the match between them (i.e., within-dyad differences); (c) incorporate interpersonal processes and dynamics between collaborating partners; (d) take into account the task, environment, and resources; (e) capture dynamic change in collaborators, task, and environment over time; and (f) address the mechanisms (e.g., behavioral, neural) leading to the potential for CC to yield positive, negative, and changing outcomes across time. Such an approach can provide structure to future research and ultimately help identify underlying processes that can serve as prevention and intervention targets for midlife and late-life cognitive aging.

## FUTURE DIRECTIONS

Our consideration of CC among middle-aged and older couples leads us to propose several considerations and directions for future work in this area. Related to methodology, researchers should keep in mind that developmental and individual differences are particularly important (Reyna & Brainerd,

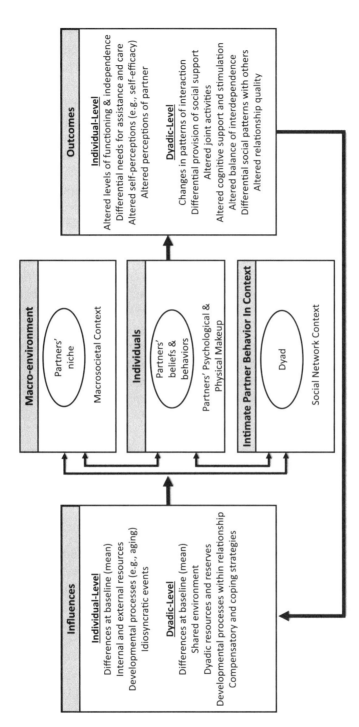

*Figure 11.3.* Bioecological model of dyadic functioning. From "The Social Ecology of Marriage and Other Intimate Unions," by T. L. Huston, 2000, *Journal of Marriage and Family, 62,* p. 300. Copyright 2000 by Wiley. Adapted with permission.

2011) as we consider normative and nonnormative cognitive aging and functioning during middle and later life. It is also important that researchers take advantage of the dyadic and multilevel data analytic tools that are now available (Ackerman, Donnellan, Kashy, & Conger, 2012). These techniques take into account the interdependence of intimate partners and allow for a clearer understanding of both individual and dyadic development as well as influences that occur at various levels (e.g., individual, couple, and larger systems). Time is a key component of the bioecological theory, and strategic consideration of time is important as the processes and outcomes of collaboration may change across learning trials (e.g., microtime; Blumen & Stern, 2011) as well as over longer periods of time, reflecting developmental change and historical trends (e.g., gender role evolution).

There are several avenues we consider very promising for future empirical study that may help to clarify equivocal findings across age groups, tasks, and real-world versus laboratory settings in the extant literature. First is the need to identify guiding principles that cut across cognitive tasks. To this end, we suggested a general theoretical framework based on bioecological and successful aging theories and provided CC examples using prospective memory and decision-making tasks. Future work can help elucidate behavioral commonalities in collaborative processes and cognitive outcomes/products across tasks. Such work can help identify common cognitive and socioemotional behaviors exhibited by intimate partners that could be the targets for prevention (e.g., avoid inhibition of memory recall by promoting individual recall prior to collaborative recall) and intervention (e.g., develop strategies and divide tasks) efforts.

A second, related issue is the transfer of collaborative experience as related to the impact of learning and performance order (Blumen & Stern, 2011; Gagnon & Dixon, 2008; Margrett, 1999). Little is known about transfer of a collaborative experience to noncollaborative performance of the same task, to collaborative (and noncollaborative) performance of a different task, and to work with a different/new partner. More work is needed to understand collaborative processes and specific strategies that serve to enhance positive transfer of performance to future collaborative as well as individual situations.

Additional empirical work is needed to elucidate the changing relationship dynamics that correspond to partners' cognitive change. Caregiving burden, social isolation, and diminished cognitive stimulation can impact the initially nonimpaired partner. Further, widowhood and divorce/relationship dissolution can result in lack of a partner and/or formation of new partnerships. Widowhood may result in loss of a "main memory collaborator," which could prove detrimental for cognitive performance (Hirst, 2013). Divorce likewise may prove challenging as prior collaborative schema for accomplishing cognitive and everyday tasks collaboratively are lost.

Finally, prior work has suggested that greater attention must be paid to both the sociocultural context of collaboration and intimate partners' motivation and perceptions (e.g., prosocial tendencies, competition, desire to engage, ability to resolve conflict; Crook, 2000; D'Angelo, Bosco, Bianco, & Brandimonte, 2012). For instance, some studies do evince gender differences. A significant example was revealed in analysis of partner influences by Margrett and Marsiske, (2002), which indicated a tendency for older male partners to be more influential in determining the outcome compared with their female partners on ambiguous cognitive tasks. Harkening back to Dixon's (2013) comments, the field will be well served by recognizing that CC is individualized and contextualized in the everyday lives of middle-aged and older adults.

CC research related to couples' navigation of everyday tasks in middle and later life has clear implications for clinical practice. Most important, social partners, such as intimate partners, need to be considered as part of the entire cognitive aging process. Incorporation of partners should span etiology as well as prevention and intervention efforts. As noted by Blumen and Stern (2011), CC research has implications for understanding how middle-aged and older adults adapt to normative and nonnormative cognitive aging. In addition, collaboration may modify individuals' neural systems (Blumen & Stern, 2011), which has implications for understanding the etiology and progression of cognitive development and impairment in the second half of life. Additionally, empirical, longitudinal investigation of gene–environment interactions among intimate partners can shed light on how these processes differ between partners and dyads. Ultimately, such investigations can inform prevention and intervention efforts related to midlife and later life cognitive development and aging.

Taken together, the CC literature has suggested that prevention and treatment efforts should perhaps be targeted at the couple instead of the individual. This may be especially true as the cognitive abilities of one or both intimate partners begin to change. Proxy reporters, such as intimate partners, can help identify the early stages of nonnormative cognitive change (e.g., Razavi et al., 2014). Caregivers sometimes express frustration that health care providers exclude the higher functioning spouse from health-related information, especially in the early stages of a partner's cognitive change when the behavioral symptoms are subtle; however, partners with dementia also express frustration when the provider directs comments toward the caregiver and not the patient (Karnieli-Miller, Werner, Neufeld-Kroszynski, & Eidelman, 2012). One benefit of aiming early prevention and treatment efforts at the level of the couple rather than the individual may be that health care providers and couples will gain experience working together, possibly easing the transition when health or cognitive disparities become more apparent.

# CONCLUSION

This chapter has addressed an important, commonplace phenomenon relevant to the everyday lives of middle-aged and older couples: cognitive collaboration. Models of everyday and cognitive functioning that focus only on an individual actor ignore the rich context in which adults perform daily tasks. Partners rely on one another to accomplish tasks ranging from remembering to take a medication on time and in the right dosage to completing a tax form and solving an interpersonal dilemma. The answer to the question "Are two heads better than one?" seems to be largely yes, with the caveat, "it depends." Collaborative cognition outcomes are determined by the collaborating partners, their interaction, and the broader context. The study of CC stems from a multidisciplinary history that enriches investigation of this lifespan phenomenon. The growing body of CC research has implications for clinical work, suggesting the importance of including intimate partners in the conceptualization and understanding of normative and nonnormative cognitive development, as well as in the implementation of prevention and intervention efforts to enhance cognition.

# REFERENCES

Ackerman, R. A., Donnellan, M. B., Kashy, D. A., & Conger, R. D. (2012). Dyadic data analyses in a developmental context. In B. Laursen, T. Little, & N. Card (Eds.), *Handbook of developmental research method* (pp. 537–556). New York, NY: Guilford Press.

Bäckman, L., & Dixon, R. A. (1992). Psychological compensation: A theoretical framework. *Psychological Bulletin, 112*, 259–283. http://dx.doi.org/10.1037/0033-2909.112.2.259

Baltes, P. B., & Baltes, M. M. (1990). Psychological perspectives on successful aging: The model of selective optimization with compensation. In P. B. Baltes & M. M. Baltes (Eds.), *Successful aging: Perspectives from the behavioral sciences* (pp. 1–34). New York, NY: Cambridge University Press. http://dx.doi.org/10.1017/CBO9780511665684.003

Baltes, P. B., & Staudinger, U. M. (1996). Interactive minds in a life-span perspective: Prologue. In P. Baltes & U. M. Staudinger (Eds.), *Interactive minds: Lifespan perspectives on the social foundation of cognition* (pp. 1–32). New York, NY: Cambridge University Press.

Basden, B. H., Basden, D. R., Bryner, S., & Thomas, R. L., III. (1997). A comparison of group and individual remembering: Does collaboration disrupt retrieval strategies? *Journal of Experimental Psychology: Learning, Memory, and Cognition, 23*, 1176–1189. http://dx.doi.org/10.1037/0278-7393.23.5.1176

Berg, C. A., Johnson, M. M. S., Meegan, S. P., & Strough, J. (2003). Collaborative problem solving interactions in young and married couples. *Discourse Processes*, *35*, 33–58. http://dx.doi.org/10.1207/S15326950DP3501_2

Blumen, H. M., & Rajaram, S. (2008). Influence of re-exposure and retrieval disruption during group collaboration on later individual recall. *Memory*, *16*, 231–244. http://dx.doi.org/10.1080/09658210701804495

Blumen, H. M., Rajaram, S., & Henkel, L. (2013). The applied value of collaborative memory research in aging: Behavioral and neural considerations. *Journal of Applied Research in Memory and Cognition*, *2*, 107–117. http://dx.doi.org/10.1016/j.jarmac.2013.03.003

Blumen, H. M., & Stern, Y. (2011). Short-term and long-term collaboration benefits on individual recall in younger and older adults. *Memory & Cognition*, *39*, 147–154. http://dx.doi.org/10.3758/s13421-010-0023-6

Bronfenbrenner, U., & Ceci, S. J. (1994). Nature-nurture reconceptualized in developmental perspective: A bioecological model. *Psychological Review*, *101*, 568–586. http://dx.doi.org/10.1037/0033-295X.101.4.568

Centers for Disease Control and Prevention. (2011). *Cognitive impairment: A call for action, now!* Retrieved from http://www.cdc.gov/aging/pdf/cognitive_impairment/cogimp_poilicy_final.pdf

Centers for Disease Control and Prevention. (2013). *Health information for older adults*. Retrieved from http://www.cdc.gov/aging/aginginfo/alzheimers.htm

Cheng, S., & Strough, J. (2004). A comparison of collaborative and individual everyday problem solving in younger and older adults. *International Journal of Aging & Human Development*, *58*, 167–195. http://dx.doi.org/10.2190/0Q2P-VMNH-4FXW-6J6A

Cherry, K. E., & Smith, A. D. (1998). Normal memory aging. In M. Hersen & V. B. Van Hasselt (Eds.), *Handbook of clinical geropsychology* (pp. 87–110). New York, NY: Plenum Press. http://dx.doi.org/10.1007/978-1-4899-0130-9_6

Crook, C. (2000). Motivation and the ecology of collaborative learning. In R. Joiner, K. Littleton, D. Faulkner, & D. Miell (Eds.), *Rethinking collaborative learning* (pp. 161–178). London, England: Free Association Books.

D'Angelo, G., Bosco, A., Bianco, C., & Brandimonte, M. A. (2012). The effects of collaboration and competition on pro-social prospective memory. *Psychologica Belgica*, *52*(2–3), 205–228. http://dx.doi.org/10.5334/pb-52-2-3-205

Dixon, R. A. (2011). Evaluating everyday competence in older adult couples: Epidemiological considerations. *Gerontology*, *57*, 173–179. http://dx.doi.org/10.1159/000320325

Dixon, R. A. (2013). Collaborative memory research in aging: Supplemental perspectives on application. *Journal of Applied Research in Memory and Cognition*, *2*, 128–130. http://dx.doi.org/10.1016/j.jarmac.2013.05.001

Dixon, R. A., & Gould, O. N. (1996). Adults telling and retelling stories collaboratively. In P. B. Baltes & U. M. Staudinger (Eds.), *Interactive minds: Life-span perspective on the social foundation of cognition* (pp. 221–241). New York, NY: University Press.

Ebbinghaus, H. (1964). *Memory: A contribution to experimental psychology.* New York, NY: Dover. (Original work published 1885)

Epstein, R. M., & Street, R. L., Jr. (2011). Shared mind: Communication, decision making, and autonomy in serious illness. *Annals of Family Medicine, 9,* 454–461. http://dx.doi.org/10.1370/afm.1301

Fong, T. G., Gleason, L. J., Wong, B., Habtemariam, D., Jones, R. N., Schmitt, E. M., . . . Inouye, S. K. (2015). Cognitive and physical demands of activities of daily living in older adults: Validation of expert panel ratings. *PM&R.* Advance online publication. http://dx.doi.org/10.1016/j.pmrj.2015.01.018

Gagnon, L. M., & Dixon, R. A. (2008). Remembering and retelling stories in individual and collaborative contexts. *Applied Cognitive Psychology, 22,* 1275–1297. http://dx.doi.org/10.1002/acp.1437

Gauvain, M., & Rogoff, B. (1989). Collaborative problem solving and children's planning skills. *Developmental Psychology, 25,* 139–151. http://dx.doi.org/10.1037/0012-1649.25.1.139

Gelatt, H. B. (1962). Decision-making: A conceptual frame of reference for counseling. *Journal of Counseling Psychology, 9,* 240–245. http://dx.doi.org/10.1037/h0046720

Gould, O., Kurzman, D., & Dixon, R. A. (1994). Communication during prose recall conversations by young and old dyads. *Discourse Processes, 17,* 149–165. http://dx.doi.org/10.1080/01638539409544863

Gould, O. N., Osborn, C., Krein, H., & Mortenson, M. (2002). Collaborative recall in married and unacquainted dyads. *International Journal of Behavioral Development, 26,* 36–44. http://dx.doi.org/10.1080/01650250143000292

Gould, O. N., Trevithick, L., & Dixon, R. A. (1991). Adult age differences in elaborations produced during prose recall. *Psychology and Aging, 6,* 93–99. http://dx.doi.org/10.1037/0882-7974.6.1.93

Henkel, L. A., & Rajaram, S. (2011). Collaborative remembering in older adults: Age-invariant outcomes in the context of episodic recall deficits. *Psychology and Aging, 26,* 532–545. http://dx.doi.org/10.1037/a0023106

Hirst, W. (2013). Commentary on: Helena M. Blumen, Suparna Rajaram, and Linda A. Henkel's "The applied value of collaborative memory research in aging: Behavioral and neural considerations." *Journal of Applied Research in Memory and Cognition, 2,* 118–119. http://dx.doi.org/10.1016/j.jarmac.2013.04.002

Huston, T. L. (2000). The social ecology of marriage and other intimate unions. *Journal of Marriage and Family, 62,* 298–320. http://dx.doi.org/10.1111/j.1741-3737.2000.00298.x

Johansson, N. O., Andersson, J., & Rönnberg, J. (2005). Compensating strategies in collaborative remembering in very old couples. *Scandinavian Journal of Psychology, 46,* 349–359. http://dx.doi.org/10.1111/j.1467-9450.2005.00465.x

Johansson, O., Andersson, J., & Rönnberg, J. (2000). Do elderly couples have a better prospective memory than other elderly people when they collaborate? *Applied Cognitive Psychology*, *14*, 121–133. http://dx.doi.org/10.1002/(SICI)1099-0720 (200003/04)14:2<121::AID-ACP626>3.0.CO;2-A

Karnieli-Miller, O., Werner, P., Neufeld-Kroszynski, G., & Eidelman, S. (2012). Are you talking to me?! An exploration of the triadic physician–patient–companion communication within memory clinics encounters. *Patient Education and Counseling*, *88*, 381–390. http://dx.doi.org/10.1016/j.pec.2012.06.014

Kimbler, K. J., & Margrett, J. A. (2009). Older adults' interactive behaviors during collaboration on everyday problems: Linking process and outcome. *International Journal of Behavioral Development*, *33*, 531–542. http://dx.doi.org/10.1177/0165025409343754

Kliegel, M., Mackinlay, R., & Jäger, T. (2008). A life-span approach to the development of complex prospective memory. In G. O. Einstein, M. A. McDaniel, M. Kliegel (Eds.), *Prospective memory: Cognitive, neuroscience, developmental, and applied perspectives* (pp. 187–216). New York, NY: Erlbaum.

Margrett, J. A. (1999). *Collaborative cognition and aging: A pilot study* (Unpublished doctoral dissertation). Wayne State University, Detroit, MI.

Margrett, J. A., & Marsiske, M. (2002). Gender differences in older adults' everyday cognitive collaboration. *International Journal of Behavioral Development*, *26*, 45–59. http://dx.doi.org/10.1080/01650250143000319

Margrett, J. A., Reese-Melancon, C., & Rendell, P. G. (2011). Examining collaborative dialogue among couples: A window into prospective memory processes. *Zeitschrift Für Psychologie/Journal of Psychology*, *219*, 100–107.

Margrett, J. A., Reese-Melancon, C., Young, S., Temple, L., & Linde, A. P. (2010, April). *Collaborative effects on adults' prospective memory performance.* Paper presented at the Cognitive Aging Conference, Atlanta, GA.

Meade, M. L., & Roediger, H. L., III. (2009). Age differences in collaborative memory: The role of retrieval manipulations. *Memory & Cognition*, *37*, 962–975. http://dx.doi.org/10.3758/MC.37.7.962

Miller, P. (1993). *Theories of developmental psychology* (3rd ed.). New York, NY: W. H. Freeman.

Morgan, S. P., & Berg, C. A. (2001). Whose life task is it anyway? Social appraisal and life task pursuit. *Journal of Personality*, *69*, 363–389. http://dx.doi.org/10.1111/1467-6494.00149

Price, E. L., Bereknyei, S., Kuby, A., Levinson, W., & Braddock, C. H., III. (2012). New elements for informed decision making: A qualitative study of older adults' views. *Patient Education and Counseling*, *86*, 335–341. http://dx.doi.org/10.1016/j.pec.2011.06.006

Razavi, M., Tolea, M. I., Margrett, J., Martin, P., Oakland, A., Tscholl, D. W., . . . Galvin, J. E. (2014). Comparison of 2 informant questionnaire screening tools for dementia and mild cognitive impairment: AD8 and IQCODE. *Alzheimer Disease and Associated Disorders, 28*, 156–161. http://dx.doi.org/10.1097/WAD.0000000000000008

Rendell, P. G., & Craik, F. I. M. (2000). Virtual and actual week: Age-related differences in prospective memory [Special issue: New perspectives in prospective memory]. *Applied Cognitive Psychology, 14*, S43–S62.

Reese, C. M., & Cherry, K. E. (2004). Practical memory concerns in adulthood. *International Journal of Aging & Human Development, 59*, 235–253. http://dx.doi.org/10.2190/8PA5-8KVB-EMNQ-BFKY

Reyna, V. F., & Brainerd, C. J. (2011). Dual processes in decision making and developmental neuroscience: A fuzzy-trace model. *Developmental Review, 31*(2–3), 180–206.

Rogoff, B., Ellis, S., & Gardner, W. (1984). Adjustment of adult–child instruction according to child's age and task. *Developmental Psychology, 20*, 193–199. http://dx.doi.org/10.1037/0012-1649.20.2.193

Ross, M., Spencer, S. J., Blatz, C. W., & Restorick, E. (2008). Collaboration reduces the frequency of false memories in older and younger adults. *Psychology and Aging, 23*, 85–92. http://dx.doi.org/10.1037/0882-7974.23.1.85

Ross, M., Spencer, S. J., Linardatos, L., Lam, K. C. H., & Perunovic, M. (2004). Going shopping and identifying landmarks: Does collaboration improve older people's memory? *Applied Cognitive Psychology, 18*, 683–696. http://dx.doi.org/10.1002/acp.1023

Staudinger, U. M., & Baltes, P. B. (1996). Interactive minds: A facilitative setting for wisdom-related performance? *Journal of Personality and Social Psychology, 71*, 746–762. http://dx.doi.org/10.1037/0022-3514.71.4.746

Strough, J., Patrick, J. H., Swenson, L. M., Cheng, S., & Barnes, K. A. (2003). Collaborative everyday problem solving: Interpersonal relationships and problem dimensions. *International Journal of Aging & Human Development, 56*, 43–66. http://dx.doi.org/10.2190/Y3XN-RW1A-7EWT-KXTC

Tudge, J. R., Mokrova, I., Hatfield, B. E., & Karnik, R. B. (2009). Uses and misuses of Bronfenbrenner's bioecological theory of human development. *Journal of Family Theory & Review, 1*, 198–210. http://dx.doi.org/10.1111/j.1756-2589.2009.00026.x

Vespa, J., Lewis, J. M., & Kreider, R. M. (2013). America's families and living arrangements: 2012. *Current Population Reports*, P20-570. Washington, DC: U.S. Census Bureau. Retrieved from http://www.census.gov/prod/2013pubs/p20-570.pdf

Vygotsky, L. S. (1986). *Thought and language* (A. Kozulin, Trans.). Cambridge, MA: MIT Press. (Abridged from 1934)

Wegner, D. M. (1986). Transactive memory: A contemporary analysis of the group mind. In B. Mullen & G. R. Goethals (Eds.), *Theories of group behavior* (pp. 185–208). New York, NY: Springer-Verlag.

Weldon, M. S., & Bellinger, K. D. (1997). Collective memory: Collaborative and individual processes in remembering. *Journal of Experimental Psychology: Learning, Memory, and Cognition, 23*, 1160–1175. http://dx.doi.org/10.1037/0278-7393.23.5.1160

# 12

# SPOUSAL INTERRELATIONSHIPS IN HEALTH ACROSS ADULTHOOD: HEALTH BEHAVIORS AND EVERYDAY STRESS AS POTENTIAL UNDERLYING MECHANISMS

CHRISTIANE A. HOPPMANN, VICTORIA MICHALOWSKI,
AND DENIS GERSTORF

Marriage is the most central relationship for many older adults, and it is well known that morbidity and mortality are considerably lower among married compared with unmarried individuals (Coombs, 1991; Holt-Lunstad, Smith, & Layton, 2010; House, Robbins, & Metzner, 1982). However, marriage per se does not guarantee good health. Adults in unhappy marriages face the same health burdens as singles (Coyne et al., 2001). Furthermore, marital characteristics have been linked to a broad spectrum of physical and mental health indices, including stress hormones, inflammation, blood pressure, functional health, health behaviors, depression, and well-being, for which the effects of marriage can cut both ways (Kiecolt-Glaser & Newton, 2001). In addition, recent meta-analytic evidence has suggested that the mortality risk associated with experiencing poor-quality social relationships may

Christiane Hoppmann gratefully acknowledges the support of the Michael Smith Foundation for Health Research and the Canada Research Chairs Program.

http://dx.doi.org/10.1037/14897-013
*Couple Relationships in the Middle and Later Years: Their Nature, Complexity, and Role in Health and Illness,* J. Bookwala (Editor)

exceed the risk of poor health behaviors such as smoking (Holt-Lunstad et al., 2010). The purpose of this chapter is to describe previous research on spousal interrelationships in health with older adults, to highlight specific behavioral and stress-related processes that may underlie interrelated spousal health trajectories, and to address potential implications of this research as well as identify future avenues for inquiry.

## OVERVIEW AND CRITICAL EVALUATION OF EXISTING RESEARCH

To date, most research looking at associations between marriage and health has focused on the individual. This makes sense, especially considering that individual appraisals of social relationship quality are key predictors of physical and mental health, over and above structural characteristics of social relationships (Coyne et al., 2001; Robles, Slatcher, Trombello, & McGinn, 2014). More recently, researchers have started to call for an inclusion of both partners' perspectives to better understand the spousal dynamics that occur within marriage when examining associations between marriage and health across the adult lifespan and into old age (Berg & Upchurch, 2007; Hoppmann & Gerstorf, 2009).

What makes older adult couples so special? Older couples are units of primary interest in health research because older spouses typically have long histories of shared experiences, possess an in-depth knowledge of each other's strengths and weaknesses, and engage in many shared activities (Carstensen, Gottman, & Levenson, 1995; Lang, 2001; Meegan & Berg, 2002). Consequently, older spouses may be well positioned to turn to each other for support, potentially achieving together what might no longer be possible alone (Dixon, 1999). Yet, by the same token, older spouses are also particularly vulnerable if something happens to the partner (Berg & Upchurch, 2007).

Recent theoretical and methodological advances have afforded new insights into spousal associations in physical and mental health as well as the interrelated nature of long-term health trajectories in older couples (Berg & Upchurch, 2007; Bookwala & Schulz, 1996; Hoppmann & Gerstorf, 2009; Lam, Lehman, Puterman, & DeLongis, 2009). We, and others, have shown that spousal health trajectories are linked across a variety of physical and mental health indices (Gerstorf, Hoppmann, Kadlec, & McArdle, 2009; Gruber-Baldini, Schaie, & Willis, 1995; Hoppmann, Gerstorf, & Hibbert, 2011; Strawbridge, Wallhagen, & Shema, 2011). It is important to note that not only do older spouses show similar initial health levels, but their health also waxes and wanes together over time (Gerstorf et al., 2009; Hoppmann,

Gerstorf, & Hibbert, 2011; Strawbridge et al., 2011). This means that linked health trajectories in older age are not simply a reflection of compositional effects in marriage with partners being similar on a host of variables even before meeting one another (Kenny, Mannetti, Pierro, Livi, & Kashy, 2002). Over and above both partners being exposed to similar environmental circumstances, something important appears to happen in couples' lives that accumulates over time and ultimately ties together spousal health in the long run (Carstensen, Graff, Levenson, & Gottman, 1996). The chapter by Berg et al. in this volume discusses dyadic coping using a lifespan perspective, reviewing the literature on dyadic coping in healthy couples as well as those coping with chronic illnesses, early developmental factors that may influence later dyadic, and early relational foundations of later dyadic coping.

Figure 12.1 shows an example of spousal health trajectories regarding depressive symptoms using 10-year longitudinal couple data from the Health and Retirement Study (Gerstorf et al., 2009). Specifically, it illustrates that more depressive symptoms at baseline among wives predicted stronger than average subsequent increases in depressive symptoms among husbands. The opposite was true as well: Fewer depressive symptoms among wives at baseline predicted smaller subsequent increases in depressive symptoms among husbands. Similarly, healthy older adults who are married to a spouse with good, as opposed to poor, health may experience very different health outcomes later on. More generally, understanding spousal interrelationships must involve acknowledging that these

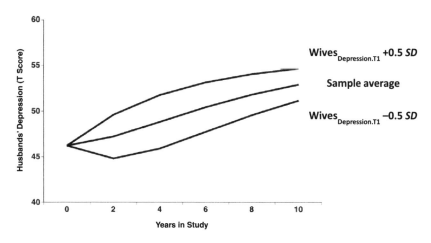

*Figure 12.1.* Model-implied means over 14.5 years from a two-variable latent growth curve model of depressive symptoms of wives and husbands. Scores were standardized to the T metric using the T1 AHEAD (Study of Asset and Health Dynamics Among the Oldest Old) couple sample as the reference ($n = 3,408$ participants; $M = 50$, $SD = 10$).

interrelationships have a gain–loss dynamic (Baltes & Carstensen, 1998; Hoppmann & Gerstorf, 2009). In other words, marital partners can both improve and hamper each other's health. It is thus crucial to identify the specific mechanisms that lead to more or less favorable outcomes for both members of the dyad.

So, what do the dyadic mechanisms that tie spousal health in older couples look like? "It takes two to tango" is an expression that is often used to describe the challenges that go along with being married. The appeal of this metaphor for a chapter on spousal interrelationships in health is that it not only figuratively, but also sometimes literally, describes some of the key processes that characterize spousal dynamics in marriage. The tango is a partner dance that originated in the Rio de la Plata region in Argentina and has made its way around the world (UNESCO, 2009). It is danced across cultures and classes, forming a multitude of different styles, and is popular among different- and same-sex couples. The comparison of marriage to the tango emphasizes that spousal dynamics must be considered in the context of key individual-difference characteristics, such as cultural norms, socioeconomic characteristics, and sexual orientation (Balsam & D'Augelli, 2006; Hoppmann & Gerstorf, 2009). Furthermore, the tango takes passion and practice because of its complexity. Analogously, dyadic characteristics, such as relationship duration, quality of and satisfaction with the marriage, and the presence of children, likely play a role in shaping spousal health (Hoppmann & Gerstorf, 2009; Robles et al., 2014). Finally, dancers may alternate between closed and open embrace figures, which involve steps that can vary widely in timing and speed, leading to an abundance of different combinations. Research on spousal interrelationships in health correspondingly needs to take into account the importance of different time scales (see also Gerstorf, Hoppmann, & Ram, 2014). For example, spousal behaviors may fluctuate across different daily life situations, requiring dense measurements, but they may also vary across different life phases, which may be captured using long-term longitudinal assessments (Hoppmann & Gerstorf, 2009). As such, comparing marriage with the tango provides useful guidance for identifying key individual, couple, and methodological issues that can potentially contribute to a richer understanding of spousal interrelationships in health across the adult lifespan and into old age. For the purpose of this chapter, we demonstrate the usefulness of taking a couples' approach to studying health by focusing on two key pathways that may underlie previously documented spousal interrelationships in long-term health trajectories: cross-spousal influences in (a) health behavior and (b) stress and emotion regulation processes. In doing so, we hope to provide additional insights into the delicate dance between individual agency and spousal affiliation in the health domain.

# NEW TRENDS AND DEVELOPMENTS THAT IMPACT THEORY AND RESEARCH

In the following sections, we highlight the potential of taking a couples' perspective when examining health behaviors as well as stress and emotion-regulation processes as potential pathways that may link the health of spouses over time. We also offer some insights into important methodological considerations.

## Health Behaviors in Couples

Health behaviors are a heterogeneous category, and it is important to recognize that health behavior research typically distinguishes between health-enhancing and health-compromising behaviors (Schwarzer, 2008; Taylor & Sirois, 2012). *Health-enhancing behaviors* are those that maintain or promote an individual's current or future health (Taylor & Sirois, 2012). Fostering health-enhancing behaviors, such as physical activity, fruit and vegetable consumption, or dental hygiene, has been a central tenet of health psychological interventions because the underlying behaviors are relatively inexpensive compared with the costs created by early disease manifestation (Taylor & Sirois, 2012). Physical activity in particular has been identified as one of the highest priorities for health promotion in North America because of its widespread health benefits (Blair, 2009; Brassington, Hekler, Cohen, & King, 2012; Sherrington et al., 2008). However, the initiation and maintenance of such key health-enhancing behaviors takes a great deal of effort and has proven to be very challenging (Schwarzer, 2008). As a consequence, in this chapter we first focus on the role of spouses for engaging in physical activity as a key health-enhancing behavior. Understanding the role of spouses in the domain of physical activity engagement may provide insights into specific dyadic mechanisms that are not only relevant to physical activity, but also have ramifications for other health-enhancing behaviors (Schwarzer, 2008; see also the chapter by Franks, Wehrspann, August, Rook, and Stephens in this volume). *Health-compromising behaviors*, such as smoking, alcohol abuse, or overeating, are those that undermine or harm an individual's current or future health (Taylor & Sirois, 2012). Health-compromising behaviors are maintained by a number of biological and psychosocial factors, and they are often difficult to change, partly because they are inherently pleasurable (Schwarzer, 2008; Taylor & Sirois, 2012). In this chapter, we also focus on recent advances in research on smoking behavior that involves couples so as to illustrate the important role of spouses in influencing this key health-compromising behavior.

*The Role of Spouses in Physical Activity Engagement*

Changing health behaviors has been a major focus of health psychological research over the past decades. Many such endeavors have targeted educating individuals about the importance of health behaviors for improving health and for reducing health risks in an effort to facilitate their commitment to a given goal (Ajzen, 1991; Schwarzer, 2008; Sheeran, 2002). The assumption underlying this approach has largely been that individuals who have set a health goal will engage in the respective behavior. Yet, there is accumulating evidence that although goals predict behaviors in a meaningful way, the effects are usually small—particularly with respect to health goals (Riediger, 2008; Sheeran, 2002). Although some individuals manage to translate their health goals into action, many struggle to realize their goals. This may be due at least in part to the limited attention that has been given to the proximal social context, such as marriage.

The important role of spouses in health-enhancing behaviors, such as physical activity, is supported by previous work indicating that everyday activities are associated in older married couples (Hoppmann, Gerstorf, & Luszcz, 2008). This effect can cut both ways. It is reasonable to assume that being married to a physically active spouse increases the likelihood of joining him or her on a walk and thereby creating or maintaining physically active lifestyles in both partners. However, it is equally reasonable to expect that having a spouse who is confined to the house because of health problems represents a barrier to physical activity engagement.

In recognition of the fact that spouses can make an important contribution to physical activity engagement, health psychological research is increasingly embracing a couples perspective. For example, it has been shown that both individual and dyadic planning are effective in promoting pelvic floor exercise in middle-aged and older men after prostatectomy (Burkert, Scholz, Gralla, Roigas, & Knoll, 2011). Research like this also answers a call for an inclusion of family members such as spouses in the caregiving literature (Zarit & Reamy, 2013). It has also been demonstrated that spousal support is positively associated with everyday physical activity in older persons with diabetes (Khan, Stephens, Franks, Rook, & Salem, 2013). However, there is also evidence that not all spousal behaviors that are aimed toward helping the respective partner to become more physically active do indeed work out as intended (see Chapter 15, this volume, for a review of research on cross-spousal influences within the context of managing a chronic illness, e.g., diabetes). For example, spouses who perceive their partner as controlling may actually engage in less exercise and physical activity (Burkert et al., 2011; Khan et al., 2013). Hence, taking a couples perspective on physical activity offers new insights into the facilitators of, as well as barriers to, health promotion, with important ramifications for interventions (see Chapter 16, this volume, for a review of current theory and research pointing to couple-based interventions as a potentially powerful tool in the management of chronic illness in married elders). For example, it may be important to pay close attention to how partners frame their involvement so that they are supportive and provide actual resources, rather than coming across as negative or controlling. This might help avoid situations where partners engage in behaviors that are meant to improve health behaviors but that actually undermine the desired outcome.

## The Role of Spouses for Smoking Behavior

There is also increasing evidence to illustrate the key role of marriage for health-compromising behaviors, such as smoking (Joung, Stronks, van de Mheen, & Mackenbach, 1995). Specifically, it has been shown that married individuals are less likely to smoke than singles and that being married to a nonsmoker is associated with a stronger desire to quit smoking (Ask, Rognmo, Torvik, Røysamb, & Tambs, 2012; Clark & Etilé, 2006; Rüge et al., 2008). However, it has also been shown that smokers are more likely to marry smokers and that spousal discrepancies in cigarette smoking are associated with reductions in marital satisfaction over time (Homish, Leonard, Kozlowski, & Cornelius, 2009). Longitudinal couple data suggest that cigarette smoking waxes and wanes in association with the respective spouse, indicating that when one partner decreases smoking, the other partner is also more likely to do so. Yet by the same token, increased smoking on the part of one spouse seems to be associated with an increased likelihood that the partner will also smoke more in young, middle-aged, and older couples (Derrick, Leonard, & Homish, 2013; Falba & Sindelar, 2008).

Beyond clear evidence for compositional effects within marriage, spousal smoking does seem to impact the respective partner over time in systematic ways, which can be a curse or a blessing. One important pathway that connects spousal smoking over time may be spousal support for quitting (Roski, Schmid, & Lando, 1996). Evidence based on middle-aged couples shows that being married to a spouse who is supportive of quitting is associated with a decrease in one's own smoking (Roski et al., 1996). However, the mechanisms underlying initial cessation and maintenance of abstinence do not seem to be the same. For instance, encouragement and positive support by a spouse has been linked to quitting attempts, whereas low rates (rather than high rates) of undermining behaviors by the respective spouse (e.g., calling smoking a "dirty habit," expressing that one is bothered by smoking) predict long-term maintenance of abstinence (Roski et al., 1996). This study also draws attention to the fact that the kinds of messages that are most effective may differ across phases of the smoking cessation process (e.g., positive encouragement at the actual quitting stage and refrainment from undermining comments at the maintenance stage). Finally, there is considerable evidence for gender differences in smoking cessation. Substantial effort is being put into bringing about smoking cessation in expecting women during pregnancy (Bottorff et al., 2006). In addition to these event-specific efforts, wives are more likely to resume smoking if their partner smokes, whereas the same does not hold true for husbands (Homish & Leonard, 2005). Though worrying about the health of the respective spouse is associated with a desire to quit smoking in middle-aged and older husbands and wives, only wives have been shown to quit smoking when their husbands reported a new chronic disease (Margolis, 2013). Hence, there is extensive evidence that spousal behaviors impact smoking and that this impact can be detrimental or beneficial. For interventions to be successful, close attention needs to be paid to individual characteristics, such as gender, and dyadic characteristics, such as marital satisfaction. There is also some indication that spousal influences on smoking depend on where in the cessation process one is because the mechanisms governing quitting and continued abstinence are different.

The aim of this section was to provide insights into the important role of spouses in shaping two key health behaviors, namely, physical activity and smoking. Even though it seems to be the case that such findings can inform research regarding other health-enhancing behaviors (e.g., eating fruits and vegetables) and health-compromising behaviors (e.g., alcohol abuse), it is crucial to take into account that spousal health behaviors often come in a package (Falba & Sindelar, 2008; Osler, 1998). Similar to recent trends focusing on health behavior change in unrelated individuals (Fleig, Lippke, Pomp, & Schwarzer, 2011), research on health behaviors in couples will also need to pay attention to how specific health behaviors may be tied to one another (e.g., smoking, alcohol consumption). Moreover, poor health behaviors can also be related to stress and coregulation of shared emotional experiences (Rohrbaugh, Shoham, Butler, Hasler, & Berman, 2009).

### Stress and Emotion Regulation in Couples

Spousal interrelationships in concurrent emotional experiences and long-term outcomes are well documented (Berg, Wiebe, & Butner, 2011; Bookwala & Schulz, 1996; DeLongis & Holtzman, 2005; Hoppmann, Gerstorf, Willis, & Schaie, 2011; Larson & Almeida, 1999). In the following section, we underline some of the mechanisms that govern the transmission of stress and negative emotions in couples. Readers are referred to Chapter 14, this volume, for a discussion of emotion regulation within the specific context of spousal caregiving.

Each partner brings his or her own problems to the relationship, and there is solid evidence that stress and negative emotions travel relatively easily between spouses (Berg et al., 2011; Larson & Almeida, 1999; Repetti, 1989). Problems may not only elicit negative emotions, but they also may affect biological stress responses (Hoppmann & Klumb, 2006). For example, problem appraisals and negative emotions may activate the body's stress system, such as the hypothalamic–pituitary–adrenal (HPA) axis, leading to the secretion of stress hormones like cortisol (Kirschbaum & Hellhammer, 2000; Piazza, Almeida, Dmitrieva, & Klein, 2010). This effect may not be limited to the spouse encountering the problem because the partner may also become affected or worried (Berg et al., 2011; Hoppmann & Gerstorf, 2013). Recognizing that encounters with problems and stress may not be limited to individual spouses, but that these experiences can also affect the dyadic unit, is pivotal for exploring potential moderators at the couple level.

Evidence has suggested that intimacy and touch, which are thought to stimulate the secretion of neuropeptides like oxytocin, may be an important target in this regard. For example, experimental research with young and middle-aged couples has compared stress reactivity to a commonly used psychosocial laboratory stressor (the Trier Social Stress Test; Kirschbaum, Pirke, & Hellhammer, 1993) in women who did not interact with their partner, in women who received verbal social support from their partner, and in women who were in a physical touch condition that used a standardized neck and shoulder massage. Findings showed that women who received a partner massage were best off as indicated by their reduced heart rate and cortisol responses (Ditzen et al., 2007). Furthermore, research using daily life assessments from midlife couples has indicated that daily exchanges of intimacy between spouses, such as a hug or a kiss, have the potential to reduce the negative association between work stress and affect, as well as cortisol secretion (Ditzen, Hoppmann, & Klumb, 2008). It would be interesting to extend experimental paradigms to research regarding the mechanisms through which intimacy may be able to undo negative associations between the experience of a problem and resulting emotional and biological stress reactions. For example, it may be fruitful to extend previous research that has been based on young and middle-aged couples by Ditzen and colleagues (Ditzen et al., 2007) by examining whether physical touch exerts its beneficial effect on stress by operating primarily through psychological (e.g., self-validation) or biological pathways (e.g., secretion of oxytocin).

Most research examining the transmission of stress and negative emotional experiences between spouses is based on relatively broad emotion categories. Such approaches may be limited in capturing the complexity of daily emotional experiences in couples (Larson & Almeida, 1999). Clinical psychologists have thus started to call for more fine-grained investigations of emotions and potential shifts in emotions (e.g., from anger in Partner A to sadness in Partner B) during emotion transmissions in couples to further our understanding of the mechanisms that link emotional experiences in one spouse with subsequent emotional experiences in the partner (Schoebi, 2008). It is important to note that social-functionalist theories of emotion propose that distinct negative emotions, such as anger or sadness, elicit different responses in social interaction partners (Keltner & Haidt, 2001). For instance, anger, as a "hard" emotion, may help mobilize energy and lead to resistance (Izard & Ackerman, 2000). Anger also tends to activate threat-related responses and rejection in close others, thus potentially leading to conflict spirals (Keltner & Haidt, 2001). In contrast, sadness, as a "soft" emotion, slows down activities and cognitive processes, thereby enabling a closer look at problems (Izard & Ackerman, 2000). Sadness can also elicit sympathy and increased proximity, thus potentially contributing to a deescalation of conflicts and an improvement in relationship functioning (Keltner & Kring, 1998; Safran & Greenberg, 1991). Important questions regarding the transmission of negative emotions in couples may thus revolve around whether, how, and when spouses reciprocate each other's anger with the same emotion and if they are able to respond with a softer negative emotion such as sadness. From a couples perspective, sadness has an important advantage over anger, in that it may help put an end to negative emotion transmission cycles between spouses—it can elicit complementary, more positive emotions, such as sympathy, in the spouse and thereby restore relationship functioning (Eisenberg et al., 1989; Keltner & Kring, 1998). Taken together, negative emotions are not all created equal and may have very different implications for the interpersonal dynamics in a given marriage.

A related line of reasoning highlights that certain spousal characteristics may be associated with more favorable emotional dynamics. One candidate that may be associated with more favorable emotion transmission dynamics in couples relates to attachment styles. Spouses often differ in the extent to which they provide each other with a secure base and a safe haven during times of distress (Baltes & Silverberg, 1994; Feeney, 2004; Fuendeling, 1998). Specifically, secure attachment styles may be associated with the ability of spouses to embrace a partner's negative emotions, thereby helping her or him to transform anger into less hurtful negative emotions, such as sadness and ultimately sympathy. Anxious attachment styles, in contrast, may be associated with spousal insecurity and maladaptive responses to negative emotions that may increase the transmission of anger and contribute to hostility in marital relationships. Positive couple characteristics, such as secure attachment styles, then may provide a good basis to contain anger, leading to improved emotion regulation in couples.

## Methodological Considerations for Studying the Interpersonal Dynamics in Marriage

Many of the theoretical considerations presented previously point to a need for better understanding of the interpersonal dynamics in marriage. To move the field forward, researchers have called for more sophisticated tools allowing for in-depth investigations of spousal health dynamics as they occur in spouses' own environments, using repeated daily-life assessments (Berg & Upchurch, 2007; Hoppmann & Gerstorf, 2009). Aside from offering insights into the individual and dyadic mechanisms underlying spousal inter-relationships in health across the adult lifespan, such an approach promises to identify key health-relevant daily life mechanisms that characterize the interpersonal dynamics within marriage. These, in turn, could be targeted at points when interventions are particularly effective, namely, before clinically relevant outcomes become manifest.

Repeated daily life assessments ("time sampling") are uniquely suited to capture the everyday dynamics that characterize marriage as spouses engage in their typical daily life routines in their natural environment, if analyzed in an appropriate way (Hoppmann & Riediger, 2009; Laurenceau & Bolger, 2005; Trull & Ebner-Priemer, 2013). We use the term *time-sampling methods* relatively loosely—there are a number of related approaches that come under different kinds of labels, such as diary methods, ambulatory assessment, experience sampling, real-time data monitoring, ecological momentary assessment, intensive repeated-measures methods, and measurement bursts (see also Ram & Gerstorf, 2009). Time sampling uses a spectrum of assessment methods, ranging from phone interviews and paper diaries to prompted pocket computer/tablet-based or cell-/smartphone-based assessments (Hoppmann & Riediger, 2009). All of these approaches offer unique insights into health-related processes, and they all have their specific benefits and pitfalls (Bolger, Davis, & Rafaeli, 2003). Therefore, time-sampling methods should be chosen on the basis of the targeted phenomenon and population. Tablets, for instance, may be the data collection tool of choice if a researcher is interested in administering timed tasks, using random schedules, or providing branched questionnaires. Although still novel, tablet-based assessments have been used successfully in many different populations, including older adults and various patient populations (Hoppmann & Blanchard-Fields, 2011). Computerized assessments, however, can pose minimum requirements regarding sensory-motor skills that render them unsuitable for certain patient populations (Hoppmann & Riediger, 2009). In this scenario, other tools such as daily telephone interviews or brief personal visits may be the assessment method of choice (DeLongis & Holtzman, 2005). Researchers can choose from a broad array of different time-sampling tools to capture daily life dynamics in marriage.

Research on spousal interrelationships in health across the adult life-span would particularly benefit from a wider implementation of time-sampling methods for a variety of reasons. First, simultaneous daily life assessments from both spouses provide insights into how husbands and wives influence each other and the transmission of emotional experiences (Berg et al., 2011). Furthermore, such an approach allows for tracking time-ordered associations, such as lead–lag relationships between spousal behaviors and subsequent pain in persons with rheumatoid arthritis (Holtzman & DeLongis, 2007). Another important feature of time-sampling methods is that they take research out of the lab into spouses' real-world environments, thus maximizing the ecological validity of health psychological research (Feldman Barrett & Barrett, 2001).

Most time-sampling studies use self-reports, but time sampling does not have to rely exclusively on self-reports (Slade & Hoppmann, 2011). This may be particularly important when the researcher is concerned about socially desirable responding. It is important to note that researchers can include combinations of self-reports with saliva-based stress hormone assessments, objective measures of intensity of movement using accelerometry, or GPS tracking (Bussmann, Ebner-Priemer, & Fahrenberg, 2009; Hoppmann & Klumb, 2006). Hence, there are many options available for supplementing self-report–based time-sampling protocols.

## POLICY IMPLICATIONS AND APPLIED SIGNIFICANCE

In closing, we would like to briefly note some promising avenues for future inquiry as well as touch on implications for policy and practice. Accumulating evidence regarding the interrelated nature of long-term longitudinal health trajectories in middle-aged and older spouses, as well as support for the transfer of stress and negative emotions in the daily lives of married couples, calls current individual-centered approaches in the health care system into question. An effective strategy could be providing special discounts in people's health insurance if both partners participate in a given prevention or intervention program. Furthermore, it seems crucial to take into account a patient's spouse's role in maintaining health-compromising behaviors. For example, knowledge of whether one or both spouses smoke may provide insights into key facilitators and barriers to smoking cessation, and one would assume that proactive coping strategies for dealing with relapse would differ as a consequence.

Furthermore, winning the spouse as an ally for health behavior interventions is still a road less travelled, but there is a lot of potential, as indicated by previous research with middle-aged and older couples (Burkert et al., 2011; Khan et al., 2013). For example, it seems more than reasonable to assume that interventions targeting dietary habits in persons with diabetes would be more successful if they involved not only the spouse who has diabetes, but also the spouse who actually does the grocery shopping and meal preparation.

Finally, time-sampling methods can be used not only as an assessment tool but also as a valuable delivery platform for interventions that promote healthy lifestyles in couples and help them to manage stress effectively. For example, it would be interesting to encourage sharing walk scores with one's partner or to offer videos that help a couple to harness their positive emotions (e.g., Fredrickson, 2000). It would also be possible to set up the data collection infrastructure such that it could allow the provision of feedback in real time (e.g., an intervention) as soon as a person moves out of his or her person-specific comfort zone (e.g., use of a data carousel; Ram, 2013). To do so, a technical infrastructure is needed that within a very brief period of time allows one to archive, visualize, prepare, model, and analyze the data that are collected in vivo as well as to compare these individual results with individual-specific norms collected earlier so as to contrast a given score obtained in a specific situation with what is typical for that person.

## CONCLUSION

This chapter contends that spousal physical and mental health are dynamically linked and shaped by a number of key individual and relationship factors. The tango metaphor implies that to better understand the delicate dance between individual agency and spousal affiliation, a consideration of the perspectives of both partners is necessary. Future research needs to study different combinations of dancers (e.g., homosexual and heterosexual couples), to explore factors that make some tango dancers shine (e.g., specific resources and strategies) while other partners trip, and to investigate the whole sequence of the dance as it is performed in real life as well as specific, particularly artful, parts of it that end up impacting everyone involved.

## REFERENCES

Ajzen, I. (1991). The theory of planned behavior. *Organizational Behavior and Human Decision Processes, 50,* 179–211. http://dx.doi.org/10.1016/0749-5978(91)90020-T

Ask, H., Rognmo, K., Torvik, F. A., Røysamb, E., & Tambs, K. (2012). Non-random mating and convergence over time for alcohol consumption, smoking, and exercise: The Nord-Trøndelag Health Study. *Behavior Genetics, 42,* 354–365. http://dx.doi.org/10.1007/s10519-011-9509-7

Balsam, K. F., & D'Augelli, A. R. (2006). The victimization of older lesbian, gay, bisexual, and transgender adults: Patterns, impact, and implications for intervention. In

D. Kimmel, T. Rose, & S. David (Eds.), *Lesbian, gay, bisexual, and transgender aging: Research and clinical perspectives* (pp. 110–130). New York, NY: Columbia University Press.

Baltes, M. M., & Carstensen, L. L. (1998). Social-psychological theories and their applications to aging: From individual to collective. In V. L. Bengtson & K. W. Schaie (Eds.), *Handbook of theories of aging* (pp. 209–226). New York, NY: Springer.

Baltes, M. M., & Silverberg, S. B. (1994). The dynamics between dependency and autonomy: Illustrations across the life span. In D. L. Featherman, R. M. Lerner, & M. Perlmutter (Eds.), *Life-span development and behavior* (Vol. 12, pp. 41–90). Hillsdale, NJ: Erlbaum.

Berg, C. A., & Upchurch, R. (2007). A developmental-contextual model of couples coping with chronic illness across the adult life span. *Psychological Bulletin, 133*, 920–954. http://dx.doi.org/10.1037/0033-2909.133.6.920

Berg, C. A., Wiebe, D. J., & Butner, J. (2011). Affect covariation in marital couples dealing with stressors surrounding prostate cancer. *Gerontology, 57*, 167–172. http://dx.doi.org/10.1159/000318642

Blair, S. N. (2009). Physical inactivity: The biggest public health problem of the 21st century. *British Journal of Sports Medicine, 43*, 1–2.

Bolger, N., Davis, A., & Rafaeli, E. (2003). Diary methods: Capturing life as it is lived. *Annual Review of Psychology, 54*, 579–616. http://dx.doi.org/10.1146/annurev.psych.54.101601.145030

Bookwala, J., & Schulz, R. (1996). Spousal similarity in subjective well-being: The Cardiovascular Health Study. *Psychology and Aging, 11*, 582–590. http://dx.doi.org/10.1037/0882-7974.11.4.582

Bottorff, J. L., Kalaw, C., Johnson, J. L., Stewart, M., Greaves, L., & Carey, J. (2006). Couple dynamics during women's tobacco reduction in pregnancy and post-partum. *Nicotine & Tobacco Research, 8*, 499–509. http://dx.doi.org/10.1080/14622200600789551

Brassington, G. S., Hekler, E. B., Cohen, Z., & King, A. C. (2012). Health-enhancing physical activity. In A. Baum & T. A. Revenson (Eds.), *Handbook of health psychology* (pp. 353–374). Hoboken, NJ: Psychology Press.

Burkert, S., Scholz, U., Gralla, O., Roigas, J., & Knoll, N. (2011). Dyadic planning of health-behavior change after prostatectomy: A randomized-controlled planning intervention. *Social Science & Medicine, 73*, 783–792. http://dx.doi.org/10.1016/j.socscimed.2011.06.016

Bussmann, J. B. J., Ebner-Priemer, U. W., & Fahrenberg, J. (2009). Ambulatory activity monitoring: Progress in measurement of activity, posture, and specific motion patterns in daily life. *European Psychologist, 14*, 142–152. http://dx.doi.org/10.1027/1016-9040.14.2.142

Carstensen, L. L., Gottman, J. M., & Levenson, R. W. (1995). Emotional behavior in long-term marriage. *Psychology and Aging, 10*, 140–149. http://dx.doi.org/10.1037/0882-7974.10.1.140

Carstensen, L. L., Graff, J., Levenson, R. W., & Gottman, J. M. (1996). Affect in intimate relationships: The developmental course of marriage. In C. Magai & S. H. McFadden (Eds.), *Handbook of emotion, adult development, and aging* (pp. 227–247). San Diego, CA: Academic Press. http://dx.doi.org/10.1016/B978-012464995-8/50014-5

Clark, A. E., & Etilé, F. (2006). Don't give up on me baby: Spousal correlation in smoking behaviour. *Journal of Health Economics, 25,* 958–978. http://dx.doi.org/10.1016/j.jhealeco.2006.02.002

Coombs, R. H. (1991). Marital status and personal well-being: A literature review. *Family Relations, 40,* 97–102. http://dx.doi.org/10.2307/585665

Coyne, J. C., Rohrbaugh, M. J., Shoham, V., Sonnega, J. S., Nicklas, J. M., & Cranford, J. A. (2001). Prognostic importance of marital quality for survival of congestive heart failure. *The American Journal of Cardiology, 88,* 526–529. http://dx.doi.org/10.1016/S0002-9149(01)01731-3

DeLongis, A., & Holtzman, S. (2005). Coping in context: The role of stress, social support, and personality in coping. *Journal of Personality, 73,* 1633–1656. http://dx.doi.org/10.1111/j.1467-6494.2005.00361.x

Derrick, J. L., Leonard, K. E., & Homish, G. G. (2013). Perceived partner responsiveness predicts decreases in smoking during the first nine years of marriage. *Nicotine & Tobacco Research, 15,* 1528–1536. http://dx.doi.org/10.1093/ntr/ntt011

Ditzen, B., Hoppmann, C., & Klumb, P. (2008). Positive couple interactions and daily cortisol: On the stress-protecting role of intimacy. *Psychosomatic Medicine, 70,* 883–889. http://dx.doi.org/10.1097/PSY.0b013e318185c4fc

Ditzen, B., Neumann, I. D., Bodenmann, G., von Dawans, B., Turner, R. A., Ehlert, U., & Heinrichs, M. (2007). Effects of different kinds of couple interaction on cortisol and heart rate responses to stress in women. *Psychoneuroendocrinology, 32,* 565–574. http://dx.doi.org/10.1016/j.psyneuen.2007.03.011

Dixon, R. A. (1999). Exploring cognition in interactive situations: The aging of N+1 minds. In T. M. Hess & F. Blanchard-Fields (Eds.), *Social cognition and aging* (pp. 267–290). San Diego, CA: Academic Press. http://dx.doi.org/10.1016/B978-012345260-3/50013-6

Eisenberg, N., Fabes, R. A., Miller, P. A., Fultz, J., Shell, R., Mathy, R. M., & Reno, R. R. (1989). Relation of sympathy and personal distress to prosocial behavior: A multimethod study. *Journal of Personality and Social Psychology, 57,* 55–66. http://dx.doi.org/10.1037/0022-3514.57.1.55

Falba, T. A., & Sindelar, J. L. (2008). Spousal concordance in health behavior change. *Health Services Research, 43*(1 Pt. 1), 96–116.

Feeney, B. C. (2004). A secure base: Responsive support of goal strivings and exploration in adult intimate relationships. *Journal of Personality and Social Psychology, 87,* 631–648. http://dx.doi.org/10.1037/0022-3514.87.5.631

Feldman Barrett, L., & Barrett, D. (2001). An introduction to computerized experience sampling in psychology. *Social Science Computer Review, 19,* 175–185. http://dx.doi.org/10.1177/089443930101900204

Fleig, L., Lippke, S., Pomp, S., & Schwarzer, R. (2011). Intervention effects of exercise self-regulation on physical exercise and eating fruits and vegetables: A longitudinal study in orthopedic and cardiac rehabilitation. *Preventive Medicine: An International Journal Devoted to Practice and Theory, 53,* 182–187. http://dx.doi.org/10.1016/j.ypmed.2011.06.019

Fredrickson, B. L. (2000). Cultivating positive emotions to optimize health and well-being. *Prevention & Treatment, 3,* 1–25. http://dx.doi.org/10.1037/1522-3736.3.1.31a

Fuendeling, J. M. (1998). Affect regulation as a stylistic process within adult attachment. *Journal of Social and Personal Relationships, 15,* 291–322. http://dx.doi.org/10.1177/0265407598153001

Gerstorf, D., Hoppmann, C. A., Kadlec, K. M., & McArdle, J. J. (2009). Memory and depressive symptoms are dynamically linked among married couples: Longitudinal evidence from the AHEAD study. *Developmental Psychology, 45,* 1595–1610. http://dx.doi.org/10.1037/a0016346

Gerstorf, D., Hoppmann, C. A., & Ram, N. (2014). The promise and challenges of integrating multiple time-scales in adult developmental inquiry. *Research in Human Development, 11,* 75–90. http://dx.doi.org/10.1080/15427609.2014.906725

Gruber-Baldini, A. L., Schaie, K. W., & Willis, S. L. (1995). Similarity in married couples: A longitudinal study of mental abilities and rigidity-flexibility. *Journal of Personality and Social Psychology, 69,* 191–203. http://dx.doi.org/10.1037/0022-3514.69.1.191

Holt-Lunstad, J., Smith, T. B., & Layton, J. B. (2010). Social relationships and mortality risk: A meta-analytic review. *PLoS Medicine, 7,* e1000316. http://dx.doi.org/10.1371/journal.pmed.1000316

Holtzman, S., & DeLongis, A. (2007). One day at a time: The impact of daily satisfaction with spouse responses on pain, negative affect and catastrophizing among individuals with rheumatoid arthritis. *Pain, 131,* 202–213. http://dx.doi.org/10.1016/j.pain.2007.04.005

Homish, G. G., & Leonard, K. E. (2005). Spousal influence on smoking behaviors in a US community sample of newly married couples. *Social Science & Medicine, 61,* 2557–2567. http://dx.doi.org/10.1016/j.socscimed.2005.05.005

Homish, G. G., Leonard, K. E., Kozlowski, L. T., & Cornelius, J. R. (2009). The longitudinal association between multiple substance use discrepancies and marital satisfaction. *Addiction, 104,* 1201–1209. http://dx.doi.org/10.1111/j.1360-0443.2009.02614.x

Hoppmann, C., & Gerstorf, D. (2009). Spousal interrelations in old age—a minireview. *Gerontology, 55,* 449–459. http://dx.doi.org/10.1159/000211948

Hoppmann, C. A., & Blanchard-Fields, F. (2011). Problem-solving variability in older spouses: How is it linked to problem-, person-, and couple-characteristics? *Psychology and Aging, 26,* 525–531. http://dx.doi.org/10.1037/a0024114

Hoppmann, C. A., & Gerstorf, D. (2013). Spousal goals, affect quality, and collaborative problem solving: Evidence from a time-sampling study with older couples.

*Research in Human Development, 10*, 70–87. http://dx.doi.org/10.1080/154276
09.2013.760260

Hoppmann, C. A., Gerstorf, D., & Hibbert, A. (2011). Spousal associations between functional limitation and depressive symptom trajectories: Longitudinal findings from the Study of Asset and Health Dynamics Among the Oldest Old (AHEAD). *Health Psychology, 30*, 153–162. http://dx.doi.org/10.1037/a0022094

Hoppmann, C. A., Gerstorf, D., & Luszcz, M. (2008). Spousal social activity trajectories in the Australian longitudinal study of ageing in the context of cognitive, physical, and affective resources. *The Journals of Gerontology: Series B. Psychological Sciences and Social Sciences, 63*, 41–50. http://dx.doi.org/10.1093/geronb/63.1.P41

Hoppmann, C. A., Gerstorf, D., Willis, S. L., & Schaie, K. W. (2011). Spousal interrelations in happiness in the Seattle Longitudinal Study: Considerable similarities in levels and change over time. *Developmental Psychology, 47*, 1–8. http://dx.doi.org/10.1037/a0020788

Hoppmann, C. A., & Klumb, P. L. (2006). Daily goal pursuits predict cortisol secretion and mood states in employed parents with preschool children. *Psychosomatic Medicine, 68*, 887–894. http://dx.doi.org/10.1097/01.psy.0000238232.46870.f1

Hoppmann, C. A., & Riediger, M. (2009). Ambulatory assessment in lifespan psychology: An overview of current status and new trends. *European Psychologist, 14*, 98–108. 10.1027/1016-9040.14.2.98

House, J. S., Robbins, C., & Metzner, H. L. (1982). The association of social relationships and activities with mortality: Prospective evidence from the Tecumseh Community Health Study. *American Journal of Epidemiology, 116*, 123–140.

Izard, C. E., & Ackerman, B. P. (2000). Motivational, organizational, and regulatory functions of discrete emotions. In M. Lewis & J. M. Haviland-Jones (Eds.), *Handbook of emotions* (pp. 253–264). New York, NY: Guilford Press.

Joung, I. M., Stronks, K., van de Mheen, H., & Mackenbach, J. P. (1995). Health behaviours explain part of the differences in self reported health associated with partner/marital status in The Netherlands. *Journal of Epidemiology and Community Health, 49*, 482–488. http://dx.doi.org/10.1136/jech.49.5.482

Keltner, D., & Haidt, J. (2001). Social functions of emotions. In T. J. Mayne & G. A. Bonanno (Eds.), *Emotions: Current issues and future directions* (pp. 192–213). New York, NY: Guilford Press.

Keltner, D., & Kring, A. M. (1998). Emotion, social function, and psychopathology. *Review of General Psychology, 2*, 320–342. http://dx.doi.org/10.1037/1089-2680.2.3.320

Kenny, D. A., Mannetti, L., Pierro, A., Livi, S., & Kashy, D. A. (2002). The statistical analysis of data from small groups. *Journal of Personality and Social Psychology, 83*, 126–137. http://dx.doi.org/10.1037/0022-3514.83.1.126

Khan, C. M., Stephens, M. A. P., Franks, M. M., Rook, K. S., & Salem, J. K. (2013). Influences of spousal support and control on diabetes management through physical activity. *Health Psychology, 32*, 739–747. http://dx.doi.org/10.1037/a0028609

Kiecolt-Glaser, J. K., & Newton, T. L. (2001). Marriage and health: His and hers. *Psychological Bulletin, 127*, 472–503. http://dx.doi.org/10.1037/0033-2909.127.4.472

Kirschbaum, C., & Hellhammer, D. H. (2000). Salivary cortisol. In G. Fink (Ed.), *Encyclopedia of Stress* (Vol. 3, pp. 379–383) San Diego, CA: Academic Press. http://dx.doi.org/10.1016/B978-012373947-6/00334-2

Kirschbaum, C., Pirke, K.-M., & Hellhammer, D. H. (1993). The 'Trier Social Stress Test'—a tool for investigating psychobiological stress responses in a laboratory setting. *Neuropsychobiology, 28*, 76–81. http://dx.doi.org/10.1159/000119004

Lam, M., Lehman, A. J., Puterman, E., & DeLongis, A. (2009). Spouse depression and disease course among persons with rheumatoid arthritis. *Arthritis and Rheumatism, 61*, 1011–1017. http://dx.doi.org/10.1002/art.24510

Lang, F. R. (2001). Regulation of social relationships in later adulthood. *The Journals of Gerontology: Series B. Psychological Sciences and Social Sciences, 56*, 321–326. http://dx.doi.org/10.1093/geronb/56.6.P321

Larson, R. W., & Almeida, D. M. (1999). Emotional transmission in the daily lives of families: A new paradigm for studying family process. *Journal of Marriage and Family, 61*, 5–20. http://dx.doi.org/10.2307/353879

Laurenceau, J.-P., & Bolger, N. (2005). Using diary methods to study marital and family processes. *Journal of Family Psychology, 19*, 86–97. http://dx.doi.org/10.1037/0893-3200.19.1.86

Margolis, R. (2013). Health shocks in the family: Gender differences in smoking changes. *Journal of Aging and Health, 25*, 882–903. http://dx.doi.org/10.1177/0898264313494411

Meegan, S. P., & Berg, C. A. (2002). Contexts, functions, forms, and processes of collaborative everyday problem solving in older adulthood. *International Journal of Behavioral Development, 26*, 6–15. http://dx.doi.org/10.1080/01650250143000283

Osler, M. (1998). The food intake of smokers and nonsmokers: The role of partner's smoking behavior. *Preventive Medicine, 27*, 438–443. http://dx.doi.org/10.1006/pmed.1998.0289

Piazza, J. R., Almeida, D. M., Dmitrieva, N. O., & Klein, L. C. (2010). Frontiers in the use of biomarkers of health in research on stress and aging. *The Journals of Gerontology: Series B. Psychological Sciences and Social Sciences, 65*, 513–525. http://dx.doi.org/10.1093/geronb/gbq049

Ram, N. (2013). *Intraindividual Study of Aging, Health, & Interpersonal Behavior.* Retrieved from http://isahib.weebly.com

Ram, N., & Gerstorf, D. (2009). Time-structured and net intraindividual variability: Tools for examining the development of dynamic characteristics and processes. *Psychology and Aging, 24*, 778–791. http://dx.doi.org/10.1037/a0017915

Repetti, R. L. (1989). Effects of daily workload on subsequent behavior during marital interaction: The roles of social withdrawal and spouse support. *Journal of Personality and Social Psychology, 57*, 651–659. http://dx.doi.org/10.1037/0022-3514.57.4.651

Riediger, M. (2008). Motivational systems and the pursuit of goals: Lessons learned from older adults. *The European Health Psychologist, 10*, 37–39.

Robles, T. F., Slatcher, R. B., Trombello, J. M., & McGinn, M. M. (2014). Marital quality and health: A meta-analytic review. *Psychological Bulletin, 140*, 140–187. http://dx.doi.org/10.1037/a0031859

Rohrbaugh, M. J., Shoham, V., Butler, E. A., Hasler, B. P., & Berman, J. S. (2009). Affective synchrony in dual- and single-smoker couples: Further evidence of "symptom-system fit"? *Family Process, 48*, 55–67. http://dx.doi.org/10.1111/j.1545-5300.2009.01267.x

Roski, J., Schmid, L. A., & Lando, H. A. (1996). Long-term associations of helpful and harmful spousal behaviors with smoking cessation. *Addictive Behaviors, 21*, 173–185. http://dx.doi.org/10.1016/0306-4603(95)00047-X

Rüge, J., Ulbricht, S., Schumann, A., Rumpf, H. J., John, U., & Meyer, C. (2008). Intention to quit smoking: Is the partner's smoking status associated with the smoker's intention to quit? *International Journal of Behavioral Medicine, 15*, 328–335. http://dx.doi.org/10.1080/10705500802365607

Safran, J. D., & Greenberg, L. S. (1991). *Emotion, psychotherapy, change*. New York, NY: Guilford Press.

Schoebi, D. (2008). The coregulation of daily affect in marital relationships. *Journal of Family Psychology, 22*, 595–604. http://dx.doi.org/10.1037/0893-3200.22.3.595

Schwarzer, R. (2008). Modeling health behavior change: How to predict and modify the adoption and maintenance of health behaviors. *Applied Psychology: An International Review, 57*, 1–29.

Sheeran, P. (2002). Intention—behavior relations: A conceptual and empirical review [Special issue]. *European Review of Social Psychology, 12*, 1–36. http://dx.doi.org/10.1080/14792772143000003

Sherrington, C., Whitney, J. C., Lord, S. R., Herbert, R. D., Cumming, R. G., & Close, J. C. (2008). Effective exercise for the prevention of falls: A systematic review and meta-analysis. *Journal of the American Geriatrics Society, 56*, 2234–2243. http://dx.doi.org/10.1111/j.1532-5415.2008.02014.x

Slade, L., & Hoppmann, C. (2011). Time-sampling research in health psychology: Potential contributions and new trends. *The European Health Psychologist, 13*, 65–69.

Strawbridge, W. J., Wallhagen, M. I., & Shema, S. J. (2011). Spousal interrelations in self-reports of cognition in the context of marital problems. *Gerontology, 57*, 148–152. http://dx.doi.org/10.1159/000318637

Taylor, S. E., & Sirois, F. M. (2012). *Health psychology* (2nd Canadian ed.). Toronto, Ontario, Canada: McGraw-Hill Ryerson.

Trull, T. J., & Ebner-Priemer, U. (2013). Ambulatory assessment. *Annual Review of Clinical Psychology, 9*, 151–176. http://dx.doi.org/10.1146/annurev-clinpsy-050212-185510

UNESCO. (2009). *Tango*. Retrieved from http://www.unesco.org/culture/ich/index.php?lg=en&pg=00011&RL=00258

Zarit, S. H., & Reamy, A. M. (2013). Future directions in family and professional caregiving for the elderly. *Gerontology, 59*, 152–158. http://dx.doi.org/10.1159/000342242

# 13

# A DEVELOPMENTAL PERSPECTIVE TO DYADIC COPING ACROSS ADULTHOOD

CYNTHIA A. BERG, KELSEY K. SEWELL, AMY E. HUGHES LANSING, STEPHANIE J. WILSON, AND CARRIE BREWER

During adulthood, couples face stressful events dealing with multiple intersecting domains of life, including work, family, finances, and health (Almeida, Piazza, Stawski, & Klein, 2011; Repetti, Wang, & Saxbe, 2011). Couples may approach such stressors individually or jointly as they appraise and cope with them (Bodenmann, Meuwly, & Kayser, 2011). For instance, a stressor such as dealing with a difficult coworker or a diagnosis of cancer may be approached individually ("this is my problem to deal with") or jointly ("this is our problem"), which may affect whether the couple uses individual or dyadic coping strategies. *Dyadic coping strategies* refer to those whereby both partners activate their joint resources to deal with the stressful event and maintain or restore a state of homeostasis in both partners.

Research on dyadic coping reveals that the coping of one partner is frequently interdependent with the coping of the other partner (Bodenmann et al., 2011), with many factors affecting whether dyadic coping is adaptive

http://dx.doi.org/10.1037/14897-014
*Couple Relationships in the Middle and Later Years: Their Nature, Complexity, and Role in Health and Illness*, J. Bookwala (Editor)

or maladaptive in dealing with stressful events. Dyadic coping can take both positive (supportive, collaborative) as well as more negative interpersonal forms (hostile and critical involvement), which affect marital satisfaction and well-being (Berg & Upchurch, 2007; Landis, Peter-Wight, Martin, & Bodenmann, 2013). Further, the benefit of dyadic coping may be moderated by a variety of characteristics of individuals such as their adjustment (Hagedoorn, Buunk, Kuijer, Wobbes, & Sanderman, 2000), gender (Bodenmann et al., 2011), and need for independence (Martire, Stephens, Druley, & Wojno, 2002).

Although a large literature now exists that demonstrates the benefit of dyadic coping across young, middle, and late adulthood for couples' physical and mental health (Bodenmann et al., 2011), little attention has been paid to developmental factors that may be involved in dyadic coping. Numerous life course differences may make dyadic coping either more or less important and effective across the adult lifespan. For instance, age-related shifts in autonomy and relational goals (Carstensen, Isaacowitz, & Charles, 1999; Hoppmann, Coats, & Blanchard-Fields, 2008) may make dyadic coping highly salient and effective during late life (Berg, Schindler, Smith, Skinner, & Beveridge, 2011). Further, dyadic coping may change across time as couples deal with stressors that occur over weeks and months, such as those that occur in dealing with a chronic illness. Given the benefits experienced from dyadic coping, understanding developmental factors that may set the stage for effective dyadic coping in middle and late adulthood may be especially important for facilitating dyadic coping processes.

In this chapter, we present a developmental perspective to dyadic coping. We first review the research on dyadic coping in healthy couples that has been conducted across a broad range of ages. This review reveals that dyadic coping is beneficial to marital satisfaction and health across the adult lifespan, although it may be especially important in late adulthood, a time when the marital relationship may be particularly satisfying and couples experience fewer social supports external to the marriage (Landis et al., 2013). Second, we use the literature on dyadic coping with chronic illness to examine developmental factors in dyadic coping as couples cope with chronic illnesses across time, allowing for an examination of dyadic coping under more extreme stressful conditions. This literature suggests that dyadic coping early in dealing with the illness may set the stage for coping throughout the illness process. Third, we posit that relational foundations of dyadic coping in adulthood are laid down in the parent–child relationship, as well as early romantic relationships that may set the stage for dyadic coping during middle and late adulthood. We conclude with implications of this developmental perspective for interventions to improve dyadic coping and future directions for research.

# DYADIC COPING IN HEALTHY ADULTS

## Two Conceptualizations of Dyadic Coping

Before discussing the specific findings in the dyadic coping literature, it is important to note that researchers have taken two different approaches to conceptualizing the term *dyadic coping*. The first approach involves statistically comparing the congruence of partners' individual coping efforts via statistical interactions or some sort of difference score. Typically, the problem-focused and emotional-focused coping efforts of both individuals are measured and compared. This approach finds quite mixed results regarding congruence (Badr, 2004; Pakenham, 1998; Revenson, 1994) in regards to relationship satisfaction and adjustment. Taken as a whole, the results seem to suggest that outcomes are best when individuals are both engaging in more effective coping strategies (e.g., congruence in problem-focused coping) versus less effective strategies (e.g., emotion-focused coping). The second conceptualization views dyadic coping as more of a systemic process and assesses how both partners cope as a couple (Berg & Upchurch, 2007; Bodenmann et al., 2011). Significant effects of dyadic coping on a number of outcomes across multiple developmental stages using both self-report and observational methods have been reported (e.g., Berg & Upchurch, 2007; Bodenmann, 2005; Landis et al., 2013; Wunderer & Schneewind, 2008). Studies comparing individual coping efforts with the systemic approach to dyadic coping find that individual coping efforts are less predictive of relationship satisfaction than dyadic coping (Papp & Witt, 2010). Further, dyadic coping can mediate the effect of individual coping efforts on relationship satisfaction (Herzberg, 2013). The following discussion of the effects of dyadic coping on outcome variables reflects the systemic approach to dyadic coping.

## Systemic Approach to Dyadic Coping

Couples are often interdependent in both their appraisal of and response to daily stressors (e.g., Berg & Upchurch, 2007; Bodenmann et al., 2011). The magnitude of the stressor's impact on the relationship depends on the intensity, duration, and origination point of the stressor, with major and chronic stressors having special impact (Randall & Bodenmann, 2009). Multiple studies link stress to negative relationship outcomes such as marital dissatisfaction (e.g., Conger, Rueter, & Elder, 1999; Neff & Karney, 2007) and deficits in important relationship skills, including communication, problem solving, and coping (Markman, 1981), even among couples who typically engage positively with one another (Frye & Karney, 2006). There also appears to be a gradual cumulative effect of stress on relationships, with divorced individuals retrospectively citing chronic daily stress as a trigger (Bodenmann et al., 2007). Taken together, these findings suggest that encountering daily stressors is a threat to the intimate relationship.

When stressors occur, couples often respond to stressors collaboratively, using common problem-solving skills. A joint response grants the couple additional resources with which to cope and may reflect a focus on "our problem," serving as a potential buffer for the negative effects of stress on the relationship (Bodenmann, 2005). Indeed, couples who approach stressors collaboratively are more likely to report the collaborative process as enjoyable (Berg, Wiebe, et al., 2008) and effective (Hoppmann & Gerstorf, 2013), and they are more likely to maintain effective communication across prolonged times of stress (Bodenmann et al., 2007). Such positive dyadic coping (i.e., a supportive and collaborative joint response to stress) may promote marital stability and prevent divorce by facilitating the management of daily stressors (e.g., Bodenmann, 2005).

Dyadic coping also is related to a number of individual and relationship outcome variables that buffer the couple from the effects of stress. For example, couples who endorse more engagement in positive dyadic coping report higher relationship satisfaction (e.g., Bodenmann, 2005; Landis et al., 2013), exhibit better communication skills and problem-solving abilities, and engage in successful coping strategies, including supportive emotional behaviors (Bodenmann, 2005). It is likely that the relationship between dyadic coping and marital satisfaction is bidirectional, with positive dyadic coping predicting better relationship satisfaction and vice versa. Further, the type of dyadic coping skills used by individuals matters. Specifically, Bodenmann and colleagues (2011) found that positive dyadic coping predicted higher relationship satisfaction and negative dyadic coping (i.e., a hostile, ambivalent, or critical style of response) predicted more conflict within the relationship.

There are also more direct effects on each individual's stress response from dyadic coping. Bodenmann, Meuwly, Bradbury, Gmelch, and Ledermann (2010) found that individuals using positive dyadic coping skills experienced less anger and verbal aggression than those using negative dyadic coping strategies, with these positive effects disappearing under high-stress conditions. They suggested that positive dyadic coping may be most helpful early in the process so that emotional reserves are not drained. In addition, the protective effects of positive dyadic coping can be observed at the physiological level. Individuals who reported their partner engaged in positive dyadic coping efforts prior to encountering stress experienced a faster reduction in cortisol levels (Meuwly et al., 2012). Further, verbal and nonverbal social interactions with a partner resulted in a decrease in ambulatory blood pressure compared with social interactions with another person, even when controlling for relationship quality (Gump, Polk, Kamarck, & Shiffman, 2001). Though these social interactions with a partner were often perceived as intimate and supportive, the characteristics of the social interaction did not mediate the effect.

Dyadic coping is often associated with outcomes beyond relationship satisfaction. Specifically, negative dyadic coping predicts anxiety and depression in both men and women; however, well-being outcomes are less well explained than relationship quality (i.e., 2%–4% in men and 2%–11% in women; Bodenmann et al., 2011). Bodenmann and colleagues suggested that mental health outcomes may not be as strongly related to dyadic coping as relational variables and might be more strongly related to individual coping. This may suggest that the primary value of dyadic coping is to maintain the intimate relationship through times of stress, whereas simultaneously using individual coping skills may be important for well-being. Dyadic coping in intimate relationships also is important for the development and maintenance of self-monitoring skills, including emotion regulation (i.e., through support seeking in times of stress; Diamond & Aspinwall, 2003) and self-growth (Overall, Fletcher, & Simpson, 2010).

Overall, dyadic coping is an important predictor of relationship and adjustment outcomes for both men and women (Bodenmann et al., 2011); however, some gender differences have emerged. Wives' distress is linked more strongly to marital satisfaction of both partners than husbands (e.g., Neff & Karney, 2007). Further, dyadic coping may affect each partner somewhat differently: Women's perceived engagement in positive dyadic coping efforts predicts both their own and their partner's relationship satisfaction (as well as decreased negative interactions), whereas men's perceived engagement in positive dyadic coping predicts only their own relationship satisfaction (Herzberg, 2013; Papp & Witt, 2010). However, Wunderer and Schneewind (2008) found that those husbands who had higher expectations for the marriage exhibited more dyadic coping behaviors compared with those who had lower expectations. Further, men's engagement in negative coping behaviors during times of stress (e.g., confrontative demand and withdrawal) was associated with both partners' negative mood, but there was no cross-spousal impact when women engaged in negative coping behaviors (King & DeLongis, 2013).

## Importance of Dyadic Coping Across the Adult Lifespan

The literature reviewed previously has largely involved married couples, frequently long-term middle-aged married couples, although age ranges vary greatly (e.g., from 17 to 84 years of age in some studies). However, a few studies have examined the relation of dyadic coping to adjustment in young adult intimate relationships of shorter duration. For example, Papp and Witt (2010) studied heterosexual couples who had been dating for at least 1 month (average 22.7 months). Similar to the research based on married couples, Papp and Witt found that positive and negative forms of dyadic coping predicted relationship satisfaction over and above individual forms of coping.

The early years of romantic initiation and marriage may be important for setting the stage for long-standing patterns of relationship satisfaction and, by extension, dyadic coping. In the early years of marriage, couples experience important developmental life tasks that affect relationship satisfaction, such as parenthood (Doss, Rhoades, Stanley, & Markman, 2009) and stressors associated with the workplace (Frankel, 2012). These experiences make such early years an important time to explore dyadic coping. Although we are unaware of any studies that explicitly examine dyadic coping strategies in newlywed couples, it is clear that stress is an interdependent phenomenon at this time (Neff & Karney, 2007).

Late life, in comparison, is a time of new developmental challenges (chronic health problems, retirement) and declines in social relationships outside of the marriage (Antonucci & Akiyama, 1987) and, as such, may increase the importance of dyadic coping. Although we are unaware of any specific studies that compare dyadic coping across age, Landis et al. (2013) found that dyadic coping was important for relationship satisfaction in late life. Dyadic coping, indeed, may be of increased importance in late life, especially as older adults have to deal with increasing challenges in health, notably chronic illness.

## DYADIC COPING WITH CHRONIC ILLNESS

Chronic illness allows for an examination of dyadic coping under more extreme stressful conditions (for a discussion of the spouse's role as a social control agent in adaptation to and management of disease, see Chapter 15, this volume; see also Chapter 16, this volume, which discusses the potential significance and efficacy of couple-based interventions in disease management). Though chronic illnesses vary in their time course, consequences for daily management, and controllability (Rolland, 1984), they all can entail extended exposure to medical, instrumental, social, emotional, and existential stressors for both partners (Kayser, 2005). In addition to individual challenges such as medical side effects for patients and the toll of observing patients' suffering on spouses (Monin & Schulz, 2009), chronic illness often requires couples to jointly make treatment decisions, redistribute familial responsibilities, and together face the possibility of death or indefinite lifestyle changes and functional decline (Kayser, 2005; Martin, Peter-Wight, Braun, Hornung, & Scholz, 2009). The severity of stressors introduced by chronic illness is evidenced in its overall disruptive effect on the adjustment of patient and spouse (Foxwell & Scott, 2011).

Dyadic coping as operationalized via the comparison of individual partners' coping strategies (Pakenham, 1998; Revenson, 1994) has found somewhat more consistent results than those found in the healthy adult literature reviewed previously. That is, couples who use congruent coping strategies, positive or negative, fare better than couples who use different strategies, perhaps because of the disruptiveness of incompatible strategies (Hagedoorn et al., 2011; Kraemer, Stanton, Meyerowitz, Rowland, & Ganz, 2011; Revenson, 1994), although there are some exceptions to this general finding (Pakenham, 1998). For instance, couples with cancer who were mismatched in their levels of self-disclosure reported slower recovery from heightened depressive symptoms than couples who were comparable in their disclosure at high and low levels (Hagedoorn et al., 2011). Fagundes, Berg, and Wiebe (2012) found that couples congruent in their highly intrusive thoughts reported less negative affect than incongruent couples. In the context of diabetes, when expectations about spouse involvement were similar, they improved the effectiveness of spousal control on patients' reports of dietary adherence (Seidel, Franks, Stephens, & Rook, 2012).

Consistent with the literature on healthy adults, dyadic coping as conceptualized via the systemic approach is associated with higher relationship satisfaction and well-being in chronically ill samples (see Berg & Upchurch, 2007, for a review). Positive dyadic coping has been examined via strategies of active engagement, relationship-focused coping (Coyne & Smith, 1991), collaboration (Berg & Upchurch, 2007), and common dyadic coping (Bodenmann, 2005). More positive dyadic coping and less negative dyadic coping were related to better relationship functioning and marital satisfaction from initial treatment to 6 months later in women diagnosed with metastatic breast cancer and their husbands (Badr, Carmack, Kashy, Cristofanilli, & Revenson, 2010). Further, appraising an illness as shared may enhance the effectiveness of support (Stephens et al., 2013) and may be especially important in the initial treatment period (Badr & Taylor, 2008). Positive illness-related communication also has been found to protect partners of ovarian cancer patients from the effects of disease recurrence on intrusive thoughts (Arden-Close, Moss-Morris, Dennison, Bayne, & Gidron, 2010).

Recently, research designs involving daily diary studies have underscored the everyday effect of dyadic coping in chronic illness. For instance, on days when couples reported more collaborative coping they also felt more positive mood, and wives reported less negative mood (Berg, Wiebe, et al., 2008), with this effect occurring through bolstering individuals' perceived efficacy to deal with stressful events. Further, work on type 2 diabetes indicates that some features of collaboration (e.g., support combined with persuasion) are associated with health behavior promotion such as dietary adherence and exercise (Khan, Stephens, Franks, Rook, & Salem, 2013; Stephens et al., 2013).

However, collaboration on daily stressors may have potential downsides through emotion transmission of one's partner's daily negative mood to the other (Berg, Wiebe, & Butner, 2011).

Chronic illness is an ideal context in which to study developmental factors in dyadic coping, although little research has examined developmental factors in couples' adjustment. Dyadic coping may change across the stages of an illness as couples identify symptoms, make treatment choices, cope with the stressful events of treatment and long-term management, and transition to new phases (e.g., survivorship of cancer). Also, with age and especially into later adulthood, chronic illness becomes more prevalent and, therefore, appraised as more developmentally on time (Hooker, 1999) and associated with better adjustment than among younger dyads (Carter, Lyons, Stewart, Archbold, & Scobee, 2010; Coyne & Smith, 1994). For instance, Carter and colleagues (2010) found that middle-aged caregivers of partners with Parkinson's disease reported greater role strain and fewer personal resources than caregiving older adults. Further, older couples dealing with prostate cancer have been reported to benefit more from collaboration than younger dyads in terms of well-being (Schindler, Berg, Butler, Fortenberry, & Wiebe, 2010).

Developmental factors may also be seen in the temporal course of the illness as dyadic coping in the early stages of an illness may lay the foundation for coping in later periods. For example, couples with a partner with lung cancer experienced better relationship functioning and greater marital satisfaction over time if both partners reported sharing tasks in the initial treatment period (Badr & Taylor, 2008). Also, couples who frequently talked about their relationship in the early phases of lung cancer treatment experienced less distress and better marital adjustment 6 months later compared with couples who talked less about their relationship (Badr, Acitelli, & Carmack Taylor, 2008). Kraemer et al. (2011) found that at the completion of breast cancer treatment, husbands' greater use of emotional approach and problem-focused coping strategies were related to wives' increased cancer-related benefit finding, and husbands' greater endorsement of avoidant coping was associated with lower marital satisfaction almost 1 year later. Also, congruence in positive (i.e., high emotion-focused and problem-focused, low avoidant) and negative (i.e., low emotion-focused and problem-focused) coping styles after treatment was associated with increases in adjustment for both members of the couple 1 year later. Conversely, for women with metastatic breast cancer, greater positive dyadic coping in the initial treatment phase was associated with their increased distress 6 months later (Badr et al., 2010). This may reflect the risk of close dyadic collaboration, with the cancer patients helping partners to manage their distress in addition to struggling themselves with the diagnosis and treatment.

"We-talk" (e.g., use of relational language when describing the illness) seems to be a sensitive marker of communal coping that can track changes in adjustment across the course of an illness. For example, couples facing cancer who underwent a series of counseling sessions saw significant improvements in depression, negative affect, and relationship satisfaction when we-talk increased (Dorros, 2010). Likewise, in the setting of a tobacco cessation intervention, couples with heart or lung difficulties who used more we-talk demonstrated better tobacco abstinence than those who used less we-talk (Rohrbaugh, Shoham, Skoyen, Jensen, & Mehl, 2012).

Continuity in dyadic coping strategies across the course of an illness seems to be adaptive for many illnesses studied, but dyadic coping in degenerative diseases and others that entail irreversible declines may differ in important ways (Martin et al., 2009; Reese, Keefe, Somers, & Abernethy, 2010). As the autonomy of one partner declines, couples shift from being able to solve problems individually, to relying more heavily on dyadic problem solving, to depending fully on the caregiving partner for task completion. To maintain well-being and relational cohesion, the caregiving partner transitions from interdependence with the ill partner, to commitment to the role of caregiving, to a willingness to sacrifice his or her resources, and to receive external support. Intermediate periods of illness where there is great variability in patients' functioning may pose the biggest challenges for couples' ability to adapt optimally, given the constant reassessment of ability and need (cf. Reamy, Kim, Zarit, & Whitlatch, 2011). The concept of "flexible coping" (Reese et al., 2010) may be helpful for couples to implement during the most tumultuous phases of an illness, whereby partners relax their expectations and appraisals of illness-related stressors as well as explore new strategies for dealing with illness challenges. For example, a couple facing medically induced sexual dysfunction may use flexible coping by framing impotence as an opportunity to explore other intimate acts rather than a relational crisis.

Dyadic coping with chronic illness occurs within the broader interpersonal context of the couple. According to qualitative studies of chronic illness, couples feel that a pre-illness history of commitment, reciprocity, and authentic communication enables them to cope effectively as a unit with the stressors of the illness (Foxwell & Scott, 2011; Kayser, Watson, & Andrade, 2007). Likewise, lower conflict in the relationship relates to increased illness-related collaboration, as shown in a group of sleep apnea patients and their spouses (Baron et al., 2011). Positive and negative forms of dyadic coping are less influential for relationship satisfaction among couples where past spousal support was high (Hagedoorn et al., 2011), consistent with the idea that couples' attributions for spousal behavior may vary relative to different levels of marital satisfaction. Further, active engagement has been found to be more beneficial for the adjustment of partners with particular relationship histories, such as high attachment anxiety. Highly anxiously attached individuals perceive a high level of need and readily accept support from others compared with those high in attachment avoidance. Past attachment relationships contribute to an internal working model for current relationships that shapes expectations about, and acceptance of, support from others (Vilchinsky et al., 2010).

In sum, similar to work with healthy couples, dyadic coping in couples where one member is experiencing chronic illness is associated with better relationship quality and better mood and adjustment. Given the importance of dyadic coping for both healthy and chronically ill couples, it is important to understand the developmental factors that may lead couples to a place in adulthood where they are able to effectively use dyadic coping strategies. We now trace these relational foundations of dyadic coping.

## RELATIONAL FOUNDATIONS OF DYADIC COPING

Dyadic coping is a social coping skill for handling stressful situations that likely develops throughout the human lifetime. We argue that parent–child relationships, as well as early romantic relationships, may set the stage for dyadic coping during middle and late adulthood. Within parent–child relationships, dyadic coping skills may be cultivated through social learning via watching parents' or other caretakers' dyadic coping behaviors, as well as through more direct coaching that parents do so that children may use more effective coping skills during stressful situations (Kliewer et al., 2006). The family environment (e.g., cohesion, communication, support) influences which social coping skills children internalize and use later on in life (Kliewer et al., 2006). When children feel stability and support from their parents, they are more willing to engage parents in managing a stressful situation using approach-oriented coping strategies (Kliewer et al., 2006). Conversely, in families where communication is low and tension is high, children are likely to engage in avoidant and self-focused strategies when handling conflict or stress. Beyond modeling dyadic coping behaviors, parents may also foster dyadic coping skills by actively coaching children in the midst of stressful situations to identify and accept emotions, as well as to engage in cognitive restructuring of the situation, problem solving, or distraction techniques (Gottman, 2001).

Skills that are foundational to dyadic coping such as cognitive and socioemotional functioning are also developing throughout childhood and adolescence within the family context (Repetti, Taylor, & Seeman, 2002). Such development of cognitive and self-regulatory skills is an additional pathway through which the parent–child relational history may contribute to the development of dyadic coping skills into adulthood. For example, across childhood and adolescence, youth experience an increase in their repertoire of coping skills and the context-specificity of those coping responses (Seiffge-Krenke, Aunola, & Nurmi, 2009). Social problem-solving skills also increase across childhood and adolescence, including the ability to engage in negotiation and collaboration during problem solving (Laursen, Finkelstein, & Betts, 2001). By later childhood and early adolescence, youth engage in collaborative exchanges on more equal footing with their parents, allowing for the emergence of dyadic coping in parent–child dyads (Berg et al., 2009). Although there is very limited research on dyadic coping in parent–child dyads that is consistent with the methodology and theory used in dyadic coping research on middle-aged and older adults, such work is beginning to show similar findings. For instance, collaborative coping in parent–child dyads is associated with better adolescent adjustment (Wiebe et al., 2005) and higher quality parent–child relationships (Berg, Schindler, & Maharajh, 2008), similar to the work on collaborative coping during adulthood.

Further support for our argument that adult dyadic coping has relational foundations earlier in development is drawn from research suggesting that early attachment relationships serve as a broad relational frame for the formation of future adult relationships. Secure attachment relationships underlie healthy parent–child relationships and contribute to better emotion regulation and coping skills across development (Diamond & Aspinwall, 2003). In turn, attachment style and emotion regulation contribute to marital satisfaction in adult relationships and health (Dinero, Conger, Shaver, Widaman, & Larsen-Rife, 2011; Pietromonaco, Uchino, & Dunkel Schetter, 2013). Links between early parent–child relationships, adult relationships, and health may be explained, in part, through the development of coping skills in childhood and adolescence. For example, when parents are accepting of children's negative emotions during a stressful situation, it validates the child's emotions and encourages the child to engage in support-seeking behavior in the future (Gentzler, Contreras-Grau, Kerns, & Weimer, 2005). If parents are punitive, abrasive, and minimize their children's emotions, the child is more likely to engage in avoidant coping behaviors and experience poorer emotion regulation (Gentzler et al., 2005). Additionally, positive parent–adolescent relationships are associated with increased adolescent self-efficacy in managing stress (Holahan, Valentiner & Moos, 1995), which is in turn an important associate of effective dyadic coping in adulthood (Coyne & Smith, 1994).

Research on dyadic coping in adulthood is supportive of the links between attachment history and the use and effectiveness of dyadic coping during adulthood. Fuenfhausen and Cashwell (2013) reported very high negative correlations among positive dyadic coping and attachment anxiety ($r = -.53$, $p < .01$) and attachment avoidance ($r = -.73$, $p < .01$) in a sample of married counseling graduate students. Furthermore, dyadic coping mediated the relationships between attachment anxiety and marital satisfaction, consistent with our idea that dyadic coping may come about through earlier relational foundations. Attachment styles in women also moderate the effectiveness of dyadic coping in supporting healthy recovery from stress. For instance, dyadic coping in response to an experimentally induced stressor (a public speaking task) was associated with faster physiological recovery (namely, cortisol) for both women and men (Meuwly et al., 2012). However, women with high attachment anxiety benefitted less from engaging in positive dyadic coping with their partner than women who were more securely attached. These results, combined with those of Dinero et al. (2011) that link parent–child relationships with romantic attachment security, are supportive of the idea that positive dyadic coping in adulthood emanates from positive parent–child relationships early in life.

Moving beyond the parent–child relationship, during adolescence the use of dyadic coping skills further continues to develop in conjunction with the development of friendships and romantic partnerships, which may serve as a training ground for adult dyadic coping skills. Across adolescence, friends and romantic relationships become increasingly important as sources of support (Beyers & Seiffge-Krenke, 2007). The success of conflict resolution within these romantic relationships is strongly correlated with the previous use of productive problem-solving strategies in the parent–child relationship (Collins, Welsh, & Furman, 2009). Thus, there appears to be an interplay between parent–child relationships, early romantic relationships, and dyadic coping skill progression. This process is likely mediated by the internalization of parents' coping behaviors (Donato, Iafrate, Bradbury, & Scabini, 2012). Adolescents internalize the coping behaviors of their parents more frequently when they have a positive, open relationship with parents, and in general, females, compared with males, seem to have greater internalization of parental coping behaviors. We theorize that when adolescents practice positive coping and problem solving in these early intimate relationships, they will be more likely to engage in effective dyadic coping later in life.

In summary, when exploring the developmental course of dyadic coping behaviors, factors such as parental coping behavior, nature of the parent–child relationship, development of foundational skills, and progression of early romantic relationships should all be considered as having an effect on the maturation and utilization of adult dyadic coping skills. Further research is needed to understand the associations of child and adolescent dyadic coping with parents and in romantic relationships with dyadic coping during adulthood. Although dyadic coping may not show complete continuity across these relationships, parent–child and early romantic relationships do provide a relational foundation for dyadic coping later in life.

# CLINICAL IMPLICATIONS AND FUTURE DIRECTIONS

We have focused in this chapter on how individuals in connection with an intimate partner appraise and cope with stressful events, both of a more minor as well as more major variety in dealing with chronic illness. We suggested that the ways in which dyadic coping occurs in adults may derive from individuals' early relational history with their parents and subsequently their friends and romantic partners. The literature clearly supports the importance of dyadic coping across the lifespan for promoting the quality of relationships both in healthy adults and in adults experiencing chronic illness. Given the high value of dyadic coping for couples, we explore in this section clinical interventions that could enhance the frequency and effectiveness of dyadic coping as well as explore future directions for the field.

## Clinical Implications

Couples who use negative rather than positive coping strategies may benefit from interventions to develop better communication and coping skills, especially when such stressors drain their limited emotional resources. Couples' intervention programs are aimed at training couples in the use of positive dyadic coping skills (Coping-Oriented Couples Training [COCT], Bodenmann, Bradbury, & Pihet, 2008; and Couples Coping Enhancement Training [CCET], Bodenmann & Shantinath, 2004). These methods involve psychoeducation about the negative impact of stress on the individual and relationship, training for each partner regarding empathic listening to identify and optimally respond to a significant other's stress (Bodenmann & Randall, 2012), and partner feedback about the listener's effectiveness at understanding and assisting the other partner. These programs share many elements that underlie cognitive–behavioral therapy, such as increasing communication skills, training in problem solving, and the use of cognitive reframing techniques. Such couple-based interventions enhance relationship quality, facilitate the use of positive dyadic coping skills, and increase the couple's communication, with longitudinal data showing strong effects immediately following intervention and continuing effects up to 2 years postintervention, though the effects do weaken over time (e.g., Bodenmann & Shantinath, 2004). Although these intervention programs have yet to be used with couples with chronic illness, couples therapy has resulted in improvements in relationship satisfaction regardless of the type of program or specific chronic illness; however, the magnitude of these effects was small (Martire, Schulz, Helgeson, Small, & Saghafi, 2010). The effectiveness of these programs may be enhanced with greater focus on dyadic coping behaviors (Martire et al., 2010; Randall & Bodenmann, 2009; see also Chapter 16, this volume). Randall and Bodenmann (2009) further noted that since COCT and

CCET primarily target coping with minor daily stressors, these interventions may need to be adapted to the chronic illness context to address issues such as illness appraisal and caregiver stress, as well as concerns unique to an illness.

Although these interventions are believed to be appropriate for couples across the lifespan, most couples who have participated in dyadic coping intervention studies have been on average middle-aged, married, and together for a moderate amount of time (i.e., around 10–15 years; see, e.g., Bodenmann & Shantinath, 2004; Ledermann, Bodenmann, & Cina, 2007; Pihet, Bodenmann, Cina, Widmer, & Shantinath, 2007). Future research needs to explicitly examine how these interventions can be best implemented in couples at different stages of the lifespan, including newlyweds, couples with children at home, blended families, and older individuals. As discussed previously, unique stressors may occur at these different developmental points, which may have implications for the effectiveness of the intervention programs. For example, although Ledermann et al. (2007) found these programs to improve relationship satisfaction among couples, they failed to find that improving dyadic coping skills reduced conflict between partners specifically related to child rearing, which is expected to be the type of stressor commonly experienced by couples during early and middle adulthood. Such results suggest that these programs may need to be adapted to address stressors specific to different stages of adulthood.

**Future Directions**

We have focused in this chapter on how individuals use dyadic coping in connection with an intimate partner, typically one's long-term married partner. However, consistent with family systems models of coping (McCubbin et al., 1980; Repetti et al., 2011), it must be noted that intimate partners are only one member of a larger family and social network, which includes siblings, children, and health care providers whose involvement has not been a focus of the dyadic coping literature. For instance, Koehly et al. (2008) found that communal coping among sisters from high-risk families who were being tested for breast or ovarian cancer reduced anxiety among sisters. Further, the role of adult children in older adults' coping processes has rarely been examined (Cicirelli, 2006) and is a ripe area for research. For couples experiencing chronic illness, health care providers also may be an important resource for coping skills as they are clearly involved in treatment decision-making processes (Zikmund-Fisher et al., 2010). These other relationships in the support network (as well as friends, pastors) may be important collaborators with whom individuals cope dyadically. Moreover, in addition to married heterosexual couples, other types of partnered relationships (e.g., cohabiting couples, gay couples) should be included in research on dyadic coping.

In summary, a developmental approach illuminates how dyadic coping is a lifelong phenomenon that is likely fostered early in parent–child relationships and extends to intimate partners, with these relationships lasting frequently for long periods of one's lifespan. Dyadic coping is fostered in the context of warm and supportive early relationships that foster the development of future relationships that, in turn, serve as essential resources as dyads face stressors both small and large. Charting the developmental course of dyadic coping will help the field understand the relational history of positive and negative forms of dyadic coping, how dyadic coping may change across time as couples deal with repeated stressful events such as those typical in the context of dealing with chronic illness, and how to assist family units cope with stressors together as an integrated system.

## REFERENCES

Almeida, D. M., Piazza, J. R., Stawski, R. S., & Klein, L. C. (2011). The speedometer of life: Stress, health, and aging. In K. W. Schaie & S. L. Willis (Eds.), *Handbook of the psychology of aging* (pp. 191–206). San Diego, CA: Elsevier. http://dx.doi.org/10.1016/B978-0-12-380882-0.00012-7

Antonucci, T. C., & Akiyama, H. (1987). Social networks in adult life and a preliminary examination of the convoy model. *Journal of Gerontology, 42,* 519–527. http://dx.doi.org/10.1093/geronj/42.5.519

Arden-Close, E., Moss-Morris, R., Dennison, L., Bayne, L., & Gidron, Y. (2010). The Couples' Illness Communication Scale (CICS): Development and evaluation of a brief measure assessing illness-related couple communication. *British Journal of Health Psychology, 15,* 543–559. http://dx.doi.org/10.1348/135910709X476972

Badr, H. (2004). Coping in marital dyads: A contextual perspective on the role of gender and health. *Personal Relationships, 11,* 197–211. http://dx.doi.org/10.1111/j.1475-6811.2004.00078.x

Badr, H., Acitelli, L. K., & Carmack Taylor, C. L. (2008). Does talking about their relationship affect couples' marital and psychological adjustment to lung cancer? *Journal of Cancer Survivorship, 2,* 53–64. http://dx.doi.org/10.1007/s11764-008-0044-3

Badr, H., Carmack, C. L., Kashy, D. A., Cristofanilli, M., & Revenson, T. A. (2010). Dyadic coping in metastatic breast cancer. *Health Psychology, 29,* 169–180. http://dx.doi.org/10.1037/a0018165

Badr, H., & Taylor, C. L. C. (2008). Effects of relationship maintenance on psychological distress and dyadic adjustment among couples coping with lung cancer. *Health Psychology, 27,* 616–627. http://dx.doi.org/10.1037/0278-6133.27.5.616

Baron, K. G., Smith, T. W., Berg, C. A., Czajkowski, L. A., Gunn, H., & Jones, C. R. (2011). Spousal involvement in CPAP adherence among patients with obstructive sleep apnea. *Sleep and Breathing, 15,* 525–534. http://dx.doi.org/10.1007/s11325-010-0374-z

Berg, C. A., Schindler, I., & Maharajh, S. (2008). Adolescents' and mothers' perceptions of the cognitive and relational functions of collaboration and adjustment in dealing with type 1 diabetes. *Journal of Family Psychology, 22,* 865–874. http://dx.doi.org/10.1037/a0013641

Berg, C. A., Schindler, I., Smith, T. W., Skinner, M., & Beveridge, R. M. (2011). Perceptions of the cognitive compensation and interpersonal enjoyment functions of collaboration among middle-aged and older married couples. *Psychology and Aging, 26,* 167–173. http://dx.doi.org/10.1037/a0021124

Berg, C. A., Skinner, M., Ko, K., Butler, J. M., Palmer, D. L., Butner, J., & Wiebe, D. J. (2009). The fit between stress appraisal and dyadic coping in understanding perceived coping effectiveness for adolescents with type 1 diabetes. *Journal of Family Psychology, 23,* 521–530. http://dx.doi.org/10.1037/a0015556

Berg, C. A., & Upchurch, R. (2007). A developmental-contextual model of couples coping with chronic illness across the adult life span. *Psychological Bulletin, 133,* 920–954. http://dx.doi.org/10.1037/0033-2909.133.6.920

Berg, C. A., Wiebe, D. J., & Butner, J. (2011). Affect covariation in marital couples dealing with stressors surrounding prostate cancer. *Gerontology, 57,* 167–172. http://dx.doi.org/10.1159/000318642

Berg, C. A., Wiebe, D. J., Butner, J., Bloor, L., Bradstreet, C., Upchurch, R., . . . Patton, G. (2008). Collaborative coping and daily mood in couples dealing with prostate cancer. *Psychology and Aging, 23,* 505–516.

Beyers, W., & Seiffge-Krenke, I. (2007). Are friends and romantic partners the "best medicine"? How the quality of other close relations mediates the impact of changing family relationships on adjustment. *International Journal of Behavioral Development, 31,* 559–568. http://dx.doi.org/10.1177/0165025407080583

Bodenmann, G. (2005). Dyadic coping and its significance for marital functioning. In T. A. Revenson, K. Kayser, & G. Bodenmann (Eds.), *Couples coping with stress: Emerging perspectives on dyadic coping* (pp. 33–49). Washington, DC: American Psychological Association. http://dx.doi.org/10.1037/11031-002

Bodenmann, G., Bradbury, T., & Pihet, S. (2008). Relative contributions of treatment-related changes in communication skills and dyadic coping skills to the longitudinal course of marriage in the framework of marital distress prevention. *Journal of Divorce & Remarriage, 50,* 1–21. http://dx.doi.org/10.1080/10502550802365391

Bodenmann, G., Charvoz, L., Bradbury, T. N., Bertoni, A., Iafrate, R., Giuliani, C., . . . Behling, J. (2007). The role of stress in divorce: A three-nation retrospective study. *Journal of Social and Personal Relationships, 24,* 707–728.

Bodenmann, G., Meuwly, N., Bradbury, T. N., Gmelch, S., & Ledermann, T. (2010). Stress, anger, and verbal aggression in intimate relationships: Moderating effects of individual and dyadic coping. *Journal of Social and Personal Relationships, 27,* 408–424.

Bodenmann, G., Meuwly, N., & Kayser, K. (2011). Two conceptualizations of dyadic coping and their potential for predicting relationship quality and individual well-being: A comparison. *European Psychologist, 16*, 255–266. http://dx.doi.org/10.1027/1016-9040/a000068

Bodenmann, G., & Randall, A. K. (2012). Common factors in the enhancement of dyadic coping. *Behavior Therapy, 43*, 88–98. http://dx.doi.org/10.1016/j.beth.2011.04.003

Bodenmann, G., & Shantinath, S. D. (2004). The couples coping enhancement training (CCET): A new approach to prevention of marital distress based upon stress and coping. *Family Relations, 53*, 477–484. http://dx.doi.org/10.1111/j.0197-6664.2004.00056.x

Carstensen, L. L., Isaacowitz, D. M., & Charles, S. T. (1999). Taking time seriously: A theory of socioemotional selectivity. *American Psychologist, 54*, 165–181. http://dx.doi.org/10.1037/0003-066X.54.3.165

Carter, J. H., Lyons, K. S., Stewart, B. J., Archbold, P. G., & Scobee, R. (2010). Does age make a difference in caregiver strain? Comparison of young versus older caregivers in early-stage Parkinson's disease. *Movement Disorders, 25*, 724–730. http://dx.doi.org/10.1002/mds.22888

Cicirelli, V. G. (2006). Caregiving decision making by older mothers and adult children: Process and expected outcome. *Psychology and Aging, 21*, 209–221. http://dx.doi.org/10.1037/0882-7974.21.2.209

Collins, W. A., Welsh, D. P., & Furman, W. (2009). Adolescent romantic relationships. *Annual Review of Psychology, 60*, 631–652. http://dx.doi.org/10.1146/annurev.psych.60.110707.163459

Conger, R. D., Rueter, M. A., & Elder, G. H., Jr. (1999). Couple resilience to economic pressure. *Journal of Personality and Social Psychology, 76*, 54–71. http://dx.doi.org/10.1037/0022-3514.76.1.54

Coyne, J. C., & Smith, D. A. F. (1991). Couples coping with a myocardial infarction: A contextual perspective on wives' distress. *Journal of Personality and Social Psychology, 61*, 404–412. http://dx.doi.org/10.1037/0022-3514.61.3.404

Coyne, J. C., & Smith, D. A. F. (1994). Couples coping with a myocardial infarction: Contextual perspective on patient self-efficacy. *Journal of Family Psychology, 8*, 43–54. http://dx.doi.org/10.1037/0893-3200.8.1.43

Diamond, L. M., & Aspinwall, L. G. (2003). Emotion regulation across the life span: An integrative perspective emphasizing self-regulation, positive affect, and dyadic processes. *Motivation and Emotion, 27*, 125–156. http://dx.doi.org/10.1023/A:1024521920068

Dinero, R. E., Conger, R. D., Shaver, P. R., Widaman, K. F., & Larsen-Rife, D. (2011). Influence of family of origin and adult romantic partners on romantic attachment security. *Journal of Family Psychology, 22*, 622–632. http://dx.doi.org/10.1037/a0012506

Donato, S., Iafrate, R., Bradbury, T. N., & Scabini, E. (2012). Acquiring dyadic coping: Parents and partners as models. *Personal Relationships, 19*, 386–400. http://dx.doi.org/10.1111/j.1475-6811.2011.01368.x

Dorros, S. M. (2010). *A content analysis of the counseling sessions of dyads with breast and prostate cancer: Linguistic predictors of psychosocial adjustment and thematic analysis of key concerns* (Unpublished doctoral dissertation). University of Arizona, Tucson.

Doss, B. D., Rhoades, G. K., Stanley, S. M., & Markman, H. J. (2009). The effect of the transition to parenthood on relationship quality: An 8-year prospective study. *Journal of Personality and Social Psychology, 96,* 601–619. http://dx.doi.org/10.1037/a0013969

Fagundes, C. P., Berg, C. A., & Wiebe, D. J. (2012). Intrusion, avoidance, and daily negative affect among couples coping with prostate cancer: A dyadic investigation. *Journal of Family Psychology, 26,* 246–253. http://dx.doi.org/10.1037/a0027332

Foxwell, K. R., & Scott, S. E. (2011). Coping together and apart: Exploring how patients and their caregivers manage terminal head and neck cancer. *Journal of Psychosocial Oncology, 29,* 308–326. http://dx.doi.org/10.1080/07347332.2011.563343

Frankel, P. (2012). Contemporary two-parent families: Navigating work and family challenges. In F. Walsh (Ed.), *Normal family processes: Growing diversity and complexity* (pp. 78–101). New York, NY: Guilford Press.

Frye, N. E., & Karney, B. R. (2006). The context of aggressive behavior in marriage: A longitudinal study of newlyweds. *Journal of Family Psychology, 20,* 12–20.

Fuenfhausen, K. K., & Cashwell, C. S. (2013). Attachment, stress, dyadic coping, and marital satisfaction in counseling graduate students. *The Family Journal, 21,* 364–370. http://dx.doi.org/10.1177/1066480713488523

Gentzler, A. L., Contreras-Grau, J. M., Kerns, K. A., & Weimer, B. L. (2005). Parent-child emotional communication and children's coping in middle childhood. *Social Development, 14,* 591–612. http://dx.doi.org/10.1111/j.1467-9507.2005.00319.x

Gottman, J. (2001). Meta-emotion, children's emotional intelligence, and buffering children from marital conflict. In C. Ryff & B. H. Singer (Eds.), *Emotion, social relationships, and health* (pp. 23–40). New York, NY: Oxford University Press. http://dx.doi.org/10.1093/acprof:oso/9780195145410.003.0002

Gump, B. B., Polk, D. E., Kamarck, T. W., & Shiffman, S. M. (2001). Partner interactions are associated with reduced blood pressure in the natural environment: Ambulatory monitoring evidence from a healthy, multiethnic adult sample. *Psychosomatic Medicine, 63,* 423–433. http://dx.doi.org/10.1097/00006842-200105000-00011

Hagedoorn, M., Buunk, B. P., Kuijer, R. G., Wobbes, T., & Sanderman, R. (2000). Couples dealing with cancer: Role and gender differences regarding psychological distress and quality of life. *Psycho-Oncology, 9,* 232–242. http://dx.doi.org/10.1002/1099-1611(200005/06)9:3<232::AID-PON458>3.0.CO;2-J

Hagedoorn, M., Dagan, M., Puterman, E., Hoff, C., Meijerink, W. J. H. J., Delongis, A., & Sanderman, R. (2011). Relationship satisfaction in couples confronted with colorectal cancer: The interplay of past and current spousal support. *Journal of Behavioral Medicine, 34,* 288–297. http://dx.doi.org/10.1007/s10865-010-9311-7

Herzberg, P. Y. (2013). Coping in relationships: The interplay between individual and dyadic coping and their effects on relationship satisfaction. *Anxiety, Stress, and Coping, 26*, 136–153. http://dx.doi.org/10.1080/10615806.2012.655726

Holahan, C. J., Valentiner, D. P., & Moos, R. H. (1995). Parental support, coping strategies, and psychological adjustment: An integrative model with late adolescents. *Journal of Youth and Adolescence, 24*, 633–648. http://dx.doi.org/10.1007/BF01536948

Hooker, K. (1999). Possible selves in adulthood: Incorporating teleonomic relevance into studies of the self. In T. M. Hess & F. Blanchard-Fields (Eds.), *Social cognition and aging* (pp. 97–122). New York, NY: Academic Press. http://dx.doi.org/10.1016/B978-012345260-3/50006-9

Hoppmann, C. A., Coats, A. H., & Blanchard-Fields, F. (2008). Goals and everyday problem solving: Examining the link between age-related goals and problem-solving strategy use. *Aging, Neuropsychology and Cognition, 15*, 401–423. http://dx.doi.org/10.1080/13825580701533777

Hoppmann, C. A., & Gerstorf, D. (2013). Spousal goals, affect quality, and collaborative problem solving: Evidence from a time-sampling study with older couples. *Research in Human Development, 10*, 70–87. http://dx.doi.org/10.1080/15427609.2013.760260

Kayser, K. (2005). Enhancing dyadic coping during a time of crisis: A theory-based intervention with breast cancer patients and their partners. In T. A. Revenson, K. Kayser, & G. Bodenmann (Eds.), *Couples coping with stress: Emerging perspectives on dyadic coping* (pp. 175–194). Washington, DC: American Psychological Association. http://dx.doi.org/10.1037/11031-009

Kayser, K., Watson, L. E., & Andrade, J. T. (2007). Cancer as a "we disease": Examining the process of coping from a relational perspective. *Families, Systems, & Health, 25*, 404–418. http://dx.doi.org/10.1037/1091-7527.25.4.404

Khan, C. M., Stephens, M. P., Franks, M. M., Rook, K. S., & Salem, J. K. (2013). Influences of spousal support and control on diabetes management through physical activity. *Health Psychology, 32*, 739–747. http://dx.doi.org/10.1037/a0028609

King, D. B., & DeLongis, A. (2013). Dyadic coping with stepfamily conflict: Demand and withdraw responses between husbands and wives. *Journal of Social and Personal Relationships, 30*, 198–206. http://dx.doi.org/10.1177/0265407512454524

Kliewer, W., Parrish, K. A., Taylor, K. W., Jackson, K., Walker, J. M., & Shivy, V. A. (2006). Socialization of coping with community violence: Influences of caregiver coaching, modeling, and family context. *Child Development, 77*, 605–623. http://dx.doi.org/10.1111/j.1467-8624.2006.00893.x

Koehly, L. M., Peters, J. A., Kuhn, N., Hoskins, L., Letocha, A., Kenen, R., . . . Greene, M. H. (2008). Sisters in hereditary breast and ovarian cancer families: Communal coping, social integration, and psychological well-being. *Psycho-Oncology, 17*, 812–821. http://dx.doi.org/10.1002/pon.1373

Kraemer, L. M., Stanton, A. L., Meyerowitz, B. E., Rowland, J. H., & Ganz, P. A. (2011). A longitudinal examination of couples' coping strategies as predictors of adjustment to breast cancer. *Journal of Family Psychology, 25,* 963–972. http://dx.doi.org/10.1037/a0025551

Landis, M., Peter-Wight, M., Martin, M., & Bodenmann, G. (2013). Dyadic coping and marital satisfaction of older spouses in long-term marriage. *GeroPsych: The Journal of Gerontopsychology and Geriatric Psychiatry, 26,* 39–47.

Laursen, B., Finkelstein, B. D., & Betts, N. T. (2001). A developmental meta-analysis of peer conflict resolution. *Developmental Review, 21,* 423–449. http://dx.doi.org/10.1006/drev.2000.0531

Ledermann, T., Bodenmann, G., & Cina, A. (2007). The efficacy of the couples coping enhancement training (CCET) in improving relationship quality. *Journal of Social and Clinical Psychology, 26,* 940–959. http://dx.doi.org/10.1521/jscp.2007.26.8.940

Markman, H. J. (1981). Prediction of marital distress: A 5-year follow-up. *Journal of Consulting and Clinical Psychology, 49,* 760–762. http://dx.doi.org/10.1037/0022-006X.49.5.760

Martin, M., Peter-Wight, M., Braun, M., Hornung, R., & Scholz, U. (2009). The 3-phase-model of dyadic adaptation to dementia: Why it might sometimes be better to be worse. *European Journal of Ageing, 6,* 291–301. http://dx.doi.org/10.1007/s10433-009-0129-5

Martire, L. M., Schulz, R., Helgeson, V. S., Small, B. J., & Saghafi, E. M. (2010). Review and meta-analysis of couple-oriented interventions for chronic illness. *Annals of Behavioral Medicine, 40,* 325–342. http://dx.doi.org/10.1007/s12160-010-9216-2

Martire, L. M., Stephens, M. A. P., Druley, J. A., & Wojno, W. C. (2002). Negative reactions to received spousal care: Predictors and consequences of miscarried support. *Health Psychology, 21,* 167–176. http://dx.doi.org/10.1037/0278-6133.21.2.167

McCubbin, H. I., Joy, C. B., Cauble, A. E., Comeau, J. K., Patterson, J. M., & Needle, R. H. (1980). Family stress and coping: A decade review. *Journal of Marriage and Family, 42,* 855–871. http://dx.doi.org/10.2307/351829

Meuwly, N., Bodenmann, G., Germann, J., Bradbury, T. N., Ditzen, B., & Heinrichs, M. (2012). Dyadic coping, insecure attachment, and cortisol stress recovery following experimentally induced stress. *Journal of Family Psychology, 26,* 937–947. http://dx.doi.org/10.1037/a0030356

Monin, J. K., & Schulz, R. (2009). Interpersonal effects of suffering in older adult caregiving relationships. *Psychology and Aging, 24,* 681–695. http://dx.doi.org/10.1037/a0016355

Neff, L. A., & Karney, B. R. (2007). Stress crossover in newlywed marriage: A longitudinal and dyadic perspective. *Journal of Marriage and Family, 69,* 594–607. http://dx.doi.org/10.1111/j.1741-3737.2007.00394.x

Overall, N. C., Fletcher, G. J., & Simpson, J. A. (2010). Helping each other grow: Romantic partner support, self-improvement, and relationship quality. *Personality and Social Psychology Bulletin, 36,* 1496–1513. http://dx.doi.org/10.1177/0146167210383045

Pakenham, K. I. (1998). Couple coping and adjustment to multiple sclerosis in care receiver–carer dyads. *Family Relations, 47,* 269–277. http://dx.doi.org/10.2307/584977

Papp, L. M., & Witt, N. L. (2010). Romantic partners' individual coping strategies and dyadic coping: Implications for relationship functioning. *Journal of Family Psychology, 24,* 551–559. http://dx.doi.org/10.1037/a0020836

Pietromonaco, P. R., Uchino, B., & Dunkel Schetter, C. (2013). Close relationship processes and health: Implications of attachment theory for health and disease. *Health Psychology, 32,* 499–513. http://dx.doi.org/10.1037/a0029349

Pihet, S., Bodenmann, G., Cina, A., Widmer, K., & Shantinath, S. (2007). Can prevention of marital distress improve well-being? A 1 year longitudinal study. *Clinical Psychology & Psychotherapy, 14,* 79–88. http://dx.doi.org/10.1002/cpp.522

Randall, A. K., & Bodenmann, G. (2009). The role of stress on close relationships and marital satisfaction. *Clinical Psychology Review, 29,* 105–115. http://dx.doi.org/10.1016/j.cpr.2008.10.004

Reamy, A. M., Kim, K., Zarit, S. H., & Whitlatch, C. J. (2011). Understanding discrepancy in perceptions of values: Individuals with mild to moderate dementia and their family caregivers. *The Gerontologist, 51,* 473–483. http://dx.doi.org/10.1093/geront/gnr010

Reese, J. B., Keefe, F. J., Somers, T. J., & Abernethy, A. P. (2010). Coping with sexual concerns after cancer: The use of flexible coping. *Supportive Care in Cancer, 18,* 785–800. http://dx.doi.org/10.1007/s00520-010-0819-8

Repetti, R. L., Taylor, S. E., & Seeman, T. E. (2002). Risky families: Family social environments and the mental and physical health of offspring. *Psychological Bulletin, 128,* 330–366. http://dx.doi.org/10.1037/0033-2909.128.2.330

Repetti, R. L., Wang, S., & Saxbe, D. E. (2011). Adult health in the context of everyday family life. *Annuals of Behavioral Medicine, 42,* 285–293. http://dx.doi.org/10.1007/s12160-011-9293-x

Revenson, T. A. (1994). Social support and marital coping with chronic illness. *Annals of Behavioral Medicine, 16,* 122–130.

Rohrbaugh, M. J., Shoham, V., Skoyen, J. A., Jensen, M., & Mehl, M. R. (2012). We-talk, communal coping, and cessation success in a couple-focused intervention for health-compromised smokers. *Family Process, 51,* 107–121. http://dx.doi.org/10.1111/j.1545-5300.2012.01388.x

Rolland, J. S. (1984). Toward a psychosocial typology of chronic and life-threatening illness. *Family Systems Medicine, 2,* 245–262. http://dx.doi.org/10.1037/h0091663

Schindler, I., Berg, C. A., Butler, J. M., Fortenberry, K. T., & Wiebe, D. J. (2010). Late-midlife and older couples' shared possible selves and psychological well-being during times of illness: The role of collaborative problem solving. *The Journals of Gerontology: Series B. Psychological Sciences and Social Sciences, 65,* 416–424. http://dx.doi.org/10.1093/geronb/gbq030

Seidel, A. J., Franks, M. M., Stephens, M. A. P., & Rook, K. S. (2012). Spouse control and type 2 diabetes management: Moderating effects of dyadic expectations for spouse involvement. *Family Relations, 61*, 698–709. http://dx.doi.org/10.1111/j.1741-3729.2012.00719.x

Seiffge-Krenke, I., Aunola, K., & Nurmi, J. E. (2009). Changes in stress perception and coping during adolescence: The role of situational and personal factors. *Child Development, 80*, 259–279. http://dx.doi.org/10.1111/j.1467-8624.2008.01258.x

Stephens, M. A. P., Franks, M. M., Rook, K. S., Iida, M., Hemphill, R. C., & Salem, J. K. (2013). Spouses' attempts to regulate day-to-day dietary adherence among patients with type 2 diabetes. *Health Psychology, 32*, 1029–1037. http://dx.doi.org/10.1037/a0030018

Vilchinsky, N., Haze-Filderman, L., Leibowitz, M., Reges, O., Khaskia, A., & Mosseri, M. (2010). Spousal support and cardiac patients' distress: The moderating role of attachment orientation. *Journal of Family Psychology, 24*, 508–512. http://dx.doi.org/10.1037/a0020009

Wiebe, D. J., Berg, C. A., Korbel, C., Palmer, D. L., Beveridge, R. M., Upchurch, R., . . . Donaldson, D. L. (2005). Children's appraisals of maternal involvement in coping with diabetes: Enhancing our understanding of adherence, metabolic control, and quality of life across adolescence. *Journal of Pediatric Psychology, 30*, 167–178. http://dx.doi.org/10.1093/jpepsy/jsi004

Wunderer, E., & Schneewind, K. A. (2008). The relationship between marital standards, dyadic coping and marital satisfaction. *European Journal of Social Psychology, 38*, 462–476. http://dx.doi.org/10.1002/ejsp.405

Zikmund-Fisher, B. J., Couper, M. P., Singer, E., Ubel, P. A., Ziniel, S., Fowler, F. J., Jr., . . . Fagerlin, A. (2010). Deficits and variations in patients' experience with making 9 common medical decisions: The DECISIONS survey. *Medical Decision Making, 30*(Suppl. 5), 85S–95S. http://dx.doi.org/10.1177/0272989X10380466

# 14

## EMOTION REGULATION IN THE CONTEXT OF SPOUSAL CAREGIVING: INTRAPERSONAL AND INTERPERSONAL STRATEGIES

JOAN K. MONIN

My husband Mike (we've been married for 43 years October 4th) was hospitalized with colon cancer. Mike has always been a strong man, rarely ill. To spend 10 days at [the hospital] was devastating. I stayed by his side and tended to his needs. I was a rock. On the way home more than once I had to pull over overwhelmed by tears. Things are better and he is expected to make a full recovery, however I was shocked at how angry he was. I told him to yell, scream, do what you will, but put it behind you. I guess he was scared too.

—Anonymous research participant, age 64

As people age, they increasingly face health conditions that challenge their ability to regulate not just their own but also their partner's emotions. As the opening quote suggests, in the context of marriage these experiences affect not only the person with the health condition, but also the spouse responsible for that person's care. Emotion regulation is often a dyadic process whereby both individuals are regulating their own as well as their partner's emotions.

This chapter integrates theory and current research on intrapersonal and interpersonal aspects of emotion regulation in spousal caregiving (for a broader discussion of emotion regulation in couples, see Chapter 12, this volume). Emotion regulation is defined, the benefits of regulating emotions are explained, and a case is made for examining emotion regulation processes in

http://dx.doi.org/10.1037/14897-015
*Couple Relationships in the Middle and Later Years: Their Nature, Complexity, and Role in Health and Illness,*
J. Bookwala (Editor)

the specific context of spousal caregiving. In addition, the role of contextual factors and moderators on emotion regulation processes, conceptual issues and opportunities for future research, and clinical implications of existing findings are discussed.

## WHAT IS EMOTION REGULATION?

Emotions are an integral part of people's lives. They profoundly affect our actions and health, even if we are not always aware of them. *Emotion regulation* involves skillful understanding and balancing of emotions, and it encompasses several components. These include being aware of and paying attention to emotions, understanding and labeling emotions, and managing or modifying emotional reactions to meet goals (e.g., Gross, 1998). Emotion regulation skills develop in infancy and childhood and mature over the lifespan. These skills are critical to mental health, achievement of life goals, and building and maintaining social bonds (e.g., Cole, Michel, O'Donnell Teti, 1994).

## WHY IS UNDERSTANDING EMOTION REGULATION IN OLDER SPOUSAL CAREGIVING DYADS IMPORTANT?

In the United States, spouses are often the first in line to take on caregiving responsibilities (Pinquart & Sörensen, 2011), and given that the baby boomers are aging and living longer, it is likely that spousal caregiving will become more common. This is a major public health concern because research has shown that providing care to a family member with a chronic condition can negatively impact caregivers' mental and physical health (Schulz & Beach, 1999; Vitaliano, Zhang, & Scanlan, 2003). This is especially true for spouses, who report more depressive symptoms, greater financial and physical burden, and lower levels of well-being than other types of caregivers (see Pinquart & Sörensen, 2011, for a meta-analysis).

There are many reasons why spousal caregivers may experience burden. These include increased physical and financial strain, social isolation, and dealing with a care recipient's changing behavior. One reason that has received less research attention is that family caregivers are often faced with their loved one's suffering on a daily basis (Monin & Schulz, 2009). Several studies have demonstrated that beyond the physical and cognitive demands of providing care, exposure to a loved one's suffering is associated with substantial negative health consequences for caregivers including depression for caregivers of persons with dementia (Schulz et al., 2008), physiological stress for spouses of persons with osteoarthritis (Monin, Schulz, Martire, et al., 2010), and cardiovascular disease and depression for older spouses (Schulz et al., 2009).

Because people are often negatively affected by a close partner's suffering, they are faced with regulating emotions such as personal distress, anger, frustration, and guilt. In the context of spousal caregiving, emotion regulation strategies can occur within an individual (intrapersonal emotion regulation) or between spouses (interpersonal emotion regulation). This chapter discusses emotion regulation strategies that occur in the context of marriages in which one spouse has a chronic condition and requires care from the other spouse, who is typically healthier. That said, it is important to remember that in many late-life marriages both partners suffer from chronic conditions and support one another (Hoppmann & Gerstorf, 2009).

## INTRAPERSONAL EMOTION REGULATION

When a care recipient is suffering or experiencing negative emotions, he or she can use emotion regulation strategies to alter his or her own experience. Likewise, caregiving spouses can use strategies to regulate their own emotions that result from the care recipient's suffering. Although the spouse's negative emotions may result from the care recipient's suffering, making this part of the process interpersonal, what is intrapersonal is that the spouse can individually act on his or her own cognitions and behaviors to regulate his or her own emotions. In other words, each partner can regulate his or her own emotions individually and separately.

Much of the work related to individuals' emotion regulation processes in the context of spousal caregiving has used the stress, appraisal, and coping model developed by Folkman and Lazarus (1985). Although the coping literature is relevant to understanding spousal caregiving dyads' emotion-related processes, coping and emotion regulation are distinct concepts (Gross, 1999). Of the two terms, *coping* is the broader category, as it includes nonemotional actions taken to achieve nonemotional goals. Coping also differs from emotion regulation in that the unit of analysis is typically longer—extended periods of hours, days, or months rather than seconds or minutes. In addition, coping does not subsume all forms of emotion regulation in that emotion regulation includes processes not typically considered in the coping literature, such as regulating expressive or physiological aspects of emotion or influencing positive emotions. That said, numerous studies have examined whether caregivers' coping styles are related to caregivers' experiences, from which we can glean information about emotion regulation. According to Folkman and Lazarus, individuals who face a stressful situation generally use a combination of problem-focused coping (taking action to change a threatening or damaging relationship between themselves and their environment) and emotion-focused coping (taking steps to regulate the emotional distress produced by the person–environment relationship). The literature mainly focuses on negative outcomes of emotion-focused coping and suggests that wishful thinking, avoidance, regression, and emotional discharge are associated with depression and anxiety; whereas problem-focused strategies such as logical analysis and taking action are associated with life satisfaction, well-being, and lower depression (del-Pino-Casado, Frías-Osuna, Palomino-Moral, & Pancorbo-Hidalgo, 2011). Similarly, when thinking about how care recipients regulate their own emotions, we can draw from a large literature examining the influence of coping strategies on psychological adjustment among older adults with chronic conditions. This research has also shown that emotion-focused coping strategies such as wishful thinking are deleterious, whereas problem-focused strategies are more effective in reducing stress (e.g., Felton & Revenson, 1984).

Another popular model of emotion regulation that has been applied mainly to intrapersonal situations, or within individuals, is Gross's (2001) process model of emotion regulation. The model details five strategies that occur sequentially during the process of generating emotion: (a) situation selection, (b) situation modification, (c) attentional deployment, (d) cognitive reappraisal, and (e) response modulation (i.e., suppression). The first four strategies are called *antecedent focused*, occurring before the emotional experience, and the last is *response focused*, occurring after the emotional experience. Using a strategy early in the process decreases the need to use a later strategy. For example, a person who is in pain may pace activities throughout the day so that negative emotions are avoided (i.e., situation selection), making it unnecessary for the person to suppress his or her negative emotions resulting from pain later in the day (i.e., response modulation). The strategies that have received the most attention are cognitive reappraisal and response modulation (e.g., emotion expression vs. suppression). For example, our research has examined the emotional consequences of caregivers engaging in cognitive reappraisal and emotion expression. Specifically, we conducted a study in which 53 caregivers of spouses with a musculoskeletal condition were audiotaped while they privately disclosed an instance of their spouse's suffering and a typical interaction (i.e., a meal together; Monin, Schulz, Lemay, & Cook, 2012). Blood pressure and heart rate were measured during their verbal accounts, and linguistic analysis determined emotion and cognitive processing word use using the Linguistic Inquiry and Word Count program (Pennebaker & Francis, 1996). Results revealed that using more positive emotion words (higher emotion expression) was associated with lower heart rate in each verbal account. Caregivers who used more cognitive processing words (e.g., think, realize, because) overall had the lowest heart rate reactivity to talking about the partner's suffering. These findings showed that expressing positive emotions was related to decreased reactivity for all caregivers, and individual differences in the use of cognitive reappraisal was related to less reactivity. The results suggest that positive emotion expression may be helpful for all caregivers when faced with their loved one's suffering, and that caregivers who try to make sense of their partner's suffering may be more resilient than other caregivers.

Together, research from the coping literature has suggested that problem-focused coping strategies are related to better outcomes than emotion-focused strategies, and research using Gross's model (Gross, 2001) has shown that cognitive appraisal is an adaptive form of emotion regulation for individuals within caregiving dyads. However, more research is needed to understand adaptive forms of emotion regulation in spousal caregiving specifically. This research should examine more strategies of emotion regulation (e.g., antecedent focused), how partners regulate both negative and positive emotions, and how emotion regulation occurs over different time scales.

## INTERPERSONAL EMOTION REGULATION

Caregivers and care recipients can also use interpersonal interactions to regulate each other's emotions. For instance, a spousal caregiver can help regulate a care recipient's emotions and a care recipient can help regulate a caregiver's emotions. Mutual emotion regulation may also occur, such that when both partners interact they regulate each other's emotions.

Gross's (2001) process model of emotion regulation has largely been used to examine intrapersonal emotion regulation; however, it can also be conceptualized in an interpersonal way. We and others have discussed how caregivers can use Gross's emotion regulation strategies to regulate care recipients' emotions (Keefe, Porter, & Labban, 2006; Monin & Schulz, 2010). For example, a strategy drawn from Gross's model that caregivers can use to help alter their own and their partner's emotions is situation modification. This can take the form of the caregiver providing support or encouragement to the care recipient to engage in activities that decrease suffering, which is likely to have a positive impact on both partners' emotions. Although providing support is not typically referred to as an emotion regulation strategy, it is a central facet of interpersonal emotion regulation as discussed by attachment theory (Bowlby, 1982) and new theoretical frameworks of interpersonal emotion regulation (e.g., Zaki & Williams, 2013). The idea that alleviating a partner's suffering can regulate a caregiver's negative emotions also fits with research showing that providing care can have positive health outcomes for caregivers (Brown et al., 2009). Although a large literature shows that caregiving is associated with negative health outcomes, we argue that caring per se may not be what is detrimental to health. What is detrimental is seeing a loved one suffer and feeling helpless.

Typically, negative health effects of being a caregiver are found when caregivers feel emotionally and physically strained. When caregivers do not feel strained and provide more help to their partners, they actually experience positive health outcomes (Beach, Schulz, Yee, & Jackson, 2000).

Care recipients can also play an important role in helping to regulate caregivers' emotions. This is especially the case for caregiving spouses who have been in long-term, committed relationships. Earlier in marriages both partners often assume equivalent obligation to respond to each other's needs if and when such needs arise (communal norms; Mills & Clark, 1982). When one partner experiences a chronic health condition and a marriage transitions to a caregiving relationship, both partners often remain responsible for emotional care, although one partner may take on responsibility for the other's physical care.

Existing research has focused mainly on caregivers' emotional experiences in isolation. Less research has examined how care recipient emotions can impact caregivers. An exception is a study that examined the extent to which care recipients were willing to express their emotions and how this related to caregiving spouses' well-being and caregiving behaviors (Monin, Martire, Schulz, & Clark, 2009). In this study, 262 care recipients with osteoarthritis reported on their willingness to express emotions to their spouse caregivers, and caregivers reported on their stress and insensitive responding to care recipients. Results revealed that care recipients' willingness to express happiness was associated with less insensitive caregiver responding, and their willingness to express interpersonal emotions (e.g., compassion) was associated with less caregiving stress. In addition, caregiving wives in particular benefited from their husband's willingness to express vulnerable (e.g., anxiety) and interpersonal emotions. The results of this study highlight the importance of taking into account both spouses' emotion expression.

Even less research has examined the extent to which both care recipients' and caregivers' emotions relate to caregivers' psychological health. An exception is a recent interview study of individuals with Alzheimer's disease (AD) and their spousal caregivers in which we examined whether both partners' compassionate love related to caregivers' psychological health (Monin, Schulz, & Feeney, 2014). This study was limited to couples in which the individual with AD scored 16 or higher on the Mini-Mental State Examination (Folstein, Folstein, & McHugh, 1975) to ensure reliable reporting. Trained interviewers also rated respondents' ability to complete the interview. *Compassionate love* was defined as

> an attitude toward other(s), either close others or strangers or all of humanity, containing feelings, cognitions, and behaviors that are focused on caring concern, tenderness, and an orientation toward supporting, helping, and understanding the other(s), particularly when the other(s) is (are) perceived to be suffering or in need. (Sprecher & Fehr, 2005, p. 630)

Previous research has demonstrated that compassionate love is associated with increased positive emotions and greater well-being in young adults (Crocker & Canevello, 2008). Consistent with this research with young adults, our results showed that caregivers who felt more compassionate love for their partners reported less burden and more positivity than caregivers who felt less compassionate love. In addition, caregivers who were high in compassionate love had partners who were also high in compassionate love. Furthermore, caregivers' compassionate love mediated the relationship between AD individuals' compassionate love and reduced burden and positive appraisals in the caregiver, suggesting that compassionate love in one partner can facilitate compassionate love in the other, with compassionate love being mutually reinforced (Clark & Monin, 2006).

Thus, emotion regulation is often a mutual process in spousal caregiving couples. However, it is important to acknowledge that this is not an entirely new idea. One emotion regulation theory that focuses on interpersonal dynamics is attachment theory. Although attachment theory has been mainly used to study relationships between parents and children and young romantic relationships, there is increasing attention to its applicability at the later stages of life (Consedine & Magai, 2003). Attachment theory identifies individual differences in people's mental representations of the self and others that evolve out of experiences with close relationship partners in times of need (primarily in early life) and that center around the regulation of distress and the maintenance of felt security (Bretherton, 1985). These mental representations organize past experiences and guide social interaction (e.g., Collins & Allard, 2001). Because not all attachment figures fulfill their roles in equally reliable ways, people develop different attachment styles that are generally assessed along two dimensions: anxiety and avoidance (Brennan, Clark, & Shaver, 1998). The anxiety dimension assesses the degree to which the self is perceived to be unworthy of love and the degree to which the individual is worried about rejection. The avoidance dimension assesses the degree to which individuals are uncomfortable with intimacy and dependence on others.

Attachment theory deals mainly with others' responses to one's own needs, but it is also useful for explaining one's own reactions to others' needs. According to Bowlby (1982), people have a caregiving system that is designed to protect and support others who are dependent and that is guided by an altruistic motive to alleviate another person's distress. However, when one's own security is disrupted, the caregiving system is inhibited, and people become self-focused on their own attachment needs, impeding the ability to behave altruistically (Mikulincer et al., 2001). This self-focus is likely to impact the extent to which caregivers perceive their partners' support-seeking cues (e.g., negative emotion expression), how they interpret those cues, and how they react emotionally (Monin, Feeney, & Schulz, 2012).

We have used attachment theory as a framework to understand care recipients' suffering and how caregiving spouses react to that suffering. In a study of caregiving spouses of persons with musculoskeletal conditions, we examined the association between caregivers' trait attachment style (anxiety and avoidance) and self-reported personal distress in response to their partner's pain (Monin, Schulz, Feeney, & Cook, 2010). We also examined whether perceptions of partner suffering mediated the associations between attachment style and personal distress. We expected that caregivers who were more anxiously attached would feel more distressed than caregivers who were less anxiously attached because they perceive more pain in their partners, whereas more avoidant caregivers would feel less distress than less avoidant caregivers because they see less pain in their partners. Fifty-three spouses watched two videos of targets (their partner and an opposite-sex stranger) perform a pain-eliciting household task, and spouses rated their own distress and perceptions of the targets' pain. Spouses also completed self-report measures of trait attachment. As hypothesized, results revealed that attachment anxiety was associated with greater personal distress in reaction to the partner's suffering, and heightened perceptions of partner pain mediated this association. Avoidant attachment was associated with less distress, but not with less perceived partner pain. This suggests that it is not that avoidant caregivers were less aware of the partner's pain, but that avoidant caregivers may have been trying to present themselves as less affected or vulnerable. Overall, the study showed that not all caregivers perceive and react to their partner's suffering the same way. Some caregivers may be more resilient in the face of partner suffering and others may feel more personal distress depending on their feelings of security in close relationships.

In another study, we examined the extent to which the attachment orientations (anxiety and avoidance) of persons with AD and their spousal caregivers were associated with each partner's report of the physical and psychological health symptoms of the person with AD (Monin, Schulz, & Kershaw, 2013). Fifty-eight individuals with AD and their spousal caregivers each completed a measure of trait attachment orientation and rated the physical and psychological health symptoms of the person with AD over the past 2 weeks. Again, data from the persons with AD were used after determining that they were able to provide reliable responses. As predicted, persons with AD who were high in anxious attachment self-reported more physical and psychological symptoms, particularly when their caregivers were high in anxious attachment. Also, caregivers perceived more physical symptoms in individuals with AD who were high in avoidant attachment. When both care recipients and caregivers were more insecurely attached, care recipients seemed to fare worse than when both partners were more securely attached. These findings support past research showing that anxious individuals, in general, report more physical health problems (McWilliams & Bailey, 2010) and more negative affect (Porter et al., 2012) than less anxious individuals. The findings also add to existing knowledge by showing that the attachment orientation of both partners may have a multiplicative influence on the symptoms of individuals with AD. Insecure care recipients may suffer when caregivers are unable to provide a secure caregiving environment (Solomon & George, 1996) and also when caregivers have increased negative affect (Monin & Schulz, 2009; Wei, Vogel, Ku, & Zakalik, 2005).

Taken together, our work on interpersonal emotion regulation in spousal caregiving suggests that partners who are willing to express vulnerability and positive emotions to one another, who feel more compassionate love for each other, and who are more securely attached tend to be more psychologically resilient. However, more work is needed to examine spouses' use of specific emotion regulation strategies and how these strategies affect both spouses' psychological and physical health. So far, we know more about individual differences in emotion regulation. We need a more process-oriented approach.

## CONTEXTUAL INFLUENCES AND MODERATORS OF EMOTION REGULATION IN SPOUSAL CAREGIVING

When studying emotion regulation processes in spousal caregiving, there are many contextual factors and moderators to take into account. Here we discuss a few. First, the gender of the caregiver and the care recipient likely relate to how both partners regulate their emotions when one partner has a chronic condition that causes suffering. Past research and theory have suggested that female caregivers may be more affected by care recipients' suffering than male caregivers because women pay closer attention to others' emotions (Hall, 1978). Women also tend to be more physiologically responsive to marital conflict than men are (Robles & Kiecolt-Glaser, 2003), and women show more cardiovascular reactivity than men in response to relational events in general (Bloor, Uchino, Hicks, & Smith, 2004). These differences suggest that female caregivers are at a higher risk for suffering the negative consequences of being a caregiver. Indeed, studies have shown that female caregivers are more distressed than are male caregivers and that female caregivers use coping strategies that are less effective in alleviating their distress (Yee & Schulz, 2000). A recent study also showed that men are less likely to report negative experiences and more likely to find positive meaning in family caregiving than women (Lin, Fee, & Wu, 2012). However, more research is needed to examine gender differences in the types of emotion regulation strategies used in spousal caregiving. Also, it is important to better understand the interpersonal dynamics that result from gender norms. Our research suggests that the emotional environment and expectations about emotional expression may be different for male and female caregivers. A study of spousal caregivers of individuals with osteoarthritis showed that male care recipients are less willing to express vulnerability to their wives, but when they do, wives experience less stress (Monin et al., 2009). Furthermore, our work with young adults suggests that women and men may differentially use network members outside of marriage to help regulate their emotions (Monin & Clark, 2011; Monin, Clark, & Lemay, 2008). Specifically, we have found that young adults (both men and women) feel and expect more communal responsiveness in their relationships with females than with males within their extended family networks. *Communal responsiveness* is the degree to which a person feels intrinsically responsible for the welfare of another and attends to the other's needs noncontingently. This can include providing instrumental and emotional support, supporting the partner's goal strivings, and conveying understanding of who the partner is (Clark & Monin, 2006). Although these findings deal with young adults, they may also have implications for how female and male spouse caregivers perceive and use support in their family networks.

Second, age is an important factor in how each spouse regulates his or her own and the partner's emotions in the context of caregiving. According to socioemotional selectivity theory (SST), older adults selectively prune their relationships and maintain only those that are emotionally meaningful, resulting in smaller social networks (Carstensen, 1992). SST argues that this is because as people become older they view time as increasingly limited, and this limited time perspective motivates individuals to make the most of their close relationships. Emotionally meaningful relationships are thought to be conducive to positive emotions; however, a small network of emotionally close individuals also has greater potential for generating negative affect when those network members suffer (Martire et al., 2013). Although Carstensen and colleagues (1995) showed that older married couples manage conflict more effectively than younger couples, older spouses may be more vulnerable to negative emotional contagion from witnessing a partner suffer from illness or disability.

Other theoretical models of age-related changes in emotion regulation suggest that older adults may be more emotionally vulnerable to stress than younger adults. Charles's (2010) Strength and Vulnerability Integration (SAVI) model posits that trajectories of adult development are marked by age-related enhancement in the use of strategies that serve to avoid or limit exposure to negative stimuli but by age-related vulnerabilities in situations that elicit high levels of sustained emotional arousal. Charles suggests that when older adults avoid or reduce exposure to emotional distress, they often respond better than younger adults; however, when they experience high levels of sustained emotional arousal, age-related advantages in emotional well-being are reduced and older adults have greater difficulties returning to homeostasis. Caregiving is one such stressor to which older adults are particularly vulnerable.

Another relevant age-related theory of emotion regulation is the lifespan theory of control (Heckhausen & Schulz, 1993; Schulz & Heckhausen, 1996). The lifespan theory of control states that striving for primary control—achieving effects in the external environment (White, 1959)—is a constant and universal motivational drive throughout the life course. However, as the capacity for primary control declines in old age, people increasingly resort to secondary control strategies of adjusting expectations, values, and attributions to cope with threats to their ability to exert primary control. Accordingly, whereas younger adults may try to use more active strategies (primary control) to try to impact their own and their partners' negative emotions, older adults may use more passive strategies (secondary control). Indeed, research has shown that older adults use more passive strategies (e.g., reappraising the situation) in dealing with everyday interpersonal problems, whereas younger adults use more active strategies (e.g., trying to change the situation or entering into conflict; Blanchard-Fields, Stein, & Watson, 2004). This suggests that in cases where a care recipient's condition cannot be ameliorated, older spouses may be better able to regulate their emotions in the face of caregiving stress than younger couples because of this shift from using active strategies to passive strategies. However, there may also be individual differences in whether people desire primary control regardless of a person's age—individual differences that may impact their psychological well-being. For example, our research showed that when older adults with severe disabilities desire higher levels of primary control (i.e., feel strongly about being functionally independent), they are more susceptible to depressive symptoms when they experience functional decline, whereas those who do not tend to experience less depressive symptoms (Monin, Schulz, Martire, Connelly, & Czaja, 2014).

Third, there are likely to be ethnic and cultural differences in emotion regulation within spousal caregiving. White Americans are more likely to be spousal caregivers, report better physical health, and use more formal services than other ethnic caregiving groups. Meta-analyses also show that White Americans report greater depression and appraise caregiving as more stressful than African American caregivers (Janevic & Connell, 2001; Pinquart & Sörensen, 2005) and that Hispanic and Asian American caregivers are more depressed than White non-Hispanic caregivers (Pinquart & Sörensen, 2005). Although differences in caregiving outcomes are often shown, less is known about the specific pathways that govern these differences. Some studies have indicated that coping processes differ between ethnic groups. For example, Knight and McCallum (1998) showed that African American caregivers use more positive reappraisal than White caregivers. However, other studies found no ethnic differences in cognitive coping (e.g., Barber, 2002), and there are inconsistent findings regarding instrumental coping (e.g., Adams, Aranda,

Kemp, & Takagi, 2002). Researchers have suggested that future studies on cultural and ethnic differences should focus on how the family network, rather than one caregiver, provides support (Aranda & Knight, 1997). Also, it has been suggested that the illness context is dealt with differently across ethnic groups (Pinquart & Sörensen, 2005). Future research should examine cultural differences in emotion regulation strategies specifically in the context of late-life marriage from both caregivers' and care recipients' perspectives.

Fourth, it is important to take into account the quality and closeness of the marriage when striving to understand emotion regulation processes in spousal caregiving. Marital closeness can be a double-edged sword. On the one hand, when spouses are healthy and in high-quality relationships, health appears to be protected and spouses live longer (Robles, Slatcher, Trombello, & McGinn, 2014). Also, when spouses report high pre-illness relationship quality, caregiving spouses are less depressed and less frequently engage in harmful behaviors (Steadman, Tremont, & Davis, 2007; Williamson & Shaffer, 2001). On the other hand, there is increasing evidence that if one partner suffers from a chronic condition, partners who report more closeness are more negatively affected by their partner's pain and negative emotions (e.g., Martire et al., 2013; Tower & Kasl, 1996). One possible reason for this is that spouses who report greater closeness are more empathetic and experience more negative emotional contagion (Batson, Turk, Shaw, & Klein, 1995). In addition to targeting relationships low in marital satisfaction, interventions may also target spouses who are extremely close and help them disengage (e.g., use respite at times) to limit exposure to partner suffering. Future research should also examine what components of relationship quality are protective or place caregivers at greater risk for negative health consequences. Perceptions of self–other overlap (Aron, Aron, & Smollan, 1992), communal responsiveness (Williamson & Schulz, 1995), compassionate love (Monin, Schulz, & Feeney, 2014), and communication (Steadman, Tremont, & Davis, 2007) may differentially affect adaptation to caregiving.

## CONCEPTUAL ISSUES AND DIRECTIONS FOR FUTURE RESEARCH

First, as alluded to earlier in the chapter, there are different ways to study emotion regulation. One way is context or process oriented in which certain situations or contextual factors evoke emotion regulation for all individuals in predictable patterns. The other way is in terms of individual differences such that people tend to favor certain types of emotion regulation strategies. Much of our research has taken an individual difference approach, but the process approach is extremely important and should be an emphasis in future research, along with studies that combine both the process and individual difference approaches. In cases of dementia care, for instance, even people who are experts at regulating their emotions are likely to face situations that challenge their ability to do so successfully.

Second, it is important to distinguish between concepts such as interpersonal emotion regulation (Monin & Schulz, 2010; Zaki & Williams, 2013), emotion coregulation (Butler & Randall, 2013), and dyadic coping (Berg & Upchurch, 2007), as these frameworks may help researchers understand distinct emotional processes in spousal caregiving research. For example, Zaki and Williams (2013) suggested that interpersonal emotion regulation is when a person uses a social interaction to alter his or her own or another person's emotion. These processes can be response dependent (a partner response is needed for the regulation to occur) versus response independent (a partner response is not needed) and intrinsic (the regulation is motivated by an individual) versus extrinsic (the individual's emotion is influenced by a partner's initiation). Zaki and Williams suggested that researchers interpret their findings using this framework to help synthesize information on interpersonal emotion regulation, which has been defined in many ways and may account for inconsistent findings in the field.

Another similar but distinct concept to interpersonal emotion regulation is coregulation. Butler and Randall (2013) defined *coregulation* as the process by which relationship partners form a dyadic emotional system involving an oscillating pattern of affective arousal and dampening that dynamically maintains an optimal emotional state for the dyad. The distinction between coregulation and other interpersonal emotion concepts is that coregulation involves an oscillating pattern of emotional interdependency within a relationship. Supportive behaviors, dyadic coping, and emotion regulation processes all describe interpersonal behavioral patterns that partners might engage in that may, or may not, promote a coregulatory state. Daily diary studies of caregiving couples' fluctuations often capture coregulation (e.g., Berg et al., 2008).

Berg and Upchurch's (2007) developmental-contextual model of couples coping is broader than interpersonal emotion regulation, although interpersonal emotion regulation is likely an important component. Their approach examined the interrelations between partners' adjustment, appraisal, and coping across development and at different stages of a chronic condition (see also Chapter 13, this volume). They emphasized that chronic illness affects the adjustment of both the patient and the spouse and that coping strategies enacted by the patient should be examined in relation to those enacted by the spouse and vice versa. Drawing from Berg and Upchurch's (2007) approach, it will be important to understand how interpersonal emotion regulation strategies change over time in a marriage, the influence of important life transitions, and contextual influences. An example of this is Levinger and Levinger's (2003) article describing their 50-year marriage in which they use a three-level conception of a couple's environment. The macrocontext refers to the prevailing cultural winds in the society that affect all its residents during a given historic era. The mesocontext pertains to the setting in which a particular relationship operates, such as its family and other social networks, physical habits, work settings, or institutions. The microcontext is the couples' own intimate environment, constructed over time by the partners' unique interactions. Each of these contexts likely influences the ways partners regulate their emotions together and separately and how these patterns change over time. For instance, expectations about emotion expression in relationships can be affected by changing societal norms, norms within the extended family or social network, and by the interplay between partners' personalities.

Relatedly, partners' beliefs about the future are likely to be an important part of the emotion regulation process. More work is needed to understand the interpersonal dynamics during the precaregiving period and how people adjust emotionally during this period (Qualls & Williams, 2013). The transition to caregiving usually does not happen overnight but is a gradual process. How people view their relationship and regulate their emotions during this transition is important. The idea that savoring limited time before illness may enhance well-being is illustrated in a quote by Levinger and Levinger (2003):

> Now we are both in our 70s and well aware of our aging. We continue to be active, but we anticipate a time when either of us may be incapacitated or when one of us is alone. In the meantime we treasure that we both still hike, swim, bicycle, and cautiously ski cross-country—and we revel in the fact that we still love being together. In choosing our travels, we try to do now what might be too difficult in the future. We are reminded of life's fragility not only by our own stiff knees and desire for extra sleep, but also by the illnesses and deaths of good friends. (p. 301)

## CLINICAL IMPLICATIONS

Spousal caregivers' and care recipients' emotion regulation experiences are interrelated and have consequences for both partners' health and well-being. Thus, simultaneously targeting care recipients and their spousal caregivers may enhance the efficacy of psychosocial and behavioral interventions (Martire, Schulz, Helgeson, Small, & Saghafi, 2010; see also Chapter 16, this volume). In the course of older adults' daily lives, it may be important for geriatricians to assess and monitor spouses' well-being when they accompany care recipients for appointments. In addition, therapy that directly enhances interpersonal emotion regulation processes for spouse caregiving dyads is likely to be beneficial, such as emotionally focused couple therapy, an empirically based psychotherapy intervention rooted in attachment theory that helps couples manage emotions (Johnson, 2003). Problem-solving therapy (D'Zurilla & Chang, 1995) may also be particularly effective in diminishing caregivers' distress by allowing caregivers the opportunity to (a) identify specific behaviors or symptoms that lead to the perception that the care recipient is suffering, (b) determine which suffering symptoms caregivers can help minimize or alleviate, and (c) come to terms with those aspects of care recipients' suffering that are out of their (the caregivers') control. Finally, it is likely that spouses' emotional well-being in particular will benefit from taking advantage of opportunities for respite (Zarit, Kim, Femia, Almeida, & Klein, 2014) and enlisting other family members to share in caregiving responsibilities (Qualls & Williams, 2013).

## CONCLUDING COMMENTS

Thus far, research has suggested that in spousal caregiving dyads, partners' emotional experiences are highly related and partners often use each other as a resource to alter emotions. Much work to date has focused on identifying individuals who are more or less effective at regulating their emotions. More work is needed to examine effective emotion regulation processes that work for spouse caregivers and their loved ones together. Although there is substantial research on age differences in emotion regulation and on a limited set of emotion-focused coping strategies for caregivers, more work is needed to understand emotion regulation processes in spousal caregiving dyads more specifically. This will require taking into account the rich relational context of late-life marriage and identifying not only problematic emotion regulation strategies, but also adaptive strategies that can lead to more effective interventions for older married couples coping with chronic conditions.

## REFERENCES

Adams, B., Aranda, M. P., Kemp, B., & Takagi, K. (2002). Ethnic and gender differences in distress among Anglo American, African American, Japanese American, and Mexican American caregivers of persons with dementia. *Journal of Clinical Geropsychology, 8,* 279–301. http://dx.doi.org/10.1023/A:1019627323558

Aranda, M. P., & Knight, B. G. (1997). The influence of ethnicity and culture on the caregiver stress and coping process: A sociocultural review and analysis. *The Gerontologist, 37,* 342–354. http://dx.doi.org/10.1093/geront/37.3.342

Aron, A., Aron, E. N., & Smollan, D. (1992). Inclusion of Other in the Self Scale and the structure of interpersonal closeness. *Journal of Personality and Social Psychology, 63*, 596–612. http://dx.doi.org/10.1037/0022-3514.63.4.596

Barber, C. E. (2002, November). *A comparison of Hispanic and non-Hispanic White families caring for elderly patients.* Paper presented at the 55th annual meeting of the Gerontological Society of America, Boston, MA.

Batson, C. D., Turk, C. L., Shaw, L. L., & Klein, T. R. (1995). Information function of empathic emotion: Learning that we value the other's welfare. *Journal of Personality and Social Psychology, 68*, 300–313. http://dx.doi.org/10.1037/0022-3514.68.2.300

Beach, S. R., Schulz, R., Yee, J. L., & Jackson, S. (2000). Negative and positive health effects of caring for a disabled spouse: Longitudinal findings from the caregiver health effects study. *Psychology and Aging, 15*, 259–271. http://dx.doi.org/10.1037/0882-7974.15.2.259

Berg, C. A., & Upchurch, R. (2007). A developmental-contextual model of couples coping with chronic illness across the adult life span. *Psychological Bulletin, 133*, 920–954. http://dx.doi.org/10.1037/0033-2909.133.6.920

Berg, C. A., Wiebe, D. J., Butner, J., Bloor, L., Bradstreet, C., Upchurch, R., . . . Patton, G. (2008). Collaborative coping and daily mood in couples dealing with prostate cancer. *Psychology and Aging, 23*, 505–516. http://dx.doi.org/10.1037/a0012687

Blanchard-Fields, F., Stein, R., & Watson, T. L. (2004). Age differences in emotion-regulation strategies in handling everyday problems. *The Journals of Gerontology: Series B. Psychological Sciences and Social Sciences, 59*, 261–269. http://dx.doi.org/10.1093/geronb/59.6.P261

Bloor, L. E., Uchino, B. N., Hicks, A., & Smith, T. W. (2004). Social relationships and physiological function: The effects of recalling social relationships on cardiovascular reactivity. *Annals of Behavioral Medicine, 28*, 29–38. http://dx.doi.org/10.1207/s15324796abm2801_5

Bowlby, J. (1982). Attachment and loss: Retrospect and prospect. *American Journal of Orthopsychiatry, 52*, 664–678. http://dx.doi.org/10.1111/j.1939-0025.1982.tb01456.x

Brennan, K. A., Clark, C. L., & Shaver, P. R. (1998). Self-report measurement of adult attachment: An integrative overview. In J. A. Simpson & W. S. Rholes (Eds.), *Attachment theory and close relationships* (pp. 46–76). New York, NY: Guilford Press.

Bretherton, I. (1985). Attachment theory: Retrospect and prospect. *Monographs of the Society for Research in Child Development, 50*(1–2), 3–35. http://dx.doi.org/10.2307/3333824

Brown, S. L., Smith, D. M., Schulz, R., Kabeto, M. U., Ubel, P. A., Poulin, M., . . . Langa, K. M. (2009). Caregiving behavior is associated with decreased mortality risk. *Psychological Science, 20*, 488–494. http://dx.doi.org/10.1111/j.1467-9280.2009.02323.x

Butler, E. A., & Randall, A. K. (2013). Emotional coregulation in close relationships. *Emotion Review, 5,* 202–210. http://dx.doi.org/10.1177/1754073912451630

Carstensen, L. L. (1992). Social and emotional patterns in adulthood: Support for socio-emotional selectivity theory. *Psychology and Aging, 7,* 331–338. http://dx.doi.org/10.1037/0882-7974.7.3.331

Carstensen, L. L., Gottman, J. M., & Levenson, R. W. (1995). Emotional behavior in long-term marriage. *Psychology and Aging, 10,* 140–149. http://dx.doi.org/10.1037/0882-7974.10.1.140

Charles, S. T. (2010). Strength and vulnerability integration: A model of emotional well-being across adulthood. *Psychological Bulletin, 136,* 1068–1091. http://dx.doi.org/10.1037/a0021232

Clark, M. S., & Monin, J. K. (2006). Giving and receiving communal responsiveness as love. In R. J. Sternberg & K. Weis (Eds.), *The new psychology of love* (2nd ed., pp. 200–224). New Haven, CT: Yale University Press.

Cole, P. M., Michel, M. K., & O'Donnell Teti, L. (1994). The development of emotion regulation: Biological and behavioral considerations. *Monographs of the Society for Research in Child Development, 59*(2–3), 73–100. http://dx.doi.org/10.2307/1166139

Collins, N. L., & Allard, L. M. (2001). Cognitive representations of attachment: The content and function of working models. In G. J. O. Fletcher & M. S. Clark (Eds.), *Blackwell handbook of social psychology: Vol. 2. Interpersonal processes* (pp. 60–85). London, England: Blackwell.

Consedine, N. S., & Magai, C. (2003). Attachment and emotion experience in later life: The view from emotions theory. *Attachment & Human Development, 5,* 165–187. http://dx.doi.org/10.1080/1461673031000108496

Crocker, J., & Canevello, A. (2008). Creating and undermining social support in communal relationships: The role of compassionate and self-image goals. *Journal of Personality and Social Psychology, 95,* 555–575. http://dx.doi.org/10.1037/0022-3514.95.3.555

del-Pino-Casado, R., Frías-Osuna, A., Palomino-Moral, P. A., & Pancorbo-Hidalgo, P. L. (2011). Coping and subjective burden in caregivers of older relatives: A quantitative systematic review. *Journal of Advanced Nursing, 67,* 2311–2322. http://dx.doi.org/10.1111/j.1365-2648.2011.05725.x

D'Zurilla, T. J., & Chang, E. C. (1995). The relations between social problem solving and coping. *Cognitive Therapy and Research, 19,* 547–562. http://dx.doi.org/10.1007/BF02230513

Felton, B. J., & Revenson, T. A. (1984). Coping with chronic illness: A study of illness controllability and the influence of coping strategies on psychological adjustment. *Journal of Consulting and Clinical Psychology, 52,* 343–353. http://dx.doi.org/10.1037/0022-006X.52.3.343

Folkman, S., & Lazarus, R. S. (1985). If it changes it must be a process: Study of emotion and coping during three stages of a college examination. *Journal* of *Personality and Social Psychology, 48,* 150–170. http://dx.doi.org/10.1037/0022-3514.48.1.150

Folstein, M. F., Folstein, S. E., & McHugh, P. R. (1975). "Mini-mental state": A practical method for grading the cognitive state of patients for the clinician. *Journal of Psychiatric Research, 12,* 189–198. http://dx.doi.org/10.1016/0022-3956(75)90026-6

Gross, J. J. (1998). The emerging field of emotion regulation: An integrative review. *Review of General Psychology, 2,* 271–299. http://dx.doi.org/10.1037/1089-2680.2.3.271

Gross, J. J. (1999). Emotion and emotion regulation. In L. A. Pervin & O. P. John (Eds.), *Handbook of personality: Theory and research* (2nd ed., pp. 525–552). New York, NY: Guilford Press.

Gross, J. J. (2001). Emotion regulation in adulthood: Timing is everything. *Current Directions in Psychological Science, 10,* 214–219. http://dx.doi.org/10.1111/1467-8721.00152

Hall, J. A. (1978). Gender effects in decoding nonverbal cues. *Psychological Bulletin, 85,* 845–857. http://dx.doi.org/10.1037/0033-2909.85.4.845

Heckhausen, J., & Schulz, R. (1993). Optimisation by selection and compensation: Balancing primary and secondary control in life span development. *International Journal of Behavioral Development, 16,* 287–303. http://dx.doi.org/10.1177/016502549301600210

Hoppmann, C., & Gerstorf, D. (2009). Spousal interrelations in old age—a mini-review. *Gerontology, 55,* 449–459. http://dx.doi.org/10.1159/000211948

Janevic, M. R., & Connell, C. M. (2001). Racial, ethnic, and cultural differences in the dementia caregiving experience: Recent findings. *The Gerontologist, 41,* 334–347. http://dx.doi.org/10.1093/geront/41.3.334

Johnson, S. M. (2003). Emotionally focused couples therapy: Empiricism and art. In T. L. Sexton, G. R. Weeks, & M. S. Robbins (Eds.), *Handbook of family therapy: The science and practice of working with families and couples* (pp. 263–280). New York, NY: Brunner-Routledge.

Keefe, F. J., Porter, L. S., & Labban, J. (2006). Emotion regulation processes in disease related pain: A couples-based perspective. In D. K. Snyder, J. A. Simpson, & J. N. Hughes (Eds.), *Emotion regulation in families: Pathways to dysfunction and health* (pp. 207–229). Washington, DC: American Psychological Association. http://dx.doi.org/10.1037/11468-010

Knight, B. G., & McCallum, T. J. (1998). Heart rate reactivity and depression in African-American and white dementia caregivers: Reporting bias or positive coping? *Aging & Mental Health, 2,* 212–221. http://dx.doi.org/10.1080/13607869856696

Levinger, G., & Levinger, A. C. (2003). Winds of time and place: How context has affected a 50-year marriage. *Personal Relationships, 10,* 285–306.

Lin, I. F., Fee, H. R., & Wu, H. S. (2012). Negative and positive caregiving experiences: A closer look at the intersection of gender and relationship. *Family Relations, 61,* 343–358. http://dx.doi.org/10.1111/j.1741-3729.2011.00692.x

Martire, L. M., Schulz, R., Helgeson, V. S., Small, B. J., & Saghafi, E. M. (2010). Review and meta-analysis of couple-oriented interventions for chronic illness. *Annals of Behavioral Medicine, 40*, 325–342. http://dx.doi.org/10.1007/s12160-010-9216-2

Martire, L. M., Stephens, M. A. P., Mogle, J., Schulz, R., Brach, J., & Keefe, F. J. (2013). Daily spousal influence on physical activity in knee osteoarthritis. *Annals of Behavioral Medicine, 45*, 213–223. http://dx.doi.org/10.1007/s12160-012-9442-x

McWilliams, L. A., & Bailey, S. J. (2010). Associations between adult attachment ratings and health conditions: Evidence from the National Comorbidity Survey Replication. *Health Psychology, 29*, 446–453. http://dx.doi.org/10.1037/a0020061

Mikulincer, M., Gillath, O., Halevy, V., Avihou, N., Avidan, S., & Eshkoli, N. (2001). Attachment theory and reactions to others' needs: Evidence that activation of the sense of attachment security promotes empathic responses. *Journal of Personality and Social Psychology, 81*, 1205–1224. http://dx.doi.org/10.1037/0022-3514.81.6.1205

Mills, J., & Clark, M. S. (1982). Exchange and communal relationships. *Review of Personality and Social Psychology, 3*, 121–144.

Monin, J. K., & Clark, M. S. (2011). Why do men benefit more from marriage than do women? Thinking more broadly about interpersonal processes that occur within and outside of marriage. *Sex Roles, 65*(5–6), 320–326. http://dx.doi.org/10.1007/s11199-011-0008-3

Monin, J. K., Clark, M. S., & Lemay, E. P. (2008). Communal responsiveness in relationships with female versus male family members. *Sex Roles, 59*(3–4), 176–188. http://dx.doi.org/10.1007/s11199-008-9420-8

Monin, J. K., Feeney, B. C., & Schulz, R. (2012). Attachment orientation and reactions to anxiety expression in close relationships. *Personal Relationships, 19*, 535–550. http://dx.doi.org/10.1111/j.1475-6811.2011.01376.x

Monin, J. K., Martire, L. M., Schulz, R., & Clark, M. S. (2009). Willingness to express emotions to caregiving spouses. *Emotion, 9*, 101–106. http://dx.doi.org/10.1037/a0013732

Monin, J. K., & Schulz, R. (2009). Interpersonal effects of suffering in older adult caregiving relationships. *Psychology and Aging, 24*, 681–695. http://dx.doi.org/10.1037/a0016355

Monin, J. K., & Schulz, R. (2010). The effects of suffering in chronically ill older adults on the health and well-being of family members involved in their care: The role of emotion-related processes. *GeroPsych: The Journal of Gerontopsychology and Geriatric Psychiatry, 23*, 207–213. http://dx.doi.org/10.1024/1662-9647/a000024

Monin, J. K., Schulz, R., & Feeney, B. C. (2014). Compassionate love in individuals with Alzheimer's disease and their spousal caregivers: Associations with caregivers' psychological health. *The Gerontologist.* Advance online publication. http://dx.doi.org/10.1093/geront/gnu001

Monin, J. K., Schulz, R., Feeney, B. C., & Cook, T. B. (2010). Attachment insecurity and perceived partner suffering as predictors of personal distress. *Journal of Experimental Social Psychology, 46*, 1143–1147. http://dx.doi.org/10.1016/j.jesp.2010.05.009

Monin, J. K., Schulz, R., & Kershaw, T. S. (2013). Caregiving spouses' attachment orientations and the physical and psychological health of individuals with Alzheimer's disease. *Aging & Mental Health, 17*, 508–516. http://dx.doi.org/10.1080/13607863.2012.747080

Monin, J. K., Schulz, R., Lemay, E. P., Jr., & Cook, T. B. (2012). Linguistic markers of emotion regulation and cardiovascular reactivity among older caregiving spouses. *Psychology and Aging, 27*, 903–911. http://dx.doi.org/10.1037/a0027418

Monin, J. K., Schulz, R., Martire, L. M., Connelly, D., & Czaja, S. J. (2014). The personal importance of being independent: Associations with changes in disability and depressive symptoms. *Rehabilitation Psychology, 59*, 35–41. http://dx.doi.org/10.1037/a0034438

Monin, J. K., Schulz, R., Martire, L. M., Jennings, J. R., Lingler, J. H., & Greenberg, M. S. (2010). Spouses' cardiovascular reactivity to their partners' suffering. *The Journals of Gerontology: Series B. Psychological Sciences and Social Sciences, 65B*, 195–201. http://dx.doi.org/10.1093/geronb/gbp133

Pennebaker, J. W., & Francis, M. E. (1996). Cognitive, emotional and language processes in disclosure. *Cognition and Emotion, 10*, 601–626. http://dx.doi.org/10.1080/026999396380079

Pinquart, M., & Sörensen, S. (2005). Ethnic differences in stressors, resources, and psychological outcomes of family caregiving: A meta-analysis. *The Gerontologist, 45*, 90–106. http://dx.doi.org/10.1093/geront/45.1.90

Pinquart, M., & Sörensen, S. (2011). Spouses, adult children, and children-in-law as caregivers of older adults: A meta-analytic comparison. *Psychology and Aging, 26*, 1–14. http://dx.doi.org/10.1037/a0021863

Porter, L. S., Keefe, F. J., Davis, D., Rumble, M., Scipio, C., & Garst, J. (2012). Attachment styles in patients with lung cancer and their spouses: Associations with patient and spouse adjustment. *Supportive Care in Cancer, 20*, 2459–2466.

Qualls, S. H., & Williams, A. A. (2013). *Caregiver family therapy: Empowering families to meet the challenges of aging.* Washington, DC: American Psychological Association. http://dx.doi.org/10.1037/13943-000

Robles, T. F., & Kiecolt-Glaser, J. K. (2003). The physiology of marriage: Pathways to health. *Physiology & Behavior, 79*, 409–416. http://dx.doi.org/10.1016/S0031-9384(03)00160-4

Robles, T. F., Slatcher, R. B., Trombello, J. M., & McGinn, M. M. (2014). Marital quality and health: A meta-analytic review. *Psychological Bulletin, 140*, 140–187. http://dx.doi.org/10.1037/a0031859

Schulz, R., & Beach, S. R. (1999). Caregiving as a risk factor for mortality: The Caregiver Health Effects Study. *JAMA, 282*, 2215–2219. http://dx.doi.org/10.1001/jama.282.23.2215

Schulz, R., Beach, S. R., Hebert, R. S., Martire, L. M., Monin, J. K., Tompkins, C. A., & Albert, S. M. (2009). Spousal suffering and partner's depression and cardiovascular disease: The Cardiovascular Health Study. *The American Journal of Geriatric Psychiatry, 17*, 246–254. http://dx.doi.org/10.1097/JGP.0b013e318198775b

Schulz, R., & Heckhausen, J. (1996). A life span model of successful aging. *American Psychologist, 51*, 702–714. http://dx.doi.org/10.1037/0003-066X.51.7.702

Schulz, R., McGinnis, K. A., Zhang, S., Martire, L. M., Hebert, R. S., Beach, S. R., . . . Belle, S. H. (2008). Dementia patient suffering and caregiver depression. *Alzheimer Disease and Associated Disorders, 22*, 170–176. http://dx.doi.org/10.1097/WAD.0b013e31816653cc

Solomon, J., & George, C. (1996). Defining the caregiving system: Toward a theory of caregiving. *Infant Mental Health Journal, 17*, 183–197. http://dx.doi.org/10.1002/(SICI)1097-0355(199623)17:3<183::AID-IMHJ1>3.0.CO;2-Q

Sprecher, S., & Fehr, B. (2005). Compassionate love for close others and humanity. *Journal of Social and Personal Relationships, 22*, 629–651. http://dx.doi.org/10.1177/0265407505056439

Steadman, P. L., Tremont, G., & Davis, J. D. (2007). Premorbid relationship satisfaction and caregiver burden in dementia caregivers. *Journal of Geriatric Psychiatry and Neurology, 20*, 115–119. http://dx.doi.org/10.1177/0891988706298624

Tower, R. B., & Kasl, S. V. (1996). Depressive symptoms across older spouses: Longitudinal influences. *Psychology and Aging, 11*, 683–697. http://dx.doi.org/10.1037/0882-7974.11.4.683

Vitaliano, P. P., Zhang, J., & Scanlan, J. M. (2003). Is caregiving hazardous to one's physical health? A meta-analysis. *Psychological Bulletin, 129*, 946–972.

Wei, M., Vogel, D. L., Ku, T., & Zakalik, R. A. (2005). Adult attachment, affect regulation, negative mood, and interpersonal problems, the mediating roles of emotional reactivity and emotional cutoff. *Journal of Counseling Psychology, 52*, 14–24. http://dx.doi.org/10.1037/0022-0167.52.1.14

White, R. W. (1959). Motivation reconsidered: The concept of competence. *Psychological Review, 66*, 297–333. http://dx.doi.org/10.1037/h0040934

Williamson, G. M., & Schulz, R. (1995). Caring for a family member with cancer: Past communal behavior and affection reactions. *Journal of Applied Social Psychology, 25*, 93–116.

Williamson, G. M., & Shaffer, D. R. (2001). Relationship quality and potentially harmful behaviors by spousal caregivers: How we were then, how we are now. *Psychology and Aging, 16*, 217–226. http://dx.doi.org/10.1037/0882-7974.16.2.217

Yee, J. L., & Schulz, R. (2000). Gender differences in psychiatric morbidity among family caregivers: A review and analysis. *The Gerontologist, 40*, 147–164. http://dx.doi.org/10.1093/geront/40.2.147

Zaki, J., & Williams, W. C. (2013). Interpersonal emotion regulation. *Emotion, 13*, 803–810. http://dx.doi.org/10.1037/a0033839

Zarit, S. H., Kim, K., Femia, E. E., Almeida, D. M., & Klein, L. C. (2014). The effects of adult day services on family caregivers' daily stress, affect, and health: Outcomes from the Daily Stress and Health (DaSH) Study. *The Gerontologist, 54*, 570–579. http://dx.doi.org/10.1093/geront/gnt045

# 15

# CHRONIC DISEASE MANAGEMENT IN OLDER COUPLES: SPOUSAL SUPPORT VERSUS CONTROL STRATEGIES

MELISSA M. FRANKS, ELIZABETH WEHRSPANN, KRISTIN J. AUGUST, KAREN S. ROOK, AND MARY ANN PARRIS STEPHENS

Among adults in their later years of life, the management of chronic illness is a common experience. By age 65, about three quarters of adults are managing at least one chronic illness, and the prevalence of chronic conditions increases with age (Fabbri et al., 2015; Weiss, Boyd, Yu, Wolff, & Leff, 2007; Wolff, Starfield, & Anderson, 2002). Demands of managing chronic illness, such as adoption and maintenance of lifestyle modifications and medication administration, can begin in the middle years for some adults. For example, in 2010 over one million adults ages 45 to 64 were diagnosed with diabetes (Centers for Disease Control and Prevention, 2011), thus the complex daily management of chronic disease often will span several decades into their later years of life. For married adults, chronic disease management often extends beyond the ill partner alone to include involvement of spouses (e.g., Berg & Upchurch, 2007; see also Chapters 13 and 16, this volume). This chapter examines spouses' efforts to promote chronic disease management

http://dx.doi.org/10.1037/14897-016
*Couple Relationships in the Middle and Later Years: Their Nature, Complexity, and Role in Health and Illness,*
J. Bookwala (Editor)

in their ill partner and the impact of such involvement on both spouses in middle-aged and older couples.

For couples who have shared much of their lives together, involving a spouse in modifying lifestyle routines, such as diet and exercise, may be a return to challenges they typically encountered earlier in their marriage. During the transition to marriage, newly married partners often work together to negotiate similar patterns of diet and exercise, drinking habits, and routine physical exams (Homish & Leonard, 2008; Leonard & Mudar, 2003). For example, in a qualitative analysis of food choices among newlyweds, eating habits of each partner gradually merged into a "joint couple food system" (Bove, Sobal, & Rauschenbach, 2003). Correspondence in partners' food choices can come about when one partner adopts the diet habits of the other and when partners modify dietary patterns together, such as consuming more fruits and vegetables.

It is increasingly recognized that health behaviors of married partners are often concordant in the later years of marriage (e.g., Graham & Braun, 1999; see also Meyler, Stimpson, & Peek, 2007, for a review). Reports from midlife and older marital partners reveal similarity in their dietary patterns (Graham & Braun, 1999) and in their body mass index (Stimpson, Masel, Rudkin, & Peek, 2006). Spouses also are similar in their alcohol consumption and smoking behaviors (Graham & Braun, 1999; Stimpson et al., 2006). Moreover, change by one partner in behaviors such as smoking, alcohol consumption, exercising, and cholesterol screenings is related to change in the same behavior by the spouse (Falba & Sindelar, 2008; Franks, Pienta, & Wray, 2002). A large, longitudinal study of social network influences on obesity documented an increased likelihood of an individual becoming obese if the spouse was obese, and this increased likelihood was similar for both husbands and wives (Christakis & Fowler, 2007). Further, married partners are similar in their readiness to change their diet or exercise patterns (Franks, Shields, et al., 2012). Considered together, these findings suggest that married partners' efforts to modify health risk behaviors may be coordinated in the context of their shared environment and lifestyles well into their later years of life.

One catalyst that may propel spouses to renegotiate their shared lifestyle routines later in life is when one partner experiences the onset of a chronic illness. When the diagnosis of a chronic illness of one partner requires sustained changes to her or his health behaviors and lifestyle, both married partners may work together to adjust daily patterns and routine health behaviors that they established in their early years of marriage to better align with current demands of illness management (Berg & Upchurch, 2007; Lewis et al., 2006). Specifically, in their model of interdependence and health behavior change, Lewis and colleagues (2006) conceptualized the adoption and maintenance of health behaviors as a process that often occurs in the context of interdependent relationships rather than solely in the context of individual efforts. Considerable attention has been given to strategies spouses use to promote the maintenance of recommended health behavior changes in their chronically ill partners and to how spouses' strategies are associated with ill partners' disease management, as discussed in the next two sections.

## SPOUSAL SUPPORT AND CONTROL
## IN CHRONIC ILLNESS MANAGEMENT

For partners managing chronic illness, spouse involvement often involves providing aid to promote their ongoing efforts to adhere to treatment recommendations, referred to as *health-related support*. Spouses may provide health-related support to ill partners in a variety of ways including sharing healthy meals together, listening to their ill partners' concerns about managing their disease, and encouraging their ill partners to sustain adherence to a healthy diet plan and regular exercise. Spousal involvement also can take the form of efforts to exert influence or control to bring about improved adherence to treatment recommendations, which we refer to as *health-related control* (e.g., Franks et al., 2006; Franks, Wendorf, Gonzalez, & Ketterer, 2004; Stephens et al., 2009) and is more generally referred to as *social control* (Umberson, 1992). Health-related control includes spouses' attempts to motivate healthier choices among ill partners such as reminding them about a treatment recommendation and why the behavior is recommended for properly managing their disease. Spouses' use of health-related control also can involve strategies intended to compel ill partners to improve their behavioral adherence, including criticizing partners' health choices and expressing irritation.

A key conceptual distinction between health-related support and health-related control hinges on the illness management efforts of the chronically ill partner (e.g., Franks et al., 2006; Stephens et al., 2013). Specifically, when ill partners are attempting to maintain adherence to treatment recommendations, involvement by their spouses can be directed at promoting their efforts through health-related support (e.g., encouraging sustained adherence to treatment recommendations, showing appreciation for importance of behavior modification). Alternatively, when efforts of ill partners to adopt and maintain recommended lifestyle modifications are irregular or absent, spouses' involvement may be directed at bringing about desired changes in their partners' behaviors to better align with disease management recommendations through health-related control (e.g., questioning their partners' poor choices, warning partners about consequences of nonadherence). Spouses' attempts to influence their ill partners' unhealthy choices through health-related control strategies can be further distinguished as efforts to persuade them to alter their behavior versus efforts to apply pressure to induce them to modify unhealthy behavior choices (Stephens et al., 2009, 2013).

Recent conceptualizations of health-related support and health-related control emphasize the interplay between ill partners' efforts to manage their disease and their spouses' efforts to facilitate proper management as well as to get their ill partners back on track after setbacks in treatment adherence. For instance, in studies of married couples managing Type 2 diabetes, spouses' diet-related support has been operationalized as doing something to help the partner stick with a healthy diet and showing understanding for the importance of following a healthy meal plan (e.g., Franks, Sahin, et al., 2012; Stephens et al., 2013). In contrast, spouses' diet-related control has been operationalized as expressing irritation with the ill partners' poor food choices (diet-related pressure; e.g., Franks, Sahin, et al., 2012; Stephens et al., 2013) and trying to persuade the ill partners to improve food choices (diet-related persuasion; e.g., Stephens et al., 2013).

Given the complexity of behaviors involved in treatment regimens for chronic illness, ill partners may be adhering well to some aspects of the regimen (e.g., avoiding high fat foods) and at the same time adhering poorly to other components of the regimen (e.g., consuming recommended amounts of fruits and vegetables). For this reason, spouses sometimes engage in both health-related support and health-related control as they traverse the demands of chronic disease management with their ill partners (Franks et al., 2004, 2006; Khan et al., 2013; Stephens et al., 2013). Although nearly all spouses report engaging in health-related support (Franks et al., 2004; Stephens et al., 2013), spouses' reports of engaging in health-related control, particularly pressure, generally are less frequent (Franks, Sahin, et al., 2012; Stephens et al., 2013).

Differences in the frequency with which spouses engage in health-related control strategies relative to health-related support strategies may be attributable, in part, to gender differences in spouses' use of health-related control to try to improve the disease management of ill partners. Among married couples, wives act as an agent of health-related control in influencing health behaviors of their partners more often than do husbands (August & Sorkin, 2010; Umberson, 1992). Consistent with gender differences in the larger literature on social control, several studies have shown that wives report receiving less health-related control (and less health-related support) than do husbands (Franks et al., 2004; Rook, August, Stephens, & Franks, 2011), but this difference is not found in other work (e.g., Franks, Sahin, et al., 2012). This variability in findings could reflect differences in ways of operationalizing social control. Gender differences have emerged thus far in studies that emphasize strategies of health-related control that do not connote irritation with or disapproval of the recipient, such as providing prompts and reminders or advice and warnings about poor health behaviors (e.g., Rook, August, Stephens, et al., 2011). In contrast, no gender difference emerged in one study that emphasized strategies of health-related control that conveyed disapproval, such as expressing irritation with or criticizing the recipient's poor health behaviors (Franks, Sahin, et al., 2012). In these studies, disapproval and criticism occurred infrequently and appears to be eschewed by husbands and wives alike.

Health-related support may be reported more frequently than health-related control, particularly in a chronic illness context, because ill partners are making efforts to adhere to their treatment regimen. Additionally, ill partners may hide their nonadherent behaviors from their spouses. As a result, ill partners' adherence (or appearance of adherence) to their treatment recommendations may elicit spouses' health-related support more often than health-related control.

It is important to reiterate that both health-related support and health-related control are conceptualized as efforts by others to promote ill partners' adherence to treatment regimens to benefit their health outcomes. Notably, however, spouses' health-related control sometimes is associated with poorer behavioral adherence and with greater emotional distress among their ill partners. In the next section, drawing from several dyadic studies focused on spouse involvement in the disease management of their ill partners (e.g., Stephens et al., 2013), ill partners' responses to health-related support and health-related control enacted by their spouses are discussed. Later in this chapter, spouses' feelings of distress and burden associated with their involvement in their ill partners' chronic disease management also are discussed.

## ASSOCIATIONS WITH ILL PARTNERS' ADHERENCE AND WELL-BEING

When spouses provide health-related support to facilitate their ill partners' treatment adherence, their ill partners often do exhibit better adherence and greater psychological well-being (e.g., Franks et al., 2006; Stephens et al., 2013). Spouse support has been found to be associated with better adherence in daily diary studies of diet and exercise behaviors among partners with type 2 diabetes (Khan et al., 2013; Stephens et al., 2013), and it has been linked longitudinally to better health behaviors among ill partners participating in cardiac rehabilitation (Franks et al., 2006). Spouses' health-related support also was associated with improved mental health over time among partners participating in cardiac rehabilitation (Franks et al., 2006). Spouses' diet-related support, however, was not associated with disease-specific distress (i.e., diabetes distress) among partners with Type 2 diabetes (Franks, Sahin, et al., 2012; Stephens et al., 2013). Notably, both health-related support and ill partners' emotional well-being have been conceptualized in different ways across studies, which may, in part, account for differences in detected associations of spouses' provision of health-related support with their ill partners' emotional well-being.

In contrast to spouses' provision of health-related support, spouses' efforts to exert health-related control are less consistently associated with improved behavioral adherence among their ill partners. When health-related control is provided by spouses in an effort to improve their ill partners' adherence, it often has been associated instead with less adherence to the treatment regimen (Franks et al., 2006; Helgeson, Novak, Lepore, & Eton, 2004; Khan et al., 2013; Rook, August, Stephens, et al., 2011; Stephens, Rook, Franks, Khan, & Iida, 2010; Stephens et al., 2013). For instance, spouses' health-related control in the form of giving warnings to try to get partners with Type 2 diabetes to improve their diet was associated with poor diet adherence. Spouses' health-related control in the form of encouraging partners to make improvements to their diet was positively associated with diet adherence, however (Stephens et al., 2010). In studies where health-related control was conceptualized as distinct strategies of pressure and persuasion, pressure was linked with poor behavioral adherence and with poor well-being (e.g., Stephens et al., 2013); was unrelated to ill partners' health outcomes (e.g., Franks, Sahin, et al., 2012); or less often, was associated with desired behavioral responses to spouses' health-related control (e.g., Stephens et al., 2009). Findings for persuasion also were mixed, with persuasion linked to better behavioral adherence among partners recovering from knee replacement surgery (Stephens et al., 2009) but related to worse diet adherence among partners with Type 2 diabetes (Stephens et al., 2013).

Several factors shape the association of ill partners' adherence and well-being with spouses' provision of health-related control, including spouses' concurrent provision of health-related support (Khan et al., 2013) as well as dyadic (Stephens et al., 2013) and ill partner (Rook, August, Stephens, et al., 2011) expectations about how spouses should behave in a relationship. For example, wives with diabetes were less likely than husbands with diabetes to hold normative expectations that their spouses should be involved in their illness management (Rook, August, Stephens, et al., 2011). Perhaps it is not surprising, therefore, that wives with diabetes who held these expectations exhibited greater behavioral resistance to their husbands' health-related control attempts. Among husbands with diabetes, in contrast, normative expectations about a spouse's role in illness management did not appear to influence their behavioral responses to health-related control. Some couples, moreover, appear to approach the tasks involved in diabetes management as a shared responsibility. Among such couples, spouses' diet-related pressure appeared to be detrimental, as those ill partners who experienced more pressure exhibited worse dietary adherence and greater diabetes distress (Stephens et al., 2013). Pressure tactics may be particularly aversive to ill partners who expect their spouses to approach their diabetes management as a collaborative task to be managed cooperatively.

It merits mention that differences in associations between ill partners' disease management and spouses' engagement in health-related support and control may depend on whether it is the ill partner or the spouse who is reporting the health-related interaction (e.g., Stephens et al., 2010). Such differences may result when spouses' health-related efforts are misinterpreted, are attributed to attempts to exert control, or are unobserved by their ill partners. For example, what a spouse may intend as a health-promoting gesture, such as encouraging a healthier food choice, may not always be interpreted as such by the ill partner. Some interactions, for instance giving warnings about nonadherence, initiated by spouses in an attempt to aid their ill partners may come across as controlling (and coercive) to ill partners and may backfire; alternatively, they may go unnoticed by ill partners and thus be ineffective. Related work has indicated that the perceptions of the health-related support and control marital partners receive from one another are not merely an account of what their spouses report providing to them, but also reflect their own provision of health-related support (or control) to their spouses (Franks et al., 2004; Hong et al., 2005). Thus, given that spouses and their ill partners may not always be in tune with one another about the quantity or quality of their health-related interactions, it is important to consider both partners' perspectives to fully understand the complex, interpersonal dynamics occurring in the context of illness management.

## ASSOCIATIONS WITH SPOUSES' OWN WELL-BEING

For a more complete understanding of how chronic disease management impacts both members of a couple, a spouse's own well-being must be considered along with adherence and well-being outcomes for a chronically ill partner. Effects on spouses of continuously providing support to ill partners have been examined in the literature on family caregiving (discussed next). Little research, however, has focused on the implications of engaging in health-related control for spouses' own well-being.

Here, we present findings and conclusions from the broader literature on spouse caregiving. Notably, much of that literature has focused on direct, hands-on provision of care to partners who are unable to take care of themselves because of physical, emotional, or cognitive difficulties. Caregiving thus involves tasks that go beyond spouses' efforts to promote proper disease management per se, such as assistance with basic activities of daily living (e.g., bathing, grooming, feeding). Because spouses are the most common, and oftentimes only, source of such intensive care to ill partners, spousal caregiving can be particularly stressful (Marks, 1998) and is associated with an increased risk of physical health problems and psychological distress (Pinquart & Sörensen, 2003; Vitaliano, Zhang, & Scanlan, 2003).

Even though negative effects of spousal caregiving have been documented extensively, it is important to note that some studies have reported positive effects (e.g., Brown et al., 2009). For example, among spouses who were caring for partners with Parkinson's disease, those who were able to find purpose in life were significantly more likely to experience positive affect (Konstam et al., 2003). In a study of family caregivers (that included spouses), the majority of caregivers could generate at least one aspect of their caregiving experience that they found to be rewarding, fulfilling, or enjoyable; these positive feelings, in turn, decreased the negative consequences of caregiving (Cohen, Colantonio, & Vernich, 2002).

More generally, providing support in the context of illness may be associated with positive emotions to the extent that it is perceived as a rewarding experience (e.g., Liang, Krause, & Bennett, 2001). For example, in a study of couples in which one member had multiple sclerosis, exchanges of instrumental support between spouses and their ill partners were related to positive mood among both members of the couple (Kleiboer, Kuijer, Hox, Schreurs, & Bensing, 2006). Spouses' positive mood likely stemmed from feelings of usefulness in being able to aid their partners, consistent with research suggesting that providing support may promote feelings of self-worth (Krause, Herzog, & Baker, 1992). Of course, it also may be that positive mood among ill partners motivates spouses' provision of support.

Consistent with the larger caregiving literature, recent research has documented that providing health-related support to promote ill partners' disease management is linked with spouses' well-being. Spouses who provided more diet-related support to ill partners with Type 2 diabetes experienced fewer negative outcomes, such as feeling less stress (August, Rook, Franks, & Stephens, 2013). Likewise, the association between provision of health-related support and well-being was documented among spouses of partners with osteoarthritis (Martire et al., 2006).

The extent to which providing health-related support has positive implications for spouses' well-being likely depends on characteristics of the disease and its treatment regimen. For example, if treatment activities involve tasks that spouses can readily evaluate and facilitate, such as preparing healthy meals, spouses may be more likely to experience positive affect (Poulin et al.,

2010). Likewise, the nature of the spousal relationship may play a role in the link between spouses' provision of support and their own well-being. Spouses who are more satisfied with their marriage and view disease management as collaborative are more likely to experience positive emotions as a result of providing support (Berg & Upchurch, 2007; Poulin et al., 2010). Notably, however, spouses who are less satisfied with their marriage and who view disease management as a task their ill partners should manage independently are less likely to experience positive emotions (and more likely to experience negative emotions) when they provide support.

As indicated earlier, few studies have investigated whether exerting health-related control affects spouses' emotional well-being. Exerting health-related control may be detrimental to a spouse's well-being because of the responsibility involved in persistently monitoring and attempting to influence the behavior of a partner who is not successfully self-regulating her or his own behavior (Miller & Brown, 2005). Spouses also may experience (and may convey) frustration and disappointment if they feel that their efforts to regulate the health behaviors of their ill partners have been unsuccessful (August, Rook, Stephens, & Franks, 2011). Frequent efforts to monitor and influence their ill partners' treatment adherence may also disrupt spouses' own routines and consume their energy (Beverly, Penrod, & Wray, 2007). Moreover, spouses' experience of negative emotions when they engage in health-related control likely depends on a number of factors such as their partners' adherence to prescribed health behaviors, partners' behavioral reactions to spouses' health-related control attempts, disease duration, and presence of other comorbid health conditions of partners. For example, negative reactions of ill partners to their spouses' efforts to exert health-related control (e.g., ignoring or doing the opposite of what spouses request) may amplify spouses' feelings of burden and stress.

Empirical work focused on the link between spouses' well-being and their provision of health-related control to partners with Type 2 diabetes has shown that providing health-related control is associated with feelings of burden and stress (August et al., 2011, 2013) and that engaging in particularly negative forms of health-related control, such as criticism or pressure, is associated with feelings of disease-specific distress among spouses (Franks, Sahin, et al., 2012). Because these studies focused only on health-related control exchanges in the context of managing Type 2 diabetes, however, links to spouses' well-being cannot be generalized to other chronic diseases, particularly illnesses that involve less complex and intensive regimens. Additional research is needed to determine the extent to which exerting health-related control is a negative experience for spouses whose partners are afflicted with other chronic conditions.

## OTHER FORMS OF SPOUSES' INVOLVEMENT
## IN CHRONIC ILLNESS MANAGEMENT

The preceding sections highlighted health-related support and health-related control as two key aspects of spouses' involvement in their partners' chronic disease management. Notably, other forms of spouse involvement (e.g., communication, undermining) and a wider range of consequences for spouses, ill partners, and their relationship as a result of such involvement have received attention in the larger research literature on marriage and health (Robles, Slatcher, Trombello, & McGinn, 2014). For instance, whether and how spouses and their ill partners communicate about behavioral adherence can shape not only disease management efforts, but also affect the well-being of each partner and the quality of their relationship. Although a detailed review of these aspects of spouse involvement and consequences for spouses and ill partners is not the purpose of our chapter, these topics merit brief mention for a more complete representation of research on spousal involvement in their ill partners' disease management.

Spouses' strategies of communicating about the illness and its management with their ill partners include engaging in problem-solving discussions about modifying a target behavior, rationing talk, and discussions about when and how to communicate with one another about their partners' adherence (i.e., metacommunication; Goldsmith, Bute, & Lindholm, 2012). For instance, willingness of ill partners to make recommended lifestyle changes opens the door for problem-solving discussions with their spouses about how to make and sustain a given change (e.g., becoming more physically active). For some ill partners, repeated discussions about maintaining a lifestyle change can be detrimental to their sense of autonomy. In these circumstances, spouses may opt to select the most opportune times to address nonadherence, rather than comment on every breach of their ill partners' treatment regimen (i.e., rationing talk). It is important to note that spouses may accompany use of restraint and rationing talk about lifestyle change with metacommunication (discussions about content and timing of communication). This combination of communication strategies is useful to inform their ill partners that spouses remain involved and concerned with their disease management, but at the same time, spouses are respectful of their ill partners' decisions and autonomy. When spouses and ill partners optimize their communication strategies to manage the meanings of their health-related exchanges in such ways, their interactions may be more effective in promoting treatment adherence among partners with chronic illness (Goldsmith et al., 2012).

In contrast to actions that spouses perform to promote effective disease management of their ill partners, spouses may at times act in ways that disrupt or weaken their partners' disease management. One study that investigated such spouse undermining in the context of Type 2 diabetes found that spouses sometimes tempted partners to eat proscribed foods, thus disrupting and interfering with their ill partners' adherence to their dietary regimen, and that spouses sometimes expressed disregard for their partners' dietary regimen (Henry, Rook, Stephens, & Franks, 2013). These spouse behaviors were reported by ill partners to have occurred relatively infrequently, but they were associated, nonetheless, with poorer dietary adherence.

The ways in which spouses and ill partners navigate the management of chronic illness can affect not only their individual well-being, but also the quality of their marriage. Notably, relationships in which both partners share responsibility for illness management and engage in joint efforts to manage the disease have been found to be associated with individual well-being (Berg et al., 2008) and relationship satisfaction of both partners (e.g., Schokker et al., 2010). Spouses' attempts to conceal their concerns, in contrast, are associated with emotional distress (Manne et al., 2007) and with lower relationship satisfaction, particularly when involvement in joint efforts to manage the illness is limited (Schokker et al., 2010).

Marital quality plays an important part in shaping marital interactions that are posited to influence individual health and well-being (Robles et al., 2014). In general, marital strain or conflict is linked with changes in physiological responses such as cardiovascular and immune functioning, and taxing these physiological processes has implications for poor physical health outcomes in the longer term (Robles & Kiecolt-Glaser, 2003). More specifically, a high-quality marriage has been identified as a key predictor of long-term survival among partners with chronic disease (e.g., Coyne et al., 2001; King & Reis, 2012). Thus, recognizing the ways in which the overall quality of the relationship can enhance (or detract from) health-protective interactions between partners is essential to furthering understanding of the benefits and costs of spouses' involvement in disease management of ill partners.

## LOOKING AHEAD: DIRECTIONS FOR FUTURE RESEARCH AND IMPLICATIONS FOR HEALTH CARE POLICY AND PRACTICE

Given the well-documented association between marriage and health (e.g., Burman & Margolin, 1992; Kiecolt-Glaser & Newton, 2001; see also Chapter 10, this volume), considerable attention has been paid to mechanisms through which this central social tie can promote individual health and well-being. As noted throughout this chapter, a key health benefit of marriage in couples' later years is spouses' provision of health-related support to facilitate disease management of ill partners. An accumulating body of work provides consistent evidence that spouses often engage in supportive efforts to facilitate partners' disease management (e.g., Rosland, Heisler, & Piette, 2012; Rosland et al., 2013; Stephens et al., 2013) and that health-related interactions with spouses are consequential for ill partners' ability to manage their disease successfully (for a review, see Berg & Upchurch, 2007). Moreover, spouses' efforts to promote their ill partners' treatment adherence include assistance with multiple complex behaviors such as lifestyle choices, self-monitoring, and medication administration as evidenced in studies of a wide array of illnesses including heart disease, diabetes, cancer, and osteo-arthritis (see reviews by Martire, Schulz, Helgeson, Small, & Saghafi, 2010; and Rosland et al., 2012).

In emphasizing the potential health advantage of a supportive spouse who is available to provide care and assistance with managing a chronic ill-ness, it is important not to overlook potential costs of spouse involvement. Foremost, spouse involvement in the form of health-related control can some-times backfire, resulting in poorer adherence to treatment recommendations among ill partners (Franks et al., 2006; Helgeson et al., 2004; Stephens et al., 2013). Such effects of health-related control are opposite to those intended by a well-meaning spouse. Moreover, spouses can experience distress as a result of their involvement in disease management with their ill partners, particularly when such involvement involves health-related control attempts (e.g., August et al., 2011). Thus, an important direction for future research is delineating interpersonal exchanges and intrapersonal resources that may enhance the benefits and limit the potential costs of spouse involvement for both spouses and ill partners.

Greater attention should be paid to the ways in which partners inter-act and communicate about managing chronic illness. Investigating patterns of communication between partners has the potential to shed light on the ways that a couple's interpersonal dynamics may shape the spouse's efforts to aid and influence the health behavior choices of the ill partners as well as the ill partner's responses to these efforts (Goldsmith et al., 2012). For example, use of control tactics, such as warning ill partners about potential overexertion, may be reduced when a spouse is engaged in a given activity with the ill partner and can directly evaluate his or her ability to perform the activity. More generally, Goldsmith and colleagues (2012) posited that when spouses recognize that each can benefit from a lifestyle change, this shared understanding uniquely frames the purpose and effectiveness of their inter-actions. Consistent with this view, couples who are concordant in enacting a given health behavior engage in more problem-solving discussions about the behavior (Goldsmith et al., 2012), have more congruent perceptions of sup-portive exchanges related to the target behavior (Hong et al., 2005), and may share greater motivation to attempt or sustain the behavior change (Reczek & Umberson, 2012) than discordant couples.

The importance of cooperative efforts of married partners to jointly modify their health behaviors is emphasized in the interdependence model of behavior change developed by Lewis and colleagues (2006). Similarly, in the context of couples coping with chronic illness, a joint understanding between spouses and their ill partners that the illness and its management are shared stressors may promote more frequent collaborative behaviors and fewer attempts by spouses to exert control over their ill partners (Berg & Upchurch, 2007). Drawing from these dyadic frameworks, cooperative efforts of spouses and ill partners to modify shared routines and lifestyles to promote one another's health may enhance perceptions of collaboration related to disease management. Further, couples' cooperative efforts may foster a supportive relational context in which spouses' attempts to exert health-related control may be less caustic to ill partners, to their relationship, and to spouses themselves (Rook, August, & Sorkin, 2011). It is anticipated that such "mutual joint effects may be the most effective in sustaining health behavior change in the context of close relationships" (Lewis et al., 2006, p. 1373).

Spouses' involvement in chronic illness management may facilitate their ill partners' adherence to treatment recommendations through bolstering intrapersonal resources of ill partners, such as self-efficacy and self-regulation (e.g., Stephens, Hemphill, Rook, & Franks, 2014). Self-efficacy consistently is associated with greater persistence in enacting target behaviors (Bandura, 2004), including health behaviors crucial to disease management. It is important to note that supportive interactions promote perceptions of self-efficacy to engage in healthy lifestyle behaviors (e.g., healthy diet) among individuals with chronic illness (Rosland et al., 2008; Williams & Bond, 2002). In this way, helpful efforts of spouses have the potential to enhance the confidence of ill partners in their ability to carry out the daily routines essential to proper disease management and thereby to promote their health and delay or offset disease-related complications. Thus, actively involving both spouses and ill partners in clinical programs and research interventions designed to improve adherence of ill partners may foster their supportive interactions, which in turn can promote proper disease management of ill partners (see Chapter 16, this volume, for a discussion of the potential efficacy of couple-based interventions in promoting better disease management).

Assistance from spouses also may aid efforts by ill partners to sustain self-regulation of their complex treatment regimen with daily management tasks. As described by Stephens and her colleagues (2014), individuals' self-regulation of health behaviors may wane from the vigilance necessary in monitoring and maintaining adherence to treatment recommendations in the context of chronic illness (see also Baumeister, Vohs, & Tice, 2007).

To counter such lapses in self-regulation, effective health-related support from spouses may serve to reenergize their ill partners' self-regulatory efforts particularly when they are taxed by the demands of illness management. Spouses' involvement in the form of health-related control strategies, however, does not appear to protect or bolster their ill partners' self-regulation of health behaviors essential to disease management (see Stephens et al., 2014), though additional research is warranted.

Although the research discussed in this chapter has emphasized spouses' efforts to foster their partners' management of chronic illness, it is important to note that such efforts are not limited to the marital context (e.g., Shaw, Gallant, Riley-Jacome, & Spokane, 2006). Individuals with chronic illness sometimes are assisted by other family members who reside with them and by those who are involved from a distance (e.g., Rosland et al., 2013). Family members and friends also may attempt to promote better disease management among individuals with chronic illness through strategies of social control (Grzywacz et al., 2012). Health-related control provided by family members and friends, like that provided by spouses, can also backfire, contributing to poorer disease management and more depressive symptoms (Grzywacz et al., 2012). In addition, recent work has investigated health-promoting interactions and gendered interpersonal dynamics, described as "health behavior work," in straight, gay, and lesbian couples (Reczek & Umberson, 2012). Increased attention to the broader relational contexts within which individuals manage chronic illness is a clear direction for future research.

Health care policy and practice may benefit from recognizing and representing the needs of spouses in the development and evaluation of educational programs designed to promote ill partners' disease management (Orvik, Ribu, & Johansen, 2010). Providing skills training and education to spouses (and other support partners) may reduce identified barriers to providing support, such as lack of knowledge about the disease and its management, and thereby enhance available support to ill partners (Rosland et al., 2013). Additionally, training about the benefits of health-promoting behaviors not only for ill partners' disease management but also for overall health might encourage spouses to jointly make modifications to their own lifestyle habits and routines.

Another policy recommendation that grows out of research on spouse involvement in disease management of ill partners is to encourage health care providers to initiate discussions with their patients about ways they can work together with their spouses most effectively to promote disease management. Increased knowledge among health care providers regarding the health-related support available to (or absent for) their patients will enable providers to tailor available formal interventions to the needs of patients and their spouses. Policies designed to recognize the involvement of spouses and programs developed specifically to include spouses in disease management training and education may have an additional advantage of reducing spouses' distress associated with attempts to improve disease management of their ill partners (Martire & Schulz, 2007). Effective couples' interventions that involve components such as education about the disease and its management and the role of relationships in disease management (Martire et al., 2010; see also Chapter 16, this volume) have the potential to improve ill partners' disease management and promote psychosocial outcomes for ill partners and their spouses.

In conclusion, effective involvement of spouses in the disease management of chronically ill partners can promote treatment adherence and reduce or delay disease complications. As such, developing and implementing strategies to bolster support and aid available to ill partners and their spouses can improve chronic disease management, thereby reducing health care costs for patients, families, and society (Centers for Disease Control and Prevention, 2011). It is crucial to recognize, however, that spouse involvement through health-related control may not always result in desirable outcomes for ill partners and their spouses. Finally, translating research findings about the potential benefits (and costs) of health-related interactions between ill partners and spouses into patient education programs and couple interventions may promote disease management and limit emotional and relational costs to ill partners and their spouses.

## REFERENCES

August, K. J., Rook, K. S., Franks, M. M., & Stephens, M. A. P. (2013). Spouses' involvement in their partners' diabetes management: Associations with spouse stress and perceived marital quality. *Journal of Family Psychology, 27,* 712–721. http://dx.doi.org/10.1037/a0034181

August, K. J., Rook, K. S., Stephens, M. A. P., & Franks, M. M. (2011). Are spouses of chronically ill partners burdened by exerting health-related social control? *Journal of Health Psychology, 16,* 1109–1119. http://dx.doi.org/10.1177/1359105311401670

August, K. J., & Sorkin, D. H. (2010). Marital status and gender differences in managing a chronic illness: The function of health-related social control. *Social Science & Medicine, 71,* 1831–1838. http://dx.doi.org/10.1016/j.socscimed.2010.08.022

Bandura, A. (2004). Health promotion by social cognitive means. *Health Education & Behavior, 31,* 143–164. http://dx.doi.org/10.1177/1090198104263660

Baumeister, R. F., Vohs, K. D., & Tice, D. M. (2007). The strength model of self-control. *Current Directions in Psychological Science, 16,* 351–355. http://dx.doi.org/10.1111/j.1467-8721.2007.00534.x

Berg, C. A., & Upchurch, R. (2007). A developmental-contextual model of couples coping with chronic illness across the adult life span. *Psychological Bulletin, 133*, 920–954. http://dx.doi.org/10.1037/0033-2909.133.6.920

Berg, C. A., Wiebe, D. J., Butner, J., Bloor, L., Bradstreet, C., Upchurch, R., . . . Patton, G. (2008). Collaborative coping and daily mood in couples dealing with prostate cancer. *Psychology and Aging, 23*, 505–516. http://dx.doi.org/10.1037/a0012687

Beverly, E. A., Penrod, J., & Wray, L. A. (2007). Living with type 2 diabetes: Marital perspectives of middle-aged and older couples. *Journal of Psychological Nursing and Mental Health Services, 45*, 24–32.

Bove, C. F., Sobal, J., & Rauschenbach, B. S. (2003). Food choices among newly married couples: Convergence, conflict, individualism, and projects. *Appetite, 40*, 25–41. http://dx.doi.org/10.1016/S0195-6663(02)00147-2

Brown, S. L., Smith, D. M., Schulz, R., Kabeto, M. U., Ubel, P. A., Poulin, M., . . . Langa, K. M. (2009). Caregiving behavior is associated with decreased mortality risk. *Psychological Science, 20*, 488–494. http://dx.doi.org/10.1111/j.1467-9280.2009.02323.x

Burman, B., & Margolin, G. (1992). Analysis of the association between marital relationships and health problems: An interactional perspective. *Psychological Bulletin, 112*, 39–63. http://dx.doi.org/10.1037/0033-2909.112.1.39

Centers for Disease Control and Prevention. (2011). *National diabetes fact sheet: National estimates and general information on diabetes and prediabetes in the United States, 2011*. Atlanta, GA: Author.

Christakis, N. A., & Fowler, J. H. (2007). The spread of obesity in a large social network over 32 years. *The New England Journal of Medicine, 357*, 370–379. http://dx.doi.org/10.1056/NEJMsa066082

Cohen, C. A., Colantonio, A., & Vernich, L. (2002). Positive aspects of caregiving: Rounding out the caregiver experience. *International Journal of Geriatric Psychiatry, 17*, 184–188. http://dx.doi.org/10.1002/gps.561

Coyne, J. C., Rohrbaugh, M. J., Shoham, V., Sonnega, J. S., Nicklas, J. M., & Cranford, J. A. (2001). Prognostic importance of marital quality for survival of congestive heart failure. *The American Journal of Cardiology, 88*, 526–529. http://dx.doi.org/10.1016/S0002-9149(01)01731-3

Fabbri, E., An, Y., Zoli, M., Simonsick, E. M., Guralnik, J. M., Bandinelli, S., . . . Ferrucci, L. (2015). Aging and the burden of multimorbidity: Associations with inflammatory and anabolic hormonal biomarkers. *The Journals of Gerontology: Series A. Biological Sciences and Medical Sciences, 70*, 63–70. http://dx.doi.org/10.1093/gerona/glu127

Falba, T. A., & Sindelar, J. L. (2008). Spousal concordance in health behavior change. *Health Services Research, 43*, 96–116. http://dx.doi.org/10.1111/j.1475-6773.2007.00754.x

Franks, M. M., Pienta, A. M., & Wray, L. A. (2002). It takes two: Marriage and smoking cessation in the middle years. *Journal of Aging and Health*, *14*, 336–354. http://dx.doi.org/10.1177/08964302014003002

Franks, M. M., Sahin, Z. S., Seidel, A. J., Shields, C. G., Oates, S. K., & Boushey, C. J. (2012). Table for two: Diabetes distress and diet-related interactions of married patients with diabetes and their spouses. *Families, Systems, & Health*, *30*, 154–165. http://dx.doi.org/10.1037/a0028614

Franks, M. M., Shields, C. G., Lim, E., Sands, L. P., Mobley, S., & Boushey, C. J. (2012). I will if you will: Similarity in married partners' readiness to change health risk behaviors. *Health Education & Behavior*, *39*, 324–331. http://dx.doi.org/10.1177/1090198111402824

Franks, M. M., Stephens, M. A. P., Rook, K. S., Franklin, B. A., Keteyian, S. J., & Artinian, N. T. (2006). Spouses' provision of health-related support and control to patients participating in cardiac rehabilitation. *Journal of Family Psychology*, *20*, 311–318. http://dx.doi.org/10.1037/0893-3200.20.2.311

Franks, M. M., Wendorf, C. A., Gonzalez, R., & Ketterer, M. W. (2004). Aid and influence: Health promoting exchanges of older married partners. *Journal of Social and Personal Relationships*, *21*, 431–445. http://dx.doi.org/10.1177/0265407504044839

Goldsmith, D. J., Bute, J. J., & Lindholm, K. A. (2012). Patient and partner strategies for talking about lifestyle change following a cardiac event. *Journal of Applied Communication Research*, *40*, 65–86. http://dx.doi.org/10.1080/00909882.2011.636373

Graham, K., & Braun, K. (1999). Concordance of use of alcohol and other substances among older adult couples. *Addictive Behaviors*, *24*, 839–856. http://dx.doi.org/10.1016/S0306-4603(99)00059-3

Grzywacz, J. G., Arcury, T. A., Saldana, S., Kirk, J. K., Bell, R. A., Ip, E., & Quandt, S. A. (2012). Social control in older adults' diabetes self management and well-being. *Behavioral Medicine*, *38*, 115–120. http://dx.doi.org/10.1080/08964289.2012.693976

Helgeson, V. S., Novak, S. A., Lepore, S. J., & Eton, D. T. (2004). Spouse social control efforts: Relations to health behavior and well-being among men with prostate cancer. *Journal of Social and Personal Relationships*, *21*, 53–68. http://dx.doi.org/10.1177/0265407504039840

Henry, S. L., Rook, K. S., Stephens, M. A. P., & Franks, M. M. (2013). Spousal undermining of older diabetic patients' disease management. *Journal of Health Psychology*, *18*, 1550–1561. http://dx.doi.org/10.1177/1359105312465913

Homish, G. G., & Leonard, K. E. (2008). Spousal influence on general health behaviors in a community sample. *American Journal of Health Behavior*, *32*, 754–763. http://dx.doi.org/10.5993/AJHB.32.6.19

Hong, T. B., Franks, M. M., Gonzalez, R., Keteyian, S. J., Franklin, B. A., & Artinian, N. T. (2005). A dyadic investigation of exercise support between cardiac patients and their spouses. *Health Psychology, 24,* 430–434. http://dx.doi.org/10.1037/0278-6133.24.4.430

Khan, C. M., Stephens, M. A., Franks, M. M., Rook, K. S., & Salem, J. K. (2013). Influences of spousal support and control on diabetes management through physical activity. *Health Psychology, 32,* 739–747. http://dx.doi.org/10.1037/a0028609

Kiecolt-Glaser, J. K., & Newton, T. L. (2001). Marriage and health: His and hers. *Psychological Bulletin, 127,* 472–503. http://dx.doi.org/10.1037/0033-2909.127.4.472

King, K. B., & Reis, H. T. (2012). Marriage and long-term survival after coronary artery bypass grafting. *Health Psychology, 31,* 55–62. http://dx.doi.org/10.1037/a0025061

Kleiboer, A. M., Kuijer, R. G., Hox, J. J., Schreurs, K. M. G., & Bensing, J. M. (2006). Receiving and providing support in couples dealing with multiple sclerosis: A diary study using an equity perspective. *Personal Relationships, 13,* 485–501. http://dx.doi.org/10.1111/j.1475-6811.2006.00131.x

Konstam, V., Holmes, W., Wilczenski, F., Baliga, S., Lester, J., & Priest, R. (2003). Meaning in the lives of caregivers of individuals with Parkinson's disease. *Journal of Clinical Psychology in Medical Settings, 10,* 17–25. http://dx.doi.org/10.1023/A:1022849628975

Krause, N., Herzog, A. R., & Baker, E. (1992). Providing support to others and well-being in later life. *The Journal of Gerontology, 47,* P300–P311. http://dx.doi.org/10.1093/geronj/47.5.P300

Leonard, K. E., & Mudar, P. (2003). Peer and partner drinking and the transition to marriage: A longitudinal examination of selection and influence processes. *Psychology of Addictive Behaviors, 17,* 115–125. http://dx.doi.org/10.1037/0893-164X.17.2.115

Lewis, M. A., McBride, C. M., Pollak, K. I., Puleo, E., Butterfield, R. M., & Emmons, K. M. (2006). Understanding health behavior change among couples: An interdependence and communal coping approach. *Social Science & Medicine, 62,* 1369–1380. http://dx.doi.org/10.1016/j.socscimed.2005.08.006

Liang, J., Krause, N. M., & Bennett, J. M. (2001). Social exchange and well-being: Is giving better than receiving? *Psychology and Aging, 16,* 511–523. http://dx.doi.org/10.1037/0882-7974.16.3.511

Manne, S. L., Norton, T. R., Ostroff, J. S., Winkel, G., Fox, K., & Grana, G. (2007). Protective buffering and psychological distress among couples coping with breast cancer: The moderating role of relationship satisfaction. *Journal of Family Psychology, 21,* 380–388. http://dx.doi.org/10.1037/0893-3200.21.3.380

Marks, N. F. (1998). Does it hurt to care? Caregiving, work-family conflict, and midlife well-being. *Journal of Marriage and the Family, 60,* 951–966. http://dx.doi.org/10.2307/353637

Martire, L. M., Keefe, F. J., Schulz, R., Ready, R., Beach, S. R., Rudy, T. E., & Starz, T. W. (2006). Older spouses' perceptions of partners' chronic arthritis pain: Implications for spousal responses, support provision, and caregiving experiences. *Psychology and Aging, 21*, 222–230. http://dx.doi.org/10.1037/0882-7974.21.2.222

Martire, L. M., & Schulz, R. (2007). Involving family in psychosocial interventions for chronic illness. *Current Directions in Psychological Science, 16*, 90–94. http://dx.doi.org/10.1111/j.1467-8721.2007.00482.x

Martire, L. M., Schulz, R., Helgeson, V. S., Small, B. J., & Saghafi, E. M. (2010). Review and meta-analysis of couple-oriented interventions for chronic illness. *Annals of Behavioral Medicine, 40*, 325–342. http://dx.doi.org/10.1007/s12160-010-9216-2

Meyler, D., Stimpson, J. P., & Peek, M. K. (2007). Health concordance within couples: A systematic review. *Social Science & Medicine, 64*, 2297–2310. http://dx.doi.org/10.1016/j.socscimed.2007.02.007

Miller, D., & Brown, J. L. (2005). Marital interactions in the process of dietary change for type 2 diabetes. *Journal of Nutrition Education and Behavior, 37*, 226–234. http://dx.doi.org/10.1016/S1499-4046(06)60276-5

Orvik, E., Ribu, L., & Johansen, O. E. (2010). Spouses' educational needs and perceptions of health in partners with type 2 diabetes. *European Diabetes Nursing, 7*, 63–69. http://dx.doi.org/10.1002/edn.159

Pinquart, M., & Sörensen, S. (2003). Differences between caregivers and noncaregivers in psychological health and physical health: A meta-analysis. *Psychology and Aging, 18*, 250–267. http://dx.doi.org/10.1037/0882-7974.18.2.250

Poulin, M. J., Brown, S. L., Ubel, P. A., Smith, D. M., Jankovic, A., & Langa, K. M. (2010). Does a helping hand mean a heavy heart? Helping behavior and well-being among spouse caregivers. *Psychology and Aging, 25*, 108–117. http://dx.doi.org/10.1037/a0018064

Reczek, C., & Umberson, D. (2012). Gender, health behavior, and intimate relationships: Lesbian, gay, and straight contexts. *Social Science & Medicine, 74*, 1783–1790. http://dx.doi.org/10.1016/j.socscimed.2011.11.011

Robles, T. F., & Kiecolt-Glaser, J. K. (2003). The physiology of marriage: Pathways to health. *Physiology & Behavior, 79*, 409–416. http://dx.doi.org/10.1016/S0031-9384(03)00160-4

Robles, T. F., Slatcher, R. B., Trombello, J. M., & McGinn, M. M. (2014). Marital quality and health: A meta-analytic review. *Psychological Bulletin, 140*, 140–187. http://dx.doi.org/10.1037/a0031859

Rook, K. S., August, K., & Sorkin, D. H. (2011). Social network functions and health. In R. J. Contrada & A. Baum (Eds.), *Handbook of stress science: Biology, psychology, and health* (pp. 123–135). New York, NY: Springer.

Rook, K. S., August, K. J., Stephens, M. A. P., & Franks, M. M. (2011). When does spousal social control provoke negative reactions in the context of chronic illness? The pivotal role of patients' expectations. *Journal of Social and Personal Relationships, 28*, 772–789. http://dx.doi.org/10.1177/0265407510391335

Rosland, A. M., Heisler, M., Janevic, M. R., Connell, C. M., Langa, K. M., Kerr, E. A., & Piette, J. D. (2013). Current and potential support for chronic disease management in the United States: The perspective of family and friends of chronically ill adults. *Families, Systems, & Health, 31*, 119–131. http://dx.doi.org/10.1037/a0031535

Rosland, A. M., Heisler, M., & Piette, J. D. (2012). The impact of family behaviors and communication patterns on chronic illness outcomes: A systematic review. *Journal of Behavioral Medicine, 35*, 221–239. http://dx.doi.org/10.1007/s10865-011-9354-4

Rosland, A. M., Kieffer, E., Israel, B., Cofield, M., Palmisano, G., Sinco, B., . . . Heisler, M. (2008). When is social support important? The association of family support and professional support with specific diabetes self-management behaviors. *Journal of General Internal Medicine, 23*, 1992–1999. http://dx.doi.org/10.1007/s11606-008-0814-7

Schokker, M. C., Stuive, I., Bouma, J., Keers, J. C., Links, T. P., Wolffenbuttel, B. H., . . . Hagedoorn, M. (2010). Support behavior and relationship satisfaction in couples dealing with diabetes: Main and moderating effects. *Journal of Family Psychology, 24*, 578–586. http://dx.doi.org/10.1037/a0021009

Shaw, B. A., Gallant, M. P., Riley-Jacome, M., & Spokane, L. S. (2006). Assessing sources of support for diabetes self-care in urban and rural underserved communities. *Journal of Community Health, 31*, 393–412. http://dx.doi.org/10.1007/s10900-006-9018-4

Stephens, M. A. P., Fekete, E. M., Franks, M. M., Rook, K. S., Druley, J. A., & Greene, K. (2009). Spouses' use of pressure and persuasion to promote osteoarthritis patients' medical adherence after orthopedic surgery. *Health Psychology, 28*, 48–55. http://dx.doi.org/10.1037/a0012385

Stephens, M. A. P., Franks, M. M., Rook, K. S., Iida, M., Hemphill, R. C., & Salem, J. K. (2013). Spouses' attempts to regulate day-to-day dietary adherence among patients with type 2 diabetes. *Health Psychology, 32*, 1029–1037. http://dx.doi.org/10.1037/a0030018

Stephens, M. A. P., Hemphill, R. C., Rook, K. S., & Franks, M. M. (2014). It sometimes takes two: Marriage as a mechanism for managing chronic illness. In C. R. Agnew & S. C. South (Eds.), *Interpersonal relationships and health: Social and clinical psychological mechanisms* (pp. 109–132). New York, NY: Oxford University Press. http://dx.doi.org/10.1093/acprof:oso/9780199936632.003.0006

Stephens, M. A. P., Rook, K. S., Franks, M. M., Khan, C., & Iida, M. (2010). Spouses' use of social control to improve diabetic patients' dietary adherence. *Families, Systems, & Health, 28*, 199–208. http://dx.doi.org/10.1037/a0020513

Stimpson, J. P., Masel, M. C., Rudkin, L., & Peek, M. K. (2006). Shared health behaviors among older Mexican American spouses. *American Journal of Health Behavior, 30*, 495–502. http://dx.doi.org/10.5993/AJHB.30.5.6

Umberson, D. (1992). Gender, marital status and the social control of health behavior. *Social Science & Medicine, 34*, 907–917. http://dx.doi.org/10.1016/0277-9536(92)90259-S

Vitaliano, P. P., Zhang, J., & Scanlan, J. M. (2003). Is caregiving hazardous to one's physical health? A meta-analysis. *Psychological Bulletin, 129*, 946–972.

Weiss, C. O., Boyd, C. M., Yu, Q., Wolff, J. L., & Leff, B. (2007). Patterns of prevalent major chronic disease among older adults in the United States. *JAMA, 298*, 1158–1162. http://dx.doi.org/10.1001/jama.298.10.1160-b

Williams, K. E., & Bond, M. J. (2002). The roles of self-efficacy, outcome expectancies and social support in the self-care behaviours of diabetics. *Psychology, Health & Medicine, 7*, 127–141. http://dx.doi.org/10.1080/13548500120116076

Wolff, J. L., Starfield, B., & Anderson, G. (2002). Prevalence, expenditures, and complications of multiple chronic conditions in the elderly. *Archives of Internal Medicine, 162*, 2269–2276. http://dx.doi.org/10.1001/archinte.162.20.2269

# 16

## HARNESSING THE POWER OF THE MARITAL RELATIONSHIP TO IMPROVE ILLNESS MANAGEMENT: CONSIDERATIONS FOR COUPLE-BASED INTERVENTIONS

LYNN M. MARTIRE, RACHEL C. HEMPHILL,
AND COURTNEY A. POLENICK

For many adults, the primary challenges of midlife and late life are brought about by one's own health problems and those of close family members such as the spouse. Evidence continues to build for the impact of the marital relationship on health (Robles, Slatcher, Trombello, & McGinn, 2014) as well as the negative effects of illness on the spouse (Berg & Upchurch, 2007; Martire & Schulz, 2012). Consequently, some researchers have incorporated the spouse in behavioral interventions for chronic illness. The most common goals of this dyadic approach are to improve psychological well-being (of the individual with chronic illness, spouse, or both), marital functioning, and illness symptoms. Much less often, couple interventions have been targeted at illness management. For many of our most common and costly chronic conditions (e.g., diabetes, arthritis), specific health behaviors, such as medication adherence,

Preparation of this chapter was supported in part by Grant K02 AG039412 from the National Institute on Aging.

http://dx.doi.org/10.1037/14897-017
*Couple Relationships in the Middle and Later Years: Their Nature, Complexity, and Role in Health and Illness*,
J. Bookwala (Editor)

exercise, dietary restrictions, blood glucose monitoring, and smoking cessation, are critical for managing illness.

The main premise of this chapter is that couple interventions for chronic illness may be strengthened by targeting the ways in which spouses influence illness management. For the purposes of this chapter, we define *illness management* as concrete, discernible behaviors that are critical for survival (e.g., medication adherence) or improving health (e.g., regular exercise). First, we summarize evidence for the efficacy of couple interventions for chronic illness and highlight findings from a small group of studies that have targeted illness management behaviors. Second, we describe findings from two relevant research literatures—observational studies of spousal influence on illness management and couple interventions for at-risk populations (i.e., overweight individuals and smokers). Third, we apply insights from this previous research to recommendations for future interventions. Throughout the chapter, our use of the terms *marriage* and *spouse* is meant to be inclusive of intimate relationships in which partners are not legally married or are of the same sex.

## STATE OF THE SCIENCE: COUPLE INTERVENTIONS FOR CHRONIC ILLNESS

Incorporating the spouse in behavioral interventions for chronic illness has been most common in research on cancer, arthritis, and chronic pain. The question of whether couple interventions are efficacious for specific illnesses is difficult to answer in that there are rarely enough studies focused on a particular population to aggregate for quantitative, or sometimes even qualitative, review. An exception is the cancer literature. A recent meta-analysis was conducted with 20 randomized controlled trials (RCTs), most of which focused on breast and prostate cancer and used communication skills training or counseling (Badr & Krebs, 2013). Couple interventions had significant but small beneficial effects on the psychological well-being (e.g., depressive symptoms), physical symptoms (e.g., pain, fatigue), and relationship (e.g., marital functioning) of individuals with chronic illness. Similar small beneficial effects were found for spouses' psychological and relationship outcomes.

We recently took a cross-disease approach to reviewing the efficacy of couple interventions, focusing on 33 RCTs for various chronic conditions (Martire, Schulz, Helgeson, Small, & Saghafi, 2010). The most common conditions were cardiovascular disease, cancer, and chronic pain. Most of these interventions were multicomponent, with educational and cognitive–behavioral interventions commonly represented. Consistent with Badr and Krebs (2013), we concluded that couple interventions for chronic illness hold promise, in that there were small improvements in depressive symptoms, marital functioning, and pain of individuals with chronic illness (too few studies assessed spouse outcomes to permit aggregation for meta-analysis). In addition, a lack of heterogeneity in effect sizes within this group of studies indicated that interventions have similar effects despite varying illness populations and content, confirming the value of a cross-disease perspective.

Intervention studies included in these two reviews were rarely aimed at illness management behaviors, in part because of the large number of studies focused on individuals with cancer and attention to improving psychological well-being and relationship functioning. A small subset of studies included in our review (i.e., four out of 33) targeted exercise, eating behaviors, use of relaxation techniques, or medication adherence. For example, as part of an educational intervention for rheumatoid arthritis, individuals with rheumatoid arthritis were provided with information on exercise and encouraged to exercise at home (Riemsma, Taal, & Rasker, 2003). Spouses were not included in this exercise component, and there was no significant improvement in exercise level for individuals with rheumatoid arthritis. In another study, both exercise and diet were targeted in a weight loss intervention for obese individuals with Type 2 diabetes and their overweight spouses (Wing, Marcus, Epstein, & Jawad, 1991). In this study, couple intervention led to reduced caloric intake (and weight loss) for women with Type 2 diabetes but not men. Spouses also showed improved adherence to weight control strategies and greater weight loss, regardless of gender.

Another study included in our review tested a couple-oriented approach to relaxation therapy for individuals with hypertension (Wadden, 1983). In this study, the spouse was encouraged to practice relaxation therapy with the individual with hypertension at least once per day or, at minimum, remind the individual to practice. Individuals with hypertension in the couple intervention practiced relaxation more often and for longer periods of time than those who were in a patient-focused relaxation intervention. Finally, an intervention for individuals with HIV that included fostering active support from the spouse was successful in improving medication adherence, albeit in the short term only (Remien et al., 2005).

In the past few years, interest in targeting illness management behaviors using a dyadic approach has grown. In one study, individuals with prostate cancer worked with the spouse to make a detailed plan for completing pelvic floor exercises after surgery (Burkert, Scholz, Gralla, Roigas, & Knoll, 2011); however, the rate of enacting this behavior did not differ significantly from that achieved through patient-focused intervention. A dyadic intervention study for individuals with Type 2 diabetes resulted in improved adherence to diet and exercise recommendations and enhanced family support (Keogh et al., 2011). Another pilot study that focused on Type 2 diabetes did not find that couple intervention resulted in better diet and blood glucose testing than patient-focused intervention (Trief, Sandberg, Ploutz-Snyder, et al., 2011).

Modifications were made to this intervention, including attention to changes in spouse communication and problem solving, and it is currently being tested in a full-scale randomized trial (Trief, Sandberg, Fisher, et al., 2011).

Although there are only a handful of couple interventions for illness management, it is worth noting that most of those described here explicitly targeted spouse support, communication, or health behaviors in an attempt to improve illness management (Burkert et al., 2011; Keogh et al., 2011; Remien et al., 2005; Trief, Sandberg, Ploutz-Snyder, et al., 2011; Wadden, 1983; Wing et al., 1991). Unfortunately, it was less common to examine change in these spousal factors (Burkert et al., 2011; Keogh et al., 2011; Wing et al., 1991), which can tell us if they are the mechanisms by which couple interventions are beneficial (or not). As we describe in the next section, there is growing empirical evidence that spouses affect illness management in both negative and positive ways.

## EVIDENCE FOR SPOUSAL INFLUENCE ON ILLNESS MANAGEMENT

There is a high rate of concordance in spouses' engagement in health-enhancing and health-compromising behaviors such as smoking (Bloch, Klein, de Souza e Silva, da Rocha Nogueira, & Salis, 2003; Franks, Pienta, & Wray, 2002), alcohol use (Graham & Braun, 1999; Stimpson, Masel, Rudkin, & Peek, 2006), dietary habits (Barrett-Connor, Suarez, & Criqui, 1982; Macario & Sorensen, 1998), and physical activity (Li, Cardinal, & Acock, 2013; Pettee et al., 2006). These findings raise the question of how spouses may affect each other's health behaviors. In the context of chronic conditions, it also is important to determine the processes by which spousal behaviors may either support or undermine illness management (see Chapter 15, this volume, for a discussion of health-supportive vs. health-controlling spousal behaviors and their relative effectiveness in disease management).

Social control theory (Umberson, 1992) is the framework most often applied in research examining effects of the spouse on illness management behaviors. According to this theory, social relationships are assumed to serve a regulatory function by which individuals promote adherence to social norms or expectations through the use of direct or indirect social sanctions (Lewis, Butterfield, Darbes, & Johnston-Brooks, 2004). Social control operates indirectly when an individual's feelings of obligation or responsibility to significant others results in the avoidance or cessation of high-risk behavior. For instance, a man might decide to quit smoking so that he can maintain his good health and optimal functioning in his roles as a husband and father. Direct social control occurs when social network members explicitly prompt or attempt to influence an individual to engage in healthy behaviors or to discontinue unhealthy behaviors (Lewis & Rook, 1999). For example, a wife might tell her husband that she is worried about how his smoking might be affecting his health with the hopes that voicing her concerns will encourage him to quit. Most research in this area has focused on social control as reported by the target of these control attempts.

Direct control strategies have been commonly categorized as positive and negative social control. Positive strategies include providing health-related information or attempting to persuade the individual to engage in a specific health behavior, whereas negative strategies involve the use of more coercive techniques such as pressure or criticism. The terms *persuasion* and *pressure control* are sometimes used in place of positive and negative social control, respectively, because they are more neutral with regard to the anticipated direction of effects on behaviors. Positive social control or persuasion strategies by the spouse have been shown to be only moderately correlated with spousal support (e.g., Fekete, Stephens, Druley, & Greene, 2006; Helgeson, Novak, Lepore, & Eton, 2004). In terms of a conceptual distinction, it has been suggested that spousal support is provided to individuals with chronic illness who are engaging, or attempting to engage, in recommended health behaviors, whereas spousal control is exerted toward individuals who exhibit limited or erratic efforts to engage in sound health behaviors (Franks et al., 2006). Thus, individuals with chronic illness may play an active role in eliciting health-related support or control from their spouses.

Four conceptual models have been proposed to describe the relationships between direct health-related social control, affective responses to control attempts, and behavioral outcomes (Okun, Huff, August, & Rook, 2007). The *dual-effects model* posits that recipients of social control show better health behaviors, but they also experience distress in response to control attempts (Rook, Thuras, & Lewis, 1990). Social control may be interpreted as intrusive by the individual with chronic illness (Rook, August, Stephens, & Franks, 2011), and negative effects on well-being may be particularly strong when punitive control strategies are used, such as those eliciting guilt or humiliation (Lewis & Rook, 1999; Tucker, Orlando, Elliott, & Klein, 2006). The *domain-specific model* predicts that positive and negative control strategies are associated with higher positive and negative affect, respectively. This model originated from research demonstrating that positive and negative affect represent separate dimensions of well-being (Diener & Emmons, 1984) and are independently influenced by positive and negative social exchanges (Ingersoll-Dayton et al., 1997).

Building on the domain-specific model, the *mediational model of health-related social control* predicts that positive affect mediates the relationship between positive social control and engagement in healthy behaviors, whereas negative affect explains the association between negative social control and engagement in unhealthy behavior. The mediational model also acknowledges that responses to social control are either compliant or noncompliant. Further, noncompliant responses may occur in several forms, such as ignoring the attempt, increasing engagement in unhealthy behavior, or engaging covertly in unhealthy behavior (e.g., hiding food). Finally, *the contextual model* expands on the previous three models by considering factors that may moderate the impact of social control on affect and health behaviors. For instance, high relationship satisfaction may buffer the impact of negative spousal control, whereas low relationship satisfaction may exacerbate such effects. These models are complementary in some ways, and each has received some degree of empirical support (e.g., Knoll, Burkert, Scholz, Roigas, & Gralla, 2012; Stephens et al., 2009, 2013).

Social control may play an important role in an individual's adaptation to chronic illness, especially when health behavior change must be initiated and maintained over time. In particular, it may be critical for individuals who are not confident in managing the illness on their own (Khan, Stephens, Franks, Rook, & Salem, 2013). However, the current literature suggests that health-related spousal control can have both positive and negative effects in chronically ill populations (for a detailed discussion, Chapter 15, this volume). These mixed findings suggest that although spouses use social control strategies to improve illness management, these attempts do not always result in positive change and may even be counterproductive. Negative control or pressure appears to be especially likely to backfire and produce negative changes in illness management. However, it is important to consider that poorer illness management may also prompt negative control by the spouse. That is, spouses of individuals with chronic illness who engage in fewer health-enhancing behaviors and more health-compromising behaviors may make more frequent social control attempts.

Research that uses repeated assessments and examines potential moderating variables may clarify the temporal ordering of social control effects as well as contextual factors that may influence responses to control attempts. A recent longitudinal study of individuals with prostate cancer and their spouses found that relationship satisfaction moderated concurrent associations between social control (assessed globally rather than as positive and negative control) and adherence to postsurgery recommendations (Knoll et al., 2012). Individuals with prostate cancer and high relationship satisfaction reported greater engagement in pelvic floor exercises when they also reported receiving more control from the spouse. Moreover, relationship satisfaction moderated the dual-effects of social control on positive affect. Among individuals with prostate cancer who reported high levels of marital relationship satisfaction, spousal control was not related to positive affect. However, for those with low relationship satisfaction, spousal control was associated with less positive affect.

Daily diary studies are valuable in determining more proximal associations between social control and health behavior as well as contextual factors that may influence these relationships (e.g., gender and how the couple appraises responsibility for illness management). Our study of individuals with knee osteoarthritis and their spouses examined the effects of daily spouse autonomy support (i.e., helping individuals find their own ways to be active), persuasion, and pressure on physical activity (Martire et al., 2013). Individuals with knee osteoarthritis were more active on days when they perceived that their spouse provided greater autonomy support and also when spouses were more active themselves. In addition, greater spousal pressure (negative control) was associated with less physical activity, but only for men with knee osteoarthritis. Contrary to expectation, spouses' daily persuasion (positive control) was not related to physical activity.

In another daily diary study, Stephens et al. (2013) examined the effects of spouses' diet-related support, persuasion, and pressure on older adults with Type 2 diabetes. Spouses' pressure and persuasion control were both associated with decreased dietary adherence, and pressure was also associated with increased diabetes-specific distress. Conversely, dietary support was related to increased dietary adherence (e.g., showing appreciation for efforts to adhere to the diabetic diet and doing something to help adherence). These supportive spousal behaviors are similar to the instrumental and reinforcing social control strategies for weight loss that have been found to be effective among healthy couples (Novak & Webster, 2011). Stephens et al. (2013) also demonstrated contextual effects in that spouse support was associated with decreased distress, and pressure was most strongly associated with decreased adherence, when couples perceived illness management as a shared responsibility rather than solely the responsibility of the individual with diabetes.

In sum, the current literature indicates that spousal social control can have a positive or negative impact on illness management and psychological well-being in individuals with chronic illness and may be a useful target of couple interventions. In addition, supportive spouse behaviors such as appreciation and encouragement of autonomy appear to have independent effects on illness management and could be enhanced through intervention. At the same time, there are many unanswered questions that call for future research. For example, what is the relative impact of the spouse on engagement in healthy behaviors versus disengagement from unhealthy ones?

# WHAT CAN WE LEARN FROM COUPLE INTERVENTIONS FOR AT-RISK POPULATIONS?

A separate research literature has focused on including the spouse in interventions aimed at poor health behaviors in otherwise healthy individuals. Findings from studies of these at-risk populations suggest specific strategies that could be incorporated into couple interventions targeting behaviors critical to illness management. Here, we focus on dyadic weight loss and smoking cessation interventions because they target health behaviors that are key for illness management as well as prevention.

## Weight Loss Interventions

Weight loss interventions have typically focused on training overweight individuals to use behavioral techniques, such as monitoring, goal setting, and stimulus control (e.g., storing food out of sight between meal times) to improve their eating habits and physical activity (Jeffery, Wing, & Stunkard, 1978). Although standard behavioral programs have been shown to produce significant amounts of weight loss, average weight loss is modest, and many participants have difficulty continuing or maintaining weight loss after treatment has ended. In the 1970s, researchers began evaluating spouse involvement in the treatment process as a means of enhancing participants' initial and long-term weight loss success (e.g., Brownell, Heckerman, Westlake, Hayes, & Monti, 1978; Saccone & Israel, 1978).

In a typical couple-focused weight loss intervention, the standard behavioral treatment is augmented by having spouses attend treatment sessions with their overweight partners. Within these sessions, spouses are often trained to model appropriate eating behaviors, reinforce positive changes in partners' eating habits, and use stimulus control techniques such as refraining from eating in the partner's presence outside of regular meal times (e.g., Brownell et al., 1978). In general, couple-focused weight loss programs have been found to be successful at modestly enhancing weight loss beyond that achieved through individual behavioral programs. In one RCT, for example, women who participated in a 6-week behavioral weight loss program with their husbands lost an average of 8.8 lb by the end of treatment, compared to an average weight loss of 4.8 lb for women who participated alone (Weisz & Bucher, 1980). Although differences in weight loss achieved by participants in couple versus individual behavioral programs have not reached statistical significance in some studies, meta-analysis shows a small but significant advantage of couple programs for postintervention weight loss (Black, Gleser, & Kooyers, 1990).

Some research has suggested that couple interventions may provide more of an advantage for maintenance of weight loss, rather than initial weight loss.

A number of these studies observed equivalent amounts of weight loss among participants in couple and individual programs at the end of treatment but found significant advantages of couple programs up to 2 years later (Brownell et al., 1978; Murphy et al., 1982; Pearce, LeBow, & Orchard, 1981). It may be that individuals who attend treatment with their spouses are better able to maintain changes in eating habits and/or physical activity after the formal treatment program has ended.

It is assumed that couple-focused weight loss interventions achieve their effects by increasing spouses' support for their partners' weight loss and behavior change. Although a handful of studies have observed greater spousal support among participants in a couple intervention, support has been broadly defined (e.g., perceived helpfulness of spouse in controlling eating habits, spouses' compliance with behaviors prescribed by the intervention) and has not always been related to participants' weight loss outcomes (Brownell et al., 1978; Pearce et al., 1981; Rosenthal, Allen, & Winter, 1980). Additional work is needed to determine which aspects of the spouse's involvement have the most impact on participants' weight loss success (e.g., increasing instrumental and/ or emotional support for participants' behavior change, decreasing unhelpful behaviors such as criticism).

One early study indicated that spousal reinforcement of behavior change (e.g., eating habits) is more effective than reinforcement of outcomes (e.g., weight loss; Saccone & Israel, 1978). Additionally, incorporating spouses into treatment may enhance weight loss by increasing the likelihood that spouses will make changes to their own eating habits. Observational research has indicated that individuals are more successful at improving a range of health behaviors, including physical activity, smoking cessation, and cholesterol screening, when their spouses engage in the behavior change at the same time (Falba & Sindelar, 2008; Pyke, Wood, Kinmonth, & Thompson, 1997).

More recent work in this area has pointed to specific strategies that may further enhance the effectiveness of couple interventions. Gorin and colleagues (2013) evaluated a weight loss intervention that targeted participants' social and home environments. In this study, an individual-focused behavioral weight loss treatment was compared with an enhanced behavioral treatment that also targeted relevant aspects of participants' homes, such as the types of foods present in the home and the availability and placement of exercise equipment and weight scales. Participants in the home environment condition also enlisted an intervention partner to participate in treatment sessions with them and to work toward the same behavior change goals; partners could be any household member who was also overweight and the majority of partners were spouses. After 6 months of treatment, weight loss was significantly greater among female participants in the home environment intervention. Partners lost significantly more weight regardless of gender. Further analysis of data from this study shows that partners' autonomy support for weight loss (e.g., minimizing pressure, providing choices and options), which was not specifically targeted in the intervention, was associated with participants' greater behavior change, whereas more directive types of support (e.g., exercising together, encouragement) were not (Gorin, Powers, Koestner, Wing, & Raynor, 2014).

A promising strategy of recent interventions targeting eating habits and physical activity is *dyadic goal setting*, also described as having partners form collaborative implementation intentions. Implementation intentions refer to if–then plans about when, where, and how an individual will perform a desired behavior (e.g., "If it's Tuesday or Thursday, then I will take a 20-minute walk after dinner"; Gollwitzer & Sheeran, 2006). Implementation intentions have been shown to be an effective component of health behavior change interventions (Adriaanse, van Oosten, de Ridder, de Wit, & Evers, 2011; Bélanger-Gravel, Godin, & Amireault, 2013). Furthermore, recent work by Prestwich and colleagues indicated that having individuals form implementation intentions with a partner about behaviors they will engage in together (e.g., "If it's Tuesday or Thursday, then *we* will go for a 20-minute walk after dinner") yields greater improvements in physical activity, diet, and waist size compared with having individuals form implementation intentions alone (Prestwich et al., 2012, 2014).

In summary, incorporating spouses into behavioral weight loss programs yields modest enhancements in overweight individuals' initial weight loss and maintenance of weight loss over time. A few studies have reported that spouses participating in couple interventions also lost a significant amount of weight (Brownell & Stunkard, 1981; Gorin et al., 2013). The eating habits that are targeted in these programs are also key to the management of chronic conditions such as diabetes and heart disease. Thus, couple interventions for chronic illness may be able to improve illness management by incorporating promising strategies of successful couple weight loss interventions, such as spouse reinforcement of behavior change, support for autonomy in behavior change, and dyadic goal setting. Furthermore, couples could be trained to problem solve regarding ways to change aspects of the home environment that hinder or facilitate behaviors needed for illness management. This would be useful for promoting a variety of behaviors including healthy eating, exercise, and healthy sleep practices (e.g., removing a television from the bedroom).

## Smoking Cessation Interventions

Smoking cessation interventions incorporate a social component using a diversity of methods, with some linking participants to a "buddy" within the program and others targeting support for smoking cessation within participants' preexisting social networks. For the purposes of this chapter, we focus our attention on the latter approach, with particular emphasis on interventions involving spouses or partners (vs. other relatives, friends, or coworkers). In contrast to the general success of couple-focused weight loss interventions, attempts to increase the effectiveness of smoking cessation interventions by incorporating spouses and other support partners have yielded mixed—and often disappointing—results.

A handful of studies have provided modest support for the utility of couple-focused smoking cessation interventions. In one early RCT, smokers received either a standard cognitive–behavioral cessation program or a couple-focused program in which spouses attended all treatment sessions with the smoking partner (McIntyre-Kingsolver, Lichtenstein, & Mermelstein, 1986). Spouses in the couple intervention were trained to increase supportive behaviors for their partners' cessation efforts, decrease negative behaviors such as criticism, and assist with problem-solving in situations that challenged cessation efforts. Although group differences did not reach statistical significance, point-prevalence abstinence rates at the end of treatment were considerably higher among participants in the couple intervention compared with those in the individual intervention (72.7% vs. 48.4% abstinent; $p < .10$).

Despite the success of a few studies, reviews of RCTs evaluating couple interventions for smoking cessation have concluded that there is little evidence that they increase cessation rates beyond those achieved by individual interventions (May & West, 2000; Park, Tudiver, & Campbell, 2012). Correlational evidence strongly suggests, however, that spouses' behaviors—namely, provision of smoking-specific and general social support as well as the spouse's own smoking—are important determinants of the ability to quit smoking and maintain abstinence over time. In fact, and as we describe next, disappointing effects of couple interventions for smoking cessation have been attributed in part to their failure to achieve substantial change in partner support or to consider the partner's smoking status.

Although the key aim of smoking cessation interventions incorporating spouses and partners is to increase supportive behaviors (and decrease unhelpful behaviors) for the smoker's behavior change, there is limited evidence that these interventions actually succeed in doing so. Few studies have observed increased support for smoking cessation among spouses in couple-focused interventions (see the review by Park et al., 2012). It has been suggested that spouse behaviors concerning smoking may be difficult to change during a relatively brief intervention (Cohen et al., 1988). Compared with dyadic weight loss interventions, which have demonstrated more success in enhancing spouse support, interventions targeting smoking cessation tend to be of shorter duration.

The literature on health-related social control suggests that spouse pressure and persuasion may be as important as spouse support for smoking cessation. To date, social control has received much less attention as a predictor of this behavior. One study of individuals attempting to quit smoking found that a spouse or partner's influence predicted smoking cessation in the short and the long term. Specifically, spouse pressure was associated with a reduction in men's smoking at 2 days and 4 months after a quit date (Westmaas, Wild, & Ferrence, 2002).

Intervention effects may also be masked by the failure of many studies to consider the partner's smoking status. Smokers whose spouses also smoke are less likely to quit and more likely to relapse (Franks et al., 2002; Homish & Leonard, 2005; McIntyre-Kingsolver et al., 1986).

Relatedly, Shoham and colleagues argued that couple interventions may be more effective if designed with the notion that the relationship may play a key but inadvertent role in maintaining smoking (Shoham, Rohrbaugh, Trost, & Muramoto, 2006). Specifically, they noted that smoking appears to have adaptive consequences for the relationship by providing a context for mutually supportive interactions, such as unwinding together after a stressful work day. Their intervention for health-compromised smokers helps partners realign their relationship in ways not organized around smoking. In a pilot study testing this couple intervention, the 50% rate of stable abstinence achieved by primary smokers at 6 months was approximately twice that of comparably intensive, individual-focused interventions (Shoham et al., 2006).

To summarize, couple interventions for smoking cessation have shown limited success overall. However, more contemporary lines of research hint at the promise of assessing and targeting spouse social control of smoking behavior as an intervention strategy and adopting a truly dyadic approach to treatment. Many individuals with chronic illness continue to smoke despite the high costs to their health. Continued attention to couple-based approaches to smoking cessation treatment is sorely needed.

## HOW CAN WE HARNESS THE POWER OF THE MARITAL RELATIONSHIP TO IMPROVE ILLNESS MANAGEMENT? CONCLUSIONS AND RECOMMENDATIONS FOR FUTURE RESEARCH

The literature on health-related social control suggests that it may be important to reduce spouse pressure of behaviors such as adhering to dietary restrictions and being physically active. Nagging, teasing, or even criticizing as a way to motivate better health behaviors seems to backfire. Support from the spouse for behavior change also is important, in terms of respecting decisions or choices and listening to how individuals with chronic illness would like to go about making changes. In contrast, the role of persuasion is less clear. It would strengthen this literature to examine a broader scope of spouse support behaviors including those that reduce barriers to illness management. People have a finite amount of mental energy for exerting self-control and will fail to make healthy choices in challenging circumstances if their ability to regulate behavior is depleted (Baumeister & Tierney, 2011). Therefore, one means by which spouses may encourage or facilitate each other's healthy behaviors is making the behaviors easier to enact (e.g., "I'll make dinner tonight so that you have time to exercise after work").

There also is accumulating evidence that behavior change in the spouse is a key predictor of improved illness management. This supports the tenets of social cognitive theory (SCT) in regard to social influences on self-efficacy for behavior change (Bandura, 1997). Applying SCT to couple interventions, one important strategy is to target spouse communications (i.e., persuasion in SCT terminology) that influence self-efficacy for illness management. A second strategy is to effect behavior change in the spouse to enhance self-efficacy through modeling.

Research that identifies moderators of spousal influence may point to potential tailoring variables in couple interventions (i.e., characteristics on which each couple can be assessed for the purpose of tailoring content to their specific strengths and resources). One such contextual factor is appraisal of illness management as primarily either the responsibility of the individual with chronic illness or shared between partners (Stephens et al., 2013). The developmental-contextual model of couples coping with chronic illness predicts that spousal involvement is beneficial when it matches the way in which partners have appraised responsibility for the disease (Berg & Upchurch, 2007). This hypothesis is likely to lead to interesting research questions that inform tailored couple interventions for illness management.

There also may be differences in the effects of spousal influence on illness management and the efficacy of couple intervention, depending on either partner's gender. However, few gender differences have been found in observational and intervention research, and there is a confounding of illness and gender in some illness populations (e.g., prostate cancer). We have argued that examining gender-linked traits (e.g., unmitigated agency or communion) may be more useful than gender and make it easier to study both same-sex and opposite-sex couples (Martire, 2013). The most consistent gender effects have been found in couple interventions for weight loss, with overweight women showing greater benefits than men (Gorin et al., 2013; Wing et al., 1991). It may be the case that the type of food brought into the home is driven by men's preferences, and therefore women benefit more than men from spouse involvement in a weight loss program. That is, participating in a couple intervention may allow women to bring food purchases in line with their dietary goals (Gorin et al., 2013).

Another recommendation for future couple interventions targeting illness management behaviors is to adopt a fully dyadic approach. In many couples, both partners are agents of influence and oftentimes both partners are living with chronic illness. Observational and intervention studies on couples and chronic illness are rarely designed in light of this reality. Partners also often share unhealthy behaviors that are enjoyable and promote intimacy, making it very difficult to break these patterns (Shoham et al., 2006). It may be useful to provide couples with appealing alternatives; for example, money saved by not buying cigarettes could be used for other shared enjoyable activities such as seeing a movie together. Partners might also set goals together even if their specific domains of behavior change differ (e.g., restricting caloric intake versus increasing the number of daily steps). We believe that the best effects might be achieved by intervening with couples in midlife, when behavioral lifestyle becomes especially important and chronic conditions begin to emerge. Finally, couples share a home environment that may not be conducive to healthy sleep practices, exercise, nutritious meals, or keeping track of medications. Couple interventions can focus on getting partners to work together to surmount such environmental challenges through facilitated problem solving.

To conclude, unhealthy behaviors are strong determinants of common health problems in midlife and late life, such as cardiovascular disease, diabetes, osteoarthritis, and respiratory disease. The ability to change these same behaviors, and to adopt new self-care strategies, also shapes the future trajectory of these chronic conditions. Couple interventions for chronic illness are a promising behavioral treatment approach, but their effects on health and well-being are small. Our goal for this chapter was to highlight ways in which couple interventions might be strengthened by targeting behaviors that are essential for illness management. Finding ways to improve illness management via the marital relationship, such as behaviors that are critical for survival or improving health, could ultimately reduce the costs of treating common chronic conditions and also benefit the health of the spouse.

# REFERENCES

Adriaanse, M. A., van Oosten, J. M. F., de Ridder, D. T. D., de Wit, J. B. F., & Evers, C. (2011). Planning what not to eat: Ironic effects of implementation intentions negating unhealthy habits. *Personality and Social Psychology Bulletin, 37,* 69–81. http://dx.doi.org/10.1177/0146167210390523

Badr, H., & Krebs, P. (2013). A systematic review and meta-analysis of psychosocial interventions for couples coping with cancer. *Psycho-Oncology, 22,* 1688–1704. http://dx.doi.org/10.1002/pon.3200

Bandura, A. (1997). *Self-efficacy: The exercise of control.* New York, NY: Freeman.

Barrett-Connor, E., Suarez, L., & Criqui, M. H. (1982). Spouse concordance of plasma cholesterol and triglyceride. *Journal of Chronic Diseases, 35,* 333–340. http://dx.doi.org/10.1016/0021-9681(82)90004-2

Baumeister, R. F., & Tierney, J. (2011). *Willpower: Rediscovering the greatest human strength.* New York, NY: Penguin Press.

Bélanger-Gravel, A., Godin, G., & Amireault, S. (2013). A meta-analytic review of the effect of implementation intentions on physical activity. *Health Psychology Review, 7,* 23–54. http://dx.doi.org/10.1080/17437199.2011.560095

Berg, C. A., & Upchurch, R. (2007). A developmental-contextual model of couples coping with chronic illness across the adult life span. *Psychological Bulletin, 133,* 920–954. http://dx.doi.org/10.1037/0033-2909.133.6.920

Black, D. R., Gleser, L. J., & Kooyers, K. J. (1990). A meta-analytic evaluation of couples weight-loss programs. *Health Psychology, 9,* 330–347. http://dx.doi.org/10.1037/0278-6133.9.3.330

Bloch, K. V., Klein, C. H., de Souza e Silva, N. A., da Rocha Nogueira, A. R., & Salis, L. H. A. (2003). Socioeconomic aspects of spousal concordance for hypertension, obesity, and smoking in a community of Rio de Janeiro, Brazil. *Arquivos Brasileiros de Cardiologia, 80,* 179–186. http://dx.doi.org/10.1590/S0066-782X2003000200006

Brownell, K. D., Heckerman, C. L., Westlake, R. J., Hayes, S. C., & Monti, P. M. (1978). The effect of couples training and partner co-operativeness in the behavioral treatment of obesity. *Behaviour Research and Therapy, 16,* 323–333. http://dx.doi.org/10.1016/0005-7967(78)90002-5

Brownell, K. D., & Stunkard, A. J. (1981). Couples training, pharmacotherapy, and behavior therapy in the treatment of obesity. *Archives of General Psychiatry, 38,* 1224–1229. http://dx.doi.org/10.1001/archpsyc.1981.01780360040003

Burkert, S., Scholz, U., Gralla, O., Roigas, J., & Knoll, N. (2011). Dyadic planning of health-behavior change after prostatectomy: A randomized-controlled planning intervention. *Social Science & Medicine, 73,* 783–792. http://dx.doi.org/10.1016/j.socscimed.2011.06.016

Cohen, S., Lichtenstein, E., Kingsolver, K., Mermelstein, R., Baer, J. S., & Kamarck, T. W. (1988). Social support interventions for smoking cessation. In B. H. Gottlieb (Ed.), *Marshalling social support: Formats, processes, and effects* (pp. 211–240). Thousand Oaks, CA: Sage.

Diener, E., & Emmons, R. A. (1984). The independence of positive and negative affect. *Journal of Personality and Social Psychology, 47,* 1105–1117. http://dx.doi.org/10.1037/0022-3514.47.5.1105

Falba, T. A., & Sindelar, J. L. (2008). Spousal concordance in health behavior change. *Health Services Research, 43,* 96–116. http://dx.doi.org/10.1111/j.1475-6773.2007.00754.x

Fekete, E. M., Stephens, M. A. P., Druley, J. A., & Greene, K. A. (2006). Effects of spousal control and support on older adults' recovery from knee surgery. *Journal of Family Psychology, 20,* 302–310. http://dx.doi.org/10.1037/0893-3200.20.2.302

Franks, M. M., Pienta, A. M., & Wray, L. A. (2002). It takes two: Marriage and smoking cessation in the middle years. *Journal of Aging and Health, 14*, 336–354. http://dx.doi.org/10.1177/08964302014003002

Franks, M. M., Stephens, M. A. P., Rook, K. S., Franklin, B. A., Keteyian, S. J., & Artinian, N. T. (2006). Spouses' provision of health-related support and control to patients participating in cardiac rehabilitation. *Journal of Family Psychology, 20*, 311–318. http://dx.doi.org/10.1037/0893-3200.20.2.311

Gollwitzer, P. M., & Sheeran, P. (2006). Implementation intentions and goal achievement: A meta-analysis of effects and processes. *Advances in Experimental Social Psychology, 38*, 69–119. http://dx.doi.org/10.1016/S0065-2601(06)38002-1

Gorin, A. A., Powers, T. A., Koestner, R., Wing, R. R., & Raynor, H. A. (2014). Autonomy support, self-regulation, and weight loss. *Health Psychology, 33*, 332–339. http://dx.doi.org/10.1037/a0032586

Gorin, A. A., Raynor, H. A., Fava, J., Maguire, K., Robichaud, E., Trautvetter, J., . . . Wing, R. R. (2013). Randomized controlled trial of a comprehensive home environment-focused weight-loss program for adults. *Health Psychology, 32*, 128–137. http://dx.doi.org/10.1037/a0026959

Graham, K., & Braun, K. (1999). Concordance of use of alcohol and other substances among older adult couples. *Addictive Behaviors, 24*, 839–856. http://dx.doi.org/10.1016/S0306-4603(99)00059-3

Helgeson, V. S., Novak, S. A., Lepore, S. J., & Eton, D. T. (2004). Spouse social control efforts: Relations to health behavior and well-being among men with prostate cancer. *Journal of Social and Personal Relationships, 21*, 53–68. http://dx.doi.org/10.1177/0265407504039840

Homish, G. G., & Leonard, K. E. (2005). Spousal influence on smoking behaviors in a US community sample of newly married couples. *Social Science & Medicine, 61*, 2557–2567. http://dx.doi.org/10.1016/j.socscimed.2005.05.005

Ingersoll-Dayton, B., Morgan, D., & Antonucci, T. (1997). The effects of positive and negative social exchanges on aging adults. *The Journals of Gerontology: Series B. Psychological Sciences and Social Sciences, 52*, S190–S199. http://dx.doi.org/10.1093/geronb/52B.4.S190

Jeffery, R. W., Wing, R., & Stunkard, A. J. (1978). Behavioral treatment of obesity: The state of the art 1976. *Behavior Therapy, 9*, 189–199. http://dx.doi.org/10.1016/S0005-7894(78)80104-X

Keogh, K. M., Smith, S. M., White, P., McGilloway, S., Kelly, A., Gibney, J., & O'Dowd, T. (2011). Psychological family intervention for poorly controlled type 2 diabetes. *The American Journal of Managed Care, 17*, 105–113.

Khan, C. M., Stephens, M. A. P., Franks, M. M., Rook, K. S., & Salem, J. K. (2013). Influences of spousal support and control on diabetes management through physical activity. *Health Psychology, 32*, 739–747. http://dx.doi.org/10.1037/a0028609

Knoll, N., Burkert, S., Scholz, U., Roigas, J., & Gralla, O. (2012). The dual-effects model of social control revisited: Relationship satisfaction as a moderator. *Anxiety,*

*Stress & Coping: An International Journal, 25*, 291–307. http://dx.doi.org/10.1080/10615806.2011.584188

Lewis, M. A., Butterfield, R. M., Darbes, L. A., & Johnston-Brooks, C. (2004). The conceptualization and assessment of health-related social control. *Journal of Social and Personal Relationships, 21*, 669–687. http://dx.doi.org/10.1177/0265407504045893

Lewis, M. A., & Rook, K. S. (1999). Social control in personal relationships: Impact on health behaviors and psychological distress. *Health Psychology, 18*, 63–71. http://dx.doi.org/10.1037/0278-6133.18.1.63

Li, K. K., Cardinal, B. J., & Acock, A. C. (2013). Concordance of physical activity trajectories among middle-aged and older married couples: Impact of diseases and functional difficulties. *The Journals of Gerontology: Series B. Psychological Sciences and Social Sciences, 68*, 794–806. http://dx.doi.org/10.1093/geronb/gbt068

Macario, E., & Sorensen, G. (1998). Spousal similarities in fruit and vegetable consumption. *American Journal of Health Promotion, 12*, 369–377. http://dx.doi.org/10.4278/0890-1171-12.6.369

Martire, L. M. (2013). Couple-oriented interventions for chronic illness: Where do we go from here? *Journal of Social and Personal Relationships, 30*, 207–214. http://dx.doi.org/10.1177/0265407512453786

Martire, L. M., & Schulz, R. (2012). Caregiving and care receiving in later life: Health effects and promising interventions. In A. Baum, T. A. Revenson, & J. Singer (Eds.), *Handbook of health psychology* (pp. 293–307). New York, NY: Taylor and Francis.

Martire, L. M., Schulz, R., Helgeson, V. S., Small, B. J., & Saghafi, E. M. (2010). Review and meta-analysis of couple-oriented interventions for chronic illness. *Annals of Behavioral Medicine, 40*, 325–342. http://dx.doi.org/10.1007/s12160-010-9216-2

Martire, L. M., Stephens, M. A. P., Mogle, J., Schulz, R., Brach, J., & Keefe, F. J. (2013). Daily spousal influence on physical activity in knee osteoarthritis. *Annals of Behavioral Medicine, 45*, 213–223. http://dx.doi.org/10.1007/s12160-012-9442-x

May, S., & West, R. (2000). Do social support interventions ("buddy systems") aid smoking cessation? A review. *Tobacco Control, 9*, 415–422. http://dx.doi.org/10.1136/tc.9.4.415

McIntyre-Kingsolver, K., Lichtenstein, E., & Mermelstein, R. J. (1986). Spouse training in a multicomponent smoking-cessation program. *Behavior Therapy, 17*, 67–74. http://dx.doi.org/10.1016/S0005-7894(86)80115-0

Murphy, J. K., Williamson, D. A., Buxton, A. E., Moody, S. C., Absher, N., & Warner, M. (1982). The long-term effects of spouse involvement upon weight loss and maintenance. *Behavior Therapy, 13*, 681–693. http://dx.doi.org/10.1016/S0005-7894(82)80024-5

Novak, S. A., & Webster, G. D. (2011). Spousal social control during a weight loss attempt: A daily diary study. *Personal Relationships, 18*, 224–241. http://dx.doi.org/10.1111/j.1475-6811.2011.01358.x

Okun, M. A., Huff, B. P., August, K. J., & Rook, K. S. (2007). Testing hypotheses distilled from four models of the effects of health-related social control. *Basic and Applied Social Psychology, 29*, 185–193. http://dx.doi.org/10.1080/01973530701332245

Park, E. W., Tudiver, F. G., & Campbell, T. (2012). Enhancing partner support to improve smoking cessation. *Cochrane Database of Systematic Reviews, 7*(3, Art. No. CD002928). http://dx.doi.org/10.1002/14651858.CD002928.pub3

Pearce, J. W., LeBow, M. D., & Orchard, J. (1981). Role of spouse involvement in the behavioral treatment of overweight women. *Journal of Consulting and Clinical Psychology, 49*, 236–244. http://dx.doi.org/10.1037/0022-006X.49.2.236

Pettee, K. K., Brach, J. S., Kriska, A. M., Boudreau, R., Richardson, C. R., Colbert, L. H., . . . Newman, A. B. (2006). Influence of marital status on physical activity levels among older adults. *Medicine and Science in Sports and Exercise, 38*, 541–546. http://dx.doi.org/10.1249/01.mss.0000191346.95244.f7

Prestwich, A., Conner, M. T., Lawton, R. J., Ward, J. K., Ayres, K., & McEachan, R. R. (2012). Randomized controlled trial of collaborative implementation intentions targeting working adults' physical activity. *Health Psychology, 31*, 486–495. http://dx.doi.org/10.1037/a0027672

Prestwich, A., Conner, M. T., Lawton, R. J., Ward, J. K., Ayres, K., & McEachan, R. R. (2014). Partner- and planning-based interventions to reduce fat consumption: Randomized controlled trial. *British Journal of Health Psychology, 19*, 132–148. http://dx.doi.org/10.1111/bjhp.12047

Pyke, S. D., Wood, D. A., Kinmonth, A. L., & Thompson, S. G. (1997). Change in coronary risk and coronary risk factor levels in couples following lifestyle intervention. The British Family Heart Study. *Archives of Family Medicine, 6*, 354–360. http://dx.doi.org/10.1001/archfami.6.4.354

Remien, R. H., Stirratt, M. J., Dolezal, C., Dognin, J. S., Wagner, G. J., Carballo-Dieguez, A., . . . Jung, T. M. (2005). Couple-focused support to improve HIV medication adherence: A randomized controlled trial. *AIDS, 19*, 807–814. http://dx.doi.org/10.1097/01.aids.0000168975.44219.45

Riemsma, R. P., Taal, E., & Rasker, J. J. (2003). Group education for patients with rheumatoid arthritis and their partners. *Arthritis and Rheumatism, 49*, 556–566. http://dx.doi.org/10.1002/art.11207

Robles, T. F., Slatcher, R. B., Trombello, J. M., & McGinn, M. M. (2014). Marital quality and health: A meta-analytic review. *Psychological Bulletin, 140*, 140–187. http://dx.doi.org/10.1037/a0031859

Rook, K. S., August, K. J., Stephens, M. A. P., & Franks, M. M. (2011). When does spousal social control provoke negative reactions in the context of chronic illness? The pivotal role of patients' expectations. *Journal of Social and Personal Relationships, 28,* 772–789. http://dx.doi.org/10.1177/0265407510391335

Rook, K. S., Thuras, P. D., & Lewis, M. A. (1990). Social control, health risk taking, and psychological distress among the elderly. *Psychology and Aging, 5,* 327–334. http://dx.doi.org/10.1037/0882-7974.5.3.327

Rosenthal, B., Allen, G. J., & Winter, C. (1980). Husband involvement in the behavioral treatment of overweight women: Initial effects and long-term follow-up. *International Journal of Obesity, 4,* 165–173.

Saccone, A. J., & Israel, A. C. (1978). Effects of experimenter versus significant other-controlled reinforcement and choice of target behavior on weight loss. *Behavior Therapy, 9,* 271–278. http://dx.doi.org/10.1016/S0005-7894(78)80112-9

Shoham, V., Rohrbaugh, M. J., Trost, S. E., & Muramoto, M. (2006). A family consultation intervention for health-compromised smokers. *Journal of Substance Abuse Treatment, 31,* 395–402. http://dx.doi.org/10.1016/j.jsat.2006.05.012

Stephens, M. A. P., Fekete, E. M., Franks, M. M., Rook, K. S., Druley, J. A., & Greene, K. (2009). Spouses' use of pressure and persuasion to promote osteoarthritis patients' medical adherence after orthopedic surgery. *Health Psychology, 28,* 48–55. http://dx.doi.org/10.1037/a0012385

Stephens, M. A. P., Franks, M. M., Rook, K. S., Iida, M., Hemphill, R. C., & Salem, J. K. (2013). Spouses' attempts to regulate day-to-day dietary adherence among patients with type 2 diabetes. *Health Psychology, 32,* 1029–1037. http://dx.doi.org/10.1037/a0030018

Stimpson, J. P., Masel, M. C., Rudkin, L., & Peek, M. K. (2006). Shared health behaviors among older Mexican American spouses. *American Journal of Health Behavior, 30,* 495–502. http://dx.doi.org/10.5993/AJHB.30.5.6

Trief, P., Sandberg, J. G., Ploutz-Snyder, R., Brittain, R., Cibula, D., Scales, K., & Weinstock, R. S. (2011). Promoting couples collaboration in type 2 diabetes: The Diabetes Support Project pilot data. *Families, Systems, & Health, 29,* 253–261. http://dx.doi.org/10.1037/a0024564

Trief, P. M., Sandberg, J., Fisher, L., Dimmock, J. A., Scales, K., Hessler, D. M., & Weinstock, R. S. (2011). Challenges and lessons learned in the development and implementation of a couples-focused telephone intervention for adults with type 2 diabetes: The Diabetes Support Project. *Translational Behavioral Medicine, 1,* 461–467. http://dx.doi.org/10.1007/s13142-011-0057-8

Tucker, J. S., Orlando, M., Elliott, M. N., & Klein, D. J. (2006). Affective and behavioral responses to health-related social control. *Health Psychology, 25,* 715–722. http://dx.doi.org/10.1037/0278-6133.25.6.715

Umberson, D. (1992). Gender, marital status and the social control of health behavior. *Social Science & Medicine, 34,* 907–917. http://dx.doi.org/10.1016/0277-9536(92)90259-S

Wadden, T. A. (1983). Predicting treatment response to relaxation therapy for essential hypertension. *Journal of Nervous and Mental Disease, 171,* 683–689. http://dx.doi.org/10.1097/00005053-198311000-00007

Weisz, G., & Bucher, B. (1980). Involving husbands in treatment of obesity: Effects on weight loss, depression, and marital satisfaction. *Behavior Therapy, 11,* 643–650. http://dx.doi.org/10.1016/S0005-7894(80)80003-7

Westmaas, J. L., Wild, T. C., & Ferrence, R. (2002). Effects of gender in social control of smoking cessation. *Health Psychology, 21,* 368–376.

Wing, R. R., Marcus, M. D., Epstein, L. H., & Jawad, A. (1991). A "family-based" approach to the treatment of obese Type II diabetic patients. *Journal of Consulting and Clinical Psychology, 59,* 156–162. http://dx.doi.org/10.1037/0022-006X.59.1.156

# INDEX

Accidents, 178
Ackbar, S., 104
AD (Alzheimer's disease), 286–289
Adaptive processes (health), 183
Adjustment, 260
Affect, 42–44
Affection, 23. *See also* Intimacy
Affiliation, 39–40, 49
African Americans. *See* Black populations
Age, 97, 119, 260
Age-related theory of emotion regulation, 291
Aging
    and living-apart-together relation-
        ships, 87
    and marital discord, 41–42
    and midlife marital satisfaction, 19
    and sexuality, 118, 125
Akers, C., 105
Alcohol use and abuse
    and couple-based interventions for
        illness management, 328
    in same-sex relationships, 99–100
    and spousal physical/mental health,
        243
    spousal similarities in, 304
Alzheimer's disease (AD), 286–289
Ambivalence, marital, 39
Ambulatory blood pressure, 262
Anderson, J. R., 21
Andersson, J., 221
Anger, 122, 248
Antecedent-focused emotion
    regulation, 284
Antidepressants, 122
Anxiety, 122, 202, 263, 284
Arthritis, 188. *See also* Osteoarthritis;
    Rheumatoid arthritis
Asian Americans, 127, 212, 291
Atchley, R. C., 158–159
Attachment theory, 20, 23, 270,
    287–289
Attentional deployment, 284
Autoimmune diseases, 183
Autonomy, 40, 81–83, 260, 312, 331
Averett, P., 103

Baby boomers
    characteristics of, 17, 19, 158
    cognitive impairment of, 220
    lesbian, gay, and bisexual, 96, 103
    life expectancy of, 282
    marital biography of, 200
Badr, H., 185, 326
Balsam, K. F., 99
Baltes, M. M., 230
Baltes, P. B., 230
Barrett, A. E., 205, 207–209
Bartlam, B., 103
Beals, K. P., 101
Bengtson, V. L., 85
Beougher, S. C., 100, 101
Bepko, C., 104
Berg, C. A., 187, 265, 293
Beth, A., 95
Biblarz, T. J., 106
Bioecological theory, 232
Black populations, 127, 168, 212, 291
Blame coping methods, 183–184
Blood pressure, 46, 262, 284
Blumen, H. M., 233
Bodenmann, G., 262, 271–272
Bonello, K., 100
Bookwala, J., 105, 143, 159, 205, 210
Bowlby, J., 287
Bradbury, T. N., 22, 262
Bridges, S. K., 100, 101
Brown, S. L., 63
Burgess, E. W., 77
Burton, L., 85
Bushfield, S. Y., 159, 163
Butler, E. A., 293
Butterworth, P., 29

CAC (coronary artery calcification), 49
Cancer
    couple-based interventions for
        management of, 326, 327,
        330–331
    and dyadic coping, 265
    and marital quality, 178
    prognosis of, 183
    and sexuality, 122, 185

Cardiovascular disease (CVD)
    couple-based interventions for
        management of, 326
    and emotion regulation in spousal
        caregiving, 283
    and marital biography, 205, 206
    and marital discord, 49
    and marital quality, 178
    and sexual functioning, 122
Caregiving
    emotion regulation in. *See* Emotion
        regulation in spousal caregiving
    in living-apart-together relation-
        ships, 86–87
    in same-sex relationships, 102–103
    and spousal role allocation, 142–145
Carpenter, L. M., 124–125, 128
Carstensen, L. L., 45, 66, 290
Carter, J. H., 266
Cashwell, C. S., 269
CBT (cognitive–behavioral therapy), 271
CC. *See* Collaborative cognition
Cerebral vascular accidents, 178
Chakravarty, D., 100
Charles, S. T., 66, 290
CHD. *See* Coronary heart disease
Childhood abuse, 100
Children
    and dyadic coping, 268–269
    and loneliness, 65
    of parents in same-sex relationships,
        101, 106
Christakis, N. A., 209–210
Chronic disease management, 303–317
    forms of spouses' involvement in,
        312–313
    future directions for research on,
        313–317
    ill partners' adherence and well-being
        in, 307–309
    overview, 304–305
    spousal support and control in,
        305–307
    and spouses' well-being, 309–311
Chronic health conditions, 185, 204,
    264–268, 282
Chronic obstructive pulmonary disease
    (COPD), 178
Chronic pain, 326
Chronic strains, 202

Clinical settings
    and dyadic coping, 271–272
    and emotion regulation in spousal
        caregiving, 294–295
    marital biography and health in, 213
    midlife marital satisfaction in, 27–28
    retirement and marital quality in,
        168–170
    same-sex relationships in, 103–105
    sexuality in, 128–129
COCT (Coping-Oriented Couples
    Training), 271–272
Cognition
    collaborative. *See* Collaborative
        cognition
    in marital discord, 42
Cognitive–behavioral therapy (CBT),
    271
Cognitive discrepancy theory, 60
Cognitive functioning, 42, 46
Cognitive reappraisal, 284
Cohabitation
    future directions for research on, 212
    increases in, 200
    and spousal role allocation, 145
*Cohabitation intermittente*, 79. *See
    also* Living-apart-together
    relationships
Cohen, H. L., 102
Collaborative cognition (CC), 219–234
    advanced theoretical perspectives
        on, 229–231
    empirical investigation of, 220–225
    future directions for, 230, 232–233
    illustrative examples of, 225–229
    and widowhood, 232
Collaborative inhibition, 222
Collectivist cultures, 27
Commitment, 81–82
Communal responsiveness, 290, 292
Communication, 292, 312
Complementarity principle, 40
Complementary coping, 184
Conflict resolution, 98–99
Contextual model (health-related social
    control), 330
Control (marital discord), 39–40, 47
Coon, D. W., 102
COPD (chronic obstructive pulmonary
    disease), 178

Coping
    dyadic. *See* Dyadic coping
    types of, 283–284
Coping-Oriented Couples Training
    (COCT), 271–272
Coregulation, 293
Coronary artery calcification (CAC), 49
Coronary heart disease (CHD), 37,
    38, 48
Couple-based interventions for illness
    management, 325–338
    evidence for, 328–331
    findings from, 332–336
    future directions for research on,
        336–338
    overview, 326–328
Couple relationships in the middle and
    later years, 3–11. *See also specific*
    *headings*
    overview, 3–4
    types of, 63–64
Couples counseling/marital therapy,
    104, 213, 271
Coyle, A., 100
Cozijnsen, R., 168
Cross, M. C., 100
Cross-cuing, 222
Cultural factors, 26, 27, 29–30
Cumulative advantage/disadvantage
    theory, 203
Cumulative marital history. *See* Marital
    biography and health
CVD. *See* Cardiovascular disease

Daily life assessments, 249
Darbes, L. A., 100
Davey, A., 165, 168
Decision making, 228
De Jong Gierveld Loneliness Scale, 59
DeLamater, J., 125
Dementia, 178, 183, 282
Depression
    and divorce, 205
    and dyadic coping, 263
    and emotion regulation in spousal
        caregiving, 283, 284, 291
    and health, 185
    and marital discord, 37, 48
    and sexual functioning, 122
    and social support, 202

Detels, R., 104
Developmental-contextual model of
    couples coping, 293
DeViney, S., 164, 168
de Vries, B., 104
Dew, J., 160
Diabetes
    and chronic disease management,
        308–311, 313
    couple-based interventions for
        management of, 327
    and dyadic coping, 265
    and marital quality, 178, 183,
        186, 189
Diemer, M. A., 99
Diet, 304, 306–308, 327, 328
Dinero, R. E., 270
Disabilities, 291
Disempowerment, 100
Ditzen, B., 247
Divorce
    in adults 50 and older, 38
    and coronary heart disease, 48
    and depression, 205
    gender differences in effects of, 209
    increases in, 78, 200
    and loneliness, 57, 65, 66
    physical effects of, 206–207, 209
    and retirement, 163, 170
    and same-sex relationships, 98, 101
    and women's equality, 89
Dixon, C. G., 105
Dixon, R. A., 224, 233
Doherty, W. J., 21
Domain-specific model (health-related
    social control), 329
Domestic violence. *See* Interpersonal
    violence
Dominance, 39–40
Dorval, M., 185
Driver, J. L., 166
Dual-effects model (health-related
    social control), 329
Dual-households/dual-residence living,
    79. *See also* Living-apart-together
    relationships
Duncan, S., 79
Dupre, M. E., 205–207
Dutton, D. G., 99
Duvall, E. M., 21

Dwyer, J. W., 144
Dwyer, Seccombe, 144
Dyadic appraisal, 178, 180, 184
Dyadic coping, 259–273
  with chronic illness, 264–268
  clinical implications of, 271–272
  conceptualizations of, 261
  defined, 259
  and emotion regulation in spousal
    caregiving, 293
  future directions for research on,
    272–273
  and health contributions to marital
    quality, 178, 180, 184
  importance of, 263–264
  relational foundations of, 268–270
  systemic approach to, 261–263
Dyadic goal setting, 334

Eckstein, D., 26
Economic hardship, 25
ED (erectile dysfunction), 120–123
Elder, G. H., 21
Elwert, F., 209–210
Emotional loneliness, 60. *See also*
    Loneliness
Emotion coregulation, 293
Emotion-focused coping, 284
Emotion regulation
  defined, 281–282
  and dyadic coping, 263
  and spousal physical/mental health,
    246–248
Emotion regulation in spousal caregiving,
    281–295
  clinical implications of, 294–295
  conceptual issues in, 292–294
  contextual influences and moderators
    of, 289–292
  future directions for research on,
    292–294
  importance of, 282–283
  and interpersonal emotion regulation,
    285–289
  and intrapersonal emotion regulation,
    283–285
Empathy, 42
Empty nest stage, 21, 24, 106,
    136–139, 147
Enduring characteristics, 180

Episodic memory, 222
Equality in spousal role allocation. *See*
    Spousal role allocation
Erectile dysfunction (ED), 120–123
Ethnic differences. *See* Racial/ethnic
    differences
Executive functioning, 42
Exercise behaviors, 307, 327

Fagundes, C. P., 265
Families
  changes in dynamics of, 77
  and same-sex relationships, 97
Family adaptation model, 21
Family life-cycle approach (spousal role
    allocation), 137
Family obligation, 86
Family therapy, 169
Fantasy coping methods, 183–184
Farr, R. H., 101
Feminism. *See* Women's liberation
Ferguson, M. L., 59
Fibromyalgia, 178
Financial stability, 202
Financial strains, 180
Finch, J., 86
Fingerhut, A. W., 100
Fitzpatrick, T. R., 159, 161, 163
Folkman, S., 103, 283
Forssell, S. L., 101
Fowers, B. J., 102
Franks, M. M., 183
Fredriksen-Goldsen, K. I., 102
Friendship, 23–24
Fuenfhausen, K. K., 269
Fung, H. H., 20, 66
Fusion, 104

Gamarel, K. E., 100
Gay marriage, 97, 103–104. *See also*
    Same-sex relationships
Gay men. *See* Same-sex relationships
Gee, E. M., 24
Gender differences
  in collaborative cognition, 233
  in dyadic coping, 260
  in health experiences, 180, 188–190
  in health related to marital discord, 48
  in living-apart-together relation-
    ships, 83–84, 88–89

in loneliness, 61, 62
in marital biography and health, 208–209
in midlife marital satisfaction, 19–20
in mortality risk, 205–206
in relationship formation, 97, 163
in repartnering, 123
in retirement preferences, 162, 166–167
in same-sex relationships, 99
in sexual frequency, 117
and sexuality over life course, 124–125
in sexual satisfaction, 118–119
in smoking cessation, 246
in social control, 306–307
in spousal caregiving, 289

Gender equality, 88, 90, 99. *See also* Spousal role allocation
Gender role ideology, 136–137, 140
Gender theory, 128
Ginsburg, P., 26
Gmelch, S., 262
Gold, D. T., 184
Goldsmith, D. J., 314
Gordon, J. R., 139
Gorin, A. A., 333
Gott, M., 123
Gottman, J. M., 45, 166
Gould, O. N., 224
Green, R.-J., 97
Greenberg, D. R., 166
Gross, J. J., 284, 285
Grov, C., 100
Growth-curve longitudinal analyses, 29
Gurevitch, J., 95

Haavio-Mannila, E., 119
Hafstrom, J. L., 182–183
Happiness
and midlife marital satisfaction, 20, 24
and sexual functioning, 122
and spousal health, 182
Harkless, L. E., 102
Hash, K., 102
Hayward, M. D., 164, 205, 206, 209
Hazan, C., 20

Health. *See also specific headings*
and living-apart-together relationships, 87
and loneliness, 62, 68
and marital discord, 37, 48–49
and midlife marital satisfaction, 19
and retirement, 164, 168
and sexuality, 116
spousal. *See* Spousal physical and mental health
Health and marital quality, 177–191, 210–211. *See also* Spousal physical and mental health
expected contributions to, 182–185
future directions for research on, 189–191
gender-specific contributions to, 188–189
theoretical framework for, 180–181
unexpected contributions to, 185–187
Health and Retirement Study (HRS), 211, 241
Health behaviors, 243–246, 304–305, 314–315
Health care policy, 316
Health-compromising behaviors, 243, 246, 328
Health-enhancing behaviors, 243, 328
Health-related support, 305
Hearing loss, 183
Heart rate, 284
Heiman, J. R., 22
Helfrich, C. A., 104
Henkins, K., 163
Heterosexism, 102, 104
Hilbourne, M., 166
Hinchliff, S., 123
Hispanic populations, 127, 212, 291
HIV/AIDS, 103, 327
Hoff, C. C., 100, 101
Hofmeister, H., 159
Holmberg, D., 166
Homophobia, 97, 102
Hong, T. B., 184
Horne, S. G., 100, 101
Hostility, 39–40, 44, 47, 49
Household labor, 99, 182, 188
Howell, L. C., 95
HPA (hypothalamic–pituitary–adrenal) axis, 247

HRS (Health and Retirement Study),
  211, 241
Huber, C. H., 21
Hueber, D. M., 101
Hughes, M. E., 206
Humor, 166
Huston, T. L., 230
Hypertension, 122
Hypothalamic–pituitary–adrenal (HPA)
  axis, 247

Iida, M., 183
Illness. *See* Health
Illness management, couple-based inter-
  ventions for. *See* Couple-based
  interventions for illness
  management
Illness-specific spousal support, 180
Impett, E. A., 101
Incontinence, 122
Independence, 260
Indifference, marital, 39
Individualistic cultures, 27
Inhibitory control, 42, 46
Interpersonal emotion regulation,
  285–289, 293
Interpersonal theory, 39, 40
Interpersonal violence, 99–100,
  104–105
Intimacy. *See also* Living-apart-together
  relationships
  and couple-based interventions for
    illness management, 338
  defined, 85
  in living-apart-together relation-
    ships, 81–82, 85–86, 88
  and marital discord, 45
  and retirement, 160
  and stress, 247
Intrapersonal emotion regulation,
  283–285

Jenkins, C. L., 103
Jenkins, K. R., 164
Johansson, N. O., 221, 223, 224
Johnson, T., 104

Kamp Dush, C. M., 18
Karney, B. R., 22
Karpiak, S., 103

Kaukinen, C., 105
Kawamura, S., 63
Keith, P. M., 146
Kelly-Moore, J., 62
Kim, H., 102
Kim, J. E., 159
Kimbler, K. J., 225
King, S. D., 95
Kitzinger, C., 100
Knight, B. G., 291
Koch, P. B., 120
Koehly, L. M., 272
Kohli, M., 85
Kontula, O., 119
Kraemer, L. M., 266
Krebs, P., 326
Kroeger, R. A., 18
Kulik, L., 141, 146, 160
Künemund, H., 85
Kurdek, L. A., 101

Landis, M., 263
Landolt, M. A., 99
LAT relationships. *See* Living-apart-
  together relationships
Laumann, E. O., 116, 121
Launching stage, 138
Lazarus, R. S., 283
Learning, 232
LeBlanc, A. J., 104
Ledermann, T., 262, 272
Lee, J. E., 25
Leppel, K., 102
Lesbian, gay, bisexual, and transgender
  (LGBT) partnerships. *See also*
    Same-sex relationships
  and gender identity, 145
  and midlife marital satisfaction, 19,
    30
  sexual experiences in, 126
Levenson, R. W., 45, 162
Levinger, A. C., 294
Levinger, G., 294
Lewis, M. A., 304, 315
LGBT partnerships. *See* Lesbian,
  gay, bisexual, and transgender
  partnerships
Li, T., 20
Life course perspective, 128, 200
Life course–stress theory, 161

Life expectancy, 136, 148, 282
Life satisfaction, 38
Lifespan perspectives, 41–42
Lifespan theory of control, 291
Lillard, L. A., 205
Lindau, S. T., 122
Liu, H., 204, 207
Living-apart-together (LAT) relation-
    ships, 77–91
    care and support in, 86–87
    defined, 63, 78–79
    and gender, 83–84, 88–89
    intimacy and social obligations in,
        81–82, 85–86, 88
    and loneliness, 63–65, 68
    motives and constructions in, 81–83
    other romantic relationships vs.,
        88–89
    prevalence of, 78–80
    Swedish context for, 79–81, 89–90
    and widowhood, 82
Living conditions, 61
Lodge, A. C., 22–23, 125
Loneliness, 57–69
    concept of, 57–58
    defined, 58
    distal antecedents of, 60–62, 67
    and marital discord, 37
    measurement of, 58–59
    and policy implications, 67–69
    proximal antecedents of, 62–67
    rates of, 57
    theoretical model of, 60
    and widowhood, 57, 65, 66
Lorenz, F. O., 204
Lundberg, S., 160

Mackaronis, J. E., 101
Mackey, R. A., 99
Mandic, C. G., 101
Manning, S. W., 205
Mansfield, P. K., 120
Margolin, G., 105
Margrett, J. A., 223–225, 233
Marital biography and health, 199–213
    clinical and policy implications of,
        213
    empirical findings on, 203–208
    future directions for research on,
        211–212

gender differences in, 208–209
and marital quality, 210–211
overview, 201–202
racial/ethnic differences in, 209–210
theoretical perspectives on, 201–203
Marital conflict. See Marital discord
Marital discord, 37–50
    aging and lifespan perspectives on,
        41–42
    correlates of, 48–50
    levels of, 43–48
    and loneliness, 67
    methods for studying, 42–43
    models of, 38–40
Marital distress. See Marital discord
Marital history, 163–164
Marital Instability Over the Life Course
    study, 182
Marital loss, 205
Marital quality
    and adjustment, 38–39
    defined, 178
    and health. See Health and marital
        quality
    and marital biography, 210–211
    and retirement. See Retirement and
        Marital quality
Marital resource model, 201–202
Marital satisfaction
    defined, 39
    midlife. See Midlife marital satisfac-
        tion
    and spousal role allocation, 146–147
Marital sequencing, 201
Marital status, 201, 204
Marital status duration, 201
Marital therapy. See Couples counseling/
    marital therapy
Marital timing, 201
Marital transitions, 204–205
Marshall, K. I., 205
Marsiske, M., 233
Masculinity, 87, 141–142, 160
Mason, J., 86
Masturbation, 116
McCabe, M. P., 19
McCallum, T. J., 291
Meadows, S. O., 206
Mediational model of health-related
    social control, 329–330

Medication, 223, 327–328
Mehl, M. R., 184
Memory, 220–223. *See also* Prospective memory
Menopause, 23, 120, 126
Mental health
    and marital biography, 208
    and sexual functioning, 122
    and sexuality, 116
    spousal. *See* Spousal physical and mental health
Meuwly, N., 262
Midlife marital satisfaction, 17–31
    and clinical work, 27–28
    conceptual and theoretical perspectives on, 20–21
    defined, 18–19
    future directions for theory and research on, 28–31
    individual, psychological, and inter/intrapersonal factors in, 22–24
    macroenvironmental factors in, 26–27
    microcontextual factors in, 24–26
    and policy, 27, 28
    shifting foci in research on, 19–20
Milbury, K., 185
Miller, R. B., 161
Mincer, S., 102
Minority stress, 100
Mitchell, B. A., 24
Moen, P., 159
Morbidity, 239
Mortality, 205, 208–210, 239
Multiple sclerosis, 178
Mumme, F. L., 21
Muraco, A., 102
Murray, Y., 102

National Longitudinal Study of Youth, 208
National Social Life, Health and Aging Project, 121, 211
Navarro, R. L., 21
Neilands, T. B., 100
Newton-John, T. R. O., 187
Normative memory, 220

O'Brien, B. A., 99
O'Rand, A., 21
Orbuch, T. L., 166

Orel, N., 95
Osteoarthritis, 282, 286, 289–290
Overeating, 243
Oxytocin, 247

Papp, L. M., 263
Parkinson's disease, 266
Parsons, J. T., 100
Parsons, M., 164
Patterson, C. J., 101
Peluso, P. R., 164
Peplau, L. A., 59, 100, 101
Performance order, 232
Personality
    and marital discord, 45
    research on, 19
    spousal similarity in, 162
Persuasion, 329, 336–337
Peterman, L. M., 105
Phillips, M., 79
Physical activity, 328
Pienta, A. M., 164
Pillemer, K., 143
Pinquart, M., 143, 144
PM (prospective memory), 223–226
Policy
    health care, 316
    and marital biography/health, 213
    and midlife marital satisfaction, 27, 28
    and spousal health, 250–251
Power relations, 141
Pressure control, 329
Primary health stressors, 180, 183
Problem-focused coping, 283–284
Problem-solving therapy, 295
Prospective memory (PM), 223–226
Prostatectomy, 244
Psychotherapy, 168–169, 294–295. *See also specific headings*

Queer theory, 128

Racial/ethnic differences
    in emotion regulation in spousal caregiving, 291–292
    in marital biography and health, 209–210
    and midlife marital satisfaction, 29–30

Randall, A. K., 271–272, 293
Reconciliation, 148
Reese-Melancon, C., 223
Reexposure to material, 222
Reis, H. T., 85
Relationship satisfaction
    and dyadic coping, 261
    in marriages. *See* Marital satisfaction
    in same-sex relationships, 98–100
    and sexual functioning, 122–123
Relative resource theory, 137, 140, 143
Relaxation techniques, 327
Rendell, P. G., 223
Repartnering, 123
Response-focused emotion regulation, 284
Response modulation, 284
Retirement, 41, 139–142
Retirement and marital quality, 25, 30, 157–170
    clinical and policy implications in, 168–170
    future directions for theory and research on, 165–168
    potential moderators in, 161–164
    research on, 158–161
Retrieval disruption, 222
Rexroat, C., 138
Rheumatoid arthritis, 327
Robbins, M. L., 184
Roberto, K. A., 184
Roberts, L. J., 166
Role allocation, 98–99. *See also* Spousal role allocation
Rönnberg, J., 221
Rook, K. S., 183
Roper, S. O., 187
Rose, S. M., 97
Rosenfeld, D., 103
Rosengard, C., 103
Rosenthal, C., 85
Rusbult, C. E., 101
Russell, D. W., 59

Sadness, 248
Same-sex relationships, 95–106
    caregiving in, 102–103
    in clinical settings, 103–105
    future directions for research on, 105–106

heterosexual relationships vs., 96–102
    methodological issues in research on, 105–106
    prevalence of, 64, 96
    and retirement, 167
    sexuality in, 125–126
    and spousal role allocation, 145–146
Sandberg, J. G., 187
*Särbo*, 79. *See also* Living-apart-together relationships
Schafer, R. B., 146
Schaffer, A. M., 160
Schneewind, K. A., 263
Schram. V. R., 182–183
SCT (social cognitive theory), 337
Seccombe, K., 144
Secondary health stressors, 180, 183
Secure attachment, 23, 248
Selection model (health and marriage), 202–203
Self-assurance, 87
Self-efficacy, 315
Self–other overlap, 292
Self-regulation, 315–316
Senn, C. Y., 104
SES (socioeconomic status), 127–128
Sexual desire, 116, 119–120
Sexual dysfunction, 116, 120–123, 127–128, 267
Sexuality, 115–129
    attitudes toward, 118
    in clinical settings, 128–129
    critique of research on, 124–128
    and desire, 116, 119–120
    dysfunction with, 116, 120–123
    and frequency of sexual activity, 116–117, 126
    and health, 184–185
    and midlife marital satisfaction, 17, 19–20, 26–27
    overview of research on, 116–124
    and relationships, 123–124
    and retirement, 160
    in same-sex relationships, 100–101
    satisfaction with, 116, 118–119
    and widowhood, 122, 123
Shaver, P., 20
Shehan, C., 138
Shiota, M. N., 162
Shoham, V., 336

Simpson, E. K., 104
Situation modification, 284
Sleep apnea, 267
Sleep disruption, 183
Smith, H. L., 184
Smith, R. D., 103
Smith, T. W., 48
Smoking behavior
    couple-based interventions for, 328,
        334–336
    and dyadic coping, 267
    and spousal interrelationships, 243,
        245–246
    spousal similarities in, 304
Sobin, J., 105
Social cognitive theory (SCT), 337
Social control, 305–307, 328–331,
    335–336
Social isolation, 58
Social loneliness, 60. See also Loneliness
Social obligations, 85
Social support, 184, 201–202
Socioeconomic status (SES), 127–128
Socioemotional collaborative processes,
    228–229
Socioemotional selectivity theory
    (SST), 41–42, 290
Sörensen, S., 143, 144
Spitze, G. D., 24
Spousal equality, 135. See also Spousal
    role allocation
Spousal health. See Health and marital
    quality
Spousal physical and mental health,
    239–251
    and health behavior, 243–246
    and interpersonal dynamics in
        marriage, 249–250
    overview of research on, 240–242
    policy implications for, 250–251
    stress and emotion regulation in,
        246–248
Spousal role allocation, 135–149
    among cohabiting heterosexual and
        same-sex couples, 145–146
    and caregiving, 142–145
    and empty nest stage, 138–139
    and marital satisfaction, 146–147
    and retirement, 139–142
    theoretical approaches to, 136–137

SST (socioemotional selectivity theory),
    41–42, 290
Stacey, J., 106
Starks, T. J., 100
Startz, R., 160
Stephens, M. A. P., 183, 315, 331
Stepparenting, 30
Stern, Y., 233
Stevens, N. L., 168
Stillman, S., 160
Strength and vulnerability integration
    model, 290
Stress
    and dyadic coping, 260–262
    and emotion regulation in spousal
        caregiving, 282
    and marital discord, 45
    and midlife marital satisfaction, 25
    and sexuality, 122, 128
    and spousal physical/mental health,
        246–248
Stressful live events, 202
Stress model of marital dissolution,
    202
Submissiveness, 39–40
Suitor, J. J., 143
Support, 86–87
Suppression, emotion, 284
Sutphin, S. T., 99
Sweden, 79–81, 89–90
Systolic blood pressure, 46
Szinovacz, M. E., 140, 160, 162, 164,
    165, 168
Szymanski, D. M., 99

Taylor, M. G., 18
Teachman, J., 208
Time, 232
Time-available approach (spousal role
    allocation), 137
Time-sampling methods, 249–251
Touch, 247
Townsend, A. L., 29
Trudel, G., 160

UCLA Loneliness Scale, 59–60
Umberson, D., 22–23, 125, 204
Unretirement, 167
Upchurch, R., 293
Urbanization, 77

Urinary tract symptoms, 122
Utah Health and Aging Study,
    44–49

Vaginal intercourse, 115–116
Van Ryzin, M. J., 21
van Solinge, H., 163
Van Tilburg, T. G., 168
Veroff, J., 166
Vickerman, K. A., 105
Vinick, B. H., 159, 161, 163
Violence, interpersonal, 99–100,
    104–105
Vulnerabilities, 180
Vulnerability–stress–adaptation model,
    178, 180–181, 190

Waite, L. J., 116, 121, 205, 206
Ward, R. A., 24
Warmth, 40, 47, 49
Warner, D. F., 62
Watts, R. E., 164
Weight loss interventions, 332–334
Weihs, K. L., 184
Weiss, R. S., 59, 60, 66
Welfare model, 81
Well-being, 19, 87
Whelan-Berry, K. S., 139
Wickrama, K. A. S., 158

Widowhood
    and collaborative cognition, 232
    and living-apart-together relation-
        ships, 82
    and loneliness, 57, 65, 66
    and marital biography, 205–207,
        209–210
    and sexuality, 122, 123
Wiebe, D. J., 265
Wight, R. G., 104
Williams, W. C., 293
Windsor, T. D., 29
Witt, N. L., 263
Womble, M. W., 21
Women's liberation
    effects of, 77
    and women in the workforce, 158,
        208–209
Wood, J. M., 120
Wunderer, E., 263

Yoon, I., 103
Yorgason, J. B., 160, 161, 169, 184,
    185, 187

Zaki, J., 293
Zand, D., 97
Zdaniuk, B., 105
Zhang, Z., 205, 206, 209

# ABOUT THE EDITOR

**Jamila Bookwala, PhD,** is a professor and head of the Department of Psychology and chair of Aging Studies at Lafayette College in Easton, Pennsylvania. She teaches courses in lifespan development, aging studies, and research design and analysis.

Dr. Bookwala's primary research interests center on close relationships, stress, and well-being over the adult lifespan. A special focus of her research is on the health-protective role of close relationships. She has examined health outcomes related to a variety of relationships (spousal relationships, kin relationships, and friendships) in the context of a range of life stressors (poor physical function, visual impairment, family caregiving, and spousal loss). Her other research interests include gender differences in adult health and well-being, ageism and attitudes toward aging, and the effects of stigma over the adult lifespan. She has expertise in survey research and secondary data analysis using large national data sets. Her research has been funded by the National Institute on Aging and by private and public funding organizations. She has presented her research findings at national and international conferences and published her research in leading peer-reviewed journals including, most recently, *Developmental Psychology*, *Health Psychology*, *Journals of Gerontology: Social Sciences*, and *The Gerontologist*. Dr. Bookwala currently serves on the editorial board of *The Gerontologist* and has served on the editorial boards of *Psychology and Aging* and *Journals of Gerontology: Psychological Sciences*. She has reviewed grant applications for the National Institutes of Health and other private and public organizations.

Dr. Bookwala received her bachelor of arts degree from St. Xavier's College, University of Mumbai, India, and a master of arts degree in psychology from the Graduate Center, City University of New York. She completed her doctoral education at the University of Pittsburgh and held a National Research Service Award postdoctoral fellowship in the Geriatric Psychiatry Division at the University of Pennsylvania from the National Institute of Mental Health.

Dr. Bookwala is a fellow of the American Psychological Association (APA); chair of the Women and Aging subcommittee of the Society for the Psychology of Women, APA Division 35; and member of the Gerontological Society of America. She is past chair of the committee for the Denmark Award for Contributions to Women and Aging and of the conference program for APA Division 20 (Adult Development and Aging).